The Encyclopedia of
CIVIL WAR USAGE

The Encyclopedia of
CIVIL WAR USAGE

AN ILLUSTRATED COMPENDIUM OF THE
EVERYDAY LANGUAGE OF SOLDIERS AND CIVILIANS

WEBB GARRISON
WITH CHERYL GARRISON

CUMBERLAND HOUSE
NASHVILLE, TENNESSEE

Published by
CUMBERLAND HOUSE PUBLISHING, INC.
431 Harding Industrial Drive
Nashville, Tennessee 37211
www.cumberlandhouse.com

Unless otherwise indicated, all illustrations are from the author's collection.

Cover design by Gore Studio, Inc., Nashville, Tennessee.

Library of Congress Cataloging-in-Publication Data

Garrison, Webb B.
     The encyclopedia of Civil War usage : an illustrated compendium of the everyday language of soldiers and civilians / Webb Garrison with Cheryl Garrison.
        p.   cm.
     Includes bibliographical references (p.)
     ISBN 1-58182-280-0 (alk. paper)
     ISBN 1-58182-186-7 (hardcover : alk. paper)
     1. United States—History—Civil War, 1861–1865—Language—Encyclopedias.   2. United States—History—Civil War, 1861–1865—Social aspects—Encyclopedias.   3. Soldiers—United States—Language—Encyclopedias.   4. English language—United States—Usage—Encyclopedias.   5. Americanisms—Encyclopedias.   I. Garrison, Cheryl, 1945- .   II. Title.
E468.9.G373 2001
973.7'03—dc21

                                                 2001028374

Printed in the United States of America

1 2 3 4 5 6 7 8 9 10—07 06 05 04 03 02

to the next generation

Contents

To the User

LANGUAGE EVOLVES from generation to generation. Dozens of word usages that were commonplace during the Civil War have since disappeared from our speech or have changed in meaning. For example, many officers on both sides reported that their troops "amused the enemy," but not a one explained specifically what his soldiers did in this process. To a military engineer of the period, *enciente* was an important term but it didn't occur to him that it might be a variant of French or Italian for *pregnant*.

Men laid their lives on the line for the commander known as "Old Granny," but few people today know to whom the title refers. "Fresh fish!" sounds as though it might be the sales pitch of a street vendor, but the men in gray or blue trembled inwardly when they heard it for the first time. Since a "false muzzle" was not part of the gear used with horses, what was it? Who gave the USS *Monitor* its name, and why did he select it?

This volume explores standard, slang, and substitute words and phrases in the vocabulary of both Billy Yank and Johnny Reb and their civilian contemporaries. It deals with syntax, battle sectors, and weapons and their components. Prisons, nicknames, generals, officeholders, named guns, horses, ships, and a few famous mascots are also treated.

A small number of unofficial titles of several well-known fighting units are briefly explained. Clothing, food, and insignia are also defined. Also described briefly are projectiles, maneuvers, and fortifications (both permanent and temporary).

Although there were relatively few dramatic and vital battles on the water, the naval war was central to the outcome of this sectional struggle. Hence a substantial number of naval terms are included (such definitions are prefaced with an N).

If the word or topic pertained to the war, almost any military, naval, or legal expression was considered for inclusion. There are, however, no biographical vignettes of general officers or short summaries of battles and campaigns, since these are readily available in sources such as *The Historical Times Illustrated Encyclopedia of the Civil War* (Patricia L. Faust), *Who Was Who in the Civil War* (Stewart Sifakis), *Generals in Blue* (Ezra J. Warner), *Generals in Gray* (Warner), and *The Civil War Dictionary* (Mark M. Boatner III; the title is a bit misleading, since few verbal usages are treated, but its vignettes concerning several hundred general officers have no easily found counterparts).

In this volume, the choice of entries was based primarily upon the language of military and naval reports and the diaries, letters, memoirs, eyewitness accounts, autobiographies, acts of Congress, and reports of key congressional bodies. Numerous terms that are not self-explanatory appear in these indispensable primary sources. These sources are listed in the bibliography, along with several reference works of the period without which this study could not have been made.

Military units identified by numbers and states are infantry regiments made up of volunteers or conscripts unless otherwise specified. Use of SMALL CAPITAL LETTERS within entries indicates that an entry exists for that subject in this volume.

The production of this work marks the culmination of thirty years of research and writing during which any word, phrase, title, or named installation not self-explanatory was filed for future reference. Numerous long entries have few if any counterparts in other works about the all-consuming and fierce struggle of Americans against Americans. There is little recorded material available on the black flag policy, for example, but some commanders on both sides resorted to it. The saga of The Immortal 600 is but a footnote to the outcome of the war, but it is a significant peephole through which to glimpse the values and attitudes that prevailed during the war.

It is my wish that this volume will be a helpful tool and will stimulate new thought among another generation of Civil War scholars. There is much that has fallen by the wayside as scholarship on the war has accumulated new insights over the almost 150 years since the conflict concluded. Some of that which has receded into the shadows is rooted in the evolution of our language, and only by rediscovering how words were used during the war years can we better grasp what our predecessors recorded of their experiences in the midst of this convulsion in the nation's history.

Webb Garrison

The Encyclopedia of
CIVIL WAR USAGE

A

A-1. N. Abbreviation for "first class, excellent, or prime." This expression grew out of the usage by insurance agents to indicate the condition of the hull of a ship (classified by letters of the alphabet) and its equipment (classified by numbers). The Lloyd's Register was maintained by a British insurance firm, and a vessel designated as A-1 had both a first-class hull and first-class equipment.

abaft. N. Toward the stern of a ship; synonymous with AFT.

abatis. Occasionally spelled "abattis," this defensive structure consisted of felled trees with their tops pointing outward and usually their limbs cut off about two feet from the trunk and sharpened. Federals and Confederates borrowed the idea from Great Britain and Europe, where it was frequently used during the early nineteenth century. Abatis played a prominent role in the defense of Atlanta and numerous other sites. CHEVAUX-DE-FRISE are similar in structure but constructed of rough or dressed lumber.

abolitionist. A derisive term applied by Southerners to any military foe in spite of the fact that great numbers of men who fought in blue did not do so for the purpose of the abolition of SLAVERY. For example, Confederate Gen. W. B. Taliaferro fumed on July 21, 1863, "Abolitionists occupied Morris Island in force." At first a minority of Union soldiers believed they were going to war to end slavery. Most of them fought to save the Union, for the sake of their pay, as adventurers, or for personal reasons.

absent without leave. With "official" added, this phrase is currently abbreviated "AWOL." In 1861–65 the designation saw far less frequent use than did DESERTER and SKULKER. In numerous instances it was used to designate men known to be prisoners of the enemy. As early as February 1, 1862, Confederate Gen. George B. Crittenden expressed embarrassment about the number of his men who were absent without leave.

absentee. A soldier not present for duty but not listed as a DESERTER, a STRAGGLER, or absent without leave. When the opening guns of the war were fired at FORT SUMTER, nearly 20 percent of the men and officers of the U.S. Army were absentees. Hundreds were too sick to report for duty, and others were on leave.

Absterdam. A 4.5-inch shell that carried a lead SABOT, or shoe, and two lead rings designed to grip the rifling of a gun. Tests showed that the majority of these projectiles tumbled in flight. Branded as inferior, they were seldom used in combat but continued to be used experimentally.

accept the gage, to. Although archaic by scholarly standards, this medieval military term was used occasionally by general officers on both sides. Occasionally a commander faced the undeniable likelihood of defeat but felt compelled by honor to

3

fight. When he reached such a decision, he considered himself much like medieval knights who stooped to pick up a gage, or glove, tossed to the ground by an opponent as a challenge. At Pea Ridge, Arkansas, Confederate Gen. Earl Van Dorn recorded the reluctance with which he "accepted the gage" from the enemy.

according to one's number. Many commanders used a system of numbers to indicate what action should be taken during combat. The death of a comrade often caused the man next to him to "take another number" (the number assigned earlier to the fallen comrade), and then to follow a new course of action.

accoutrements, accouterments. This term was almost always used in the plural. It referred to the equipment (not including clothing) carried by a uniformed soldier, sailor, or marine. Accoutrements varied from one service to another but incorporated such items as belt, CAP BOX, CARTRIDGE BOX, MUSKET or RIFLE, scabbard and SWORD. Long established usage usually excluded a man's canteen, haversack, and knapsack. In mid-December 1860 in Charleston, military storekeeper F. F. Humphreys sent forty muskets and accoutrements to Fort Moultrie and almost immediately began begging Maj. Robert Anderson to

return these items. News of the shipment made "a violent demonstration" likely, he warned. During the fiscal year that began on July 1, 1863, Federal quartermasters provided 509,578 accouterments for INFANTRY and 91,410 for CAVALRY.

Ace of Spades. A name of admiration bestowed upon Robert E. Lee as a tribute to the skill with which he directed his men to dig trenches in front of Petersburg.

acknowledge the corn, to. Widely used by Rebels but seldom heard among Yankees, this phrase was employed to mean confession to a hoax, deception, or trick.

acoustic shadow. Although only a few official reports mention this phenomenon, it was a common occurrence. Theories of the time suggested that unknown forces sometimes caused very loud sounds, such as the firing of ARTILLERY, to be stifled in some, but not all, nearby areas. High-ranking officers experienced what they and newspaper correspondents called "silent battles" at several sites. This phenomenon was reported from Port Royal, Hampton Roads (during the *Monitor-Virginia* fight), Perryville, and Fair Oaks. At Chancellorsville, Thomas J. "Stonewall" Jackson's smashing attack on the right of the Federal line

Reports of acoustic shadows included the May 31–June 1, 1862, battle at Fair Oaks, Virginia.

was not heard at the Union command post. At Gettysburg, Confederate Gen. Richard Ewell was accused of dawdling, but he claimed that he did not hear Gen. James Longstreet's opening bombardment, and so he did not know when to move his men. Acoustic shadows were probably produced by chance combinations of terrain, barometric pressure, fog, and smoke. There is, however, no clear and consistent explanation for all of the reported incidents.

action. A widely used but loosely defined term for an engagement between enemy forces; often treated as synonymous with BATTLE.

NATIONAL ARCHIVES

Adams grenade. John S. Adams of Taunton, Massachusetts, developed a hand grenade that received an 1865 patent too late for it to see effective use. Had it been available earlier, it probably would have saved many a man's hand and arm. It was activated by a hook fastened to a wrist strap, meaning that it had to be thrown with considerable force to set the FUSE. Live shells with burning fuses, tossed toward the enemy, were often termed GRENADES.

Adams revolver. In England, Robert Adams developed a series of double-action side arms, which allowed the cylinder to rotate at the same time the trigger was pulled to cock the hammer and allow it to fall. These revolvers were manufactured in quantity in at least three calibers: .32, .44, and .50. A few were made in Massachusetts under license from the parent firm. Letters and diaries, chiefly Federal, abound with references to its usefulness.

adjutant. Derived from a Latin term meaning "to assist," this title was applied to a staff officer by both Gray and Blue. The communication of orders was high on the list of an adjutant's responsibilities. An adjutant-general often published orders in the name of his commander.

admiral. N. Denoting the highest rank among naval officers. The first Union officer to receive this rank was David G. Farragut after his capture of New Orleans in April 1862. The first Confederate admiral was Franklin Buchanan, a man who tried to rescind his resignation from the Federal navy when his state (Maryland) did not secede from the Union, and who went on to command the CSS *Virginia* in its successful attack on the Federal fleet at Hampton Roads in March 1862.

Advance. This 902-ton side-wheel steamer was one of the most successful BLOCKADE-RUNNERS of the war. The ship was built in 1862 at Greenock, Scotland, and purchased under the name *Lord Clyde* by the state of North Carolina in 1863. Renamed *Advance* (sometimes recorded as *A. D. Vance*), the vessel made more than twenty voyages prior to being captured off Wilmington, North Carolina, on September 10, 1864, by USS *Santiago de Cuba*. The blockade-runner was adopted by the Union navy and in 1866 was renamed *Frolic*.

The Advance, *renamed* Frolic, *in Naples after the war.*

NAVAL HISTORICAL CENTER

advanced lunettes. These earthworks resembled BASTIONS and RAVELINS but were thrown up beyond the GLACIS of defensive fortifications.

advertise, to. To make public deliberately or by chance. At New Orleans in September 1862, Union Gen. Benjamin F. Butler expressed annoyance at the fashion in which steamers advertised their approach "from a distance of three miles." He protested that this impeded the likelihood that his forces could capture anyone or seize supplies that could be moved out of the way.

advice. Information secured from CAVALRY, SCOUTS, spies, or other sources that aided a commander in making decisions about troop movements. Gov. Andrew G. Curtin of Pennsylvania provided Federal leaders with a stream of advice that came so frequently that some of his colleagues wished he would keep his information to himself.

aerial reconnaissance. Some commanders encouraged reconnaissance from free-floating and tethered balloons in 1861. Most of this work was done for Federal forces by men organized by Thaddeus Lowe. Early in the conflict, this term was applied to sightings made from elevated signal towers, such as those erected by Southerners near the field of Manassas prior to the battle of First Bull Run. Four signal towers were built under the direction of Capt. E. Porter Alexander, and some analysts suggest that these contributed significantly to the ensuing Confederate victory.

aeronaut. Borrowed from eighteenth-century British usage, this name was used to designate members of Thaddeus Lowe's crews and other pioneer military balloonists.

affair. An ENGAGEMENT of minor size and consequences.

afloat. (1) N. Aboard ship or being borne by a ship. (2) In an uncertain or ambiguous position. In June 1862 U.S. Secretary of the Navy Gideon Welles reported to Cmdr. Samuel F. Du Pont, "The [U.S. Naval] school is afloat."

aft. N. Toward the stern of a vessel; synonymous with ABAFT.

NAVAL HISTORICAL CENTER

***Agawam*, USS.** This 1,173-ton Sassacus-class double-end steam GUNBOAT was built in March 1864 at Portland, Maine, and assigned to the North Atlantic Blockading Squadron. She was detailed to the James River for mine-clearing operations, including an August 13, 1864, engagement with shore batteries. In December 1864 the vessel was in the Norfolk Navy Yard for repairs while her crew was assigned to the initial assault on FORT FISHER, North Carolina. From February 1865 to the end of the war, *Agawam* was assigned to the inland waters of North Carolina.

Ager, occasionally spelled "Agar." Inventor Wilson Ager perfected a single-barrel rapid-fire gun. Despite its price tag of eight hundred dollars, many officers were initially anxious to adopt it because it was considered capable of firing 120 rounds per minute. Because a handle had to be turned for cartridges to drop into place from a hopper, the weapon bore a superficial resemblance to a coffee grinder. As a result, it was ridiculed as the coffee-mill gun. Less than one hundred of these "Union Repeating Guns" were purchased during the war, and afterward some were offered as surplus at five dollars apiece.

aggregate, to. To bring together or unite. This term was sometimes used by an officer who brought together units scattered by combat under his command. Writing of his experiences during 1863, Confederate Gen. John B. Imboden said that a commander "aggregated several detachments into their respective temporary brigades."

agnew. Despite being named for an obscure early user, the name of this garment was seldom capitalized. A variant of the standard Federal army shirt, it was worn by many female nurses of the U.S. SANITARY COMMISSION. Most users kept the collar open, rolled up the sleeves, and draped it over their skirts.

ague. A nonspecific term for chills and fever, often but not always occasioned by malaria.

aide-de-camp. Often an ex officio position on a general officer's staff. Consequently it was sometimes filled by civilians and foreign OBSERVERS. Aide functions were so numerous and varied that the title appears countless times in documents of 1861–65.

aiguilette. An ornamental tassel plus the cord from which it is suspended, designed to identify the wearer's branch of service.

air, to be in the. Usually used in connection with accounts of troop movements, this term indicated the consequences of being forced into an area without protection or support on either flank.

Ajax. A sorrel horse presented to Robert E. Lee after the battle of Second Manassas (Bull Run).

Alabama, CSS. Built at Liverpool, England, by John Laird Sons and Company, this 1,050-ton screw sloop-of-war was sold to Confederate agents for £47,500. The vessel was commissioned

on August 24, 1862, as CSS *Alabama*. She could carry 285 tons of coal and had a maximum speed of nearly 13 knots. Her 1862 battery consisted of only eight BLAKELY guns, but the fast raider became the bane of North Atlantic shipping and carried the war on the water into the West Indies and passed the Horn of Africa en route to the East Indies. Her exploits claimed more than sixty prizes worth $6 million. On June 11, 1864, she arrived at Cherbourg, France, for repairs. The Union sloop-of-war *Kearsarge* arrived three days later and waited for the Confederate raider to appear. The Federals were not disappointed when the *Alabama* sailed out to engage on June 19. After a little more than an hour's engagement, the Southern vessel was a wreck. The *Kearsarge* rescued most of the Confederate crew, but a British yacht rescued the raider's commander and about forty others.

Alabama, USS. Built at Portsmouth, New Hampshire, and rated at 1,448 tons when launched, this vessel had a battery of fifteen guns, eight of which were 9-inch PIECES. Despite her size and strength, her accomplishments were vastly outshone by the Confederate raider of the same name.

Alabama claims. An international legal case in which the United States demanded compensation from Great Britain for damages done by Confederate raiders. Several of these vessels were built in the island kingdom; the *Alabama* was the most successful and notorious of them. Argued in Geneva, Switzerland, over a period of fifteen months, the case led to a complicated verdict under whose terms both nations received monetary damages.

Britain paid the United States $15.5 million for losses brought about by British-built ships, and the United States paid Britain a trifle less than $2 million to compensate British citizens for losses incurred because of the Civil War.

alarm rattle. N. A wooden rattle about one foot long, similar to those carried by some watchmen on shore. Regulations called for at least one rattle to be aboard every U.S. warship, ready for use to signal that trouble had been sighted.

NAVAL HISTORICAL CENTER

Albemarle, **CSS.** Built at Edwards Ferry, North Carolina, in 1864, this 158-foot IRONCLAD ram lasted only six months. On April 19, she attacked a number of Federal ships off Plymouth, North Carolina, driving off most of the vessels and sinking USS *Southfield.* On May 5, *Albemarle* struck again at Union ships in the North Carolina Sounds but was lightly damaged. She was attacked at her berth in Plymouth and sunk on October 28, 1864, by a spar torpedo boat. When Union troops occupied Plymouth again, *Albemarle* was refloated and taken to Norfolk.

alert. Frequently used as a noun, this term labeled a member of a formal or informal organization whose announced goal was "feeding and clothing our boys." Confined to the North, the alert movement included many children among its members. The name possibly stems from the election of 1860 in which "wide awakes" stayed on the alert and helped to score a win for Abraham Lincoln.

alien enemy. Largely but not exclusively used by Confederates, this term identified a loyal citizen of the United States residing in a seceded state. Unlike UNIONISTS, such people were openly sup-

portive of the North. On August 14, 1861, Confederate president Jefferson Davis issued a proclamation requiring all male citizens of the United States, age fourteen or older, to leave the Confederacy within forty days. Any U.S. citizen who failed to act on this warning was to be treated as an alien enemy. Numerous persons of Northern birth or loyalty who would not or could not leave suffered SEQUESTRATION of everything they owned. Col. Charles Anderson of the U.S. Army, a brother of Union Maj. Robert Anderson, was treated as an alien enemy at San Antonio during the autumn of 1861.

Allegheny Ed. An adaptation of "Old Allegheny," the nickname of Confederate Gen. Edward Johnson. He was a veteran of the Mexican and Seminole Wars and served under Thomas J. "Stonewall" Jackson in the Shenandoah campaign of 1862. He commanded the STONEWALL BRIGADE at Gettysburg, the Wilderness, and Spotsylvania, where he was captured. After his exchange, he was sent to the western theater and participated in the 1864 battles of Franklin and Nashville, where he was

captured again. He spent the rest of the war in the OLD CAPITOL PRISON and was not released until July 1865.

allegiance barracks. A special set of barracks erected at FORT DELAWARE that housed Rebel prisoners who had taken the oath of allegiance to the United States.

"All Quiet Along the Potomac." An 1861 poem by Ethel L. Beers included this phrase. Employed frequently by Union Gen. George B. McClellan to mean "no action now," the poem that borrowed his term elevated it into use throughout the North. Part of the work entitled "The Picket Guard" read: "All quiet along the Potomac tonight, / No sound save the rush of the river, / While soft falls the dew on the face of the dead / The picket's off duty forever."

Alton. The first Illinois state prison was erected at this Mississippi River town in 1831. Public indignation was aroused when Dorothea Dix published an exposé describing it as being situated in an undrained area where many prisoners and guards were frequently ill. As a result of her crusade, a new state prison was built at Joliet and Alton was abandoned. Early in the war, Union Gen. Henry W. Halleck secured permission from Gen. Lorenzo Thomas to turn Alton into a military facility. Gov. Richard Yates gave his approval, and prisoners began arriving early in 1862. Just one week later the place was crowded beyond its capacity. When a smallpox epidemic broke out in the Alton facility, six to ten men died daily for many weeks. Other maladies that afflicted the prisoners were malaria, pneumonia, and diarrhea. About eight thousand men were confined at the grossly inadequate prison. Of these an estimated 20 percent died. Only a few prisons in the North or in the South had a worse record for the medical care of their inmates. At war's end, the antiquated penitentiary was demolished, but mass graves in which the unidentified dead were dumped are still there.

alvine flux. Another medical phrase for diarrhea.

amalgamation. A reference to interracial sexual activity and children of mixed heritage. Outspoken abolitionist William Lloyd Garrison charged in his newspaper *The Liberator* that Southern planters practiced "unbridled lust and filthy amalgamation" with slave women. The record shows that Garrison was accurate. A Bostonian was criticized in the North as well as the South for preaching that "the blending of the two races by amalgamation is just what is needed for the perfection of both."

ambrotype. A photograph generated by a process perfected in 1854 by Boston and Philadelphia inventors James Cutting and Isaac Rehn. Simpler and less expensive to produce than DAGUERREO-TYPES, ambrotypes were widely available by 1861. A lasting image of this variety was made by means of a light-sensitive collodion process that yielded photographic positives on glass plates.

U.S. ARMY MILITARY HISTORY INSTITUTE

ambulance. A two- or four-wheeled horse-drawn vehicle used to transport the wounded. Napoleon Bonaparte allegedly coined the name, calling the then common "walking hospital" *l'hopital ambulant.* Away from the battlefield, ambulances were often commandeered by officers for their personal use or for use by their wives. The U.S. Congress delayed until 1864 an act that attached the ambulance corps to the army. Numerous surgeons preferred to call the vehicle an AVALANCHE.

American Bastille. A reference to Washington's OLD CAPITOL PRISON and referring to the Bastille prison in France, which housed a great many political prisoners before the French Revolution.

American Colonization Society. Organized in 1817 with the goal of raising funds to transport free blacks to Africa, the movement was supported by many prominent men, including Henry Clay, John Marshall, and James Monroe. Abraham Lincoln publicly endorsed the society and its goals in 1853 and a few years later became one of the managers of its Illinois chapter. During an 1857 speech, he told a Peoria audience that his first impulse was to send all freed slaves to the tiny Republic of Liberia. Some of his biographers omit all mention of this aspect of the future president's views about SLAVERY. He strongly favored a three-step process of ending slavery: (1) gradual emancipation, ending about 1900, (2) compensation to owners, and (3) overseas COLONIZATION.

American flag dispatch. On January 29, 1861, three days after the secession of Louisiana, U.S. Secretary of the Treasury John A. Dix sent instructions to his agents in New Orleans that ordered the captains of the revenue cutters in the port city to relinquish their vessels to the appropriate Federal authorities. Dix subsequently learned that Capt. J. G. Breshwood of the *McClelland* boasted that he would deliver his vessel to the Secessionist Party in Louisiana. The Treasury secretary sent follow-up orders to the U.S. authorities in New Orleans and authorized them to seize the vessel. The dispatch gained

John A. Dix

immortality of a sort by a single sentence of the text: "If anyone attempts to haul down the American flag, shoot him on the spot."

ammo. A universal abbreviation of ammunition. Short supplies in the early months of the war influenced Federal and Confederate quartermasters to maintain tight controls over the flow of ammunition to troops. During training, many citizen-soldiers were limited to ten rounds per week. Numerous sizes and kinds of ammunition created problems. After the July 1–3, 1863, battle

of Gettysburg, a tabulation by READY FINDERS revealed that at least twenty-four thousand fully loaded weapons were recovered from the field. About 20 percent of these held three or more rounds; one rifle contained twenty-three loads, one on top of the other. At the close of the 1863 fiscal year, Federal arsenals held close to 1.2 million cannonballs, shells, and other projectiles for heavy guns. At the same time, almost one-half million artillery pieces were on hand. Cartridges, percussion caps, friction primers, and fuses for small arms were inventoried separately—a total of more than two hundred million items.

ammunition chest. (1) A wooden chest that held a substantial quantity of ammunition from which soldiers filled their cartridge belts. (2) With regard to artillery, these wooden chests were used to store ammunition in the field. They were carried on LIMBERS (which usually held one chest) and CAISSONS (which could hold at least two chests) and provided seating for the gun crew. An empty chest weighed 185 pounds, but depending on the type of ammunition, each could weigh as much 560 pounds. The interior of the chests were specifically designed for each type of projectile.

amnesty. A formal pardon of an individual or a group of persons, often involving a proclamation by a high-ranking military or civil official. Abraham Lincoln issued a March 10, 1863, proclamation offering amnesty to all Federal deserters who returned to their units by April 1. One year later he again offered a similar pardon. Southern civilians who took an OATH OF ALLEGIANCE or LOY-

10

ALTY OATH to the United States were offered amnesty on December 8, 1863, and March 26, 1864. A very small number of people responded to these offers. Earlier amnesties announced for Federal soldiers had no discernible effect upon the rate of desertion. On May 9, 1862, Confederate president Jefferson Davis ordered deserters to return to their ranks but offered no pardon. Numerous generals—among whom were Braxton Bragg, Theophilus Holmes, and Leonidas Polk—followed up Davis's order with offers of amnesty. On August 1, 1863, a desperate Davis gave deserters twenty days to return to their ranks without punishment. Like the offers made by Lincoln, the Davis order had little impact. Individual Confederate generals were allowed to offer amnesty as they deemed appropriate, but Davis abandoned the use of amnesties to refill his armies' ranks made ragged by combat and illness.

amnesty oath. The solemn vow that former Confederates were required to make in order to have their citizenship restored. Like the LOYALTY OATH, which had a similar effect, this affirmation had a variety of forms. On August 8, 1864, the U.S. War Department issued instructions governing the administration of amnesty oaths offered by Abraham Lincoln on March 6 of that year. After the surrender at Appomattox, Robert E. Lee took the amnesty oath as soon as he was offered a chance to do so. His signed document was, however, misplaced by either chance or malice. When the document was found almost a century later, the U.S. citizenship of the commander of the Army of Northern Virginia was restored by President Jimmy Carter.

amputee fork. Manufactured by a major maker of cutlery, this implement was a long, curved fork with a knife blade at the back of its curve. Some amputees found it extremely useful.

amuse, to. To take action calculated to keep the enemy occupied without risking an escalation that could lead to battle. This unusual expression, which did not survive the Civil War by many years, was in constant use during about fourteen hundred days of conflict. At Fort Lincoln, Missouri, in early September 1861, James H. Lane, the commander of the Kansas Brigade (U.S.), reported that his CAVALRY engaged a large Confederate force near Fort Scott. In the face of superior numbers and firepower, Lane fell back to Fort Lincoln. He reported, "I left my cavalry to amuse the enemy until we could establish ourselves here and remove our good stores from Fort Scott."

Anaconda Plan. Eager to oust Gen. Winfield Scott and take his place, Gen. George B. McClellan ridiculed a plan proposed by the aging head of the U.S. Army. Scott suggested slowly moving Federal forces down the Atlantic Coast and the Mississippi River in order to isolate the South and choke off the supply lines of the Confederacy. McClellan dubbed it the "boa constrictor plan." Newspaper correspondents modified the term to "anaconda," and cartoonists were quick to deride the passive offensive. Yet an adaptation of this early plan—revised and executed by Ulysses S. Grant and William T. Sherman—keyed the ultimate Federal victory.

Ancient of Days. A satirical title bestowed upon Abraham Lincoln in the North.

Andersonville. The most infamous of Civil War prisons, the Andersonville prison was established in February 1964 in Sumter County in

southwestern Georgia, not far from the Georgia Southwestern Railroad line. The facility was founded to reduce the number of Union prisoners being detained in camps around Richmond (thus relieving the food shortages being experienced in the Confederate capital) and to deliberately remove the prisoners from the battle lines (so as to make escape unfeasible and reduce the number of guards needed to watch over the large number of captives). Initially known as Camp Sumter, the open stockade into which the Federal prisoners were herded eventually took its name from nearby Anderson Station. Built to hold about ten thousand captives, the facility came to be crowded with more than three times that number. Most of the captives arrived weak and sick from the Richmond prisons. Bad food and limited rations were compounded by diarrhea and scurvy. The prisoners became walking skeletons, and the death rate was horrendous—thirteen thousand men were buried in the camp cemetery. Although he was not directly responsible for the atrocities at Andersonville, commandant Henry Wirz was hanged as the only man convicted of war crimes during the Civil War. A separate and smaller officers prison, known as Castle Reed, was only a half mile from the notorious stockade. Conditions were not much better than in the stockade, and this little-known prison was crowded with three hundred officers. When conditions at the stockade reached their lowest,

Confederate authorities moved to relieve the crisis by transferring some prisoners to other camps in South Carolina, specifically in Charleston, Columbia, and Florence. Other plans were made to construct a larger stockade at Millen, Georgia, that was known as Camp Lawton. The work, however, was halted and then abandoned because of shortages of building materials and a fear that, after seizing Atlanta, Gen. William T. Sherman would march through southwestern Georgia to free the prisoners.

Andersonville of the North. See ROCK ISLAND.

Andrews pump. One of the most efficient pumps of the period, it was widely used in permanent fortifications and on naval vessels.

anemometer. An instrument designed to measure the velocity and force of wind. One of the most widely used forms of this instrument consisted of four cups mounted on the ends of crossed rods.

Angel of Cairo. A title of gratitude bestowed upon Mary J. Safford of the U.S. SANITARY COMMISSION. Working tirelessly at Cairo, Illinois, she was regarded by many sick or wounded men as a surrogate mother. A spinal injury suffered after the April 1862 battle of Shiloh removed her from active service as a volunteer.

Angel of Marye's Heights. On December 13, 1862, Federal troops made repeated futile charges against the powerful Southern position on Marye's Heights at Fredericksburg. That night hundreds of wounded men who lay where they had fallen that afternoon moaned and cried for water and for help. They lay in a "no man's land" into which no soldier on either side was supposed to venture without risking fire. Nineteen-year-old Sgt. Richard Rowland Kirkland of the 2d South Carolina Infantry requested permission to take water to the fallen Northerners. When his BRIGADE commander, Joseph B. Kershaw, granted the request,  Kirkland spent part of the bitterly cold night taking canteen after canteen to the wounded men and even covered one of the men with his own coat. Both sides were struck by the act of compassion, and Federal soldiers cheered the man who offered some small comfort to their comrades. Nine months later Kirkland was killed during the September 20, 1863, battle of Chickamauga. His act is marked with a statue on the Fredericksburg battlefield and a fountain to the "Angel of Marye's Heights" in Camden, South Carolina. Kirkland is also commemorated by Virginia's Sgt. Kirkland's Museum.

angle of defense. In field works, the junction of a flanking face with a face of a field work or the fields of fire from one field work across the face of another.

ankle boot. Commonly worn by cavalrymen of the U.S. Army since the mid-1830s, this ankle-high boot was used in the Civil War by those who could afford it. Because it had several eyelets, it was unlikely to be lost in combat.

Annie. A 32-pound smoothbore piece named for the wife of Irish-born Lt. Richard Dowling. Southern defenders used "Annie" with tremendous effect during the September 8, 1863, battle of Sabine Pass.

annoy, to. To keep the enemy on the move or alert without making an attack. Some commanders chose to have their ARTILLERY throw an occasional shell in the direction of the enemy. Others preferred to harass their opponents by having small squads of riflemen fire at the enemy's flanks from distant points of concealment. When Gen. Benjamin F. Butler was placed in command at FORT MONROE, Virginia, Gen. Winfield Scott cautioned him not to let the enemy "annoy" him.

antebellum. In general speech this term designates the period between 1812 and 1860. Strictly speaking, the Latin phrase means "before the war" and could be applied to any prewar period. In the United States, the label is still used to designate the prewar South.

***Antietam*, USS.** Constructed at the Philadelphia Navy Yard, this huge warship displaced 2,354 tons and was powered by thirty steam boilers. Two of her great engines had cylinders that were sixty inches in diameter. Her name commemorated the September 17, 1862, battle of Antietam, the bloodiest day in American history.

appendage. Anything that gained its importance by virtue of being attached to or associated with something else. For example, a tool needed for taking a musket or rifle apart or assembling it was an appendage to the weapon. In February 1862 Union Gen. Henry W. Halleck directed Gen. William S. Rosecrans to make Fort Heiman an "appendage" to FORT HENRY.

Appomattox. A common reference to Appomattox Court House, Virginia, where on April 9, 1865, Robert E. Lee surrendered the Army of Northern Virginia to Ulysses S. Grant.

appreciate, to. To comprehend or understand. Officials were assembled at Montgomery,

Alabama, during the spring of 1861 to form a provisional Confederate government. Their reaction to a series of telegrams from Charleston led observers in the South as well as the North to say that these men did not appreciate the delicacy of the situation at the port city.

approach. (1) The line of attack. (2) In siege works, a trench facilitating the advance of an attacking force, under cover, against a fortified position. In general, these trenches were wide enough to accommodate four men abreast and deep enough to allow troops to move upright. At Vicksburg, the approaches were as much as eight feet wide and seven feet deep. The soil excavated in the digging of the trench was used to shield the trench from enemy fire. To avoid enfilading fire from the opposing side, trenches zigzagged from one line (called PARALLELS) to the next. (3) Trenches designed to allow troops to enter defensive works from the rear and under cover.

apron. Long before the war began, veteran gunners knew that the touch-hole of a cannon could be very dangerous. As a result some unknown artisan designed a piece of leather to cover this opening when a GUN was fired. Similar to a miniature baker's attire, it took that name. Federal ARTILLERY regulations required that the apron be over the vent when a piece was not in use. Leather was so scarce in the South that many a Confederate gun had no apron.

Archer. Ammunition for numerous kinds of guns was prone to drop its cup, or disc, upon friendly troops over whose heads it was fired. In an effort to eliminate this source of danger, ammunition that was tapered toward the rear came into use. An obscure Confederate named Archer developed a shell of this type, and his surname came to be attached to it.

ardent. An enthusiastic or fervent person. This descriptive term was also applied to especially potent alcohol by many men and their commanders. In March 1861 Union Gen. George B. McClellan tried to stop the transportation of most ardent spirits in Ohio. He made an exception for "hospital and subsistence stores" and "the private stores of officers."

argee. This humorous adaptation of initials standing for "rot gut" was used to name any kind of decidedly inferior whiskey.

NAVAL HISTORICAL CENTER

Arkansas, **CSS.** Built at Memphis and on the Yazoo River in 1861 and 1862, this IRONCLAD ram was powered by twin screws and could attain a speed of eight miles per hour. Two of her seven guns were 100-pound COLUMBIADS. On July 15, 1862, she engaged three Federal vessels then ran past a fleet of thirty-three more Union vessels, fighting her way to Vicksburg. In early August the vessel was dispatched to Baton Rouge but suffered a breakdown during an encounter with USS *Essex* and was scuttled to prevent her capture.

Arkansas toothpick. Some northern-reared soldiers used this term to label a SIDE-KNIFE; among Southern troops, the usage was universally employed and understood.

Arlington Mansion. The Virginia estate that was owned by Mrs. Robert E. Lee under the terms of her father's will. Because it was close to the Federal capital, Lee feared for his wife's safety as soon as hostilities broke out. At his urging, she eventually left, and it was soon occupied by Federal forces

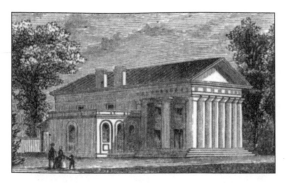

under Gen. Irvin McDowell. The decision to turn the place into a Federal cemetery was almost certainly made in a bid to deprive Lee of the use of the home after the war.

arm. Any of the various branches of service on land. A general officer might say, "The chief duty of the cavalry arm is to supply intelligence useful to the infantry arm and the artillery arm."

armor. Perhaps because metal and artisans were scarce in the South, use of body armor was largely a Northern experiment. In a few cities, small industrial plants turned out "steel vests" for sale by sutlers. Although touted as extensively tested, these metal pieces seldom served to deflect small-arms projectiles. Most men who bought armor discarded it after their first exposure to hostile fire.

arms, all. A shortened term by which to designate all branches of military service.

arms, to stack. To form a freestanding pyramid by placing MUSKETS or CARBINES butt down and held in place by their interlocking stacking swivels or their bayonets. This maneuver was frequently performed at the end of a day's exercises in camp. To stack arms was a vivid gesture of surrender when performed in the field by

forces such as those of Confederate Gen. Joseph E. Johnston at Durham's Station, North Carolina. When a body of men in a state of rebellion against authority stacked arms, this move was a nonverbal statement of a refusal to fight. Hence it was sometimes performed just prior to a mutiny.

Armstrong gun. Southerners imported these banded rifled cannon from England in both breech- and muzzleloading versions. Field guns used special studded Armstrong ammunition that served as both canister and spherical shell. They were known to be accurate long-range weapons, but the Confederate ordnance department apparently preferred BLAKELY and WHITWORTH guns in the field. A few large-caliber Armstrongs appeared in the South, but their special ammunition limited their application. The first of these weapons to be used in the Civil War was purchased by an anonymous Charleston citizen who contributed it to Secessionists for use against FORT SUMTER.

army. The largest organizational body in Confederate and Federal forces, usually named after the military department in which it was organized or functioned. Most of the sixteen Union armies bore the names of rivers. The Army of the Potomac and the Army of the Tennessee were among the most prominent of these. Nearly all of the twenty-three Confederate armies, such as the Army of Northern Virginia and the Army of Tennessee, were named for states or regions. The commanders of the armies normally established their headquarters in areas well to the rear of combat. As a result of this practice, Gen. James M. McPherson was the only Federal commander of an army to die from wounds on the battlefield. His only counterpart in gray to suffer a similar fate was Albert Sidney Johnston. A full general who commanded all Confederate forces west of the Allegheny Mountains, Johnston was struck in the back of his knee and bleed to death during the April 6, 1862, battle of Shiloh. On January 1, 1861, the U.S. Army—consisting of "regulars" only—numbered about fifteen thousand men. Over the course of the war, Federal armies may have totaled close to two million men in uniform, and Southerners approached nine hundred thousand under arms.

army grayback. An ordinary body louse whose name was derived from its color. Frequently a source of annoyance to the soldiers in the field, this insect was minute but prolific. It was the bane of many a man held prisoner, whether in the South or in the North. Even during weeks or months in the open, soldiers became infested with the pests.

artificer. In theory, this title designated a workman with experience and skill in making guns ready or repairing them. In practice, the term was applied to any civilian or soldier who had mechanical skills of any sort that were useful to the armed forces. Artificers were badly needed by industries producing martial and other essential goods. Although they were exempt from conscription, many of them volunteered. Since these men were likely to be assigned to a gun crew, large numbers of them were battle casualties.

artillery. Soldiers trained, armed, and equipped to use large-caliber GUNS, MORTARS, and HOWITZERS.

artillery, field. Cannon light enough to accompany INFANTRY or CAVALRY into the field and capable of rapid deployment against the enemy. A favorite weapon of this sort was the brass NAPOLEON, named for the French emperor. Heavy artillery was designed for stationary use, often in

U.S. ARMY MILITARY HISTORY INSTITUTE

defensive works that protected forts and cities. Light artillery, much of it even smaller than the Napoleon, was used chiefly by cavalry units. Field artillery played crucial roles in almost every action of the war.

assassination of the president. Several early chief executives received serious threats, and a few zealots set out to kill an American head of state prior to the outbreak of war. No attempt before 1865 had succeeded, however, and so Abraham Lincoln became the first president to die at the hand of an assassin.

assassination sympathizers. Although their names are not known with certainty, a number of Union soldiers were given this designation. These men allegedly registered their approval of John Wilkes Booth and the outcome of the president's death.

assembly. A signal from a drum or bugle calling every man in a post or command to come together at a designated central spot.

assessment. A term employed by military officers and elected officials on both sides. It normally meant "an enforced levy of cash or goods" that might be exacted from civilians—friendly or enemy. Rates of assessments varied widely, since they were often made at the discretion of commanders. At Cairo, Illinois, late in 1861, Union Gen. Ulysses S. Grant directed that an assessment be collected in Kentucky and Missouri. He had reason to believe that some citizens of Northern birth and rearing were among active Secessionists. Hence he directed that such persons should "be taxed 50 percent more than Southern men of their class and means."

asylum. Civilians used this term to designate any place of refuge, especially an institution whose mission was to care for those who could not care for themselves. In military parlance, the name was quite specific, referring to the SOLDIERS' HOME in Washington. This institution's primary mission was to give medical and other care to disabled veterans and other honorably discharged military personnel. It was generally known in the capital that Lincoln frequently visited this institution and sometimes spent the night there. At one time John Wilkes Booth planned to kidnap the chief executive while he was at the asylum or returning to Washington. This particular scheme collapsed when an announced visit was canceled.

A-tent. A canvas tent, quickly and easily erected, whose sides sloped downward from the ridge pole to form a shape approximately like the letter *A*. Although designed to hold only four men, such a structure was often packed with five to six soldiers. The floor of the tent was only about fifty square feet in size. When an A-tent was crammed with sleeping men, all of them had to turn simultaneously.

NAVAL HISTORICAL CENTER

***Atlanta,* CSS.** This British-built BLOCKADE-RUNNER was originally known as the *Fingal.* The

Atlanta was later refitted as a fighting vessel and renamed. The new Confederate warship never saw action, however. She was bottled up by the BLOCKADE and could not leave Wassaw Sound, Georgia. On June 17, 1863, she was captured by men aboard the USS *Weehawken* and *Nahant.*

***Atlanta,* USS.** Converted into a Federal warship after her capture, the onetime BLOCKADE-RUNNER had an undistinguished career in the U.S. Navy. This despite the fact that her battery was raised by her captors to include two 150-pound pivot RIFLES. She was stationed on the James River to support the Federal siege of Petersburg.

Atlantic cable. An especially designed submarine cable whose function was to establish a telegraph link between the United States and England. Despite several early failures, financiers such as Chicago's Marshall Field continued to put money into the venture until it achieved its goal.

attack. A movement designed to make direct contact with the enemy. An INFANTRY attack was often made with men deployed in LINE OF BATTLE. This formation was long but only two ranks deep. A variant was to attack in COLUMN, a formation relatively narrow but having eight to twenty ranks.

at the word. The interval after which action was taken by a body of men who waited for a verbal command such as "Load and fire!"

Attick. Because makers of this heavy-duty GUN guarded the process of its manufacture as a trade secret, little is known about it. Experts who examined 7-inch seacoast guns said that they were sure brass was used in making its bands.

Austrian Lorenz rifle. Second only to the British ENFIELD, the Austrian Model 1854 Lorenz .54-caliber RIFLE was one of the most popular imported shoulder arms of the war. The South acquired approximately 100,000 between 1862 and 1864. They were sometimes referred to as

Enfields, because a number of them had blued barrels and lockplates like the British weapon. Southerners used the Lorenz throughout the central and Trans-Mississippi areas. Meanwhile, more than 225,000 Lorenz rifles were acquired by the North, at first to preclude their sale to the South but then issued to Federal units when ORDNANCE inspectors approved the rifle. Prior to distribution to Union soldiers, the rifles were rebored to accept .58-caliber ammunition. The Lorenz was lighter than the U.S. Model 1861 SPRINGFIELD and Enfield rifles and longer than the U.S. Model 1841 "MISSISSIPPI" and two-banded Enfield model.

autumn divers. Organized bands of thieves who flourished in New York and other large eastern cities after the middle of 1862. These fellows lurked in the vicinity of conscription offices and relieved many a enlistee of his BOUNTY only minutes after his enlistment.

avalanche. Although not nearly so widely used as the four-wheel variety, this ambulance with only two wheels saw action on many fronts. It jolted and lurched so badly that it was dangerously unsafe. Many wounded men who had been stuffed into one of these vehicles compared its movements with the rushing of a mountain avalanche.

As a result the improvised name frequently appears in diaries and letters but was seldom mentioned in dispatches and reports. Some officers used its name interchangeably with that of the four-wheel AMBULANCE.

awkward squad. Veteran soldiers liked to apply this label to a unit of GREEN TROOPS whose members knew little or nothing about military commands and responses.

axle grease. A majority of outfits carried this essential material, typically in flat tin cans that held sixteen to twenty cubic inches. Without it, wagons, AMBULANCES, and FIELD ARTILLERY would have been quickly damaged. Much grease used during the war consisted of animal fat that was similar to but softer than tallow.

B

---

baby waker. First shot of a CANNONADE.

bait, to. To give food or drink to an animal, especially a horse.

Balaclava. A wool hood covering the head and neck, first worn by troops in the Crimean War. Balaclava (or Balaklava) was the focal point of the "Charge of the Light Brigade."

Bald Eagle. The nickname of Confederate Gen. Martin W. Gary, whose command may have been the last to leave Richmond in the aftermath of the breakthrough at Petersburg in April 1865.

baldrick. A wide decorative sash that was worn over one shoulder and across the chest by drum and band majors. An occasional AIDE-DE-CAMP displayed such sashes adapted from earlier ornamented leather belts used to support a bugle or a sword. Usage during the Civil War influenced the adoption of the baldrick by many civilian bands.

Baldy. (1) A nickname for Union Gen. William F. Smith. (2) A bright bay horse acquired by George G. Meade soon after the battle of First Bull Run (First Manassas) that carried him through the battles of Antietam, Fredericksburg, Chancellorsville, Gettysburg, and the Overland campaign, remaining with him until Meade's death. After the animal's death, its head was mounted in Philadelphia's Civil War Library and Museum.

baled hay. Dried and compressed mixed vegetables such as string beans, turnips, carrots, beets, and onions, issued in an attempt to prevent scurvy. Soldiers claimed that it included leaves, stalks, and roots. Officially known as desiccated compressed mixed vegetables, it was also known as DESECRATED VEGETABLES.

balk. (1) N. A rafter or tie beam on warships. (2) A twenty-seven-foot timber, five inches square, used as the base for the treadway over a pontoon bridge.

ball. A general reference to ammunition, such as cannonballs and MINIÉ BALLS. Balls used by the regular army prior to the war were regarded as superior to the shot manufactured during the war.

ball and chain. Heavy iron shackles used to prevent offenders from escaping.

Ballard rifle. A single-shot .45-, .46-, or .56-caliber weapon nearly four feet long. Patented in 1861, Ballards were manufactured chiefly between 1862 and 1863.

ballast. N. Any heavy material not listed on a cargo manifest that was used to stabilize a vessel and keep it in proper draft or trim. A vessel in ballast carried no cargo. Thousands of tons of waste granite, carried to Charleston as ballast in the decades before the war, were used to form the artificial island on which FORT SUMTER was built.

Balloon Corps. This aerial reconnaissance service was organized by pioneer balloonist Thaddeus Sobieski Constantine Lowe. During the first two years of the war, it functioned remarkably well. Lowe and those he recruited to occupy his balloons sent telegraph messages from the airborne baskets to the ground and frequently directed artillery fire. Observations from balloons proved valuable to mapmakers working under the direction of Gen. George B. McClellan. When Gen. Joseph Hooker was named to command the Army of the Potomac in early 1863, he reduced Lowe's staff and Lowe resigned. No successor was appointed. Although Southerners managed to launch a few balloons, they lacked the materials to manufacture these "gas bags" and did not hold sufficient gas reserves to lift them.

ball screw. A surgical bullet extractor developed late in the war, too late to be distributed to all military hospitals. The brainchild of Arthur de Witzleben, the device had projecting edges, much like the threads of a screw, on its two augerlike points and provided a more reliable grip on the bullet during extraction.

Baltimore rations. A sarcastic term designating shiploads of stone that were key to the futile attempt to block key Southern harbors with the sunken hulks of ships, the cargoes carried by the STONE FLEETS.

Baltimore riot. On April 19, 1861, prosecession citizens of Baltimore provoked an exchange of gunfire with the 6th Massachusetts volunteers en route to Washington. During the movement of some railway cars from one station to another, the mob gathered and pelted the vehicles with various objects. Although nine cars were moved successfully, a tenth was untracked, and the volunteers opted to march to the connecting station. Objects again were hurled at the men from the Bay State, but this time shots were fired. Afterward at least four soldiers were killed and thirty-nine injured; twelve citizens died and an unknown number were wounded, but these numbers were never confirmed. That evening bridges were burned to prevent more soldiers from arriving in Washington, and on April 20 Abraham Lincoln suspended all troop movements through Baltimore. The 6th Massachusetts returned on April 13 and occupied Federal Hill overlooking the city. Baltimore was treated as an occupied city for the remainder of the war.

band box regiments. These were Federal regiments formed late in the conflict from affluent and professional men, many of whom wore white gloves when they drilled.

banishment. A form of punishment that required an offender to leave the area in which he had been accused or convicted of a crime. Never officially legalized in either the United States or the Confederacy, it had been practiced earlier in some New England colonies. During the war, a number of offenders were banished from Union soil, among whom Rose O'Neal Greenhow and Clement L. Vallandigham were the most prominent. In the case of Vallandigham, an Ohio political leader and outspoken peace advocate, double banishment was meted out. Almost as soon as he passed into the Confederate lines by order of Abraham Lincoln, he was also banished from the Confederacy and spent some time in Canada as an exile from both warring nations. His sensational case inspired the

Clement L. Vallandigham

Reverend Edward Everett Hale of Boston to write the short story, "The Man Without a Country," first published in the *Atlantic Monthly* in 1863. In Kansas, Union Gen. Thomas Ewing ordered the banishment of all civilians from four counties in Missouri because many were suspected of aiding Confederate guerrillas, particularly those led by William Quantrill. Ewing's GENERAL ORDERS NO. 11 of 1863 has no precise parallel, and these families were scattered across the adjoining states.

banquette. A low "bank" or impromptu BREAST-WORK thrown up below the crest of a PARAPET. Its height was determined so as to accommodate the shortest man in the defending unit.

baptism of fire. A soldier's first exposure to combat. A more formal expression than to "see the ELEPHANT."

bar. N. An elevated portion of a basin, usually formed by tidal action, over which a vessel had to pass in order to enter a harbor.

bar, to cross the. (1) N. To get a ship across a natural barrier at a port. (2) A euphemism for death.

bar shot. Two balls connected by an iron bar, designed to cut the rigging and masts of warships; similar to CHAIN SHOT. The inability to control the trajectory of bar shot, however, rendered it useless.

barbette. An elevated position designed to permit gunners to fire over a PARAPET that had lacked openings or EMBRASURES. When guns were placed in this fashion, they were described as being en barbette.

bark. N. A three-masted vessel whose fore and aft mast were rigged as a ship, but whose mizzenmast was like that of a SCHOONER.

bark juice. Slang for hard liquor.

Barnes machine cannon. A Lowell, Massachusetts, inventor won an 1856 patent for an early rapid-fire gun with a rate of fire determined by a hand crank.

***Baron de Kalb,* USS.** This 512-ton Cairo-class IRONCLAD river GUNBOAT was built in St. Louis for the Western Gunboat Flotilla and named USS *St. Louis.* After the vessel had been commissioned in January 1862, she participated in the actions at FORTS HENRY and DONELSON, Tennessee; Columbus, Kentucky; Island No. 10; Fort Pillow, Tennessee; Memphis; and on the White River in Arkansas. When the ship was transferred to the Union navy, it was renamed *Baron de Kalb* and engaged in operations on the Yazoo River and in

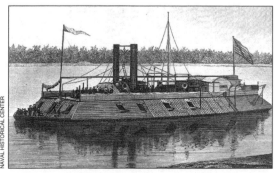

the capture of Fort Hindman, Arkansas. On July 13, 1863, during an expedition on the Yazoo, the gunboat was sunk by a Confederate mine.

barrack hack. (1) A soldier who avoided drilling. (2) A prostitute; also called a BAT.

barrage. A continuous discharge of artillery from numerous guns.

barrel drill. Euphemism for a punishment in which an offender was required to stand for a specified time on top of a barrel and usually hold a notice that labeled his crime.

barrel jacket or **barrel shirt.** A punishment device comprised of a wooden barrel in which holes were cut for the offender's head, arms, and legs.

barrier. A fence erected in the midst of a passageway or entrenchment. A barrier gate was securely fastened during an attack for the convenience of men in the defensive work.

Bars, the. A vernacular reference to the Confederate banner known as the Stars and Bars.

bastion. A work that projected toward the field at a SALIENT ANGLE with its apex pointing toward the enemy, constructed so that its defenders could fire on an attacking force even if it reached the walls.

bat. A prostitute, also called a BARRACK HACK.

battalion. (1) A command made up of two or more companies whose members were often detached for special duty as PIONEERS, SAPPERS, or SHARPSHOOTERS. (2) Companies of INFANTRY temporarily serving apart from a parent body. They were commanded by a lieutenant colonel or major and included a HEADQUARTERS company and several artillery batteries.

battery. (1) In the Union army, a cluster of six guns of the same caliber. In the Confederate army,

a cluster of four of the same kind of cannon. Batteries were commanded by a captain and also divided into sections, each of which was commanded by a lieutenant and had two guns. Each gun was designated a platoon and included a sergeant and two corporals. In general practice, the term referred to any number of PIECES or the place where they were situated. (2) A promenade or park adjoining the waterfront.

battery wagon. A wagon designed to transport tools and other materials needed to repair carriages and other segments of artillery batteries.

Battle Above the Clouds. The November 24, 1864, battle of Lookout Mountain, where low-hanging clouds shrouded the mountain's summit during the fighting.

battle cry. Any distinctive sound, word, or phrase chanted loudly and repeatedly to intimidate the enemy. The most famous of these during the war was the REBEL YELL.

battle flag. A banner that was carried into battle and served as a focal point for a company since battlefields quickly were filled with powder smoke and the din of fighting drowned out the orders of officers. Many units on both sides inscribed upon their flags the names of the engagements in which they had fought. Such battle flags were trophies whose capture was second in importance only to that of a battery.

battle flag of the Confederacy. The Confederate Stars and Bars was sometimes mistaken for the Stars and Stripes during the early engagements of the war. To address this situation, Confederate Gen. P. G. T. Beauregard designed a banner with a red field, a blue St. Andrew's cross, and thirteen white stars (Kentucky and Missouri were represented on the flag despite the fact that neither state officially seceded). The new emblem was adopted and appeared in both rectangular and square shapes, depending on the materials available.

battle for Kilpatrick's pants. During the evening of March 9, 1865, Confederate horsemen under Gen. Joseph Wheeler surprised Union Gen. H. Judson Kilpatrick's command at Monroe's Crossing, South Carolina. Adding insult to injury, the Southerners were also poised to capture the Federal commander while he was still in bed, but Kilpatrick managed to flee the camp—allegedly without his trousers.

H. Judson Kilpatrick

"Battle Hymn of the Republic." During the early months of the war, the 12th Massachusetts camped in Washington, D.C. The unit's commander, Fletcher Webster, son of Daniel Webster, addressed the morale of his men by encouraging the formation of a quartet, whose members popularized music and adapted a camp meeting song that itself had been modified as "John Brown's Body." Julia Ward Howe heard the foursome, and because the melody "kept floating through her head," the experience contributed to her writing a poem that she sent to the *Atlantic Monthly*. It appeared on the front cover in February 1862 and became the most popular song of the war.

battle pin. A decorative pin that listed the engagements in which the wearer had participated.

battle streamer. A long narrow flag used by Federal units to display the names of the battles in which a unit had participated.

Bayard. A light brown horse upon which Union Gen. Philip Kearny was riding when he was killed at Chantilly, Virginia, on September 1, 1862.

bayonet. (1) An elongated dagger that could be attached to the muzzle of a MUSKET or RIFLE. Although it was seldom used in combat, it proved useful in hand-to-hand fighting. (2) Sometimes used as a synonym for soldier; e.g., some persons habitually referred to the number of bayonets in a command rather than the number of men.

bayonet exercise. A drill in the use of bayonets in combat. Observing a regiment performing the drill, an observer noted that the men resembled "creatures compounded of the sentinel crab, the frog, the grasshopper, and the sand-hill crane."

B.C. An abbreviation for "Brigade Commissary," which was customarily stamped on hardtack containers. Soldiers claimed that it indicated the unpalatable staple had been prepared "before Christ."

Beardslee telegraph. An alternative to the usual telegraph key on which an operator tapped out letters by Morse Code, this instrument was equipped with a disk on which letters could be dialed and transmitted. Skilled operators were required to use the Morse system, but it took little practice and no skill for anyone to use a Beardslee. The wiring used by this system was insulated with gutta percha, a latex product. A pair of men could easily handle a lengthy spool of Beardslee wire, making the system very mobile and especially useful in combat areas. Its range, however, was limited to five miles, and the system—used exclusively by Union forces—was discontinued in late 1863.

Beast. Perhaps the best-known nickname of Gen. Benjamin F. Butler; a reference to his infamous WOMEN'S ORDER in New Orleans, an attempt to halt the disrespect being shown the Northern occupying army. See GENERAL ORDERS NO. 28.

beat. (1) An area of responsibility; e.g., a picket on sentry duty. (2) A shirker or loafer, a.k.a. deadbeat.

beat up, to. (1) To disturb, alarm, arouse, or dislodge an enemy from a position. (2) N. To sail against the wind, a movement requiring skill and frequent repositioning of a vessel's sails.

Beauty. A playful nickname for Confederate Gen. J. E. B. "Jeb" Stuart acquired during his time at the U.S. Military Academy at West Point. His classmate Fitzhugh Lee once joked that the title "described personal comeliness in inverse ratio to the term employed."

bed. The heavy rigid metal or wooden foundation on which an artillery piece rested.

bed quilt regiment. A derisive reference to a Federal unit raised in northern Alabama. These volunteers had only lightweight clothing, and so during the colder months many wrapped themselves with everything they had, including their bedding.

Beecher's Bible. A RIFLE, dubbed thusly from the widespread belief that the Reverend Henry Ward

Beecher of Brooklyn's Plymouth Congregational Church aided free-soilers and abolitionists in the Kansas Territory by shipping weapons to them in the years before the war in crates marked "Bibles."

bee gum. A broad-brimmed slouch hat with a conical top, resembling a "gum" or hive for bees.

beehive. A soldier's knapsack.

beetle-crunchers. A jocular synonym for INFANTRY who advanced or retreated over untrodden ground, i.e., crushing beetles under their feet.

beeves. Beef cattle.

belaying pin. N. A piece of oak, about one and a half inches in diameter and a bit more than a foot long, used to secure lines on naval vessels. They could also be used as clubs.

belch, to. A term applied to guns and to the men who fired them and referred to their ability "to fire or throw projectiles."

bell buoy. N. A floating marker used to warn of nautical dangers. The bell enhanced the marker's usefulness at night.

Belle Isle. A small island in the James River at Richmond. It was used as a stockade for Union prisoners. When more than ten thousand captives occupied the island, Confederate authorities shifted great numbers of prisoners farther south, to places such as ANDERSONVILLE and CAHABA.

Belle of Alabama. A 12-POUNDER Confederate GUN used at Resaca, Georgia, until its battery was overrun and the piece was turned against Southern soldiers.

bell tent. A SIBLEY TENT.

belly band. A strip of cloth, usually flannel, that was worn about the waist. Many soldiers believed that a salve or some other household remedy, when applied to a belly band, would prevent or ease dysentery.

belly robber. A mess sergeant or cook.

Bench Leg. A nickname for Confederate Gen. Roger W. Hanson, whose first battle in this rank was at FORT DONELSON, Tennessee. He was wounded in a duel before the war and, as a result, walked with a noticeable limp that gave rise to the nickname. Hanson was captured at Fort Donelson, and was eventually exchanged for Col. Michael Corcoran, who had been captured at the battle of First Bull Run (First Manassas).

benchrest. A Federal RIFLE adapted from weapons used by buffalo hunters. No benchrest weighed less than fifteen pounds, and some exceeded forty pounds. It was almost impossible to use one unless it rested on a support or bench, hence its name.

Bengal Tiger. A nickname bestowed on U.S. Gen. David E. Twiggs, who surrendered Texas and all of its military installations to Secessionists.

Benner's Hill. An area of the Gettysburg battlefield on a ridge from which Confederate Maj. J. W. Latimer's thirty-two cannon pounded Federal positions on Cemetery and Culp's Hill. until Latimer was killed and his guns were silenced.

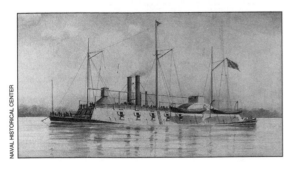

NAVAL HISTORICAL CENTER

Benton, **USS.** Shipbuilder James B. Eads purchased this 1,033-ton snagboat and converted it into an IRONCLAD river GUNBOAT for the Western Gunboat Flotilla. Its battery consisted of seven 32-POUNDERS, two 9-inch PIECES, and seven 42-pounder RIFLES. Commissioned in February 1862, she participated in Mississippi River actions that included the captures of Island No. 10, Fort Pillow, and Memphis. In the summer of 1862 the

gunboat engaged the Confederate ironclad *ARKANSAS* near Vicksburg and joined the Yazoo River expedition. In October 1862 the ship was transferred to the Union navy and was made the flagship of the Mississippi Squadron. The vessel participated in the run past Vicksburg on April 16, 1863, and the action against Grand Gulf, Mississippi, later that month as well as the May 1863 attack on Fort DeRussy, Arkansas, before returning to support the siege of Vicksburg. In the spring of 1864 *Benton* participated in the Red River campaign in Louisiana and remained in the area until the end of the war.

Berdan's Sharpshooters. The 1st and 2d U.S. Sharpshooter Regiments. The commander, Col. Hiram Berdan, had a reputation as the finest RIFLE shot in the country for a dozen years preceding the outbreak of war. These regiments, though raised by the individual states, were enlisted into the U.S. Army. No applicant was accepted until he had passed a rigorous test of his marksmanship.

berm. A narrow ledge, sometimes sloping, between a parapet and a moat or other body of water, frequently used as a walkway.

Bermuda bacon. This contraband was a product of "financial fraternization." Purchased by meat speculators in the North, this pork was transported to Bermuda and transferred to Confederate BLOCKADE-RUNNERS. Should the cargo reach a Confederate port, it was sold at exorbitant prices in the meat-starved South.

besiege, to. To envelop or surround an enemy position. Heavy artillery was often used to shell the opponent, but military might alone was seldom sufficient to bring a SIEGE to a successful conclusion. Sieges starved an enemy into submission.

Bethel Regiment. The nickname of the 1st North Carolina, based on its participation in the first significant engagement of the war at Big Bethel, Virginia, during which it was claimed that the first Confederate soldier was killed in action—Henry Lawson Wyatt. The regiment was originally organized in May 1861, reorganized in November 1861 as the 11th North Carolina, and participated in every major battle of the eastern theater. At Gettysburg the unit was said to have driven the farthest into the Union line, and at Appomattox it was said to have been among the last regiments to surrender. Thus its soldiers claimed to be "First at Bethel, farthest at Gettysburg, last at Appomattox."

between wind and water. N. Any spot on a warship above the water line and below its sails.

Bible Company. This unit, the 125th Pennsylvania, was raised in the Keystone State by devout coal mine operator William Wallace. A staunch Scotch Presbyterian, Wallace founded the unit "in the name of God and of religion" and provided each recruit with a musket and a Bible. His men cheerfully adopted the slogan "In God We Trust," which may have contributed to that inscription being placed upon Civil War–era coins.

Big Foot. (1) A mule that was the favorite mount of artist William Travis, who made many sketches in the field. (2) The nickname of Union Gen. Lew Wallace.

Big Little General. Union Gen. Egbert Ludovickus Viele, an accomplished engineer whose prewar design for New York's Central Park was accepted but later shelved. During the war Viele was the military governor of Norfolk.

big ticket. A document certifying a soldier's honorable discharge from Federal forces.

bilged. N. Confinement in the bilge, the lowermost portion of the hull of a ship in which stagnant water collected.

Billinghurst-Requa battery gun. A multiple-fire gun invented by Isaac Requa and manufactured by the Billinghurst firm. It consisted of twenty-five side-by-side RIFLE barrels and a movable slab equipped with twenty-five chambers. It was not a machine gun but fired a volley as gunpowder ignited and raced from one end to the other.

binnacle. N. A sturdy container that held a ship's compass and a light to illuminate the dial at night.

Birago or **Birago trestle.** A versatile support useful in building both conventional and pontoon bridges.

bird-cage. A game of chance in which players bet on the total of the numbers that would appear when three dice were rolled.

birdie. A prisoner of war.

Birney. An experimental projectile made by dividing the cavity of a PARROTT shell with a thin strip of metal, placing a bursting charge in the front and an incendiary substance in the back of the chamber. As used at Fort Brady late in 1864, such shells held about six pints of inflammable liquid. Most of them burst and flared on contact, but twenty-nine destroyed a cluster of six wooden Confederate buildings.

bite the bullet, to. To undertake a repugnant or dangerous task. The term likely stems from the practice of placing a lead bullet between a patient's teeth while surgeons operated on the man. Some linguists observe that the reference may be to a comrade who had to bite a paper cartridge to extract the bullet for the patient's use.

bivouac, to. To camp while on the march.

blackberry picker. A STRAGGLER, i.e., one who leaves his line under the pretext of gathering foodstuffs, preferring the risk of imprisonment to that of being maimed or killed in an engagement.

blackbirder. N. A ship or a person engaged in the importation of slaves.

Black Bob. The nickname of Confederate Col. Robert McCulloch, who commanded a BRIGADE of CAVALRY for nearly two years but never received the rank appropriate to that responsibility, possibly because he was out of favor in Richmond.

black codes. A series of legislative acts in the South designed to control the rights of freedmen (former slaves) after the Southern states had been readmitted to the Union. Although the laws were viewed as unconstitutional by the North, many remained on the books until sweeping new measures concerning civil rights became effective in the 1950s and 1960s.

Black Dave. The nickname of Union Gen. David Hunter of the District of Columbia, who accompanied Abraham Lincoln in 1861 on his journey from Springfield to Washington for his inauguration. The moniker stemmed from his role in the organization of the 1st South Carolina Volunteers, whose ranks were filled by former slaves. Also it was said that Hunter left behind many Southern towns and villages that were only masses of blackened ruins.

black flag policy. A policy of taking no prisoners. The black flag referred to the skull and crossbones of pirates, who showed no mercy to their captives. During the Civil War, the black flag was discussed but rarely practiced. Since it was considered an unpopular tactic, there is little record of Northern troops flying the black flag in combat. What few references appear in the record largely are laid at the feet of Confederate forces. The most notorious incident was alleged to have occurred at the April 12, 1984, battle of Fort Pillow, Tennessee.

black gang. N. A reference to naval engineers.

Black Hat Brigade. An early reference to the all-Western BRIGADE comprised of the 2d, 6th, and 7th Wisconsin and the 19th Indiana Regiments. Under the command of Gen. John Gibbon, HARDEE HATS—tall black felt headwear—were distributed to the Westerners to give the units a distinctive look. Following the battle of South Mountain, the unit was dubbed the IRON BRIGADE.

***Black Hawk*, USS.** This 902-ton side-wheel tinclad river GUNBOAT was built in 1857 at New Albany, Indiana, as *New Uncle Sam,* a civilian steamer. The Union navy purchased the ship in 1862 and later renamed it. Her large size led to her being made the flagship of the Mississippi Squadron, and Adms. David Dixon Porter and Samuel Phillips Lee utilized her accordingly. The vessel was involved in all major actions on the river, including the siege of Vicksburg, the attack on Fort Hindman, and the Red River campaign. On April 22, 1865, the ship caught fire and sank near Cairo, Illinois.

NAVAL HISTORICAL CENTER

Black Horse Cavalry. (1) One of the squadrons of the 4th Virginia Cavalry, commanded by J. E. B. "Jeb" Stuart. (2) The 2d New York Cavalry, led by Col. A. J. Morrison.

Black Jack. The nickname of Gen. John A. Logan, a prominent Illinois Democrat. The reference is to a comment by his soldiers that he was "as tough as a blackjack locust [tree]."

blackjack. (1) A club made of wood and usually weighted at one end, "the business end," and usually carried by both Northern and Southern prison guards. (2) A concoction of molasses laced with rum, probably named for the tar-coated leather containers of ale and beer that were commonplace in many public houses or clubs.

black powder. Gunpowder.

black rascal. N. A Federal GUNBOAT. These pragmatic rivercraft played a significant role at the April 6–7, 1862, battle of Shiloh.

Black Republican. (1) A scornful Southern epithet for the members of the Republican Party. (2) A Congressman who consistently elevated abolition above all other causes. As a group, these men frequently opposed any actions proposed by Abraham Lincoln.

black snake. A derisive designation for abolitionists.

Black Terror. N. A dummy GUNBOAT built at the direction of Union Comdr. David D. Porter and dispatched on the Mississippi River to test the accuracy of Confederate gunners.

black troops. Washington did not approve the use of black troops in the Union army until the EMANCIPATION PROCLAMATION was issued on January 1, 1863. One of the first uses of African-American soldiers occurred in Kansas under the command of James H. Lane. The first formal use of former slaves as soldiers occurred in South Carolina, when Gen. David Hunter authorized the organization of three regiments at Hilton Head. By the end of the war, approximately two hundred thousand African Americans had fought in the Federal

army. Of these, almost half were former slaves. A few black soldiers served as officers (mostly as chaplains), but the vast majority served under white officers.

Blakely gun. This British banded rifled GUN—known for its accuracy—was used extensively during the war, particularly in the South, in both field and GARRISON versions. Two of the largest weapons in the Confederacy were 12.75" Blakelys installed in Charleston, South Carolina, batteries. The guns themselves weighed more than fifty thousand pounds and were distinguished by an unusually large breech.

blanket boat. A boat devised by Union Gen. Herman Haupt from a sheet of rubber. The frame was made of wood and displaced only four inches of water, yet it was capable of conveying a fully loaded soldier across a river. When several blanket boats were lashed together, they formed a raft upon which a wagon could be taken across a stream.

blaze a trail, to. To mark a pathway by knocking chunks of bark off trees at frequent intervals. PIONEERS were assigned this task, which was performed when troops were dispatched to an unfamiliar site in a densely wooded area.

blenker, to. To appropriate forcibly the benefit of another person's labor. The phrase may stem from 1862, when Union Gen. Louis Blenker regularly dispatched his men into the Virginia countryside to plunder and FORAGE.

blind. A screen of shrubs or branches used to conceal troops.

blind shell. A projectile with no charge, used for target practice.

blind shot. A stray or undirected shot of the battlefield.

blizzard. A long and heavy volley of MUSKET or RIFLE fire or canister.

blockade. (1) N. A system of interdiction of traffic into and out of a port. Abraham Lincoln's proclamation by which a portion of the coastline of the seceded states was declared to be under blockade was issued on the heels of the surrender of FORT SUMTER. At the time, however, the U.S. Navy did not have sufficient vessels to enforce the directive. Only over the course of the war did the blockade become an effective measure in depriving the South of supplies with which to prosecute the fighting. (2) Whiskey obtained by illicit means and against orders. As a general rule, officers were permitted to drink whenever they wished, but alcohol was usually forbidden to enlisted men.

blockade cotton. Cotton that Southern growers were unable to get to British or European markets because of the Federal BLOCKADE. Considerable quantities of cotton therefore went upriver to Northern buyers and manufacturers despite the fact that such trade was illicit.

blockade-runner. N. A vessel whose mission was to thwart the Federal BLOCKADE of Southern ports. Many blockade-runners, including some of the finest and swiftest, were British owned and operated. Before the Union navy increased in size, blockade-runners kept the South supplied with weapons and goods from Europe.

blockhouse. A defensive structure constructed of logs or heavy timbers. Originally many-sided and several levels high, it gradually evolved into a large one-level post whose top was often but not always covered with a thick layer of earth.

Blockhouse Bridge. A landmark in the May 1864 battle of Spotsylvania.

Blood of Boone. An early name used in and around Kentucky for the Confederate unit from the state that was later dubbed the ORPHAN BRIGADE.

Bloody Angle. (1) A point of the Federal line at Gettysburg that was critical to the action of the third day. During PICKETT'S CHARGE, Confederate Gen. Lewis A. Armistead and most of the 150 men he led against the center of the Union line broke through here temporarily, but they were either killed or captured during the failed assault. (2) A segment of the field at Spotsylvania where nearly 20,000 casualties were suffered.

Bloody Bill. The nickname of Confederate partisan leader William T. Anderson.

Bloody Hill. The rugged and heavily wooded terrain near Wilson's Creek, Missouri, where combatants exchanged fire at less than forty yards, reformed, and fought again at the same distance.

U.S. ARMY MILITARY HISTORY INSTITUTE

Bloody Lane. A long-traveled farm road on the Antietam battlefield that residents knew as the SUNKEN ROAD. The roadway was a two or more feet below the prevailing surface levels, having been worn down over the years. During the battle, it marked the center of the Confederate line on the morning of September 17, 1862. The road was approximately one mile west of the creek. So many men died in the road that it was said that one could walk across the area and never touch the ground.

Bloody Pond. A small body of water just north of the Peach Orchard on the Shiloh battlefield. During the night after the first day of battle, wounded Northerners and Southerners dragged themselves to the pond to get water and to wash out each other's wounds.

Bloody Salient, the. A segment of the Spotsylvania battlefield, a.k.a. the MULE SHOE.

Bloody 17th. The moniker of the 17th Virginia Infantry, which was formed at Manassas on June 10, 1861. The regiment was comprised of militia units from Alexandria, Fairfax, Fauquier, Loudon, Prince William, and Warren Counties. During the war, the unit participated in the battles of First Manassas, the Peninsula campaign, the Seven Days' battles, Second Manassas, Antietam, the siege of Suffolk, Cold Harbor, the siege of Petersburg, and Five Forks. The 17th earned its nickname, suffering more than twelve hundred casualties during the conflict.

blow the call, to. N. A signal, by no means uniform, by which men away from a warship were notified to return immediately.

blow off steam, to. To reduce the pressure in a steam engine, such as a locomotive or the boiler of a warship, by releasing superheated vapor through a valve designed for that purpose.

blower. N. A device that produced a strong and steady stream of air into burning coal. If a blower was disabled, the furnace to which it was attached quickly dropped in temperature. Sailors considered blowers the life of a ship.

blown horses. Animals that had been ridden to the point of exhaustion.

blueback. Confederate currency, one side of which was printed with blue ink.

blue cockade. An ornament worn on one's hat to symbolize that the wearer was an advocate of secession. This practice, which was firmly rooted in antebellum South Carolina, was adapted from a time-honored custom of displaying such symbols as badges of protest.

blue light. (1) N. A signal light. (2) A designation for a turncoat, traitor, or GALVANIZED soldier. The phrase possibly originated during the War of 1812.

blue mass. Civil War surgeons used this poisonous compound of mercury, chalk, licorice, and honey almost indiscriminately.

Bluff Ben. A nickname for Sen. Benjamin F. Wade of Ohio, who was prone to speak his mind regardless of the consequences and who led a contingent of BLACK REPUBLICAN lawmakers (that is, strong advocates of abolition) in perpetually finding fault with the Lincoln administration's conduct of the war.

boarder. (1) N. An enemy attempting to come aboard a warship. (2) A prostitute.

boarding pike. N. A lancelike wooden shaft about eight feet long and tipped with a metal hook and often a spike. The weapon was designed to be used by BOARDERS.

boat battery. N. A vessel mounting heavy guns and usually covered with a skin of iron. It was not designed to fight other vessels but to bombard fixed fortifications from the water.

boatswain. N. A warrant officer on a warship charged with manning the anchor, cable, riggings, and other lines. The boatswain's mate was a petty officer who served as an assistant to the boatswain.

Bobbin Boy. The nickname of Union Gen. Nathaniel P. Banks, who began his career as a child laborer in a Massachusetts cotton mill.

bodyguard. (1) A formally designated body of men assigned to guard their commander with their lives, if necessary. In ordinary use, the term was treated as being equivalent to ESCORT. The size of a bodyguard and the respect or lack of it with which its members were treated varied widely. (2) A louse.

body of the place. The complete works that enveloped a fortified area. A few general officers preferred to call such an installation an ENCIENTE.

body servant. An employed servant or a slave who performed chores for his master. Hundreds of officers, including many Federal officers, took body servants with them when they went to war. Under battle conditions, body servants were expected to fight alongside their employer-masters.

bog-trotter. A soldier of Irish ancestry, used by both sides in the war.

Bohemian. A newspaper correspondent who traveled with the army but was not subject to the restrictions imposed upon the soldiers. Partly to avoid retaliation in the event of capture, many correspondents used pen names.

Bohemian Brigade. A epithet bestowed in the eastern theater upon newspaper correspondents, and artists who traveled with an army.

boiled rye. Derisive reference to Southern efforts to brew coffee from substitutes such as parched rye.

Bold Dragoon. A reference to Confederate Gen. J. E. B. "Jeb" Stuart.

Bold Emory. West Point nickname for Union Gen. William H. Emory, Class of 1831.

bolt. A RIFLE or artillery projectile.

bomb. A hollow projectile carrying an explosive charge. During the Civil War that charge was seldom more powerful than black powder.

Bombast. A sarcastic reference to Confederate Gen. Richard L. Page, a thirty-seven-year veteran of the U.S. Navy who resigned and served as naval aide to Virginia Gov. John Letcher.

Bombastes Furioso. A satirical prewar nickname for Union Gen. John Pope.

bombproof. A refuge from cannon fire, such as a cave or an underground shelter. In fortifications,

the walls were made of such thicknesses so as to absorb multiple impacts of solid shell and shell without losing the ability to prevent penetration of the structure. During the war the term was applied to shelters built into the base of batteries in field-works so as to shelter the garrison. These usually followed post-and-joist framing that was covered with several layers of planking and enough soil to absorb the impact of incoming fire. Some military installations included bombproof doors; others were equipped with bombproof barracks. The bombproof at Fort Wagner on Morris Island near Charleston held as many as fifteen hundred men; it suffered little damage during the siege of 1863.

Bomford cannon. George Bomford, inventor of the COLUMBIAD, developed this huge SMOOTH-BORE for seacoast defense. One of these 12-inch PIECES weighed about twenty-five thousand pounds and required eighteen pounds of powder for a 180-pound shot. These weapons were reinforced with an iron band around the base of the GUN tube, but few were ever involved in combat.

bond, to. N. To secure a legal pledge from a captured vessel that a specified sum would be paid at a designated place—a condition upon which many commercial ships taken at sea were freed instead of burned.

bone butter. A butter substitute produced in many prisons. Scraps of bone were boiled in water then filtered through a piece of cloth to yield a residue that hardened when cooled. Fashioned into cubes, these also served as a medium of exchange.

bone yard. A prison cemetery, often little more than a trench into which the dead—stripped of shoes and clothing—were placed.

Bonnie Blue Flag. One of the earliest secession flags; it displayed a single white star on a rectangular blue field. The banner first appeared in 1810 when the Republic of West Florida (which included parts of Alabama and Mississippi) rebelled against Spain. Twenty-five years later it was revived during the Texas revolution against Mexico. During the January 9, 1861, Convention of the People of Mississippi, the Bonnie Blue Flag was adopted as the banner of the Republic of Mississippi. The flag inspired a song that rivaled "Dixie" in popularity in the South, perhaps because all the states of the Confederacy were listed in the lyrics. The banner, however, was not adopted officially, possibly because its legacy was limited to Texas and the coastal regions of Louisiana, Mississippi, and Alabama.

boom, to. To charge a position so that large clusters of soldiers would strike simultaneously and overwhelm the defenders.

bootee. A laced boot that rose only to the ankle. See JEFFERSON BOOT.

boot hook. An iron implement designed to aid one in pulling on knee-high boots quickly.

bootleg. An artillery shell. The etymology is unknown.

border free state. A state in which SLAVERY had been practiced but had diminished over time; for example, Delaware and Maryland.

border ruffians. A reference to violent proslavery groups in Missouri that were dedicated to intimidating and driving out FREE SOILERS (antislavery) settlers in Kansas.

border slave state. A state strategically situated between the South and the North with sympathetic ties to the South and SLAVERY; for example, Kentucky and Missouri. Both tried to declare neutrality, but the arrival of Federal troops led to the founding of provisional Confederate governments, and the two states were admitted to the Confederacy—in name only. Men from the Border States joined the ranks of both armies, and Missouri was plagued with guerrilla warfare.

bore. (1) The tube of a MUZZLELOADING GUN. (2) The portion of a BREECHLOADER's tube before the breechlock, which held both powder and shot chambers. The diameter of the bore was used to indicate the size of the gun.

Bormann time fuse. A metal cap FUSE used with SMOOTHBORE ammunition. Developed before the war by and named for its Belgian inventor, it allowed artillerists to set a shell to explode as much as five seconds after it was fired. The fuse was accurate 75 percent of the time. The top of the fuse resembled a clock face and was marked in quarters of a second; the base was threaded so it could be screwed into a shell. A hole bored into the top allowed the gunpowder flash following discharge to ignite the fuse and detonate at the prescribed interval.

borrowed. A euphemism for theft, foraging, and pillaging.

bosque. A substantial clump of trees or a grove.

Bottle. A point on the James River about three miles north of City Point, Virginia, and also known as Bermuda Hundred.

bottom. Another word for a ship of any description. Many fleet, flotilla, and squadron commanders were prone to speak of the number of

bottoms they commanded rather than the number of vessels.

bottom scraper. A raft-supported device designed by John Ericsson (architect of the USS *MONITOR*) to scrape the bottom of a waterway for mines (also called torpedoes). It was first used in 1863 in Charleston Harbor.

bought the farm. Died on the field of battle.

Bounding Bet. An 8-inch HOWITZER whose sixty-eight-pound shells had a tendency to bounce after hitting the ground.

bounty. A financial inducement to enlist for military service. Most Northern states and numerous cities and a few Southern locales offered bounties so as to meet recruitment quotas. The amount of these inducements grew as the war continued. In some rare instances a recruit might legitimately draw bounties from federal, state, and ward sources, thus pocketing a sum equal to a lifetime's income.

bounty broker. A recruiter who received a commission on the bounties for which he enlisted soldiers.

bounty jumper. A deceptive practice of enlisting so as to draw a bounty, deserting at the first opportunity, and then enlisting again in another district so as to drawn additional bounties. One bounty jumper, after he was apprehended, admitted to more than thirty enlistments.

bow gun. N. A GUN mounted on the bow of a ship, usually a PIVOT GUN.

Bowie knife. A single-edge knife with a blade twelve to eighteen inches long. Styled by Rezin Bowie of Louisiana and made famous by his brother, Jim, Bowie knives were manufactured in a wide range of shapes and lengths. The weapon was common on the frontier, and when war broke out in 1861 it appeared in both Union and Confederate hands, but no branch of service ever sponsored its issuance. No doubt it played a role in much of the fighting of the war; it also likely satisfied more mundane daily needs around the campfire.

bowlegs. A cavalryman, so called because of the characteristic outward curvature of a horseman's legs at the knees.

bowsprit. N. A heavy spar or boom that projected forward from the STEM of a vessel.

box. A CARTRIDGE BOX.

boyau. In SIEGE work, these were trenches that allowed troops to advance from one PARALLEL to the next. Like APPROACHES, they were laid out in a zigzag pattern, but they differed in that they lacked a PARAPET for defense.

boys of the sod. Irish immigrants.

Braden. Part of a military bridle constituted from the snaffle and rein. Many horsemen valued it because it could be used independently of the bit.

Bragg's bodyguard. A body louse, coined by soldiers under the command of Confederate Gen. Braxton Bragg and a reflection of the disdain he elicited from his men.

braid. A woven band, usually gold in color, used as trim on the uniforms of officers. Also known as CHICKEN GUTS.

Brain of the South. A nickname for the vice president of the Confederacy, Alexander H. Stephens of Georgia, also known as "LITTLE ALEC" due to his short stature. Before the war he was a close friend of  Abraham Lincoln and was never an advocate of secession. Although elected to the office of vice president, he had severe disagreements with Jefferson Davis, and thus spent most of the war in self-imposed exile in Georgia. During his tenure of office, he conducted only two official acts: as commissioner to the Virginia secession convention in 1861 and as a representative at the Hampton Roads Peace Conference in 1865.

Brain Regiment. A reference to the 33d Illinois, which was formed almost exclusively of teachers and students. The unit was also known as the TEACHERS REGIMENT.

Brains of the Confederacy. A nickname for Judah P. Benjamin, a native of the Virgin Islands and a U.S. senator prior to the war. He served the Confederacy in three positions: attorney general, secretary of war, and secretary of  state. After the war, he managed to escape the country and became a barrister in England.

braveo. A proud or boastful man.

bread bag. A haversack made of rubberized fabric, considered waterproof.

bread basket of the Confederacy. A reference to Virginia's Shenandoah Valley, renowned for its fertile farms.

Bread Riot. A civil disturbance in Richmond, the Confederate capital, on April 2, 1863. A group of several hundred men, women, and children began a march on the city's business district to demand food, but the matter escalated and the mob swelled to more than a thousand people and businesses were looted. Jefferson Davis rushed to the scene and appealed to the crowd to disperse. When reason failed, he announced that soldiers would be brought in to restore order and gave the people five minutes to disband before they might be fired upon. The mob dissolved.

bream, to. N. To scrape clean the bottom of a vessel.

breastwork. A hastily constructed defensive work of earth and wood, erected to protect defenders from artillery and RIFLE fire. In most instances the the front of the work was protected by a ditch—from which the breastwork was made—and other obstacles, such as ABATIS or CHEVAUX-DE-FRIZE.

Brecht tent. Union soldier T. C. Brecht devised a type of waterproof fabric that could be inflated to form a bed, a prototype of the sleeping bag. When not inflated, the same fabric could serve as a cloak or as a tent. The contrivance saw limited use.

Breckinridge's slaughter-pen. An area of the Stones River battlefield where Confederate Gen. John C. Breckinridge's command took heavy casualties from Union batteries.

breech. The rear portion of a cannon or other firearm, behind the BORE or barrel.

breeching. N. A device that conveyed the smoke from the flues of a steamer to its smokestack.

breechloader. A weapon that was loaded at its breech instead of through its muzzle. Although initially disdained by the ORDNANCE department of the U.S. War Department, breechloaders were eventually adopted for Federal use, although usually issued only to CAVALRY. Despite this radical change in design and manufacture, MUZZLELOADERS continued to be used because adequate supplies of newer weapons were not available. A few breechloading cannon were introduced (notably WHITWORTH GUNS and some ARMSTRONG GUNS), but their numbers were few by comparison to the vast number of muzzleloading guns.

breech sight. A marksman's sight designed to be mounted at the rear, or breech, of a GUN.

brevet. An honorary rank among Federal forces that elevated the recipient a single grade. While in force, brevet rank entitled its holder to wear the uniform and collect the pay attached to the rank. Many brevet ranks conferred on the battlefield, however, were never confirmed by Congress. Disturbed by what he considered the gross abuse of the brevet system, Union Gen. Edward D. Townsend lobbied for a better way to recognize gallantry. The end result was the MEDAL OF HONOR. Despite the fact that many medals were conferred hastily and carelessly, at war's end lawmakers still awarded brevets to hundreds of officers, some of whom returned to civilian life.

brevet horse. An army mule.

brick. A block of DESICCATED VEGETABLES, regarded by the soldiers as being as hard and inedible as a clay brick.

Bricktop. A notorious red-haired prostitute of New Orleans. She allegedly killed at least four men prior to 1861 and was in jail when the city was surrendered to Federal forces in April 1862. She was freed by military governor George F. Shepley, probably because Shepley believed that most of the occupants of the cells were UNIONISTS.

bricole. A harness twenty feet or more in length that was used to haul guns by manpower when horses were not available or could not negotiate steep terrain.

bridge burners. A term for civilians and soldiers who burned bridges with the expectation that they would impede the progress of an opposing force. Bridge burning was a serious civil and military offense, but it began in the aftermath of the BALTIMORE RIOT and continued until after Appomattox.

bridle cutter. A sharply curved hooked blade on the end of a pike. This device was sold as a means to render a horseman ineffective by slashing the bridle of his animal.

Brierfield. The Mississippi plantation of Kentucky native Jefferson Davis about twenty-five miles from Vicksburg. It was a special target of Federal forces, and the acreage became an assembly point for freed slaves.

brig. N. (1) A square-rigged vessel with two masts. (2) On a vessel of the U.S. Navy, a compartment reserved for the confinement of offenders.

brigade. A unit consisting of four or five REGIMENTS and a HEADQUARTERS staff. As casualties mounted, six or seven decimated regiments were sometimes included in a single brigade. Brigades often included a BATTERY of ARTILLERY and a COMPANY of CAVALRY. Nominally commanded by a brigadier general, in practice many brigades were led by colonels, majors, and even captains who survived the other ranking officers lost in combat.

brigand. A civilian fighter often considered "an independent volunteer" and likely to have the same or even more freedom of action than a partisan ranger or GUERRILLA.

bridgehead. An advanced position in enemy-held country.

bridging. The process of throwing a bridge across a creek, river, run, or stream, normally assigned to engineers who were listed as PIONEERS.

bring a brick, to. To return drunk from a leave or furlough. Soldiers who did not hold commissions were forbidden to drink alcohol except when permission was granted under special circumstances. Drunkenness was a serious offense, despite the fact that alcohol flowed freely among the officers. In the U.S. Navy, tradition allowed a ship's captain to dispense a daily ration of grog to each member of the crew, but this practice was suspended during the war.

bring hair, to. To bring back the scalp of an enemy from battle; could also be used figuratively.

bring to. N. To cause an enemy or suspected vessel to drop her anchor or lower her sails—an action expected in response to a shot across her bow.

Britt projectile. A British-made shell, equipped with a SABOT, that bore the name of its developer, Ashley Britt.

broadside. (1) A printed notice on a single sheet of oversized paper, such as an advertisement or public notice (e.g., calls for volunteers). (2) N. The simultaneous discharge of all guns that could be brought to bear upon a target from one side of a warship.

broadsword. A formidable weapon. Some officers wore broadswords in preference to comparatively slender sabers.

brodequens. Calf-length leather boots popularized by Gen. Benjamin F. Butler.

brogan. A Gaelic term for *shoe* and applied to coarse flat-heeled footgear at least ankle high and fastened with laces.

Brooke rifles. Considered by many to be comparable to or even an improvement over PARROTT guns, these excellent heavy artillery PIECES were designed and manufactured in the South during the war. They were developed by James M. Brooke, a former U.S. naval officer who also contributed to the conversion of the *Merrimack-Virginia* and later served as chief of the Confederate Bureau of Ordnance and Hydrography. Both SMOOTHBORE (particularly for the navy) and rifled versions were produced at the Tredegar Iron Works at Richmond and the Confederate Naval Ordnance Works at Selma, Alabama, in a variety of sizes, including 6.4-, 7-, 8-, and 11-inches. Distinguishing ele-

ments of the weapons were a hemispheric breech contour, a straight tapered barrel, unturned exterior surfaces, and seven-groove rifling. The cast-iron barrel was reinforced by unwelded single-, double-, or triple-banded breech rings. Brooke rifles were used extensively in coastal and waterway defense as well as aboard ship.

Buck. (1) The nickname of Confederate Gen. Earl Van Dorn. (2) The nickname of Missouri guerrilla Frank James.

buck, to. A punishment in which offenders were bent over a log or barrel and then lashed a specified number of times.

buck and ball. A musket load made up of three buckshot and a one-ounce ball, the whole of which was wrapped in paper. Used primarily by Confederates, the load was not effective beyond two hundred yards.

buck and gag, to. A punishment that forced an offender to take a sitting position and then draw his knees to his chin and place his arms around his shins. Once in position, the hands were tied together and a gag forced into his mouth. Duration of this punishment varied, depending upon the offense committed and the judgment of the officer who prescribed it.

Buckland Races. A reference to the rout of Union Gen. George A. Custer at Buckland Mills, Virginia, in October 1863.

Buckshots. A Northern secret society also known as the MOLLY MAGUIRES. More than fifty murders in Schuylkill County, Pennsylvania, were attributed to the Buckshots, most of whom were Irish immigrants. Seventeen were eventually executed for inciting terrorism in the mining regions during and just after the war.

Bucktail Brigade. The nickname of the 2d Brigade, 3d Division, 1st Corps of the Union Army of the Potomac, which was comprised of the 143d, 149th, and 150th Pennsylvania Infantry Regiments. The units were MUSTERED INTO Federal service during late 1862 and participated in every campaign in the eastern theater from Gettysburg to Petersburg.

Bucktails. A reference to the regiment recruited from the lumbermen of the Bucktail region of Pennsylvania. A prospective recruit was allegedly required to bring the tail of a buck (deer) as part of his enrollment process. True or not, the majority of men in the outfit wore deer tails on their forage caps or hats. The Bucktails were good marksmen and had a reputation as a boisterous and rowdy group with their own peculiar battle yell. The unit entered Federal service in June 1861 as the 42d Pennsylvania but was also known as the 13th Pennsylvania Reserves, Kane's Rifles (after Col. Thomas L. Kane), and the Bucktailed Wildcats. The regiment participated in the battles of Second Manassas (Bull Run), Antietam, Fredericksburg, Gettysburg, the Wilderness, and Spotsylvania.

budge barrel. A special container for artillery charges used to transport them from powder magazines to batteries.

budget. A synonym for "quantity."

buffalo. (1) A robe fashioned from an undressed buffalo hide. (2) A UNIONIST of North Carolina.

built-up gun. A heavy weapon whose manufacture was a radical departure from earlier methods.

COLUMBIADS or DAHLGRENS were cast in a homogeneous system, in which the bulk of the guns was poured as a single segment. ARMSTRONGS, PARROTTS, and several other guns were made up of a number of individual parts that were welded, forged, or shrunk together.

Bull. (1) The nickname of professional detective Lafayette C. Baker, who is sometimes credited with having launched the U.S. Secret Service and who organized the pursuit of John Wilkes Booth in the aftermath of the Lincoln assassination. (2) The nickname of three-hundred-pound Union Gen. William Nelson, who was shot and killed in a Louisville hotel by fellow officer Jefferson C. Davis. (3) The nickname of Confederate Gen. Elisha F. Paxton. (4) The nickname of Confederate Gen. Thomas L. Rosser. (5) The nickname of Edwin V. Sumner, the oldest corps commander in the Federal Army of the Potomac.

Bull of the Woods. The nickname of Union Gen. Oliver O. Howard, who fought throughout the war and was one of fifteen generals to receive the formal Thanks of Congress.

bullpen. An enclosed segment of a stockade; sometimes the specific area in which prisoners were kept.

bull pups. Small mountain HOWITZERS that some Confederate units favored for use in steep and heavily wooded terrain.

Bull Run. A nickname for William H. Russell, a British correspondent who had won international recognition for his reporting during the Crimean War. Russell's detailed account of the rout of Federal forces at  the battle of First Bull Run (First Manassas) led to his expulsion from the United States.

bull's-eye canteen. A regulation issue U.S. Army CANTEEN developed just before the war; it was strengthened by numerous concentric rings pressed into its sides.

bully. An expression of strong encouragement and affirmation.

Bully Dutchmen. A nickname for the 9th Ohio Infantry, which was made up of German immigrants and raised mostly at Cincinnati. Originally the unit was formed for three-months' service on April 22, 1861, then reorganized for three-years' service on May 28, 1861. The regiment served in western Virginia, Kentucky, Tennessee, and Georgia, and suffered its heaviest losses at the battle of Chickamauga (51 percent casualties). During the Atlanta campaign, the enlistment expired, and the men were mustered out on June 7, 1864.

bully soup. A hot cereal that was made from cornmeal and crushed HARDTACK that had been boiled, usually in a mixture of water, ginger, and wine.

bumblebee. A bullet.

bummer. (1) A forager, often a man who left his unit to become an independent raider. Such bummers were especially prominent during William T. Sherman's March to the Sea. Also any person safely in the rear and away from combat; a SKULKER, cook, or wagon driver. (2) N. To Federals who manned it, the slow and clumsy vessel to which they gave this name seemed to be about as bad as it could be. Its flat bottom permitted it to move into shallow water, but its metal sides made it heavy and hard to maneuver. Numerous bummers, usually armed with a single mortar whose crew could sometimes get off a round every ten minutes, were used against Confederate positions on the Mississippi and other major rivers.

bummer's roost. Any spot well to the rear of combat and considered to be safe by the surgeons, correspondents, and other noncombatants.

bump, to. To bombard or shell with the certainty of causing death.

bunked. A wounded man who has been assigned to and placed in a bunk of a hospital ship.

Bunsby. A nickname for London *Times* correspondent William H. Russell, whose early dispatches were viewed to influence Great Britain to extend diplomatic recognition to the Confederacy.

buoy. N. A floating marker anchored to the bottom, commonly used to guide pilots through channels and to warn them of underwater boulders and shoals.

burden car. A railroad car designed to carry heavy machinery and commodities rather than passengers; a freight car.

Burns. A black horse ridden by Union Gen. George B. McClellan.

Burnside blouse. A loose-fitting blue blouse, much favored by Federal INFANTRY, named in honor of Ambrose E. Burnside.

Burnside carbine. Ambrose E. Burnside developed three experimental carbines at a factory in Bristol, Rhode Island, and made a sale of about one thousand of the third model in 1860. Less than satisfied with the performance of his single-shot weapon, another variant was perfected and

patented. This seven-pound shoulder weapon, which used .54-caliber cartridges, used a rifled barrel and was extremely accurate. Partly due to his prestige as a military commander but largely because his carbine was superior to many on the market, more than fifty thousand were purchased by Federal quartermasters during the war years.

Burnside hat. Union Gen. Ambrose E. Burnside fought at Manassas in July 1861 wearing the HARDEE HAT that was favored by professional soldiers of the U.S. Army. Afterward he modified this headgear by lowering its crown. Hat makers began producing the new version in quantity, and it was widely used throughout the rest of the war.

Burnside stew. HARDTACK soaked in water and fried in pork fat.

Burnt District. A four-county section of southern Missouri that was evacuated by GENERAL ORDERS NO. 11, which was issued by Union Gen. Thomas Ewing Jr. in an attempt to curb the activities of Confed-erate GUERRILLA leader William C. Quantrill, whose men had families in the region. Federal troops burned homes and barns in the region to deny shelter to the guerrillas.

Burton shell. A Confederate shell equipped with a SABOT, or "shoe."

busby. An elaborate military headpiece made of bearskin.

bush, to. To equip parts of a GUN or machinery with bushings, designed to reduce friction in shafts, axles, pivots, and other movable parts.

bushwhacker. Confederate PARTISAN RANGERS or GUERRILLAS.

busthead. Slang for a home-brewed alcoholic beverage.

butcher's bill. Slang for casualty lists.

Butler Medal. An unofficial award given by Union Gen. Benjamin F. Butler to about two hundred members of the 25th Corps for their gallantry during combat in September 1864. Most or all went to African-American enlisted men and noncommissioned officers.

butterfly poles. Ash poles adorned with gayly colored triangular streamers and augmented with scythes. During an acute shortage of MUSKETS and RIFLES, the Confederate War Department sent these "weapons" to the otherwise unarmed men of the 5th Virginia Infantry.

Butterflies. The nickname of the 3d New Jersey Cavalry, which was also known as the FLYING BUTTERFLIES. The men wore one of the most distinctive uniforms in the Union army: braided hussar jacket, visorless cap, and hooded cloak. They were armed with SPENCER CARBINES and served in the Shenandoah campaign of 1864 and in the last engagements of the Appomattox campaign.

buttermilk ranger. A derisive phrase used by Confederate INFANTRY of Southern cavalrymen in the early months of the war, because mounted troops were often sent to the rear before combat.

butternut. A reference to Southern soldiers on the basis of the butternut color of their uniforms.

With so many materials becoming rare in the South as the war progressed, textile mills turned to substitutes, resulting in various shades of light brown and brownish gray for military use.

button board. A sturdy slab of hardwood or metal that was placed under blouses, coats, and other segments of uniforms to protect the cloth while the metal buttons were being shined.

buttons with hens. The metal buttons of a Confederate uniform, which were prized as souvenirs by Union soldiers.

buzz. A card game reputedly developed by Federal prisoners at CAMP SORGHUM. The distinctive feature was for a player to make a buzzing sound whenever a seven card appeared.

buzzard. (1) A derisive reference to a straggler who deliberately tried to lag behind a body of men in order to plunder—regardless of whether the residents of the region were friendly or not. (2) A professional thief who circulated around military camps and recruitment offices in order to relieve veteran soldiers and newly enlisted men of their cash and valuables.

by the mark twain, N. The cry of the landsman of a riverboat when he found his vessel was in water only two feet deep.

by the numbers. The series of stages by which soldiers prepared a MUSKET or RIFLE to fire.

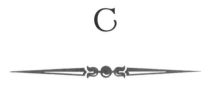

C

C. An abbreviation for *coward* sometimes branded on a soldier for desertion in the face of the enemy.

cabbaging. Slang for stealing.

cacolet. A device whereby two seats or litters could be placed on the back of a horse or mule. It was designed for use in areas too rough or heavily wooded for conventional wagons.

Cactus. A nickname for Union Gen. William T. Sherman, likely a reference to his beard.

cadet gray. A grayish blue color, the official designation of the color of a regulation Confederate coat.

Cahaba. A Confederate prison in Alabama at the confluence of the Cahaba and Alabama Rivers.

Cairo, **USS.** A wooden GUNBOAT of the seven-vessel "Pook Turtle" class built at Mound City, Illi-nois, by James B. Eads. Launched in January 1862, the 512-ton vessel participated in the battles of Forts Henry and Pillow and Plum Run Bend. On December 12, as part of a five-boat flotilla dispatched up the Yazoo River during an attack on the Confederate stronghold at Vicksburg, Mississippi, the *Cairo* struck two torpedoes (mines) and sank in less than fifteen minutes with no loss of life. The wreck was discovered in 1956 and restoration was begun at the Vicksburg National Battlefield Park.

caisson. A two-wheeled cart designed to carry ammunition for a field GUN. In Federal batteries, a single gun required  two caissons, each of which carried as many as 150 projectiles. Generally speaking, a caisson carried two ammunition chests, a limber carried one.

calcium light. A light generated by a high-intensity flame and lime. Union Gen. Quincy A. Gillmore trained one of these floodlights on South Carolina's Fort Wagner, and his gunners maintained their fire around the clock, which played a significant role in the capture of the installation.

caliber. The diameter of the BORE of a CANNON or the barrel of a handgun. The caliber of artillery was, however, usually expressed in terms of the weight of the projectile it was designed to fire. At

41

times the size of a GUN was expressed in terms of both the diameter of the bore and the weight of its ammunition.

Calico Colonel. A nickname for Mary Ann Ball Bickerdyke, a widow from Galesburg, Ohio, who delivered medical supplies to a company of soldiers from the town and then remained as a nurse in the Union armies in the western theater. She was present at nineteen major battles, which included the siege of Vicksburg and the Atlanta campaign.

California Brigade. A Union BRIGADE made up of four "California regiments," each of which was recruited from the Philadelphia area and organized by English-born U.S. Sen. and Union Col. Edward D. Baker, a friend of the Lincoln family and the namesake of the president's second son. Baker was a good politician who had spent several years in California after the Mexican War, and he believed that the state would remain loyal to the Union if it had some representation in the Federal army. Thus while the members of Baker's brigade were Pennsylvanians, their numbers were credited to the quota of soldiers to be raised by California (funding for the brigade, however, was to come from California). The regiments were designated the 1st, 2d, 4th, and 5th California, but after Baker's death in the October 21, 1861, Federal debacle at Ball's Bluff, Virginia, the honorific title of this unit was changed to the Philadelphia Brigade, and the regiments were reorganized as the 69th, 71st, 72d, and 106th Pennsylvania.

call. A request for troops. Abraham Lincoln's initial call for seventy-five thousand men to enlist for ninety days was answered with such enthusiasm that it was oversubscribed. Some of the later calls for troops evoked immense popular enthusiasm but brought in few recruits. When calls no longer satisfied the need for men, the North resorted to conscription.

Cally. The family nickname for John Hunt Morgan, a veteran of the Mexican War and a talented Confederate cavalry commander. His horsemen executed several successful raids in Tennessee and Kentucky.

Morgan himself was captured and imprisoned in the Ohio State Penitentiary, but he escaped in sensational fashion and returned to his command. Morgan was killed on September 3, 1864, in a surprise engagement near Greenville, Tennessee.

caltrop. A four-pointed anti-cavalry device fashioned so that one point always projected upward, designed to maim a horse's hoof. Also known as a CROW'S FOOT.

camel. N. (1) A watertight float lashed below the water line of an IRONCLAD to temporarily reduce the vessel's draft. (2) A wooden float designed to protect the sides of a vessel tied to a pier.

camouflet. An explosive mine designed to direct the force of the explosion downward should an opponent attempt to tunnel into an installation.

Camp Butler. An Illinois training site for the state militia, near Springfield, that was converted into a prisoner-of-war camp in early 1862. The camp was named for William Butler, the state treasurer.

camp canard. Gossip.

Camp Chase. Situated a short distance west of Columbus, Ohio, this Federal prisoner-of-war camp was named for Ohio native Salmon P.

Chase, the U.S. secretary of the Treasury. Originally a training facility for state troops, by 1863 it housed eight thousand captives.

camp colors. A banner used to identify a REGIMENT in camp, usually a piece of bunting about eighteen inches square and placed atop an eight-foot pole. Such colors displayed the regiment's numerical designation and identified its branch of service: white for INFANTRY and red for ARTILLERY.

Camp Defiance. A training camp adjacent to Cairo, Illinois, and the launching point for a number of significant Federal movements in the western theater.

Camp Distribution. A Washington, D.C., camp directed by the U.S. SANITARY COMMISSION for men declared unfit for additional military service and awaiting formal discharge. The facility was also known as Camp Misery by those who were processed here.

Camp Douglas. This sixty-acre Union training base just south of Chicago was converted into a prisoner-of-war camp and held as many as thirty thousand captives.

camp fever. A reference to typhoid fever, which was usually contracted from contaminated water.

camp followers. Any nonmilitary personnel camping with or following an army on campaign. This category included newspaper correspondents, religious representatives, sutlers, artists and photographers, and prostitutes.

Camp Ford. Originally a Confederate training facility at Tyler, Texas, it was converted into a prisoner-of-war camp during the summer of 1863. Because the climate was judged as mild, no shelters were built for the inmates. Originally considered an alternative stockade to CAMP GROCE, Camp Ford quickly mushroomed into the largest prison camp west of the Mississippi River.

Camp Groce. A Confederate prisoner-of-war camp near Hempstead, Texas. It received its name from the land baron who offered the acreage to the state in 1863. The facility was equipped with barracks, but the inmate population swelled beyond the camp's capacity.

Camp Hoffman. Situated on the point where the Potomac River enters Chesapeake Bay and best known as POINT LOOKOUT, these forty acres were set aside as a Union prison camp. Prior to the war the area was a resort, but it was leased to the federal government in 1862. See POINT LOOKOUT.

Camp Lawton. A Confederate prisoner-of-war camp in Georgia that was designed to receive the overflow population from the ANDERSONVILLE prison camp, but the facility was never finished.

Camp Morton. A Union prisoner-of-war camp founded at the state fair grounds in Indianapolis, Indiana, and named for the state's wartime governor, Oliver P. Morton. During the early months of the war, it functioned as a training camp for state troops. In February 1862 it was first used as a prisoner-of-war facility, and Morton personally oversaw the operation of the camp. In August 1862 it reverted to a training center, and in early 1863 Morton was again converted into a prison camp. For the remainder of the war, few if any other facilities of this sort equaled the exemplary record of this prison. Soon after the war, Col. Richard Owen became the only former prison commandant to be honored with a monument erected by grateful former inmates.

camp of parole. Following the Confederate surrenders in Virginia and North Carolina, a number of prison camps became holding areas for former prisoners awaiting parole.

Camp Sorghum. The nickname of a Southern stockade at Columbia, South Carolina. Union prisoners complained at being given sorghum syrup with which to sweeten their food, but conditions here never approached those of the most notorious prison camps of the war North or South.

Camp Sumter. The official but seldom-used designation of the Confederate prison at ANDERSONVILLE, Georgia.

Canaan. The hereafter.

candlestick. A sarcastic nickname for a BAYONET, referring to its use as a candlestick when thrust into the ground so that the socket could hold a taper.

canister. An antiper-sonnel artillery projec-tile filled with metal balls and packed with sawdust. Its effective range was less than 350 yards, but it was most lethal at one-third to one-half that distance.  The standard canister for a Federal 12-POUNDER NAPOLEON SMOOTHBORE contained twenty-seven balls; canister for a 12-pounder HOWITZER held forty-eight.

canned hellfire. A Confederate term for Union canister.

cannon. A term applied to guns ranging in size from brass NAPOLEONS, designed for use in the field, to massive seacoast artillery.

cannon fever. Battle fatigue.

cannon quick step. A mocking term used by veterans to describe the chaotic pace of green troops in full fight.

cannonade. A barrage of cannon fire.

canteen. A personal container designed to carry water. Confederate canteens were practically anything that would hold liquid—a clay or porcelain jug, a bottle covered with leather or straw, or a simple container made of tin. The Federal canteen was made of tin and had a pewter spout; it was covered with dark blue cloth and equipped with a cloth strap. See also BULL'S-EYE CANTEEN.

canvas. A reference to any tent made of canvas.

canvas pontoon. A pontoon with a wooden frame over which canvas was stretched. Because this device was much lighter than those made entirely of wood, it was widely used in field operations by armies in numerous theaters.

cap. (1) A small piece of paper or very thin metal that held an explosive charge for use in a MUSKET or RIFLE. Caps were sometimes packed in standard-issue sets of ten. (2) Headgear.

cap-a-pie. Informal dress.

cap box. A small pouch, often made of leather, into which sufficient caps could be placed to fire forty cartridges—the standard number carried by a soldier entering combat.

cap container. A tin cylinder in which rifle caps were packed by the manufacturer.

caponniere. (1) A covered passageway leading from one part of a fortification to another, designed to allow communication with the outer works. (2) A small FIELDWORK constructed as a BLOCKHOUSE within a larger fieldwork.

capstan. N. A massive spool-like timber used to raise or lower anchors or other great weights.

Captain Chatters. The nickname of the duke of Chartres, a great-nephew of the French king Louis Philippe and an observer of the war.

Captain Parry. The nickname of the duke of Paris, a brother of the duke of Chartres and an observer of Federal strategy.

carbine. A lightweight shoulder arm that was shorter than a RIFLE. This BREECHLOADER was manufactured chiefly for use by CAVALRY, although MOUNTED INFANTRY sometimes were issued it.

carabine a tige. Named for a central raised area or "tige" that was screwed into the chamber of a weapon from the back, this Belgian system addressed the problem of forcing the charge of a MUZZLELOADING GUN to engage the rifling in the barrel. Powder surrounded the tige, and a lead ball was placed on top. When struck by the RAMROD, the soft ball spread outward—sufficiently to engage the rifling grooves. This process was easily susceptible to corrosion, and the tige was often broken or bent as a result of ramming the ball. The introduction of the MINIÉ BALL addressed these shortcomings.

carbine tool. A multifaceted tool containing a screwdriver, a bullet mold, and a rear-sight screwdriver. Other small tools could be added.

carcass. A spherical incendiary shell. In addition to the FUSE hole, this projectile had three vent holes that admitted sufficient air for the contents to burn for eight to ten minutes.

cards. Small loaves of cornbread, the ends of which were approximately the size of playing cards.

carga. A Mexican measure for flour used in the western theater in general and by Texas troops in particular.

cargo. A Mexican unit of weight equivalent to three hundred pounds.

Caribbean Empire. A reference to the prewar Southwestern Conspiracy, a southern idea to conquer Mexico and other Latin American nations where cotton and SLAVERY could prosper. See KNIGHTS OF THE GOLDEN CIRCLE.

NAVAL HISTORICAL CENTER

***Carondelet*, USS.** This 512-ton Cairo-class IRON-CLAD river GUNBOAT was built at St. Louis and commissioned in January 1862. The ship participated in the captures of Forts Henry and Donelson and Island No. 10 as well as the engagements against Fort Pillow and Memphis and then was severely damaged in an encounter with the Confederate ironclad *Arkansas*. In October 1862 the gunboat was transferred to the Federal navy and participated in the April 16, 1863, run past Vicksburg and the action at Grand Gulf, Mississippi, later that month before returning to support the siege of Vicksburg. River operations occupied the gunboat for the rest of the war, including the Red River campaign. The vessel was decommissioned in June 1865.

carpetbagger. A Northern political or economic adventurer who went to the South during the post-war RECONSTRUCTION period (1865–70). The reference was to a carryall made of carpet materials.

carpet knight. A soldier in the BODYGUARD or ESCORT of a Federal commander. Although occasionally involved in combat, these men did not have to face the same hardships as most foot soldiers.

carpet soldier. A contemptuous reference to state guard or militia soldiers who avoided front-line military service.

carriage. A wheel-equipped support for a GUN used in CASEMATES of permanent and semipermanent fortifications.

carronade. N. A short cannon designed to throw a heavy projectile at low velocity. It was designed to break or to smash, rather than pierce, the hull of an opponent.

catamaran. N. A small flat-bottom boat designed by Napoleon for his projected invasion of England. Since the French emperor's tactics were studied and imitated by Civil War commanders on both sides, some Federal warships were equipped with catamarans.

carte de visite. A 2¼" x 3¾" photographic card. These small, inexpensive images were easily reproduced, and so they became lasting mementoes of the soldiers to their families as they marched off to war. These were produced in both formal studios and by photographers in the field, all of which were decorated with the props appropriate to the subject. At the same time, a market developed for images of politicians and celebrities, and albums were produced for collectors. The demand was usually greater than the supply but tapered off somewhat after a Federal tax was placed on the cards in 1864.

cartel. A formal written agreement negotiated by nations at war. Although the United States never recognized the Confederacy as a nation, numerous cartels were executed between the two govern-

ments addressing such things as the treatment of wounded and prisoners of war and the exchange of letters and telegrams.

cartridge. A charge of powder and a ball for a RIFLE. Initially, the majority were wrapped in paper, but metal cartridges became standard for some rifles. Arsenals used women and children to prepare individual cartridges.

cartridge bag. A canvas pouch designed to hold cartridges.

cartridge box. (1) A small rigid or semirigid container designed to hold forty cartridges, the standard number issued to each soldier before an engagement. (2) A large ammunition box with a capacity of one thousand rounds.

cartridge class. A civilian volunteer group, usually comprised of women, that met at regular intervals to make cartridges.

cartridge tearer. A metal device fitted near a RIFLE muzzle and used to open paper cartridges.

cascabel. The part of a cannon behind its base ring.

Casco. A class of IRONCLAD warships of the same basic design as the USS *MONITOR* but built to draw only four feet of water instead of the original's ten-foot draft.

case knife. A knife with a blade that retracted into a sheath of metal or horn.

casemate. A chamber designed to withstand artillery fire. A fortification's outer casemates usually mounted guns that were fired through EMBRASURES.

case shot. See SPHERICAL CASE SHOT.

cashier, to. To dismiss from military service dishonorably or with ignominy. This course of action was rarely taken with enlisted men, most of whom were punished and retained.

casket. A coffin; a metallic or wooden container for a corpse. Before the war this word referred to a small box that held jewelry.

cast the lead, to. N. To make a sounding or measure the depth of water with a lead weight attached to a chain or rope.

Castle Morgan. The Union prisoners' nickname for CAHABA Prison in Alabama, a token of admiration and respect for the ingenuity and courage of Confederate Col. John Hunt Morgan. Captured during a daring raid in the North, Morgan was confined at the Ohio State Penitentiary but managed to escape.

Castle Pinckney. A Revolutionary War–era military installation at Charleston Harbor. Named for Charles C. Pinckney, by 1860 it was of little use as a fortress but served as a prison. Federal prisoners from the July 17, 1861, battle of First Bull Run (First Manassas) were sent to Pinckney, where they enjoyed considerable liberty and a climate they praised as "congenial."

Castle Thunder. (1) A Richmond prison comprised of three buildings linked by a highboard fence. The central structure was formerly Gleanor's tobacco factory, which stood at the corner of Cary and Eighteenth Streets. The name was suggested by the original inmates, most of whom were black marketers who believed their imprisonment was the result of their having tempted the gods. It was originally a place of confinement for deserters and political prisoners—spies and skulkers and criminals—including a number of women. Although capacity was estimated at around fourteen hundred, more than three thousand captives were confined here during the war. (2) In Petersburg, Virginia, a facility for Union prisoners of war was dubbed by this name because the inmates were held during the siege of the city and regularly endured the thunder of Federal artillery.

catarrh. A generic name for any inflammation of the nose and throat.

cattle. A Southern battlefield designation for Union soldiers.

cavalier. (1) An inner defensive position within a seacoast fortification that was separated from the outer works and had a commanding field of fire. (2) A raised PARAPET of an inland fortification, such as some of the defensive works around Petersburg.

Cavalier of Dixie. Confederate Gen. J. E. B. "Jeb" Stuart, whose bold dress and gallant ways were carefully cultivated.

cavalry. Soldiers trained, armed, and equipped to fight on horseback. The branch was distinguished from DRAGOONS (horse soldiers trained to fight on foot or in the saddle) and MOUNTED INFANTRY (which was trained to fight on foot).

cavalry bell. A bronze or steel bell used to mark a makeshift corral in the field. One belled animal was sufficient to locate a unit's horses in the dark.

centaur. A Federal nickname for Terry's Texas Rangers, skilled riders who seemed to be united with their horses much as mythical centaurs, creatures half-man and half-horse.

Cerro Gordo. The nickname of Confederate Gen. John S. Williams, whose men bestowed the title on him following the battle of Cerro Gordo during the Mexican War. When the Civil War broke out, he helped to raise a BRIGADE in Virginia and saw action in that state as well as Kentucky and Tennessee.

chain. A surveyor's chain of standardized length, used to measure distances.

Chain Bridge. Spanning the Potomac River at Washington, D.C., this was perhaps the most used bridge of the capital, named for the heavy chains used in its construction.

chain firing. Accidental discharge of all cartridges in a percussion REVOLVER, caused by flashover from the mouth of one chamber to the next.

chain shot. Two cannonballs linked with a short chain and designed to sever masts and the rigging of ships. It proved too erratic for general use.

chair. An iron socket that connected railroad track to a tie, or sleeper, on a rail line.

chandelier. A device fashioned of timber to constitute a frame for a quantity of FASCINES—wood bundles—and used to elevate artillery batteries or to stabilize the sides of trenches.

change one's breath, to. A swallow of hard liquor.

chapeau, chapeau bras. This "bicorne" hat had a distinctively European look. It varied in length from seventeen to nine-  teen inches and could be flattened and carried under one's arm. Such headgear was part of the formal dress uniform of the different services. Per prewar regulations, the chapeau bras was to be worn only by field officers and commandants of installations. The hats were also edged with black silk and displayed "at each end a gold and scarlet tassel." Other decorations, such as colored plumes, were mandated by each service.

chaplain's coat. Federal chaplains were expected to wear a plain black frock coat, plain black trousers, and a black felt hat.

charger. A horse trained to charge upon command or signal.

Charleyville musket. A SMOOTHBORE .69-caliber weapon used by more sailors than soldiers.

Charlie. One of the guns used to defend Fort Powhatan in Virginia during Confederate Gen. James Longstreet's command there.

chase. That portion of a GUN that lay between its TRUNNIONS and the spot at which its muzzle swelled. When the chase was obscured by gunsmoke, gunners could not aim accurately.

chatoyant face. A compass face having a changeable luster. In 1862 Jedediah Hotchkiss acquired one of these instruments in Warrenton, Virginia, for use in his mapmaking for Confederate Gen. T. J. "Stonewall" Jackson.

Chattanooga Southern on Wheels, The. Chattanooga's *Daily Southern* newspaper continued to be published after the town fell to the Union army. Editor F. M. Paul retained the name but took the publication to Atlanta, and when the railroad center threatened to fall to Federal forces in the summer of 1864, Paul moved the paper to Alabama.

chattel. Slaves.

chebang. A dirt hut of considerable length erected by the Federals who were trapped in Chattanooga during the winter of 1863. It was later imitated at sites where conventional tents or other housing could not be had. Although possibly related to SHEBANG because of a similar pronunciation, the two kinds of structures were quite different.

cheeks. Seasoned timber used to form the sides of GUN CARRIAGES.

cheer ship, to. N. To salute a passing ship with cheers, usually from men in the rigging.

cheesebox on a raft. A nickname for the USS *MONITOR* and similar vessels whose decks were just above the surface of the water and on which a single turret was mounted.

cheese knife. A sword or saber carried by an officer, and an example of the sarcasm of which enlisted men were capable.

chesses. Boards placed transversely on the balks, or stringers, of a pontoon bridge to form a treadway.

chevaux-de-frise. Defensive obstructions fashioned from tree trunks. Holes were bored into the trunks, and sharpened poles were inserted in such fashion that they pointed toward the direction

from which an attack was likely to come. They were used to obstruct gaps, plug a breach, or form a line of obstructions in front of a fixed fortification or breastworks. Southerners usually placed such a line fifty to one hundred yards in front of their trenches.

chevrette. A device used to hoist heavy guns onto their CARRIAGES.

chevrons. Emblems that indicated the rank of a noncommissioned officer. Usually made of silk or worsted wool, in Federal forces half-inch pieces were sewed upon both sleeves of a regulation coat and overcoat. Confederate noncoms used a similar pattern of stripes and arcs to indicate their rank.

***Chickamauga,* CSS.** This 585-ton cruiser was constructed in London as the BLOCKADE-RUNNER *Edith*. She was purchased by the Confederate navy in 1864 at Wilmington, North Carolina, and converted into a warship. After a short cruise in the western North Atlantic as a COMMERCE RAIDER, during which *Chickamauga* captured several Yankee merchant ships, the ship returned to the Cape Fear River and remained there until she was scuttled on February 25, 1865, to prevent her capture.

NAVAL HISTORICAL CENTER

NAVAL HISTORICAL CENTER

Chickasaw, **USS.** This 1,300-ton Milwaukee-class twin-turret IRONCLAD river MONITOR was built at Carondelet, Missouri, and commissioned in May 1864. She was eventually assigned to the West Gulf Blockading Squadron and participated in the August 5, 1865, battle of Mobile Bay, where she contributed to the capture of the Confederate ironclad *TENNESSEE. Chickasaw* remained in Mobile Bay for the remainder of the war. She was decommissioned at New Orleans in June 1865.

chicken guts. Elaborate braiding on an officer's uniform, especially the cuff braiding.

chicken heart disease. Cannon fever, also known as battle fatigue.

children by brevet. Children whose fathers were not known to them.

chimney. N. A smokestack of a steam-powered vessel that burned coal. Some Confederate raiders had movable chimneys that could be lowered when a captain chose to present the profile of a sailing vessel.

Chimneyville. Although uncounted villages and towns were burned to the ground during the war, Federal soldiers applied this descriptive name chiefly to Jackson, Mississippi.

chinch. A bedbug.

chin music. Slang for conversation.

chipping. Damage caused to wooden structures, such as the treadways of bridges, by the hooves of horses and the iron rims of wagon wheels. When a column of animals, wagons, and guns were moved quickly across such structures, the treadway could be splintered in a short time unless covered with a thick carpet of straw.

chit. Fractional paper currency issued by SUTLERS and redeemable only by the person or unit to whom it was issued.

chivalry, the. A colloquial phrase for prewar residents of California who were born in the North.

chock. A wooden wedge used by gunners to block the wheels of a CARRIAGE into position after a GUN had been aimed.

Choctaw. A member of a Southern secret society whose paramount goal was the secession of slaveholding states from the Union.

Christian Commission, U.S. This aid society for Union soldiers was founded in New York City on November 14, 1861, by the Young Men's Christian Association. The group worked in concert with the U.S. SANITARY COMMISSION and offered alternatives to the usual sutler's options by providing free box lunches and coffee wagons. Women volunteers focused on the fairly constant need for nurses. The commission addressed more than the physical needs of the soldiers by establishing reading rooms with Bibles, magazines, and newspapers and by providing writing materials and postage to encourage soldiers to write home. By the end of the war, Christian Commission efforts had provided six million dollars' worth of aid to Federal troops.

Christian Soldier, the. A reference to Union Gen. Oliver O. Howard, who was known for his piety and his integrity as well as his performance in the field. A member of the West Point Class of 1854, Howard served throughout the war. He lost his right arm at the May 1862 battle of Seven Pines and received the THANKS OF CONGRESS for his performance at the July 1863 battle of Gettysburg. After the war Howard headed the FREED-MEN'S BUREAU, helped to establish Howard University, and served as superintendent of the U.S. Military Academy.

chuck-a-luck. A comparatively simple game of chance that used dice.

Cincinnati. A large horse, almost eighteen hands tall, presented to Union Gen. Ulysses S. Grant after the November 23–25, 1863, battle of Chattanooga.

circular order. An order addressed to all officers of a designated rank, as opposed to an order directed to a single officer.

circumvallation. An earthen wall and trench erected at the rear of besieging troops so as to prevent an attack by a force sent to relieve a city under siege.

climbing iron. A foot-long metal bar with a pointed spike opposite a footrest, used by telegraphers when climbing poles.

clockwork torpedo. A MINE (TORPEDO) equipped with a mechanism by which it detonated after a chosen interval. Many of these relatively sophisticated devices were placed in wooden tubs and set adrift in rivers. Each torpedo had a vertical shaft attached to a propeller, and currents caused the propeller to turn against a spring-loaded plunger that detonated a primer.

close around, to. To surround an objective.

close confinement. Definitions varied from prison to prison, but the order was generally interpreted to mean that a prisoner's activity was to be greatly restricted and could include manacling and/or shackling.

close order. A precision drill formation in which each soldier maintained an exact distance from his comrades.

close ranks, to. This maneuver kept men together as much as possible after the ranks had been depleted. Prevailing tactics assumed that massed men equaled massed firepower and only massed men could break through an opponent's line.

coach. A four-wheel carriage with two interior seats and a capacity for at least four people. Coaches were used when AMBULANCES were not available. These vehicles were also central to many occasions of state.

coaling. A cleared flat spot in a forest used by the residents as an area in which to burn wood for charcoal.

coal wheeler. A laborer whose principal task was to haul coal.

cockade. A knot or elaborate rosette often worn on hats as a symbol of rank.

coehorn. A portable SMOOTHBORE MORTAR, invented in the seventeenth century by Dutch Baron Menno van Cohoorn, that fired a seventeen- or twenty-four-pound projectile over a range (depending on the amount of powder used) between twenty-five and twelve hundred yards. The small size allowed it to be moved easily and manned by a crew of only four men.

Cofer revolver. Manufactured in Virginia under Confederate patent no. 9, this .36-caliber weapon with a split cylinder used a metallic CARTRIDGE.

coffee boiler. A straggler. Also called a coffee cooler, because he was prone to start his duties only after his coffee had cooled.

coffee-mill gun. An experimental weapon. See AGER.

cold steel. A reference to BAYONETS.

colonization. A reference to the colonization of freed slaves overseas by the AMERICAN COLONIZATION SOCIETY or similar agency. Colonies were envisioned in Africa, Colombia, and Haiti.

color. A banner, a source of unit pride and honor.

color-bearer. A soldier entrusted with the task of carrying a flag, especially into combat. The honor also included greater risk, because the high visibility of the emblem made color-bearers major targets on the battlefield. During  the course of an action, it was not unusual for a unit to lose several color-bearers.

color guard. A hand-picked group charged with protecting the COLOR-BEARERS during combat. They faced the same risks as the color-bearers and were only less vulnerable by virtue of their weapons.

color line. A line of stacked MUSKETS or RIFLES at which the colors rested.

colors. Strictly speaking, the plural form referred to a unit's flag and the national banner. In practice, the term generally meant a single flag, usually that of a regiment.

Colt revolver. Manufactured by Samuel Colt in both army and navy models, this was the most popular handgun of the war. The Colt Model 1860 Army revolver was a .44-caliber six-shot weapon that weighed almost three pounds. An estimated two hundred thousand were manufactured during the war. The Colt 1861 Navy model was a .36-caliber that resembled the army revolver in all other aspects, including weight. Thirty-eight thousand were produced, but only forty-five hundred were purchased by the Federal government. Sales were hampered by high pricing. Individuals could purchase the revolvers for a little less than fourteen dollars, but Remington and Starr revolvers were available at lower cost. Government purchases ended in 1863, and a fire at the manufacturing plant in 1864 greatly limited production.

Colt repeating rifle. The Colt-Root Model 1855 percussion repeating RIFLE was the first rapid-fire weapon to be issued in quantity during the war. It was available in a wide variety of calibers, a variety of barrel lengths, and both five- and six-shot cylinders. The weapon was not distributed throughout the ranks because the ignition of one round had a tendency to ignite the others. (See CHAIN FIRING.)

Columbiad. A MUZZLELOADING SMOOTHBORE that fired both shot and shell and was capable of a wide range of elevation. Well suited to defend narrow channels, it was deployed throughout the country's coastal fortifications. Columbiads were cast according to the RODMAN process in which the BORE of the GUN was integral. A number of models were available from the prewar years, mostly 8- and 10-inch guns, but during the war Northern foundries produced 8-, 10-, 13-, 15-, and 20-inch calibers. Confederate Columbiads were cast solid and then bored. Many of these were banded to strengthen the firing chamber, and the bore was rifled.

column of companies. A column of ten ranks instead of the two that usually formed a line of battle. This maneuver required participants to get as close together as possible, known as "close in mass." As a result, a column of companies created the best of all targets for enemy gunners.

Comanches. The nickname of the 35th Virginia Cavalry, allegedly bestowed by Confederate Gen. Thomas L. Rosser during the Mine Run campaign of November-December 1863.

come booming, to. To trot or run toward the enemy behind skirmishers three ranks deep.

comin' with a bone in her teeth. N. A vivid description of a fast-approaching vessel marked by foaming water at the prow.

commerce raider. An armed vessel operated by Southerners whose goal was to sink or capture commercial vessels of the North.

commissary. (1) A camp store that stocked equipment and provisions not likely to be issued by military authorities. (2) A person operating such establishment or otherwise providing goods for soldiers. (3) Inferior whiskey dispensed by most commissaries.

Commissary Banks. A mocking nickname for Union Gen. Nathaniel P. Banks, because he permitted Southerners to capture enough supplies at Port Royal, Virginia, in the summer of 1861 to stock fifty to one hundred commissaries.

committee of safety. A militia or home-guard organization in a seceded or Border State.

Committee on the Conduct of the War. The Congressional Joint Committee on the Conduct of the War was founded to investigate the Federal disasters at the July 17, 1861, battle of First Bull Run (First Manassas) and the October 21, 1861, battle of Ball's Bluff. Over the course of the war, the committee exercised broad investigative powers into the Union war effort. Dominated by RADICAL REPUBLICANS, the body targeted conservative and Democratic generals, such as George B. McClellan. Rather than attack him directly, McClellan's subordinates were frequently grilled in closed sessions. Several Republican generals, despite their demonstrations of incompetence, received the endorsement of the committee. Later the committee launched investigations into engagements and affairs that held a potentially high propaganda value in Northern eyes; for example, the April 12, 1864, massacre at Fort Pillow, Tennessee, and the treatment of Union prisoners of war. The committee had little influence on the conduct of the war, however. Abraham Lincoln consulted it when to do so furthered his purposes, and he ignored the committee when he disagreed with it.

commodore. N. An officer whose rank was above a captain and below a rear admiral, roughly equivalent to a brigadier general.

common time. The normal rate at which men marched without special instruction, approximately ninety steps per minute.

commutation. (1) Cash paid in lieu of such stipulated necessities as housing, food, and fuel. (2) An exemption fee of three hundred dollars paid by a draftee to avoid enlistment. After the first Federal draft, the U.S. Treasury received fifteen million dollars in commutation fees. (3) An exemption fee of five hundred dollars paid by a Southern draftee to avoid military service. Strict laws, however, limited Southern commutation to members of religious bodies such as Quakers and Mennonites.

company. A basic organizational unit ideally comprised of one hundred men and commanded by a captain. For practical purposes, companies and REGIMENTS were the principal INFANTRY and CAVALRY groups of the war. Most of the men in a company came from the same town or general locale. They had been acquainted with each other for years prior to becoming soldiers; most maintained as close ties as possible with their home communities. At the beginning of the war, nearly all companies elected their captain from within the ranks. Such units were fiercely protective of their identity, and when mauled in combat the men were prone to protest when ordered to fill their ranks with replacements not from the same geographical hometown or county.

company bean boiler. The company cook.

Company Darling. Company D of John S. Mosby's renowned Confederate Partisan Rangers.

Company Q. (1) The sick list. (2) A Federal unit comprised of former Confederates sent west to maintain peace on the frontier between the settlers and the native tribesmen.

compensated emancipation. A plan to reimburse slaveowners for freeing their slaves.

complement. N. The body of officers and men who constitute a ship's personnel.

Condemned Yankees. A Confederate reference to the special organization known as the Federal Invalid Corps.

condonation. An act of implied forgiveness, treating an offense as though it did not happen.

Confederate beef. Mule meat.

Confederate candle. A substitute candle made from animal fat, rosin, beeswax, turpentine, or other combustibles.

Confederate gas. A substitute for illuminating gas, such as pine cones or double-distilled turpentine.

Confederate Gray. The designation for the color of Confederate uniforms. Although the majority of Southern uniforms were some shade of gray or butternut by 1864, there were notable exceptions. In some instances, especially at the beginning of the war, Southern soldiers wore the uniform of their state militia. ZOUAVE units were known for distinctively colorful clothing. Some units wore impeccable uniforms ordered from European suppliers. Yet not all Confederate soldiers wore uniforms, and what they wore varied according to their location and at different times during the war.

Confederate grayback. A piece of Confederate currency of any denomination, so called because

poor paper and ink often caused it to take on a gray hue after brief circulation.

Confederate Military History. This compilation of military accounts and biographies was launched in 1899 under the editorship of former Confederate Gen. Clement A. Evans. Arranged into seventeen volumes, it was called the South's response to the government-issued *Official Records.*

Confederate paper. Southerners relied upon whatever substitutes could be found for linen, and much of the paper produced from these inferior substances tore readily and quickly turned yellow. Substandard paper accounts for the low number of Southern documents that survived the war.

Confederate Veteran, The. A magazine "published monthly in the interest of Confederate veterans and kindred topics." Launched at Nashville, Tennessee, in January 1893, the magazine had a life of forty years and published hundreds of firsthand observations and recollections of the war.

Confederate winged shot. A projectile equipped with spring-loaded "wings," or fins, that were supposed to stabilize it in flight.

confide, to. To consign to or commit to the care of another.

Confiscation Act of 1862. The Second Confiscation Act was approved on July 16, 1862, and was part of the first legislation to address the emancipation of slaves. Enacted by RADICAL REPUBLICANS against the expressed wishes of Abraham Lincoln, the law provided for the confiscation of the property—including slaves—of all political and military Southern officials and proposed procedures for colonizing freed slaves abroad. The president signed the bill into law when its proponents agreed to limit any confiscations of land by the government to the lifetime of the Confederate officials involved. The act also addressed a long-standing problem for Federal commanders in the field: runaway slaves were now considered freed after entering Union lines. This Confiscation Act, however, was limited in jurisdiction to the Confederacy; in the Border States, runaway slaves were to be returned to their owners, provided the owners proved their loyalty to the Union. Many of the act's provisos were incorporated into and expanded by the EMANCIPATION PROCLAMATION that followed, but for the time being, the legislation addressed the pressing matter of what to do with fugitive slaves who had sought refuge behind Union lines.

Congreve rocket. A cylinder filled with gunpowder and topped by an explosive shell with a separate FUSE. In use since the War of 1812, the rocket's effect was more psychological than tactical. Few were used during the war.

conscription. The draft. The first conscription act was passed by the Confederate Congress on April 16, 1862; Federal lawmakers enacted the first Union conscription acts less than a year later. Partly because both sides had numerous provisions for exemption and because BOUNTIES were offered to volunteer recruits early in the war, conscription was among the most conspicuous failures of either side's war measures.

consumption. A synonym for tuberculosis.

contraband. (1) Goods deemed to benefit an opponent and therefore subject to seizure. (2) A runaway slave. The term was first applied to fugitive slaves when a Confederate officer demanded the return of a runaway under the terms of the Fugitive Slave Act of 1850. Union Gen. Benjamin F. Butler refused to relinquish the slave, citing that the act applied only to the states of the Union, of which the officer claimed to no longer

be a constituent. The Federal commander was also motivated not to return runaway slaves since they were used as laborers in erecting Confederate fortifications.

contribution. A euphemism for theft by foragers, looters, and pillagers.

contribution, under. To exact a ransom from a party unable to pay.

convention. A formal agreement between two or more parties.

Cook and Brother musketoon. Manufactured at a New Orleans plant that was later moved to Athens, Georgia, this CARBINE was patterned after the ENFIELD RIFLE. Considerable numbers were distributed to Southern forces.

cooking canteen. A metal cup in which a bottle was securely enclosed. When filled with water, the bottle served as a miniature boiler.

coosh. Softened HARDTACK fried in bacon grease.

copperbottom. A Secessionist of Missouri or Kansas.

coppered. N. A warship whose hull was sheathed with copper to protect it from marine worms.

Copperhead. A Northerner, usually a Democrat, who was opposed to the war and favored a negotiated peace. The earliest reference appeared in the September 11, 1862, issue of the *Lawrence (Kans.)*

Republican, which noted the application of the term to Southern sympathizers in Indiana.

Coquette. A high-stepping horse belonging to Southern partisan commander John S. Mosby.

coracle. N. An open one-man boat made of leather stretched over a wicker frame.

cordage. (1) The capacity of a vehicle, measured in terms of the number of 128-cubic-foot cords it could carry. (2) N. Lines in the rigging of a ship.

corduroy road. A temporary road surface made up of small-diameter tree trunks, usually erected in muddy or swampy regions.

corked in a bottle. A situation in which movement was seemingly impossible.

Corncrackers. Kentuckians.

corn dodger. Cornbread shaped into sticks or patties.

Corn Exchange Regiment. The 118th Pennsylvania Infantry, which was raised and partly funded by merchants of Philadelphia's Corn Exchange—an early commodities market. Organized in May 1862, the unit participated in most eastern theater engagements from Antietam to Appomattox and mustered out on June 1, 1865.

corn rigs. A stack or pile of cornstalks gathered at harvest time.

corps. (1) An organizational unit composed of two or more divisions. Reorganizations often renamed these units as LEGIONS, GRAND DIVISIONS, or WINGS. The size of a corps varied from twelve thousand to more than twenty-six thousand men, commanded by a major general. During the war the Federal army had forty-three corps, which were designated by number. (2) The Confederate army adopted the corps system in November 1862. There were thirty corps in the Southern army during the war, and their size was not as structured as their counterparts in blue. In various Confederate armies, corps were numbered separately and usually designated by the names of their commanders—a source of no small confusion. (3) A special Southern unit, such as a hand-picked group of sharpshooters in the Army of Northern Virginia.

corps badge. An ornament or patch worn on a soldier's hat or uniform that identified the corps to which he belonged. Union Gen. Philip Kearny is credited with the idea of using corps badges after he reprimanded officers in the field not under his command. When Joseph Hooker assumed command of the Army of the Potomac, corps badges were mandated throughout the ranks. These were designed and implemented by Gen. Daniel Butterfield, using such shapes as circles, diamonds, half-moons, triangles, stars, and hearts. No such identification badges evolved in Confederate ranks.

Corps d'Afrique. A name attached to the Louisiana Native Guards, Union regiments formed of freed slaves. When a regiment of the Native Guards was MUSTERED INTO Federal service by Gen. Benjamin F. Butler, it was the first black regiment to serve in any U.S. army. For a period, all black units in Union service were listed as part of the Corps d'Afrique. Later this segment of the Union army came to be known as the U.S. Colored Troops (USCT).

corvette. N. A warship with a flat deck and only one GUN deck.

Cosmopolitan carbine. Also known as the Union CARBINE, this was a shoddy weapon.

Cotton Belt. The southern portion of the eastern United States, made up of the states in which cotton could be produced at a satisfactory profit.

cottonclad. A river steamer protected from enemy fire by means of cotton bales—an effective substitute for iron armor.

cotton press. An industrial device designed to compress cotton into four-hundred-pound bales for shipping.

countermarch. A march made with the purpose of countering the movement made by the enemy.

counter mine. A tunnel dug by a fortification's defenders to thwart a besieging force suspected of tunneling toward the defenders.

counter scarp. The exterior slope of a ditch dug to protect a PARAPET.

countersign. An oral response to a challenge or an identification signal to authenticate the background of the person or persons approaching a picket line or accidentally encountered in the field.

countervallation. An earthwork consisting of a trench and a wall of earth that was erected behind a besieging force to protect it from attack by a relieving army.

coupe de main. Borrowed from the French, this expression described a sudden strong attack meant to overwhelm a position quickly.

coupe d'oeil. A sudden unanticipated decision or move by which a commander tried to make the best of a difficult situation.

court-martial. A trial court composed of officers and convened to hear evidence and judge a person accused of violations of the military code.

couteau. A mountain ridge whose summit was a sharp peak.

covert. A flat covered walkway above the exterior slope of a defensive ditch.

covered-bridge gun. A reference to the rapid-firing BILLINGHURST-REQUA GUN. The term may stem from the notion that a single Billinghurst-Requa gun mounted at one end of a bridgeway was sufficient to halt any adversary's advance through the structure.

covered way. A gallery sheltered from enemy fire that allowed troops to move from one fieldwork to another.

cows' horn turban. Southern women made these hats by attaching shavings from the horns of cows to cardboard.

Cracker Line. A supply line opened by Federal forces in 1863 to bypass the railroad leading north into Chattanooga, portions of which were under Southern control.

cracker outfits. The wagons of SUTLERS.

craps. A game of dice and the most popular form of gambling in both gray and blue ranks.

Crazy Delawares. The 2d Delaware Infantry Regiment, which was formed as a three-year unit in May 1861 and included recruits from Maryland and Pennsylvania. The unit fought in all major battles of the Army of the Potomac from 1861 to 1865.

Crazy Jane. A 20-pound PARROTT in a Confederate battery at Vicksburg that fired constantly during the forty-seven days while the river city was under SIEGE, from May 22 to July 4, 1863.

crib. A storage crate or bin made of wood.

crimp. (1) N. A felon who specialized in getting men drunk and signing them on to the crew of a ship about to sail. (2) A BOUNTY BROKER who profitted by supplying Union forces with recruits who had serious disabilities or criminal records. Numerous crimps operated in Canada, seizing underage boys or getting men drunk and carting them to the nearest recruiting station.

critter company. A CAVALRY unit smaller than a regulation company.

crooked shoe. A shoe cut to fit a right or a left foot and used exclusively by Federal soldiers.

cross-draw holster. A holster worn on the right side, permitting a man to draw the firearm with his left hand while wielding his saber with his right.

crossfire. Massed fire from two or more directions on the same target or point in front of a fieldwork.

cross on Confederate pontoons, to. A sarcastic Federal reference for wading across a waterway.

crow's foot. A CALTROP. A four-pointed anti-cavalry device fashioned so that one point always projected upward, designed to maim a horse's hoof. It was rarely, if ever, used during the war.

Crossing on "Confederate pontoons"

crumb. A nickname for a body louse.

Cump. A nickname for Union Gen. William Tecumseh Sherman.

curtain. A segment of a fortification's wall that served to join two structures, such as BASTIONS or towers.

cush. Cornmeal fried in bacon fat and stewed meat.

cutlass. A short sword with a heavy curved blade; a regulation weapon on warships.

cutter. (1) N. A vessel with a broad and almost square stern whose primary function was to transport stores and/or passengers over relatively short distances, usually between a dock and a large ship. (2) N. A member of a ship's crew who was dispatched to sever any obstruction that was placed in a waterway to hinder an opponent's advance.

Czar of Pennsylvania. The nickname of Simon Cameron, Abraham Lincoln's first secretary of war who was made the U.S. minister to Russia in January 1862.

D

D. An abbreviation for DESERTER sometimes branded on a soldier for desertion in the face of the enemy.

daguerreotype. An early photographic process in which an image was burned into a sheet of thin silver or thin silver-coated copper.

Dahlgren. A classification of three types of naval ORDNANCE designed by John A. Dahlgren during his tenure as director of ordnance at the Washington Navy Yard, which began in 1847. The first was a model of 12- and 24-pound bronze boat HOW-ITZERS and RIFLES that were developed just after the Mexican War. In the 1850s Dahlgren refined a series of 9-, 10-, and 11-inch iron SMOOTHBORE shellguns capable of firing both shell and shot. He added 15- and 20-inch versions during the first years of the war. Because of their shape, they were nicknamed "SODA-POP GUNS." By 1860 Dahlgren had devel-

oped 50-, 80-, and 150-pound rifles, of which the 50-pound version was the most successful.

Dan the Magnificent. The nickname of Union Gen. Daniel Butterfield, judged by some of his peers and most of his subordinates as thinking extremely highly of himself.

dance. A lighthearted synonym for "the beginning of a battle."

dandyfunk. N. A stew made of HARDTACK, molasses, and salt pork.

Daniel Webster. A dark bay horse ridden by Union Gen. George B. McClellan.

daughter of the regiment. Following a common practice among European armies in the eighteenth century, many REGIMENTS elected a woman as an honorary "daughter." Some were wives or children of officers; others were attractive young women in the community from which the regiment was subscribed. Several Federal and Confederate regiments chose "daughters" during the early months of the conflict. See also VIVANDIÈRE.

David. N. A Federal term referring to a class of steam-powered cigar-shaped semisubmersible warships with a SPAR TORPEDO. The original vessel that gave its name to this boat class was built in Charleston in 1863 and measured fifty feet

NATIONAL ARCHIVES

long. The moniker was based on the biblical story of David and Goliath. Only four men were required to operate the *David*, and its maximum speed was seven knots or less. Still, armed with a torpedo that weighed one hundred pounds or more, the tiny ship was a formidable foe. Three attempts were made to attack the Federal ships blockading Charleston Harbor; the first severely damaged but did not sink the USS *New Ironsides*, and the other two were not successful.

David's Island. An eighty-acre island in Long Island Sound. Initially used as a Federal hospital site, it was converted into a prison whose population seldom dropped below twenty-five hundred.

Davis boot. A hightop shoe that reached slightly above the ankle and was tied with laces. Extremely popular with men in both blue and gray, it was named for former U.S. Secretary of War Jefferson Davis, whom many consider to have been one of the most effective men to execute that office during the nineteenth century.

Davisdom. A Federal designation for the eleven states of the Confederacy.

Davis Guards Medal. The only Confederate decoration to be awarded during the war, it was bestowed on the forty-four members of the Davis Guards, a militia company from Houston, Texas, for their performance in the September 8, 1863, battle of Sabine Pass, Texas, and the repulse

of more than six thousand Federals. A forty-fifth medal was sent to Confederate president Jefferson Davis, who carried it until it was taken away from him during his imprisonment at FORT MONROE after the war.

Davy Jones. N. A reference to the sea; the unmarkable "graveyard of the sea."

Dead Angle. A sector of the battlefield at Kennesaw Mountain.

dead cart. An AMBULANCE.

deadening. A soldier at the battle of Shiloh defined this type of field as "a vast, open, unfenced district, grown up with rank, dry grass, dotted here and there with blasted trees, as though some farmer had determined to clear a farm for himself and had abandoned the undertaking in disgust."

dead ground. Any spot on a battlefield that could not be reached by the enemy's shot and shells.

dead-head. (1) A coward. (2) An empty railroad train or ship in transit.

dead-house. A structure within a prison in which dead inmates were placed before burial.

deadline. An area, not always marked by a DEAD ROPE, beyond which prisoners could pass without risking death from the guards. Some evidence exists that desperate and hopeless men violated the deadline rather than struggle for life under intolerable conditions.

dead march. A slow-tempo march to a grave site by a burial party, frequently accompanied by a military band.

dead rope. A rope that marked the DEADLINE beyond which prisoners were not allowed.

dead shot. A weapon capable of delivering an accurate shot at a distance of six hundred feet.

deadwood. Incompetents and cowards who were useless in battle.

death bells. A derogatory term for HARDTACK.

death-shot. The single shot from a REVOLVER, MUSKET, or RIFLE that killed a man.

Decatur. The war horse of Union Gen. Philip Kearney.

debouche. An opening or pathway capable of allowing a unit to move from a wooded area or other difficult terrain into a relatively clear area.

debouche, to. To move into open ground from a swamp, a wood, or some other difficult terrain.

debts, repudiated. In May 1861 the Confederate Congress enacted legislation that required Southern citizens to submit payments for debts incurred in the North prior to the war to the Confederate Treasury. Special provisos exempted the treatment of such debts owed in the Border States and areas having significant populations of Southern sympathizers, such as Maryland, Delaware, the District of Columbia, Kentucky, or Missouri. Most Confederate debtors, however, simply ceased to make the payments. At the war's end, "repudiated debts" were cleared by negotiated settlements.

deer, small. A term for rats eaten by prisoners of war and citizens under SIEGE. During the siege of Vicksburg, several Southerners observed that small deer were just as tasty as normal deer.

defile. A narrow passageway, such as a mountain pass, a trail bordered by heavy trees, a bridge, a road running through a village, or a site at which a river could be forded.

defilade, to. To shield from enemy fire or observation from a given point by means of a natural or artificial barrier.

demand note. Federal currency carrying the promise that it could be redeemed for silver or gold; also known as a sight bill.

demonstration. A show of strength staged without intention of doing battle.

department. A territorial organization usually named and occasionally numbered. In many but not all cases, an army stationed or operating within a department took its name from that geographical region.

D'Epineuil Zouaves. The nickname of the 53d New York Infantry, which was MUSTERED INTO service between August 27 and November 15, 1861. The colonel of the REGIMENT, Lionel Jobert D'Epineuil, claimed to have served in the French army and to have been decorated by Napoleon III. When the regiment was dispatched to North Carolina, it arrived in such disarray and confusion that it was sent back to Annapolis, where it was discovered that D'Epineuil's claims were false and he was brought up on charges. The men of the 53d were reassigned, and the unit disbanded on March 21, 1862.

deploy, to. (1) To increase the length of a line of troops by depleting the depth of the line. (2) The placement of units in line of battle or in a desired position on a battlefield.

depot prison. A facility, such as a city jail, used as a temporary holding area for prisoners of war en route to a larger installation. The men were rarely integrated with the prison population.

desecrated vegetables. A phrase commonly applied to DESICCATED VEGETABLES by the soldiers whose rations included this forerunner of dehydrated food.

deserter. A soldier or sailor who knowingly and willfully abandoned his unit or his ship with no intention of returning.

desiccated vegetables. A mixture of common vegetables from which most or all water had been extracted. Issued in solid form, usually as a BRICK, the mixture was a substitute for fresh vegetables. Most cooks used it to make soup.

detached service. Formal release of a soldier for a stated period of time from the duties associated with his rank and unit. Men assigned to special noncombat duty, such as the construction and destruction of roads, bridges, and earthworks, were listed as being on detached service.

detached volunteers. INFANTRY soldiers who volunteered to serve temporarily in the ARTILLERY.

detail. (1) A man or men selected for a specific task. (2) A written list of orders for the day, applicable to an entire command or any portion of it. (3) A Rebel order for the furlough or assignment to noncombat duty of an individual soldier.

detail, in. To attack smaller segments of an opposing force with all units or components fully involved.

develop, to. To determine, assess, ascertain, or reveal the facts in a given situation; to probe an opponent's position to discover his precise location and strength.

devil. N. A device used to detect TORPEDOES and remove them from the paths of vessels.

Devil Dan. A nickname for Union Gen. Daniel E. Sickles.

devil fish. A Federal reference to a Confederate TORPEDO shaped to resemble a fish.

deviling. Hazing newcomers and other forbidden activities in which West Point cadets regularly engaged.

Devil's Bridge or **Grapevine Bridge.** A long and unstable bridge over the Chickahominy River.

Devil's Errand Boy. The nickname of Confederate Gen. Thomas L. Rosser.

Devil's Pulpit. A natural rock formation on Lookout Mountain, the name being a Federal transformation of an earlier nickname: Pulpit Rock.

Dictator. The nickname of a 13-inch seacoast MORTAR mounted on a railroad flatcar and utilized during the siege of Petersburg. A.k.a. the PETERSBURG EXPRESS.

die of January fever, to. False notions that the war would be over by January 1, 1862, and January 1, 1863, led dispirited soldiers to describe themselves as having died of January fever—that is, having to continue to fight.

Dingus. The nickname of Jesse James, who served for a time in the Missouri guerrillas.

dinkey. N. A ship judged as too small and all but worthless.

direct fire. Fire delivered from positions perpendicular to the enemy's front line.

Dirty Bill. The nickname of Como. William D. Porter of the U.S. Navy.

Dirty Dick. The nickname of Irish-born Union Gen. James Shields.

disaffection. A spirit of mutiny or outright revolt against authority.

diseases of indulgence. Venereal diseases, such as syphilis and gonorrhea.

disgorge, to. To yield or relinquish something firmly in one's possession.

dispart. A triangular plank lashed to a GUN at its sight and meant to enhance the accuracy of gunners at short ranges.

dispatch. An official message transmitted by courier and, in the latter years of the war, by telegraph.

dispatch case. A container for carrying dispatches.

dispatched, to be. To be killed.

displacement. N. The weight of water displaced by a warship or a commercial vessel.

dispose, to. To move the elements of an army into prearranged positions in preparation for action.

disposition. An opponent's location and strength.

distinguished from the dead, to be. To be found alive on a battlefield, lying among the dead.

ditch hunter. A Federal disparagement of Southern soldiers, implying that their opponents were cowards who ran for the nearest ditch when fighting erupted.

ditty bag. N. A small carry-all closed by a drawstring and used to hold a sailor's personal effects.

diversion. An action designed to distract the attention of an opponent.

diving bell. N. A hollow vessel, airtight except at the bottom, used to salvage items from the floor of the ocean.

division. A basic organizational unit of three BRIGADES commanded by a major general; a subdivision of a CORPS.

Dixie silk. Any nonsilk fabric.

dog collar. A stiff strip of leather, about two inches wide at the middle, that was fastened around the neck to prevent the head from drooping. It was used to correct the posture of new soldiers in the drill.

dog robber. A servant of an officer or prosperous enlisted man who was derided as enjoying the scraps (i.e., perks) that otherwise would have been given to dogs.

dog's body. N. A sailor's derisive term for a meal of dried peas boiled in a cloth sack.

dog tent. A small, portable tent.

Dolly. One of the numerous nicknames bestowed upon Union Gen. William T. Sherman.

Don MacGregor. A name conferred by Confederate Gen. William J. Harden upon a GUN in the aftermath of the December 31, 1862–January 2, 1863, battle of Stones River.

donkey. A portable steam engine. Such engines were used to rotate the turrets of Union monitors.

donkey pump. N. An auxiliary pump powered by a donkey engine, generally used aboard ships.

Doodle. A sarcastic Southern nickname for Union soldiers, probably referring to "Yankee Doodle."

double-barrel cannon. An experimental Southern CANNON with side-by-side barrels. Projectiles were linked by a chain with the expectation that the discharge would mow down Union soldiers "like ripe wheat before a scythe." The idea failed in practice when it proved impossible to detonate the two cannon at exactly the same instant. As a result, the linked cannonballs helicoptered in bizarre patterns and could not be aimed with confidence.

NAVAL HISTORICAL CENTER

double ender. N. A shallow-draft, paddle-wheel GUNBOAT, tapered at both the bow and the stern, with a rudder at both ends. Theoretically capable of changing direction without having to turn—a useful maneuver on most interior waterways.

double envelopment. A complex maneuver during which a line is flanked on both sides.

double-quick. A rate of march approximately twice as rapid as that of the QUICK STEP, approximately covering a mile in seven and a half minutes.

double shotting. Two loads of ammunition in a CANNON. To increase their firepower, gunners double- and sometimes triple-shotted their weapons if the enemy threatened to overwhelm the guns.

doughboy. A derisive term used by cavalrymen of the INFANTRY.

doughface. A Northerner—especially an office-holder—who showed Southern sympathies.

down the line. A brothel district.

doxy. A mistress.

draft. A lottery in which the names of those eligible for military service were placed in a container and then drawn out at random until a quota had been reached. The first American draft act was passed by the Confederate Congress early in April 1862, and the U.S. Congress followed within a year's time. In the Union states, CONSCRIPTION—including the draft in all of its forms—proved not to add a great many men to the armies of itself, but it did help to motivate others to enlist and to take advantage of the bounties offered for joining up.

drag. N. A low-weight anchor sufficient to steady a vessel but not to hold it in place during a gale.

drag bar. A link or bar for attaching railroad cars not equipped with standard couplings; also known as a drag-link or draw-link.

dragoon. Unlike CAVALRY, which was trained to fight from the saddle, or mounted troops, who used horses for transportation but fought on foot, dragoons were trained to fight from the saddle and on foot. Prior to the war, the U.S. Dragoons were stationed on the frontier, where this style of fighting was appropriate for the clashes with the native tribes of the plains. When the war broke out, several dragoon units were reassigned to the eastern theater, although other units remained on the frontier. During the general reorganization of the regular army in August 1861, the 1st Dragoons were renamed the 1st U.S. Cavalry, and the 2d Dragoons became the 4th and 5th U.S. Cavalry.

dragoon, to. Equivalent to IMPRESSMENT. Military commanders sometimes resorted to force to fill their ranks.

dragoon pistol. A handgun designed to be worn in a holster.

drag rope. A twenty-eight-foot length of four-inch hemp equipped with a hook on one end. It was designed to move a GUN CARRIAGE over difficult terrain or drag a piece by sheer manpower, usually by six men per rope.

draught. N. Draft; the depth of water displaced by a fully-loaded vessel.

draw-head. A device attached to a railcar coupling to reduce the shock when the cars were jolted together.

draw over the left, to. Any act of thievery.

dredging box. A container of finely ground cornmeal. These particles were sprinkled over mortar fuses to enhance their ability to catch fire.

dress, to. To straighten a line of men and maintain a specified interval between each man.

dressed rats. Rodents sold in Southern butcher shops when conventional meats were not available.

dresser. A volunteer or medical student assigned the task of dressing wounds.

drift. A shortened term for driftwood.

drifting torpedo. A floating explosive device, or TORPEDO, suspended from a barrel or other object and set adrift in a river or lake.

drill, to. To impart military skill by repetitive training and by emphasizing the execution of simple maneuvers which then evolved into more complex tasks.

Drummer Boy of Chickamauga, The. John Lincoln "Johnny" Clem, a nine-year-old Ohioan who persisted in his efforts to enlist until he was more

or less "adopted" by the 22d Michigan Infantry (the officers pooled their money to pay Clem the standard thirteen dollars a month due Union enlisted men). He first gained fame at the April 6–7, 1862, battle of Shiloh, where a Confederate round smashed his drum. Newspaper accounts dubbed him "Johnny Shiloh" and made much of the smallest drummer on the field. At the September 19–20, 1863, battle of Chickamauga he won national attention for refusing to surrender. Between the two battles, he was allowed to enlist. Although he was unable to enroll at the U.S. Military Academy at West Point, he never left the army, remaining in uniform until 1916, when he retired as a major general.

Drummer Boy of the Rappahannock, The. Robert H. Hendershot, a thirteen-year-old whose exploits during the December 13, 1862, battle of Fredericksburg attracted the interest of Abraham Lincoln. The boy was a drummer for Company B of the 8th Michigan and volunteered to push off the boats being used to cross the river under fire. When he came to the opposite bank, a shell shattered his drum and so Hendershot picked up a RIFLE. Somehow he captured a Confederate and brought him back to the Union line. The story made him a hero at a battle desperately in need of Union heroes. After Hendershot relinquished his uniform and drum, the president secured for him a job in the U.S. Treasury Department.

drum out, to. To escort, at the cadence of a drum, a dishonorably discharged soldier from his company, regiment, or camp.

drum-sling. A mesh band used to carry a drum.

Duck Bill. A prewar nickname of James Butler "Wild Bill" Hickock.

duff. N. A dish of flour and molasses, sometimes embellished with dried fruits or nuts.

duty. A tax collected on imported goods and a chief source of government revenue.

Dyer's *Compendium*. Frederick H. Dyer, a Union army veteran of the 7th Connecticut, spent forty years researching the makeup, movements, and other general information concerning 3,500 Federal units during the Civil War, as well as cataloging the battles, campaigns, and commanders for each. His 1,796-page landmark work, entitled *A Compendium of the War of the Rebellion,* consisted of three parts and was published as a single volume in Des Moines, Iowa, in 1908. It has subsequently been published in a three-volume format.

dying tree. A stately tree near a battlefield that was chosen as the area in which the mortally wounded were placed and left to die.

dyspepsia. Equivalent to biliousness, this term was applied to a wide range of gastrointestinal maladies.

E

⊷∙⊶

Eads ironclads. A number of Union GUNBOATS built by James B. Eads for use on rivers and other interior waterways. The construction work was

done primarily at Eads's Union Marine Works at Carondelet, Missouri. The first of these were the City-class IRONCLADS, also known as POOK TURTLES, but Eads was also involved in the construction of the GUNBOAT *Fort Henry;* the ironclad *ESSEX;* the river MONITORS *Neosho, OSAGE, Milwaukee,* and *CHICKASAW;* the ironclad RAM *Choctaw;* the double-turreted river monitor *Winnebago;* the light-draft ironclad monitors *Etlah* and *Shiloh;* and the converted snagboat that eventually became the ironclad gunboat *BENTON.*

eagles. In the parlance of prisoners, the buttons on Federal uniforms.

easy sail. N. Favorable sailing conditions that sped a vessel along without her having to use much of her canvas.

eat the dishrag, to. Eating a piece of bread that had been used to clean a plate.

echelon. A formation of a number of INFANTRY units arranged with each component standing or moving forward in parallel and maintaining a set interval to the right or left of the unit it followed. Borrowed from the French, the word meant "a rung of a ladder."

edged weapons. Weapons having one or more sharpened blades, such as knives, BAYONETS, SWORDS, and SABERS.

Edith. A 10-inch COLUMBIAD originally mounted at Fort Moultrie in Charleston Harbor. Serviced by cadets from The Citadel, this GUN participated in the action on the morning of January 9, 1861, that thwarted President James Buchanan's attempt to resupply the Federal garrison at FORT SUMTER. Although not the GUN to claim to have fired the first shot of the war, Edith's gunner, H. M.

Clarkson, fired the second warning shot at the chartered supply ship *Star of the West*.

effective. A combatant present and ready for duty.

effective total. The total number of able-bodied men in a REGIMENT, BRIGADE, or other combat unit. Confederate commanders included noncommissioned officers in their totals, but commissioned officers were not counted.

Egypt. A horse presented to Ulysses S. Grant by admirers from his home state of Illinois. Grant named him for the southern Illinois area where the horse had been bred.

El Capitan Colorado. A nickname of Confederate Gen. John B. Magruder.

electric telegraph. Samuel F. B. Morse's invention for transmitting messages by means of electricity.

electric torpedo. Floating MINES (TORPEDOES) were connected by wire to a shore operator who controlled detonation.

elephant. (1) A designation for combat, regardless of its scale. To see or meet the elephant was to have been in combat for the first time, one's baptism under fire. (2) The nickname of Thomas W. Knox, a correspondent of the *New York Herald*. His huge girth, which many said was smaller than his ego, effected this name.

elevating screw. A screw device designed to control the elevation of a GUN.

elevation. The angle to which a GUN was raised from the horizontal.

eligible point. A spot or position considered to be usable or suitable for artillery batteries.

Ellet ram. A river steamer whose hull was heavily reinforced to allow the vessel to ram another, but

NAVAL HISTORICAL CENTER

whose power plant and superstructure were only lightly protected; no armament was added. These modifications were made under the supervision of Charles Ellet, a long-time proponent of "ramboats." The first official to lend credence to the idea was Secretary of War Edwin M. Stanton, who commissioned Ellet as a colonel and allowed him to prepare nine rams: *LANCASTER, Dick Fulton, Monarch, QUEEN OF THE WEST, SWITZERLAND, LIONESS, Mingo, Samson,* and *T. D. Horner.* The first combat for these vessels occurred during the June 6, 1862, battle of Memphis. The only casualty aboard the ram boats was Ellet; he died of his wounds fifteen days later. When the Union army's Western Gunboat Flotilla was transferred to the Federal navy, the ram fleet remained under army command. The vessels were subsequently deployed effectively near Vicksburg and remained there until the Confederate stronghold surrendered. When the threat of Southern warships declined on the Mississippi, the ram fleet was reorganized as the Mississippi Marine Brigade and used in amphibious operations along the waterway. In August 1864 the ram brigade was discontinued and the ships reassigned.

Ellsworth's Avengers. Following the death of Union Col. Elmer Ellsworth, a nationally recognized drill organizer, during the May 24, 1861, occupation of Alexandria, the 40th New York Infantry Regiment adopted this nickname. Enlistment was restricted to single men less than thirty years old and at least five feet eight inches tall.

Ellsworth gun. A 300-pound SMOOTHBORE named for Union Col. Elmer Ellsworth, the first martyr of the war in the North. Guns of this type were used by Union Gen. John Charles Frémont in Missouri, and a few captured PIECES were for a time used by Confederate Gen. John H. Morgan.

Elmira. Originally a training camp, this prison camp was founded in May 1864 and came to be one of the most notorious camps of the war. The population at its highest numbered more than twelve thousand. Living conditions were awful, with barracks available for only half the men, and the Confederate prisoners were plagued with serious health and sanitation problems. Camp doctors feuded constantly with the camp commander over the quality of food and medical care, but not even an ominous report by the surgeon general contributed to any improvements.

Emancipation Proclamation. A formal decree by Abraham Lincoln, issued on January 1, 1863, that declared all slaves in Confederate-held territories to be free. States and regions firmly under Union control, however, were not affected by the proclamation, and Washington lacked the means to enforce the declaration in the Confederate areas in

which it was allegedly in effect. Thus, on the one hand, the proclamation's impact was less than it appeared to be—and it did not represent the president's earlier preference for the COLONIZATION of slaves abroad. Yet in response to the decree, thousands of slaves were admitted through the Union lines and allowed to fight in the Federal army alongside newly enlisted free men of color of the North, albeit under white officers and, at first, for less pay than white soldiers. In the end, almost two hundred thousand African Americans fought for the North—a considerable swelling of the ranks of the Union army in the field. At the same time, the proclamation preempted the possibility that the Confederacy might gain recognition and military aid from Europe.

embalmed beef. Canned or "tinned" beef.

embody, to. To unite as a group.

embrasure. An opening in a CASEMATE that permitted artillery to fire through it. These openings could also be shuttered closed when the GUNS were not in action.

Emerald Light Infantry. A South Carolina Militia unit made up entirely of Irishmen.

emeute. A small riot. In Civil War usage, a desperate attack.

emplacement. A position in which a GUN or a group of guns was situated; also the PARAPET or platform on which a gun or guns could be found.

en barbette. A battery in plain sight of an opponent, clearly visible with no attempt made to conceal it.

enciente. The body or main wall of a fortification, including its RAMPART or ramparts and PARAPET.

Enfants Perdus. An independent ZOUAVE battalion raised in New York by Col. Felix Confort.

Enfield rifle. The Enfield was a British weapon, but none of the Enfield RIFLES used in the Civil War were, strictly speaking, Enfields. Those were manufactured at the Royal Small Arms Factory in Enfield, and the British government, in painstakingly trying to appear neutral in the American conflict, refused to export Enfields to either side. The "Enfields" that were imported—approximately eight hundred thousand by both sides—were copies of the British government-issue .577-caliber Model 1853, manufactured privately in London and Birmingham. The singular distinction between the government-issue rifles and the privately produced rifles was that Enfield parts were interchangeable and the parts of the privately manufactured models were not, which might be problematic in combat should a soldier grab another man's rifle by mistake. Yet the Enfield was the second-most common rifle of the war; the .58-caliber Model 1861 SPRINGFIELD RIFLE was the most widely used rifle of the conflict.

enfilade, to. To fire along the length of an opponent's line or trench, usually with artillery, making each shot potentially more effective and less likely to over- or undershoot the target.

enfilade fire. Fire delivered from positions parallel to the enemy's front line.

enginry. A collective term designating numerous and varied engines.

enlistment. A volunteer or conscript's term of military service. The first enlistments of the war were for a ninety-day period. When problems arose, such as the refusal of a few Federal REGIMENTS to fight at the July 17, 1861, battle of First Bull Run because their terms of enlistment had expired, and the war's appearing to be much longer than anyone had anticipated, three-year terms became standard until even these were superceded by enlistments for the duration of the conflict. The arbitrary extension of enlistments by some commanders in the field was a major cause of discontent and desertion in both Northern and Southern armies late in the war.

ensign. (1) A flag, banner, or standard. (2) N. A commissioned officer of the navy whose rank was equivalent to that of a second lieutenant in the army.

entertain, to. To ponder or decide upon a plan of action.

entrenchment. A defensive work of trenches and parapets.

envelopment. An offensive move to gain a position at the flank or rear of an opponent from which enfilading fire could be directed.

epaulement. A hastily erected mound of soil that functioned to protect troops from flanking fire from an opponent. These were usually created using sandbags or GABIONS.

epaulette. (1) A shoulder ornament, especially a fringed strap. (2) A leather device to protect the shoulder on which a musket was borne.

eprouvette. A small mortar used to test the projectile force of gunpowder. Although not considered a combat weapon, at the July 30, 1864, battle of the Crater at Petersburg, several members of the 16th Virginia used these to hurl small charges into the Union ranks.

equipments. A designation of a class or body of gear; e.g., horse equipments.

equivalent. An opponent of the same rank. When exchanges of prisoners were effected, they were done in terms of equivalents and a graduated scale was adopted. A brigadier general equalled so many colonels, majors, captains, lieutenants, sergeants, corporals, and privates. Occasionally the idea of equivalents was set aside, and exchanges were negotiated on a case-by-case basis.

Ericsson's Folly. A contemptuous epithet for USS *MONITOR* prior to its March 9, 1862, engagement with CSS *VIRGINIA* at Hampton Roads, Virginia.

Ericsson's raft. A heavily armed floating BATTERY devised by John Ericsson and used during the war-long siege of Charleston.

Erlanger loan. This was the largest and most important foreign loan secured by the Confederate government during the war. On October 28, 1862, commissioner John Slidell negotiated an arrangement with the Paris banking firm of Emile Erlanger and Company to conduct a £5 million bond issue secured by cotton futures. The Southern Congress approved the venture on January 29, 1863, but reduced the issue to £3 million (approximately $14.5 million). The twenty-year 7 percent bonds were convertible to cotton at well below the world market price, making the offer highly lucrative to European investors. The issue was also enhanced by the military successes of the South following the Federal defeat at Fredericksburg and the change of commanders of the principal army of the North—the Army of the Potomac. At the same time, cotton was selling in Europe for fifty cents a pound; in the South the price was twelve cents per pound. Therefore the Confederate Treasury planned to stockpile cotton and use it to redeem the bonds within six months of the end of the war. The Erlanger bonds went on sale on March 19, 1863, in Paris, London, Amsterdam, and Frankfurt, and the issue was oversold immediately. Prices, however, declined over the following weeks, and the Confederate defeats at Gettysburg and Vicksburg all but collapsed the price. Yet Confederate purchasing power had been buoyed during the spring of 1863, and Southern agents had been able to acquire much-need materials for

John Slidell

the Confederate military. Bond sales continued for the remainder of the war, and by February 11, 1865, more than 80 percent of the issue had been sold. Confederate profits were estimated to be between $6 and $8 million.

escalade. An assault with scaling ladders.

escarp. The side of a ditch nearest the PARAPET of a fortification.

escort. A select group of soldiers who served as guardians of a commander; BODYGUARDS.

essence of coffee. A prototype of instant coffee.

***Essex*, USS.** This 1,000-ton IRONCLAD river GUN-BOAT was originally the steam ferry *New Era*, constructed in 1856 at New Albany, Indiana. The vessel was purchased by the Union army for its Western Gunboat Flotilla and converted into a timberclad GUNBOAT. Renamed in 1862, the ship was badly damaged in the attack on FORT HENRY, Tennessee. While the vessel was under repair, her commander, William D. Porter, called for radical upgrades until she was one of the most powerful gunboats on the river. In July 1862 *Essex* ran past Vicksburg, engaged and damaged the Confederate ironclad *ARKANSAS*, and joined in the August 1862 action at Baton Rouge. In October 1862 *Essex* was transferred to the Union navy. She remained active on the river for the rest of the war, participating in

NAVAL HISTORICAL CENTER

operations against Port Hudson, Louisiana, and Baton Rouge as well as joining the Red River expedition in early 1864. The ship was decommissioned in July 1865.

European Brigade. A Confederate BRIGADE comprised of REGIMENTS of immigrants—French, Italian, and Spanish—in Louisiana. More than forty-five hundred men were recruited to serve as a home guard, notably in New Orleans prior to the Federal occupation in April 1862.

European stovepipes. Inferior MUSKETS and RIFLES acquired by Federal agents from Belgium and the German states. One analyst of the Union arms purchase program suggested, "The refuse of every European army was put into the hands of American volunteers."

Evacuating Lee. A moniker of Robert E. Lee during his unsuccessful stint in 1861 as a commander in western Virginia.

evacuation of Corinth. Coined by Federal soldiers after the dysentery they experienced in and around Corinth, Mississippi, just prior to the April 6–7, 1862, battle of Shiloh.

Excelsior Brigade. Departing from the usual fashion in which REGIMENTS were first formed and then BRIGADES, New York Democratic congressman Daniel E. Sickles set out to raise a brigade, which he dubbed Excelsior on the basis of the state motto. This brigade was comprised of the 1st, 2d, 3d, 4th, and 5th Excelsior Regiments, which were eventually renamed the 70th, 71st, 72d, 73d, and 74th New York Infantry Regiments. In December 1862 the 120th New York joined the brigade, and in March 1864 the unit was increased with the addition of the 11th Massachusetts and the 84th Pennsylvania. Sickles commanded the brigade only during the summer of 1862, at the battle of Fair Oaks and during the Seven Days' battles. The unit served with little distinction at Chancellorsville but

made significant contributions in the battles of Williamsburg, Bristoe Station, Second Bull Run (Manassas), Gettysburg, Mine Run, the Wilderness, Spotsylvania, North Anna, Cold Harbor, and Petersburg. Only the 73d and 120th New York remained in service at the surrender at Appomattox; the other units were mustered out as enlistments expired.

Excelsior hat. The Confederate reference for the WHIPPLE HAT.

exchange. According to an agreement known as the Dix-Hill Cartel (negotiated on July 22, 1862, by Confederate Gen. Daniel Harvey Hill and Union Gen. John A. Dix and based on the cartel established between Great Britain and the United States during the War of 1812), North and South consented to exchange prisoners rather than confine them. At the time, Union prisons held approximately 20,000 Confederate prisoners and Southern prisons housed between 9,000 and 12,000 Federal captives. The cartel established a "rate of exchange" for soldiers depending on rank rather than a simple one-for-one barter. Exchanges were not new; after many battles early in the war, the two sides exchanged prisoners with the stipulation that they not fight until formally PAROLED. In some instances, such transactions were not completed until months after a soldier had been paroled. When the cartel was accepted by both sides, exchange points were established at Aiken's Landing and City Point, Virginia, in the east and at Vicksburg in the west. By the fall of 1862 the prisons were virtually empty, and the cartel continued to work well for almost a year. Yet prisoner exchange was one of the thorniest questions that Lincoln's generals faced. Initially, the president was wary of this practice, because he felt that it implied recognition of the Confederacy as a nation. Eventually the officers in charge of the cartel—Union Gen. Ethan Allen Hitchcock and Confederate Col. Robert Ould—began to quibble over how well exchanged prisoners observed their paroles not to fight. The EMANCIPATION PROCLA-

MATION also confused the situation once black soldiers were allowed to enlist in the Federal army. In 1864 Ulysses S. Grant suspended all exchanges, ostensibly because he had been informed that Southerners would not exchange captured black soldiers. Grant, however, knew that Union manpower resources were greater than those of the Confederates. By curtailing exchanges that would have liberated many starving Federal prisoners, Grant was able deprive the South of manpower and drain other resources to guard the growing population of Union prisoners.

exchange numbers, to. N. To swap identification of a naval vessel with a sister ship.

execute a flank movement, to. To attempt to frustrate body lice by turning one's underwear inside out.

exemption. To be eliminated from the draft rolls. This issue contributed to DRAFT riots in the North. In both North and South, entire classes of men were exempted because of occupation or age. The first bill calling for the enrollment and drafting of men in the North provided the following exemptions: anyone physically or mentally unfit, convicted felons, numerous civil officials, and anyone who was the only source of support for orphans or aged parents. By August 1862 the list had been expanded to include a number of exempted trades and occupations: telegraph operators, engineers, artificers, armory workmen, members of Congress, customs officials, postal workers, stage drivers, merchant mariners, and "all persons exempted by the laws of their respective states." Likewise, Southern exemptions were also mandated for "men having agricultural or mechanical skills," which was then more specifically defined as an owner or overseer of twenty or more slaves. Most Southern physicians and clergymen were also exempted, but in early 1864 Confederate lawmakers attempted to end exemptions for men who had earlier furnished SUBSTITUTES. In both sections, the prevalence of exemptions fostered the bitter phrase "rich man's war, poor man's fight."

executor. The credentials of a consul, issued by the country he represented and of special importance in major Southern ports such as Charleston, Savannah, Mobile, and New Orleans.

exercise, to. N. To test a GUN to ensure that it was in usable condition.

expanding bullet. The MINIÉ BALL.

expedition. With great haste; top speed.

explosive bullet. Erroneously used as a synonym for MINIÉ BALL. Several experimental bullets carried percussion caps and chambers of packed powder that was primed to explode on impact. Most soldiers regarded the ammunition as too barbaric and inhumane.

exposure. To be unprotected from an opponent's fire.

Extra Billy. Confederate Gen. William Smith, a former governor of Virginia. While operating a mail-coach service between Washington, D.C., and Milledgeville, Georgia, he received payment  in addition to postage for the mileage covered, which gave rise to his nickname. When the war broke out in 1861, at age sixty-three Smith refused a commission as a brigadier in order to fight at First Bull Run (First Manassas) as the colonel of the 49th Virginia. A brave man in combat, he lacked any tactical skill. He participated in the Peninsula campaign and the Seven Days' battles. At the battle of Antietam, he was wounded three times, knocking him out of action until early 1863. Smith was promoted to brigadier general and

U.S. ARMY MILITARY HISTORY INSTITUTE

fought at Gettysburg. As his shortcomings were being revealed, he was again elected governor of Virginia. Promoted to major general shortly before he assumed the governor's office, Smith was out of action for the remainder of the war. After the war he was a wanted man, but Federal authorities paroled him almost as soon as he surrendered.

Eyes and Ears of the Army of Northern Virginia. A reference to Confederate Gen. J. E. B. "Jeb" Stuart, who gained lasting fame by four daring and flamboyant reconnaissances ("rides") around the Federal army.

F

faces. The lengths of PARAPETS extending from one angle of a work to the next. They were designed to facilitate direct fire on an attacking force.

face, to. To direct a body of troops into a prescribed direction.

facings. The collar and cuffs of a coat plus the symbolic trimmings on them.

faith paper. A term applied to currency by men who were accustomed to only coins.

fall in, to. To take one's place in the ranks.

fall out, to. To be dismissed.

false muzzle. A short tube attached to the muzzle of a MUSKET or RIFLE to form a temporary extension that reduced abrasion on the barrel by the RAMROD and aided in centering the bullet when the weapon was fired.

Fancy. See LITTLE SORREL.

fancy female. A prostitute. Also known as "fancy girl."

fanega. A Mexican measure of 160 pounds; one-half CARGA.

Fannie. (1) A nickname for Union Gen. George Armstrong Custer. (2) The name of one of the mounts of Confederate Gen. Joseph E. Johnston.

faro. A popular card game.

farrier. An ironworker devoted to shoeing horses and mules.

fascine. Also spelled as *facine*, these were tightly bound bundles of two-inch-thick sticks used to elevate BATTERIES, to line the sides of trenches to prevent them from collapsing, and to cover marshy ground. They  were incorporated much as sandbags or cotton bales were utilized as reinforcing materials.

fascine knife. A BAYONET with a saw-toothed edge used to cut branches and saplings with which to fashion FASCINES.

Fast-footed Virginians. A scornful mangling of the phrase "First Families of Virginia" applied to any Confederate retreat.

fast little trick. A prostitute.

fatigue cap. A head covering to be worn when soldiers were out of uniform.

fatigue duty. Manual labor not to be performed while in uniform.

fatigue party. A group of soldiers assigned to FATIGUE DUTY.

fatigue slacks. N. A pullover shirt that extended from the shoulders to below the hips, this was appropriate dress for performing fatigue duty aboard ship.

feather-bed fighter. Slang for a soldier who habitually wrangled easy jobs far from the battle lines.

feel, to. To probe an enemy force or position to discover its strength.

feint, to. An offensive move against an opponent designed to deceive the opponent as to the location and/or time of an actual offensive action.

Felix. A good-natured nickname for Confederate Gen. P. G. T. Beauregard implying that he had found favor with the  gods of war, particularly after the bombardment of FORT SUMTER and the Confederate victory at the July 21, 1861, battle of First Manassas (Bull Run). Such praise contributed to poor relations between the general and Jefferson Davis and led to Beauregard's reassignment to the west.

felloe. The rim of a wheel, or a portion of it.

fencing bayonet. A training BAYONET with a rounded tip.

ferrule. A ring placed around a flagstaff or a wooden pole to prevent it from splitting.

ferryboat. A scornful nickname for a nearly shapeless shoe meant to be worn on either foot.

fez. A head covering with no brim, copied from or adapted from headgear worn in the Near East and displayed in many colors and patterns by members of ZOUAVE units.

field battery. A specified number of artillery PIECES equipped for both offensive and defensive actions and capable of accompanying either CAVALRY or INFANTRY in their movements in the field. When serving with infantry, these guns were usually categorized as mounted artillery. When serving with cavalry, they were categorized as horse artillery.

field-grade officer. Any officer who functioned in the field of battle rather than at a command post. In practice, this category included all commissioned officers below the rank of brigadier general. When a colonel, major, or captain commanded a brigade, he was considered a GENERAL OFFICER.

field fortifications. Hastily improvised defensive works erected on a field of battle, as simple as shallow trenches scraped out by men lying prone or as elaborate as REVETMENTS connected by a maze of trenches.

field of fire. An unobstructed area across which GUNS had a clear line of sight.

field telegraph. A portable telegraph unit used in the field.

fifth wheel. (1) A spare wheel carried on a gun LIMBER. (2) A disparaging reference to the U.S. SANITARY COMMISSION by those who considered the volunteers to be more of an encumbrance than an asset to the troops in the field.

fieldworks. Fortifications that provided troops or areas with relative degrees of safety from sudden assaults by forces of superior numbers. These defenses had PARAPETS of earth, fieldstones, or other available indigenous materials and were designed to withstand bombardments and assaults. They were usually designed by engineers, but when an army advanced or withdrew rapidly, individual soldiers excavated pits or dug entrenchments.

fight it out on the existing line, to. To announce one's determination not to retreat farther.

Fighting Bishop, the. Confederate Bishop Gen. Leonidas Polk of Louisiana.

Fighting Bob. The nickname of Union Rear Adm. Robley D. Evans.

Fighting Dick. (1) The nickname of Confederate Gen. Richard H. Anderson, earned at the May 31–June 1, 1862, battle of Seven Pines. (2) The nickname of Union Col. Isaac B. Richardson, a Mexican War veteran.

Fighting Joe. The nickname of Union Gen. Joseph Hooker, acquired during the Seven Days' battles from news reports headed "Fighting—Joe Hooker."

Fighting Parson, the. The nickname of the Rev. John Milton Chivington, who left his congregation to fight for the Union in the 1st Colorado Regiment.

file, to. To maintain formation when moving to the right or left.

file-closer. A soldier charged with the responsibility of keeping troops in formation and directing the movement of wounded men to the rear. During combat situations, these men remained slightly behind their squads to ensure that the men would fight and not desert. During the siege of Petersburg, Confederate commander Robert E. Lee boosted the number of file-closers in his army to one for every ten men in the ranks.

file leader. A soldier charged with the responsibility of leading a file of men.

filibuster. A military adventurer in search of political and personal gain; for example, William Walker, a native of Tennessee, who led an armed contingent into Nicaragua in the prewar years with the hope of establishing a Caribbean empire (the SOUTHWESTERN CONSPIRACY).

finger stall. A protective leather covering for the finger of a gunner in closing the vent of a CANNON to extinguish any remaining sparks in the GUN TUBE.

fire and fall back, to. Slang for vomiting.

fireball. (1) *Military.* A projectile made from a canvas sack filled with a combustible substance, such as GREEK FIRE. The shell was designed to light up an opponent's position in order to direct projectiles accurately. (2) *Civilian.* Coal dust mixed with dampened sawdust or clay and formed into a ball, used as a substitute for coal.

fire by battery, to. To detonate all the guns of a BATTERY in sequence.

fire by files, to. To volley the fire of every soldier in a formation in sequence with other rows of men.

Fire Eater. The bay horse ridden by Confederate Gen. Albert Sidney Johnston at the April 6–7, 1862, battle of Shiloh. Johnston was wounded by a ball in the back of his knee and bled to death on the battlefield. Some have speculated that he was wounded by his own men.

fire-eater. A prewar term describing one as an ardent advocate, a true believer. As the leaders of the North and the South took increasingly hard-line positions in 1860, the term came to be applied to zealous secessionists, particularly in South Carolina.

fireman's shirt. A garment worn by some ZOUAVE units whose members had been recruited from the fire departments of eastern cities.

Fire Zouave. A reference to the 5th New York, a ZOUAVE company composed almost exclusively of firemen from New York City; later the phrase was applied to similar regiments of firemen recruited elsewhere in the North.

fires, to spread. N. To scatter burning coal in a ship's furnace or furnaces so as to keep the vessel's boilers ready for action.

firing line. A line of as many as four ranks of men arrayed to mass their fire directly upon an opponent. If two or more ranks were involved, the men were required to aim, fire, and reload through a tightly choreographed drill so as to maximize their fire and reduce the chance for mishaps among the ranks.

first-callers. Volunteers who responded to Abraham Lincoln's April 1861 call for seventy-five thousand ninety-day men and subsequently signed up for three-year enlistments after their initial term of service had expired.

first light. A time of day just prior to the rising of the sun, when dim and somewhat eerie light can be perceived.

fish. N. (1) A small fish-shaped strip of well-seasoned wood used to strengthen YARDS and masts. (2) A protuberance used to steady a rope being used to "FISH THE ANCHOR" upward.

fish the anchor, to. N. To hoist anchor by muscle power alone.

Fishing Creek. A designation of the January 19, 1862, battle of Mill Springs, Kentucky; a.k.a. Beech Grove, Logan's Cross Roads, and Somerset.

fixed ammunition. Any artillery charge in which the projectile, SABOT, and powder bag formed a cohesive, inseparable unit. Such charges could be loaded with only one movement by a gunner, thus increasing the GUN's rate of fire.

fixed battery. Siege works that held long-range heavy-caliber GUNS and MORTARS. Such batteries usually held between three and seven guns.

flag, personal. N. The distinctive pennant of a naval commander, used to indicate that he was aboard a particular vessel, which made that the flagship from which other vessels were to receive orders.

flag-bearer. Although technically the duties of this soldier were different from those of a COLOR-BEARER, in practice the terms were synonymous.

flagitious. An offense whose prescribed punishment was flagellation, or whipping—a form of severe discipline administered to both civilian and military offenders.

flag lieutenant. N. A naval officer who ordered and directed the use of signal flags in transmitting orders to other vessels. Especially zealous and talented flag lieutenants devised coded systems of signal flagging.

flag officer. N. An officer in command of a squadron or fleet who was permitted to fly at the masthead of the ship he was aboard a flag or pennant designating both his rank and his presence.

flagship. N. The vessel that carried the commander of a squadron or fleet and displayed his command pennant.

flag signal. A signal transmitted by flags and using the semaphore system, which positioned flags to represent letters or abbreviated phrases. At night, flares and torches were used in the same way as flags.

flambeaux. Torches made by coating especially thick wicks with wax.

flamethrower. Several devices for projecting a flame toward or upon enemy positions were demonstrated during the war; e.g., the Berney flamethrower. None were ever purchased by the Federal Quartermaster Corps for use in combat.

flaming. A descriptive term for official reports and news stories bearing particularly important and time-sensitive information.

flank. (1) The right or left sides of a military or naval command regardless of whether the men or vessels had been formed in line or in column fashions. (2) A portion of a BASTION that extended from its curtain to its face. It was designed to provide an ENFILADING or slanted column of fire on an attacking force.

flank, to. To gain a position on either side of an opponent's line that allows one to ENFILADE his ranks. Emulating the tactics of Napoleon, commanders in blue and gray placed the highest priority on flanking one another at every opportunity.

flashover. The accidental discharge of multiple charges at one time. This frequently occurred when a soldier failed to lubricate a REVOLVER, particularly a Remington, or a repeating RIFLE.

flat. A small boat with a shallow, broad bottom, designed for but not restricted to river use. In some instances, flats were used as ferries and pulled by rope from one side of a river to the other.

fleche. A V-shaped earthwork.

flimsy. A newspaper dispatch written or printed on very thin paper. Most flimsies were sent simultaneously to a number of newspapers. The GOLD HOAX of May 1864 was due to the distribution of flimsies and their immediate printing in several New York papers.

flintlock. A device that held a flint in a hammer to ignite a supply of gunpowder and cause a weapon to fire. In usage, the lock gave its name to the weapon on which it was carried. Although long obsolete by the time of the July 21, 1861, battle of First Manassas (Bull Run), some flintlocks were used as late as the battle of Shiloh in April 1862. This weapon quickly became burdensome when soldiers were forced to carry it on long marches. The weight of individual pieces varied between nine and ten pounds.

floating battery. (1) One or more guns mounted on a raft or a barge that could be maneuvered to positions not accessible by land. (2) A disparaging term for bread, often stale and nearly inedible.

NAVAL HISTORICAL CENTER

floating railway bridge. A bridge constructed of prefabricated wooden sections that were assembled on shore and towed into position and secured by anchors or piles.

flood. A synonym for high tide.

Florence Nightingale of the South. Mrs. E. K. Newsom, a wealthy widow, who devoted her time, energy, and fortune to hospital work in Memphis, Bowling Green, Nashville, Corinth, and Atlanta.

Florida, **CSS.** This 700-ton steam screw cruiser was built in England in 1862 under the name *Oreto*. The Confederate navy secretly purchased the vessel and outfitted the ship as a commerce raider. In 1863 she cruised the Atlantic and West Indies, taking twenty-two prizes. In 1864 the ship claimed eleven prizes before docking at Bahia, Brazil. While there, the vessel was attacked, captured, and towed to sea by USS *Wachusett*, but the matter violated neutrality issues and the courts ordered the ship returned to Brazil. Before the order could be carried out, *Florida* was sunk off Newport News, Virginia, on November 28, 1864.

NAVAL HISTORICAL CENTER

flukes. N. The pointed tips of an anchor that fastened into the bottom.

flux. Roughly equivalent to dysentery and meaning excessive discharge from one's bowels.

fly. A small tent. Most flys were expected to accommodate three to eight men, but a hospital fly was large enough to shelter a dozen.

flying battery. A group of two or more PIECES of horse-drawn FIELD ARTILLERY that could be moved quickly from one spot to another. Some commanders used flying batteries to convince an opponent that he faced a great many GUNS since the batteries could be fired from one position after another in rapid succession. See also HORSE ARTILLERY.

flying bridge. A hastily constructed bridge that used a heavy rope to anchor a line of rafts or a group of small boats covered with planks. An experienced team could erect one in about three hours. If a rudder was attached to a partial bridge segment, the anchored floating structure was made to swing from one bank to the other.

Flying Butterflies. A nickname for the 3d New Jersey Cavalry, also known as the BUTTERFLIES.

flying fougasse. A mobile version of the FOUGASSE, an "infernal machine" made by filling a barrel with fist-size stones packed around a central powder charge. Thrust over a wall toward an advancing opponent, a flying fougasse would explode upon impact when it hit the ground and send its deadly load into the oncoming ranks.

flying hospital. A mobile medical facility.

flying telegraph train. A short TRAIN made up of two wagons that were loaded with the gear used to operate a BEARDSLEE TELEGRAPH system.

flying torch. A metal cylinder containing an inflammable substance. The torch was ignited by a wick then hurled into an opponent's lines. It usually flared long enough to allow SHARPSHOOTERS a clear sighting.

foamy boiler. If contaminated water were used in the boiler of a locomotive or steamship, the boiler emitted a foam as well as steam.

fog of war. The gray haze generated by powder smoke. Often the acrid smoke became so dense that the effective vision of fighting men was limited to a few feet.

fool soldiers. A derisive nickname for the Native American guides and allies utilized by Federal commanders during the Sioux uprising of 1864 in Minnesota.

foot cavalry. A term of admiration used to express awe at the speed with which Confederate Gen. Thomas J. "Stonewall" Jackson's corps marched over great distances in the Shenandoah Valley during the summer of 1862.

foot up, to. To reach the foot, or bottom, of a column of figures—usually by adding them.

forage. Grass, hay, or vegetables suitable for horse feed.

forage, to. (1) To seek food for horses from non-military sources. (2) To plunder the countryside, stripping friendly or unfriendly civilians of food, clothing, and valuables. Initially prohibited by numerous Federal commanders, this activity came to be condoned and even encouraged as RATIONS and other essentials grew scarcer.

forced march. A march against time; INFANTRY being quick marched to the point of exhaustion.

LIBRARY OF CONGRESS

Ford's Theatre. John T. Ford, a former Baltimore bookseller, in 1861 bought Washington's former First Baptist Church building. The building was

lost to fire, and Ford built a substantially larger structure on the Tenth Street lot that was hailed as one of the finest theatrical venues in the nation when it opened in late 1863. While attending a play there on April 12, 1865, President Abraham Lincoln was assassinated by actor John Wilkes Booth in the theater. Ford was questioned at length about his possible complicity in the assassination plot, but he was eventually cleared.

fore-and-aft sail. N. Any sail not supported by a YARD or yards; also often termed a GAFF.

forecastle. N. The forward portion of a ship, named for the fact that the front of many medieval warships was built to look like a fortified castle.

forefoot. N. That point at the forward end of a ship where its keel and STEM were joined.

forlorn hope. (1) A body of about one thousand handpicked volunteers who were used in a suicidal charge at the March 14–July 8, 1863, battle of Port Hudson, Louisiana. The men who volunteered for this charge knew that many of them would not survive it. (2) Any group of soldiers who spearheaded an advance or faced certain doom. When PIONEERS (engineers) laid their lives on the line by cutting a path through an enemy's outworks, such men were dubbed a "forlorn hope" band.

fore-spencer vangs. N. Ropes suspended from a GAFF, or spar, at the head of a fore-and-aft sail suspended upon a small supplementary mast.

Fort Damnation and Fort Hell. Coined by Ulysses S. Grant's army while besieging Petersburg

in 1864, these names designated fortifications in the defensive lines outside the city and were called Fort Sedgwick and Fort Mahone by Southerners.

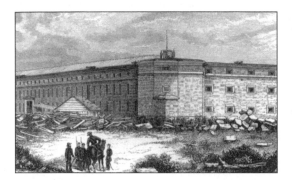

Fort Delaware. A Federal prisoner-of-war camp on Pea Patch Island in the Delaware River. The fort had been built in the 1850s as part of the nation's coastal defense system. Categorized as a third-system fort, the pentagonal structure was built of solid granite, with walls thirty-feet thick and thirty-five feet high. The facility was garrisoned in 1860 and received its first prisoners of war in July 1861. It became overcrowded quickly, which made the situation wretched for the captives. In addition to the usual problems of such a large prisoner population, Fort Delaware was notorious for its severe discipline, bordering on torture. From 1863 to 1865 the number of captives ranged from seven thousand to eight thousand on land that was not capable of supporting such a large number of men. The men who comprised THE IMMORTAL 600 were gleaned from the fort's prisoner rolls. By the end of the war, as many as thirty thousand Confederates had been imprisoned here.

Fort Donelson. Situated on the Cumberland River, this fortification was used by Southerners to guard the interior of Tennessee. It was here that Ulysses S. Grant became known as "Unconditional Surrender" because he refused to discuss any other terms with the Confederate commander, a friend from his days at West Point. Grant's February 16, 1862, success at Fort Donelson was the first significant Federal victory of the war and brought him to the interested attention of Abraham Lincoln and eventually to command of all Union forces in the war.

Fort Fisher. Erected to guard the harbor of Wilmington, North Carolina, this was the last major Confederate bastion to fall in the war. So long as Fort Fisher's guns were active, Wilmington could continue to be a haven for BLOCKADE-RUNNERS. Two expeditions were mounted against the Southern stronghold. The first faltered under the command of Union Gen. Benjamin F. Butler, who attempted to breach the fort's defenses by exploding a powder boat offshore and swarming over the stunned Confederates. When that failed, no other attack was made until a joint army-navy effort in January 1865 by Alfred H. Terry and David D. Porter succeeded in taking the position.

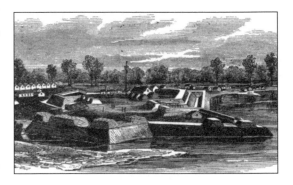

Fort Henry. Located not far from FORT DONELSON, on the Tennessee River, Henry was the smaller of the two installations. By making the most of the GUNBOATS temporarily under his command, Ulysses S. Grant forced the Confederates to abandon this fort on February 6, 1862, and move to FORT DONELSON.

Fort Lafayette. A Federal prisoner-of-war facility on a tiny island off the tip of Staten Island, New York. This octagonal military installation was built in 1822 and was considered escape-proof.

The first prisoners arrived from western Virginia on July 15, 1861.

Fort Lawton. Another name for the Confederate prisoner-of-war facility known as ANDERSONVILLE.

Fort McHenry. This small Federal prisoner-of-war facility at Baltimore, Maryland, held fewer than one thousand prisoners during the winter of 1862–63. Four months later its prisoner population had passed seven thousand. When Southern prisoners kept coming, an estimated six hundred were herded into the city jail, where the Federal government was charged twenty cents per day per man for food and lodging. When a new facility was opened in Maryland, the population of the prison fell to four hundred.

Fort Mifflin. Not far from Philadelphia, Fort Mifflin was converted into a military prison during 1863. Situated on Mud Island, for a time it had a mixed population of Southern prisoners, Southern sympathizers, and Federal soldiers awaiting trial or serving time. This was one of the smallest prisons in the North.

Fort Monroe. This vast installation at the tip of Virginia's Peninsula was among the most imposing fortresses in the United States. Protected by a huge moat, it remained in Federal hands throughout the war. Here Union Gen. Benjamin F. Butler coined the term CONTRABAND as a designation for runaway slaves. After the war, former Confederate president Jefferson Davis was imprisoned here.

Fort Pickens. Located not far from Pensacola, this large but poorly defended fortress was one of the few in the South that remained in Federal hands once the secession movement got under way. It was the intention of Abraham Lincoln simultaneously to relieve Pickens and FORT SUMTER early in April 1861. The Sumter effort failed, but Pickens was relieved and remained in Federal hands throughout the war.

Fort Pickens Medals. These were unofficial awards struck by the New York Chamber of Commerce and presented to the men who participated in the April 1861 defense of FORT PICKENS, Florida. Designed by Charles Miller of New York, they were struck in four styles—commander of the GARRISON, officers, noncommissioned officers, and privates—and four sizes varying from two to six inches in diameter. One side bore the likeness of Lt. Adam J. Slemmer, the fort's commander, and the other side depicted an allegorical image of quashed secession with the words, "Cerebus, or the Monster of War, Chained to Fort Pickens."

U.S. ARMY MILITARY HISTORY INSTITUTE

Fort Pulaski. Just as numerous other pentagonal third-system forts on the Atlantic Coast were constructed to protect major shipping ports, Pulaski was built on Cockspur Island to protect the city of Savannah. Work began on the facility in the 1830s, but the fort was not yet completed when the war began. Georgia state forces seized and occupied the structure on January 3, 1861. Despite more than a year's work to make the fort viable, the Union occupation of Port Royal, South Carolina, blunted the usefulness of Savannah as a port of entry for much-needed supplies from abroad. When Robert E. Lee visited Pulaski, he concluded that its walls were well beyond the effective range of Federal gunners. Union Gen. Quincy A. Gillmore, however, erected eleven batteries with thirty-six guns (ten of which were Parrott and James RIFLES) on Tybee Island, roughly a mile away. Gillmore's gunners opened fire on April 10, 1862, and the fort surrendered the next day, after a wall had been breached and the bombardment threatened to explode the fort's magazine.

Fort Skedaddle. This "installation" was a Confederate earthwork erected close to Munson's Hill, within view of Washington, D.C.; it was named following the July 17, 1861, battle of First Bull Run (First Manassas) by German immigrants in a Federal REGIMENT.

Fort Sumter. A part of the harbor defenses of Charleston, South Carolina, this fort was one of the largest and strongest of the third system of Federal fortifications constructed since 1816 (American Revolution forts were called first system, the forts of the War of 1812 were called second system, and forts built afterward were called third system). It was a pentagonal brick fortress erected on a man-made shoal in the middle of the entrance to Charleston Harbor. Work began in 1829, but the fort was not finished when hostilities began here between North and South on April 12, 1861. The structure appeared impressive, but few GUNS had been mounted and no GARRISON had occupied the facility until U.S. Maj. Robert Anderson relocated his command here from Fort Moultrie on December 26, 1860. Because government property was liable to be seized as part of a state's secession from the Union, Forts Sumter and Pickens became focal points of sectional struggle that erupted into war. Beginning on August 17, 1863, the fort came under the Union BATTERIES erected on Morris Island. A steady bombardment breached the walls, but the fort did not fall. By war's end, Sumter endured more than eleven separate bombardments. The post was abandoned on February 17, 1865, and occupied by Federal soldiers the next day.

Fort Sumter Medals. The New York State Chamber of Commerce commissioned these medals to commemorate the defense of FORT SUMTER at the same time that similar medals were commissioned for the GARRISON of FORT PICKENS. Designed by Charles Miller of New York, they were struck in four styles—commander of the garrison, officers, noncommissioned officers, and privates—and four sizes varying from two to six inches in diameter. One side bore the likeness of Robert Anderson, the fort's commander, and the other side bore an image of Liberty supporting the flag on the PARAPET of the fort with the words, "The Genius or Guardian Spirit of America Rising from Fort Sumter."

Fort Warren. A granite pentagonal fortress on George's Island in Boston Harbor. Initially used as a training camp for volunteers, Warren was garrisoned by the 14th Massachusetts until converted to a prison. At first, these prisoners were a few smugglers and political prisoners from the Border States. Following the August 1861 capture of the Hatteras Inlet forts in North Carolina, prisoners of war began arriving. The influx, however, exceeded the fort commander's expectations, so an appeal for assistance went out to the people of Boston, who responded with food and other necessities that contributed to something like an elite status for the prison. By comparison to other prisoner-of-war facilities, Warren's captives had ample room, sufficient food, and a comfortable existence. Some officers were even allowed private cells. Only twelve men died at the fort during the war, and these deaths were from wounds or illnesses that occurred prior to incarceration.

forty acres and a mule. This phrase summarized the notion that every freed slave should be given a tract of land from the property confiscated from Southern planters. Gen. William T. Sherman set the idea and the expression in motion in a GENERAL ORDER issued in early 1865, during his MARCH TO THE SEA. Under its terms, which were never implemented, large sections of coastal land in Georgia and South Carolina were to be set aside and allotted to freedmen.

forty dead men. A Federal soldier's allotment of forty cartridges prior to going into battle.

forty-eighters. Immigrants who participated in 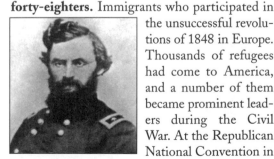 the unsuccessful revolutions of 1848 in Europe. Thousands of refugees had come to America, and a number of them became prominent leaders during the Civil War. At the Republican National Convention in

Carl Schurz 1860, David Davis, Abraham Lincoln's campaign manager, made a special effort to secure the votes of forty-two German-born delegates, and as a token of the president's gratitude, Carl Schurz was made a brigadier general in April 1862.

Forty-eight Hours. A nickname for Union Gen. Abner Doubleday, who was known to be cautious in reaching a decision and some said even slower to act upon it.

forty-rod. The worst possible whiskey, said to be lethal at a distance of forty rods.

fosse. A moat, trench, or ditch designed to be filled with water.

fougasse. A prototype land MINE. Large charges of gunpowder were buried in the anticipated path of an oncoming opponent. It was detonated by a FUSE, but this was not an exact science as yet. One of the first instances of use was allegedly at Charleston, where Maj. Robert Anderson drew on all possible defenses of his GARRISON at FORT SUMTER.

foul ammo. Ammunition that had been mishandled and appeared to be defective. Although regulations required it be destroyed, in emergencies all resources were exhausted.

foul anchor, to. N. To handle an anchor in such fashion that it becomes entangled with cables, a wreck, or another anchor.

Fox. A roan horse ridden by Union Gen. Ulysses S. Grant at the early 1862 engagements at FORT DONELSON and Shiloh.

fractional currency. Paper currency or metal coin token with a face value of less than one dollar.

85

fraise. A defensive work, on the outward slope of an earthwork, constructed with sharpened stakes projecting outward in an oblique or horizontal fashion. These PALISADES were to be an overhead obstacle to an attacking force, positioned at least seven feet above the ground so as not to be used by the enemy to scale the PARAPET. See ABATIS and CHEVAUX-DE-FRISE.

Francis lifeboat. N. A lifeboat made of metal.

Frank Leslie's Illustrated Newspaper. A rival of *HARPER'S WEEKLY,* this illustrated weekly was also published in New York. *Leslie's* never achieved the circulation of *Harper's,* but it built a reputation on its excellent illustrations. In 1842 Frank Leslie had been an engraver for the *London Illustrated News,* the pioneer illustrated newspaper in the world. He immigrated to the United States in 1848 and worked for several illustrated papers until he launched his own illustrated fashion guide in 1854. This success led him to publish his own illustrated newspaper in 1855, which struggled to compete with the other illustrated weeklies of the day. That situation changed, however, with the coming of the war. Leslie dispatched several field artists to the front and reproduced their images in his newspaper within two weeks of the portrayed event, which was much quicker than his rivals, save *Harper's.* The paper appeared on Sundays at eight cents an issue and was a best-seller throughout the 1860s. After the war, Leslie reproduced the war images in numerous pictorial histories, and his publications flourished until the end of the century.

fraternization. Unlawful INTERCOURSE with the enemy. Strictly forbidden at every level of command on both sides, the practice was impossible to prevent. It began very early, during the period when multitudes of persons were confident that there would be only one or two small-scale encounters to determine a victor. Sometimes taking place on the eve or at the conclusion of a battle, the soldiers swapped sugar, coffee, and tobacco. Occasionally these meetings were arranged by shouting from one line to the other, such as an occasion near Falmouth, Virginia, when two Confederate REGIMENTS negotiated with some nearby New Yorkers to trade tobacco for coffee, overcoats, and shoes.

freedman. (1) A former slave who had purchased his or her freedom or been freed by an owner. (2) A runaway slave who had escaped or been separated from an owner by the exigencies of war. These fugitive slaves were also called CONTRABANDS.

Freedmen's Bureau. A Federal bureau created by Congress at war's end. Officially titled the Bureau

of Refugees, Freedmen, and Abandoned Lands, this agency addressed many of the problems encountered by former slaves.

free soiler. A resident of any western territory, but especially in Kansas, who advocated the prohibition of SLAVERY in the region whenever it should become a state and seek admission to the Union.

freight train. An incoming projectile. The term referred to the scream of the shell in flight.

French leave. Being absent without leave but with the supposed intention of returning. Some soldiers encountered situations in which the normal procedure of requesting leave took too much time when they simply wanted to visit loved ones briefly. Punishment upon their return was usually lengthy picket duty.

fresh fish. (1) New recruits. (2) Newcomers to a prisoner-of-war camp. Long-time inmates often fell upon newcomers to relieve them of any valuables or potables.

fresh meat. A first-year cadet at West Point.

Fretwell-Singer torpedo. A highly sophisticated explosive device, by comparison with the earliest torpedoes of the conflict. A spring-loaded trigger was installed on top of the device and was designed to explode on impact.

friction primer. A metal tube, two inches in diameter, that was filled with gunpowder and a smaller tube packed with combustibles. It was placed in the VENT of a GUN. The friction generated by pulling a lanyard through the smaller tube ignited the primer. The resulting flash traveled down the vent to the charge, igniting the powder and discharging the gun.

frigate. A vessel whose size lay between that of a sloop of war and a ship of the line. Typically such ships carried twenty-eight to forty-four guns,

which were placed in batteries on the main and spar decks.

frog. (1) Any small device shaped like a frog, such as the fastener by which an officer's scabbard was linked to his belt. The same term was also applied to buttons on coats and cloaks and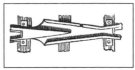

railroad frog

junctions of railroad track. (2) A scornful Federal epithet for Southerners.

front, to. To form a line of battle with a body of soldiers.

frontal attack. One of the costliest maneuvers of attack, an attacking force focused on the front of an opponent's line rather than a flank or other segment. Such movements were rarely undertaken and always generated the highest possible casualties.

frumenty. A meal of wheat bran, milk, and sugar. Fruit was added when available. Confederate Gen. Richard S. Ewell, who suffered from chronic DYSPEPSIA, allegedly ate frumenty at every meal.

full dress. An officer's formal attire.

fulminate. An explosive formed from a compound including mercury; a basic component of percussion caps.

furlough. A soldier's formal leave of absence for a stipulated length of time. Prior to the election of 1864, some Federal commanders furloughed their men by COMPANIES or REGIMENTS so that they could return home and vote. This practice proved to be of great importance, for the soldier vote played a large role in reelecting Abraham Lincoln to the White House.

furniture. A designation for ACCOUTREMENTS. A cavalryman would say that the furniture for his horse included the saddle cloth, housings, and other gear. Infantrymen would have said that the furniture of their RIFLES consisted of trigger guards and such ornamental items as barrel bands.

fuse. Spelled *fuze* during the war. A combustible device that served to detonate an explosion such as that of a shell, a mine, or case shot. At the siege of Petersburg, initial attempts to set off the gigantic explosion that created the Crater were unsuccessful because the lengthy fuse went out before reaching the charge. Fuses were customarily cut by hand, but this was not an exact method, often causing projectiles to fall short of their mark (and into the ranks of one's comrades) or overshoot it.

fuse box. A container, usually leather, made for fuses four and a half inches long.

fuse extractor. Wooden fuses were required by some PIECES. When they were driven too far into a GUN's VENT, a wormlike extractor was used to remove the spent FUSE.

fuse mallet. A hardwood tool used for installing wooden FUSES in a field piece.

fuse plug. A brass seating device for a FUSE.

fuse saw. A small saw used to cut wooden fuses to a desired length.

fuse setter. A brass instrument used in conjunction with wooden fuses.

fuse wrench. A wrench used for seating fuses in a GUN VENT.

G

gabion. These open-ended cylindrical wicker baskets, usually three feet high and two feet in diameter, could be rolled into position then filled with rocks and dirt to create or bolster BREASTWORKS or other field fortifications.

gabionade. A fieldwork constructed of GABIONS.

gaff. N. A spar designed to hold the upper edge, or head, of a FORE-AND-AFT SAIL.

gaiters. A canvas, leather, and/or rubber leg covering that reached from the instep to above the ankle or midcalf or knee.

Gallant Egyptian. A nickname for Union Gen. John A. Logan, because he was from Little Egypt in southern Illinois.

Gallant Pelham. Confederate Maj. John Pelham, an Alabama native and a commander of HORSE ARTILLERY in Jeb Stuart's CAVALRY. He withdrew from West Point ten days after the bombardment of FORT SUMTER, just weeks before he would have been graduated. During the war he was assigned to Stuart's cavalry and placed in charge of an eight-gun battery  of horse artillery. Pelham fought in more than sixty engagements and refined the concept of flying artillery, that is, the constant deployment and redeployment of artillery on the field during the course of an engagement. He was dubbed "the gallant Pelham" by Robert E. Lee after the battle of Fredericksburg. While on leave on March 17, 1863, he observed an action near Kelly's Ford, Virginia, and impetuously joined a charge during which he was mortally wounded by shrapnel from Union artillery.

gallery. An underground passageway large enough to accommodate men and equipment that was used to link a fortification's outer works with its inner works. In permanent fortifications, galleries usually led to the powder magazine.

galley. N. The kitchen of a vessel.

gallinipper. A large insect, especially a mosquito.

galoot. A soldier who had not as yet seen battle; a replacement; GREEN; considered awkward and all but worthless in combat.

galore. An abundance.

galvanized Confederate. A Federal DESERTER or prisoner of war who declared allegiance to the Confederacy. Some saw action in or near Savannah. Records, however, are scarce, so little is known specifically about this allegedly small number of men.

galvanized Yankee. A Confederate DESERTER or prisoner of war who took the OATH OF ALLEGIANCE to the Union. They were also called "repentant Rebels," "transfugees," and "whitewashed Rebels." By 1864 six thousand Southerners were recruited into the Union army from prison camps and formed into six regiments. They were sent to the frontier, the Trans-Mississippi Department, where authorities believed they could do little or no harm. Largely consigned to duties such as mail service, escorting wagon trains, and survey and scout work, these six thousand men were nevertheless engaged in several skirmishes and one battle. After the war, few returned to the South to face the scorn of their former comrades, and they were not welcomed into the ranks of Union veterans, so they scattered and found new lives apart from their war service.

Game Cock Brigade. A Confederate brigade whose commander, Gen. Philip St. George Cocke, committed suicide on December 26, 1861, in Powhatan City, Virginia, eight months into the conflict. A West Point graduate (Class of 1832), Cocke had resigned from the army in 1834 and developed a reputation as an agriculturalist and served on the board of visitors of the Virginia Military Institute. He played a role in Virginia's secession and accepted command of a brigade in western Virginia. Cocke was commended by Robert E. Lee and P. G. T. Beauregard. The only reason given for his suicide was failing health.

Playing upon his name, the brigade adopted the title before Gen. George E. Pickett was appointed its commander in early 1863.

gammoning. N. Any device, such as an iron band or lashing, that served to secure the BOWSPRIT of a vessel to its STEM.

GAR. See GRAND ARMY OF THE REPUBLIC.

Garde Lafayette, La, or **Garde des Fourchettes, Les.** The 55th New York Infantry Regiment, which was known originally as La Garde Lafayette due to the large number of French immigrants who comprised the unit. The cooks for the officers mess were renowned chefs, and the Gallic flavor of the regiment included the occasional rounding up of frogs for the chefs. The phrase Les Garde des Fourchettes translates as "guards of the forks" and reflected this gastronomical aspect of the regiment. The 55th was led by Col. Régis de Trobriand, a Frenchman who had immigrated to New York in 1847 and had reputations as an author poet, novelist, philanderer, and newspaper editor but also a love for the life of a soldier. The 55th was a ZOUAVE regiment and, during the Peninsula campaign, performed gallantly at the battle of Fair Oaks. De Trobriand served with distinction through the end of the war as a brigade commander then as a divisional commander.

Gardner bullet. Perhaps the most widely used explosive bullet of the war. The projectile had a copper core surrounded by a casting of lead. Filled with powder and having an opening that extended to the base of the bullet, the Gardner ignited upon discharge. Although the resulting explosion was too small to be significant, it left a fire trail that aided SHARPSHOOTERS in determining how close they were to hitting their marks.

Garibaldi Guard. The 39th New York, which was raised by a Hungarian, Col. Frederic D'Utassy. The regiment was made up of seven ethnic groups: Hungarians, Italians, Poles, Germans, Czechs,

Spaniards, and Portuguese. The multinational flavor of the regiment complicated communication. Both D'Utassy and his second in command, Alex Repetti of Italy, were court-martialed for misusing government property.

garrison. (1) INFANTRY or other units assigned to occupy a fort with permanent quarters and specific duty areas. (2) Artillery assigned to such fixed fortifications.

garrison flag. A twenty-foot-by-thirty-six-foot banner to be flown over fortresses and other permanent installations. The Confederate flag displayed eleven stars even though Kentucky and Missouri remained in the Union. The Federal flag exhibited thirty-four stars, including the Southern seceded states and the recent admission of Kansas to the Union in January 1861, and thirty-five when West Virginia separated from Virginia and was admitted to the Union in June 1863.

Gath. The pen name of veteran newspaper correspondent George A. Townsend, who added an *H* to his initials in the postwar years. He was dispatched to cover the Peninsula campaign for Horace Greeley's *New York Herald* and then went overseas to lecture and write on the Union cause. Townsend returned to cover the last battles of the war for the *New York World;* he found national fame for his writing and insights into the assassination of the president.

Gatling gun. Frequently misidentified as an early machine gun, this rapid-firing weapon was invented by a North Carolina physician, Dr. Richard J. Gatling. Motivated by humanitarian motives, Gatling argued that in devising this weapon he wished to make war so terrible that it would no longer be waged. The hand-cranked gun with six revolving barrels was displayed and demonstrated in Indianapolis in 1862. Among the spectators was Gov. Oliver P. Morton, who urged the War Department to adopt it since it fired six hundred rounds per minute. No action was taken in Washington, however, partly because many viewed rapid-fire weapons as a waste of ammunition. Nevertheless, Gatling produced twelve of the .577-caliber guns. Finally Union Gen. Benjamin F. Butler agreed to purchase all of them for twelve thousand dollars. In the field, the Gatling gun was less than accurate and displayed other flaws. It is thought that the guns saw action during the lengthy siege of Petersburg, and Gen. Winfield Scott Hancock allegedly requisitioned a dozen of the guns for his Veteran Corps. In 1865 Gatling adapted his invention to use rimfire cartridges, rather than the more expensive paper cartridges, and in 1866 the War Department officially adopted it.

General. A locomotive of the Western and Atlantic Railroad that was hijacked on April 12, 1862, near Atlanta by Federal volunteers known as Andrews's Raiders. The band had planned to disrupt Confederate communications so as to facilitate the fall of Chattanooga. Wet weather and the dogged pursuit of the raiders foiled the plot. The locomotive was abandoned twelve miles south of Chattanooga, but the raiders were rounded up and tried and convicted of spying. Eight men, including the leader, James J. Andrews, were executed. Eight others escaped, and the remainder were exchanged as prisoners of war. The raiders were among the first recipients of the Medal of Honor.

general call. Sounded by fife and drum, this signal alerted encamped troops to strike their tents and get ready for combat.

general muster. N. Before departing from port, commanding officers were required to call all hands to the main deck for inspection.

general officer. Any officer with a rank above colonel; that is, brigadier general, major general, lieutenant general. In Federal forces, only Ulysses S. Grant held the highest rank; Winfield Scott had held the rank by BREVET. Confederates conferred all three GRADES upon some of their commanders. In addition to RANK, seniority was important and was the subject of several bitter controversies among commanders. Long-standing codes of conduct suggested that general officers should remain in the rear, but generals were not required to avoid EXPOSURE to enemy fire. A field commander who was not a general officer could assume the prerogatives of a general officer if casualties placed him in command of a BRIGADE or CORPS. During and immediately after the conflict, nearly two thousand Federal officers attained the rank of general; Confederates included fewer than five hundred. An estimated fourteen hundred Union generals held their rank by brevet, many of whom were promoted by Congress almost as soon as the war ended, and some of them used the honorary title for the rest of their lives.

general orders. A set of orders that outlined the action to be taken by specified bodies of soldiers. Most commanders of armies issued general orders, each of which was numbered separately, and a few came from high-ranking civil officials.

General Orders No. 8, Union Gen. Ambrose E. Burnside. According to historian William K.

Goolrick, these orders of January 23, 1863, constitute "one of the most remarkable and intemperate documents in the annals of the U.S. Army." After berating Gen. Joseph Hooker at length, Burnside called him "unfit to hold an important commission" and recommended his dismissal. Abraham Lincoln alone had the power to dismiss, and after pondering the evidence and meeting with Burnside, he chose to retain Hooker and reassign Burnside.

General Orders No. 9, Gen. Robert E. Lee. Issued at Appomattox on April 10, 1865, and known as "Lee's Farewell to the Army of Northern Virginia." Perhaps the most poignant general

orders issued during the war, Lee commended the Southern soldiers, saying: "You will take with you the satisfaction that proceeds from the consciousness of duty faithfully performed; and I earnestly pray that a Merciful God will extend to you His blessing and protection. With an unceasing admiration of your constancy and devotion to your Country, and a grateful remembrance of your kind and generous consideration for myself, I bid you all an affectionate farewell."

General Orders No. 11, Union Gen. Thomas Ewing. Ewing was a foster brother of Gen. William Tecumseh Sherman. He was responsible for the Border District, which included the Colorado Territory, but commanded only twenty-five hundred men. Because Southern sympathizers were rife in Kansas, which was plagued with GUERRILLA activity, and because the civilian population regularly sheltered the guerrillas, Ewing proclaimed on August 25, 1863, that all people living more than one mile from any military post in a three-and-a-half-county area—Jackson, Cass, Bates, and part of Vernon Counties—were to leave by September 9. The order effectively depopulated the region involved, causing about 94 percent of its residents to relocate. Many refugees were harassed and victimized en route to other states. Federal troops swept through the area, leaving behind many burned-out farms, which led to the region's designation as the BURNT DISTRICT. The eviction of the population was depicted on canvas by Missouri artist George Caleb Bingham, and the forced exodus of thousands of people is regarded as the war's sternest measure directed against civilians.

General Orders No. 11, Gen. Ulysses S. Grant. Issued at Holly Springs, Mississippi, on December 17, 1862, this directive came close to bringing censure upon Grant. It constituted one of the most comprehensive anti-Jewish regulations issued in the United States, because it branded all Jews within the area as violators of trade regulations laid down by the Treasury Department and ordered their expulsion

within twenty-four hours. Prominent and indignant Jews quickly took the matter to Abraham Lincoln. Apparently unaware of the edict prior to their visit to the Executive Mansion, on January 4, 1863, the president ordered General in Chief Henry W. Halleck to revoke Grant's order. This action, however, did not quell the storm of protest from common folk and high officeholders.

General Orders No. 28, Gen. Benjamin F. Butler. Issued in occupied New Orleans on May 15, 1862, this directive is also known as the "Woman's Order." Southern women demonstrated their patriotism by insulting Union soldiers and even emptying chamber pots on the men as they walked down the city streets. Butler therefore ordered that if the demonstrations continued, the women would "be regarded and held liable to be treated as a woman of the town plying her avocation." This order outraged the Confederacy, and Confederate president Jefferson Davis branded Butler as "a felon deserving of capital punishment . . . no longer simply a public enemy of the Confederate States of America, but an outlaw and common enemy of mankind [who should] be immediately executed by hanging." The insults, however, ceased. A few women persisted and were arrested and imprisoned for a short while.

General Orders No. 45, Confederate Gen. Samuel Cooper. Under this directive, all captured Federal medical officers were to be immediately released. This action was a response to established Federal precedents that medical officers should not be held as prisoners of war.

General Orders No. 91, U.S. Secretary of War Simon Cameron. At Cameron's urging, Congress approved this order on July 29, 1862, which solidified the role of Abraham Lincoln as commander in chief, including the right to dismiss any officer from further service.

General Terror. The nickname of Union Gen. Albin Francisco Schoepf, a native of Poland and a refugee who commanded the Union prison at FORT DELAWARE. One of the most notorious of Federal prisons, the marshy site on Pea Patch Island held as many as eight thousand captives who were punished severely for any infraction of the camp

rules. Schoepf was not personally involved in the punishment, but he allowed his subordinates great latitude, bordering on torture.

General War Order No. 1, President Abraham Lincoln. From the Executive Mansion on January 27, 1862, Lincoln ordered a general movement of all Union forces on February 22. Few official orders from a head of state or army commander have been so patently impossible to execute. No significant offensive was undertaken on the appointed day.

General War Order No. 3, President Abraham Lincoln. During the movement of Union troops from their Washington camps to FORT MONROE, Virginia, as the prelude to the Peninsula campaign, Abraham Lincoln issued this general order on March 8, 1862, stipulating that a sufficient number of men should remain in the area of the national capital to make the city "entirely secure." This vexed his generals, particularly George B. McClellan, since the president's vague language called for more troops than were deemed necessary by the military leaders. The campaign conducted in May by Confederate Gen. Thomas J.

"Stonewall" Jackson in the Shenandoah Valley flummoxed the Union commanders and seemed to threaten Washington, which panicked the Lincoln administration into demanding that Irvin McDowell's forty-thousand-man corps be diverted from joining the fighting on the peninsula. When McClellan protested, Lincoln responded, "I think the time is near when you must either attack Richmond or else give up the job and come to the defense of Washington." McDowell's army moved toward the valley, and McClellan remained on the peninsula.

general reserve. A reserve force that could be called into action only by the commanding general of an army. Subordinate officers had discretionary authority with regard to reinforcements that were deemed to be "local reserves."

General Shaler. A horse valued by Confederate Gen. John B. Gordon, who named the animal for the Federal officer from whom it was captured. Union Gen. Alexander Shaler had earlier captured the animal from Southerners.

general signal. N. A signaled message designed to go to all commanders of a SQUADRON or fleet.

gentleman private. A son of a plantation owner or respected professional who was eligible for an officer's commission but who preferred to fight as a private.

Georgia, **CSS.** This 1,150-ton iron screw steam cruiser was built in Dumbarton, Scotland, in 1862 as the merchant ship *Japan,* but was secretly purchased by the Confederate government in March 1863 and converted to a commerce raider. That year she cruised the North and South Atlantic, taking nine prizes. When the vessel arrived at Cherbourg, France, in October 1863, it was found that her hull was heavily encrusted with marine growth. The ship was decommissioned and sold to private interests. In August 1864 the vessel was seized at sea by USS *Niagara* and claimed as a

prize. After the war she was used as a merchant steamer until lost off the Maine coast in 1875.

Georgia reel. A descriptive term applied to the 1865 movements of William Tecumseh Sherman's and Joseph E. Johnston's armies through northern Georgia after the MARCH TO THE SEA.

Gettysburg of the West. A descriptive term referring to the March 26–28, 1862, battle of Glorietta Pass in the New Mexico Territory. Fought on the old Santa Fe Trail, this Federal victory ultimately forced the South to give up any hope of adding the Southwest to the Confederacy.

ghost. A reference to a white horse. Instead of being hard to see on a battlefield cloaked with gray powder smoke, white horses stood out against this background and their riders were easy targets.

Gibbs carbine. Only a thousand of these weapons were produced and delivered to Federal quartermasters before the New York City factory where they were manufactured was destroyed by fire during the draft riots of 1863.

Gibraltar of the West. A nickname for Vicksburg, Mississippi. Situated on an extremely high river bluff, the town was considered safe from naval guns. Because the only good approaches by land were from the south, the Vicksburg defenders believed that no Federal army would ever get close to the city.

gig. N. A longboat built for speed and reserved for a ship's commander.

Gillmore Medal. A bronze medal commissioned by Union Gen. Quincy A. Gillmore from Ball, Black, and Company of New York to award enlisted men who had distinguished themselves during the summer of 1863 in the siege of Charleston. One side depicted the ruins of FORT SUMTER, the other bore Gillmore's signature, and the clasp bore the recipient's name, RANK, and REGIMENT. Regimental commanders nominated soldiers, who also received certificates setting forth the basis for their selection. Four hundred medals were manufactured.

gimbal. A device that allows an object to maintain a level plane regardless of the incline of its base. Aboard ships, gimbals enabled a compass to maintain an even level, and during the war, gimbals were used to mount the sight of an artillery piece.

Gimlet. The horse of John Babcock, a Federal scout. As a result of his friendship with photographer Alexander Gardner, Babcock became one of the most publicized of Federal scouts. He eventually became chief of an intelligence unit operated by the Army of the Potomac.

ginger beer. A beer substitute in the South made from ginger, water, molasses, and yeast.

give the vermin a parole, to. To discard body lice rather than kill them.

glacis. (1) A mound of earth outside a ditch or wall designed to deflect or absorb cannon fire. (2) The outer bank of a ditch situated so that an attacking force would be exposed to fire from the defenders.

glass. A telescope.

Glengary. A soft cap prized by Scotsmen in the Federal army.

glory hole. A gap in the enemy's line where one had to be very cautious in order to keep from "being blown to glory."

glue pot. A double-chambered pot, the outer section of which was filled with water. When the water was heated, hardened glue was melted in the inner chamber.

gobble, to. To win an overwhelming victory quickly.

gobble talk. A derisive reference to soldiers from Louisiana.

go in search of his rights, to. A sardonic allusion to a soldier who had fled the battlefield rather than fight.

going down the line. To visit a brothel.

gold brick, to. A soldier who performed his duties in slovenly or worthless fashion.

gold hoax of 1864. A scheme by which Joseph Howard, an editor of the *Brooklyn Eagle,* hoped to inflate gold prices after he had acquired a quantity that he could then resell. Howard drafted a bogus presidential proclamation calling for the immediate draft of four hundred thousand men. Issued as a FLIMSY from the White House, the report appeared in two prominent New York newspapers on May 18, 1864. The stock market swooned, and the price of gold increased 10 percent, but then stories began circulating that the call for troops was false. The Lincoln administration ordered the seizure of the offices of the two newspapers that had printed the report as well as the telegraph office accused of sending the dispatch. Howard was arrested on May 30. He absolved the newspapers and the telegraph office of any responsibility and was held for three months before being released at the behest of the Reverend Henry Ward Beecher. Ironically, Lincoln had entertained the idea of issuing a call for more men, but the hue and cry evoked by Howard's scheme caused the president to delay the call by two months. Howard may have never known that his scheme could have deprived the Union army of badly needed men with whom the war might have ended sooner.

goober grabber. (1) A Southern soldier from North Carolina. (2) A native of Georgia.

good earnest. Genuine striving. In S. H. M. Byers's laudatory biography of Ulysses S. Grant, Grant's failures as a farmer and tanner were dismissed as enterprises into which the man had not entered with "good earnest."

goose question. A covert reference to the issue of SLAVERY.

gopher. (1) A nickname for soldiers in general and infantrymen in particular because so many of them spent a great deal of time digging holes and trenches. (2) A reference to natives of Florida.

gopher hole. A hole in the ground large enough for one man.

gorge. The side of a fort or the face of fieldwork that held the SALLY PORT, the entrance to the fortification. Open-ended fieldworks (e.g., REDANS and LUNETTES) were considered "open at the gorge" because their entrances were not covered by a PARAPET.

gorge line. A line that was determined by the position of the rear entrance to a fortification.

go South, to. To turn in one's commission as an officer in the U.S. Army or Navy in order to fight for the Confederacy. Many of the most capable leaders of Southern forces were West Point graduates and experienced fighting men who placed loyalty to their state or region above loyalty to the nation.

go up, to. To die on the battlefield or in a hospital, supposedly ascending to heaven.

Governor's Island. Situated off Manhattan, this island was the site of Fort Columbus, built in 1794. Its only facility that could be used as a prison was an officers quarters, and Southern officers were confined here. At its peak, the population of this impromptu prison was no more than three hundred.

government livery. An army uniform.

government on wheels. A reference to Confederate officials who, fleeing from Richmond in April 1865, had to be on the move perpetually to avoid capture.

grade. The RANK of a commissioned officer.

grain. A unit of weight based upon the average weight of a grain of wheat taken as the average of the weight of grains from the middle of the stalk. Armorers measured the amount of powder per bullet in grains. During the war, regulations specified that bullet cartridges should hold sixty grains of powder.

Grand Army of the Republic (GAR). Founded in 1866, this was one of several veterans organizations that arose to address the situation of former soldiers in the hard times that followed the war. Gens. Richard J. Oglesby and John A. Logan, both of Illinois, led the formation of this all-inclusive organization of veterans. The first local body, or post, was established at Springfield on or about April 1. Both Logan and Oglesby had political aspirations, and the GAR soon became a potent political force. Within eighteen months of its founding, the GAR had hundreds of posts in the North and a few in the South. The body successfully campaigned for such benefits as pensions and homes for the orphans of veterans, and leadership in the politically powerful GAR often served as a stepping-stone to national office. The organization was closely allied with the Republican Party, so much so that the acronym GAR was explained by some as "Generally All Republicans." Some analysts credit the GAR with providing the crucial votes necessary in 1868 to propel Ulysses S. Grant into the White House. Logan, who had aspirations for the nation's highest office, made skillful use of his GAR base. Although he never won the presidency, he was regarded as a political "king maker." Throughout the late 1800s the power of the GAR fluctuated to the degree its support was deemed crucial to the Republican Party. GAR membership peaked in 1890 at close to 428,000. In addition to standardizing benefits for veterans of the war, the GAR also devoted considerable energy to raising civic consciousness through its endorsement of patriotic exercises in public schools and other reminders of the price of freedom. Some analysts believe that, lacking the influence of the GAR, the nation would not have seen the succession of Civil War veterans to the White House. Following Grant were Rutherford B. Hayes, James A. Garfield, Benjamin Harrison, Chester A. Arthur, and William McKinley.

grand division. An oversized grouping of troops, usually temporary, in which segments of more than one division were placed under a single command. Preparing to launch an all-out attack upon Fredericksburg late in 1862, Union Gen. Ambrose E. Burnside reorganized the Army of the Potomac into three grand divisions, each of which included two CORPS. This reshuffling of commands demonstrated little improvement over the previous organization, however, and after Burnside was reassigned, the army reverted to its prior corps organization under Joseph Hooker.

Grand Review. To celebrate the Union victory, on May 18, 1865, the War Department ordered a grand review in Washington of the main Union armies: George Gordon Meade's Army of the Potomac and William T. Sherman's Army of Georgia and Army of the Tennessee. Two days were required for the armies—about 145,000 veterans—

to pass before a presidential reviewing stand. On May 23 Meade led 80,000 men along the Pennsylvania Avenue route. Sherman, somewhat concerned over the tattered appearance of his men in comparison to Meade's, led his men across the course on the following day. Many spectators believed that Sherman's armies put on the better show of the two. His bands played "The Battle Hymn of the Republic," which had also been played throughout the march through the Carolinas, and the troops were accompanied by an assortment of cattle, mules, goats, and former slaves as well as groups of BUMMERS who brandished goods from their foraging missions.

grand rounds. The formal inspection of a line of sentinels by high-ranking officers.

Granny. (1) A nickname for Union Gen. Robert Patterson, who was sixty-nine years old when he entered Federal service. His failure to prevent Confederate Gen. Joseph E. Johnston's troops from reaching Manassas caused Patterson to be mustered out a few days after this first major battle of the war. (2) A moniker for Union Gen. Theophilus Holmes, who was fifty-seven years old when the conflict started. (3) A nickname for Robert E. Lee, whose early war exploits were directed toward evaluating entrenchments and assessing coastal defenses.

grant quarter, to. To show mercy to defeated or surrendered men.

grapeshot. A projectile assembled with iron plates and rings and holding a cluster of shot together. A SABOT, usually wooden, was attached to the "stand" of shot. One version, known as quilted grape, encased the shot with a canvas bag that also held a powder charge. Highly effective against troops at short range, the army dis-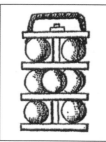continued the use of grapeshot in favor of CANISTER. The navy, however, continued to use it throughout the war. Union grapeshot usually held nine balls; Confederate versions frequently held more, in some cases as many as twenty-one, but the shot was usually smaller than that used in the Federal ammunition.

grapevine bridge. A bridge hastily constructed across a river in much the same way as the bridge erected by Federal forces over the Chickahominy

River during the Peninsula campaign of 1862. Heavy ropes were suspended from trees, and then planks were laid upon them. Although the structure shook and quivered, it held up to heavy traffic.

grapevine telegraph. Any clandestine or informal means of conveying information. This jocular moniker was based on the growing importance of the telegraph as a formal means of communication. Undocumented stories try to account for the name by referring to downed lines that looked like tangled grapevines.

grapnel. N. A small anchor designed to hold boats or small vessels. Grapnels were fitted with four or five instead of the customary two FLUKES of larger anchors. Known also as "claws," its flukes gained sufficient notoriety that the name of the device came to designate any instrument designed to hold or grapple.

Gratiot Street. This address in St. Louis referred to a three-story prison that had formerly housed a medical college. It was substantially larger than some improvised prisons but was used primarily to process prisoners to long-term incarceration at ALTON or another permanent facility.

graveled. A sudden onset of night blindness, probably due to exhaustion and inadequate diet.

grayback. An allusion to a Confederate soldier, also known as a gray-coat.

Graybeard Regiment. The 37th Iowa Volunteer Infantry, a three-year REGIMENT, was created by a special order of the U.S. War Department and enrolled no man under forty-five years of age. Fifty-year-old George W. Kincaid raised the regiment in December 1862 and served as its colonel. His men were destined to relieve able-bodied men from GARRISON, prison, and guard duty for front-line assignment. The average age of the 914 officers and men who made up the regiment was fifty-seven; the oldest member of the regiment may have been eighty-year-old Curtis King of Muscatine. In addition to guard duty, the regiment also provided escorts for supply trains that were susceptible to GUERRILLAS. When the unit was discharged in May 1865, it had almost half as many men as when it was formed. Disease and rail accidents took their toll, but the vast majority were discharged from the service due to the infirmities of old age.

Gray Eagle. The personal mount of Union Capt. Andrew Hickenlooper of the 5th Ohio Artillery. This horse gained widespread fame during the April 6–7, 1862, battle of Shiloh. Gray Eagle's performance on the battlefield reputedly strengthened Federal resistance to the Confederates' surprise attack.

Gray Fox. Union Gen. George Cook acquired this name as an Indian fighter during the years before the war.

Greasy Dick. A nickname for Union Gen. Israel B. Richardson.

greatcoat. A British term for an overcoat.

Great Confederate Murat, The. An allusion to Confederate Gen. Nathan Bedford Forrest, whose almost legendary exploits as a cavalry commander  in the western theater led his many admirers to compare him with Napoleon's famous cavalry leader, Joachim Murat. After Forrest's stunning victory at Brice's Cross Roads, Mississippi, Union Gen. William T. Sherman urged his subordinates, "Follow Forrest to the death if it costs ten thousand lives and breaks the treasury."

Great Creole, The. A reference to Confederate Gen. P. G. T. Beauregard, who was lauded for the capture of FORT SUMTER and the victory at First Manassas (Bull Run).

Great Scott! An exclamation of astonishment that was also a sly dig at the enormous girth and weight of Union Gen. Winfield Scott. Although Scott was the most respected military leader in the army, in his later years he was too huge and too plagued with gout to mount a horse. His swaggering campaign for the presidency in 1852 is believed to have given rise to the expression.

Great Peppering, The. An allusion to Union Gen. George G. Meade, known for his fiery temper.

Greek fire. An incendiary combination of phosphorus and bisulfide of carbon used in some artillery ammunition. Frequent or prolonged firing of Greek fire was likely to cause a CANNON tube to explode, such as occurred in the August 1863 destruction of the so-called SWAMP ANGEL on Morris Island, South Carolina. Confederates later attempted unsuccessfully to launch a campaign of fire in New York City, but it failed largely due to the instability of the solutions of Greek fire that they carried into the city.

green apple quickstep. Acute diarrhea, possibly due to the ingestion of immature, green apples.

greenback. Paper currency was issued by the Federal government to be used in lieu of gold following the Legal Tender Act of February 1862. The non-interest-bearing notes came to be called "greenbacks" because one side was printed with green ink. In 1860 the nation's stock of gold and silver coins amounted to $228 million, which, in the opinion of U.S. Secretary of the Treasury Salmon P. Chase, was inadequate to finance the Union war effort. Shortages of money mounted as the war progressed and increasing numbers of fighting men had to be provided with uniforms, food, clothing, shelter, and weapons. During the war approximately $450 million in greenbacks were issued. The supply of gold and silver coins dropped by about 31 percent between 1861 and 1865, but in the last year of the war $379 million in greenbacks and $146 million in national bank notes were in circulation. In December 1865 Congress acted to retire the notes, but the legislation was never carried out because paper currency had found favor with the public.

greens. A nickname for the paper currency issued by the U.S. government, also known as GREEN-BACKS and SHINPLASTERS.

green troops. A body of soldiers with little or no military training. The manpower needs of armies on both sides meant that few battles of any consequence lacked green regiments. European observers of the war suggested that a few regulars from the U.S. Army should be included in every green unit so as to demonstrate proper soldiering to the newcomers.

grenade. An explosive device usually thrown by hand. Although some kinds were developed for this specific use, the majority of Civil War references to grenades refer to FUSE-ignited shells hurled by hand toward the enemy. Some of these were  unexploded shells that were hastily thrown back to their points of origin.

Greyhound Division. A reference to Confederate Maj. Gen. John G. Walker's Texas Division. The unit was composed of four brigades organized at Camp Nelson in Austin, Arkansas, in October 1862. One of its distinctives is that it was the only division in the Southern military to be manned with troops from a single state throughout the war. Another hallmark was the unit's nickname, the Greyhound Division (or Walker's Greyhounds), which was a tribute to the division's reputation for executing long, forced marches across the Trans-Mississippi Department. The unit participated in efforts to relieve the siege of Vicksburg by attacking Federal elements at Milliken's Bend in July 1863 as well as other points in Louisiana. In early 1864 the Greyhounds helped to thwart the Red River campaign at the battles of Mansfield and Pleasant Hill and Jenkins Ferry. During the confusion at the end of the war, the division disbanded at Hempstead, Texas, in May 1865.

Grim Chieftain, the. An allusion to Union Gen. George B. McClellan.

Grimes. A reference to Union Col. Benjamin Franklin Davis, who recruited the 8th New York Cavalry by standing on a Rochester street corner with a placard.

grog ration. Long before the war it was customary for a ship's master to issue twice daily a specified amount of grog—a mixture of rum or whiskey and water—to every sailor. In the years before the war, several campaigns were launched in Congress to abolish the grog ration in the U.S. Navy, all of which were soundly defeated by representatives from the South and West. Adjustments were made, however, in that the ration was slightly reduced and sailors could choose between grog and a sum of money. During the Civil War, soldiers in the field loudly protested that they were forbidden to have alcohol of any kind. Possibly as an economy measure rather than in response to the complaints from the landsmen, the grog ration was abolished in the Union navy in September 1862. It continued in the Confederate navy, however, throughout the war, although a sailor could opt for payment in lieu of the grog ration.

Grumble. The nickname of Confederate Gen. William E. Jones. Although Jones was highly regarded by his men and was commended by both

Robert E. Lee and Thomas J. Jackson, he was scorned by Jeb Stuart. In September 1863 Jones insulted Stuart and was court-martialed, convicted, and reassigned to the Department of Western Virginia. Again he performed admirably, but in June 1864 he was killed on the field.

guard line. The extreme boundary of a prison camp or a stockade, beyond which there were no guards.

guards. N. Fencelike rails erected on ships to prevent sailors from falling overboard.

guerre imminente. A term used in the South to refer to the inevitable coming war.

guerrilla. In the context of the Civil War, a distinction, usually based on the level of regular-army control rather than tactics, is made between the PARTISAN RANGERS of the eastern theater and the guerrilla units of the western districts. Guerrillas were loosely organized clusters of men drawn from the civilian population for the purpose of harassing the enemy behind the

lines, but they were not members of the regular army. These men were also characterized by a criminal element that evoked terror and fear rather than a sense of protection. In the western states their actions were influenced more by the prewar violence in that region, which was translated into action during the war more by a sense of revenge and personal grudges than the pursuit of tactical military objectives. Likewise, the legacy of the war in the West is colored by the brutal reprisals executed by the Federal authorities, the most notorious of which, following the August 13, 1863, guerrilla raid on Lawrence, Kansas, was the banishment of Southern sympathizers from three Missouri counties and the wide-scale destruction of farms and homes. Guerrillas were not bound by the rules or regulations of an army, and so they obeyed no law and pillaged friendly and hostile civilians alike. Likewise, captured guerrillas were not accorded protection as prisoners of war but were summarily executed. By 1863 the Confederate military disavowed their effectiveness, always excepting certain partisan ranger commands in Virginia. Two of the most notorious guerrilla leaders were William C. Quantrill and William "Bloody Bill" Anderson. Approximately ten thousand guerrillas harassed the Federals in the West, and after the war several of these men became the most notorious outlaws of the era—the Jameses, Daltons, and Youngers—and recruited gang members from their wartime colleagues.

guide. A circumlocution for spy.

guide left, right, or center. A command used to align a marching unit.

guidon. A swallow-tailed pennant used by CAVALRY and light ARTILLERY units during the Civil War. At the beginning of the war, Union army regulations did not allow Federal cavalry to carry a national flag; they did require regimental standards and company guidons (which displayed the letter used to designate the unit). The article mandated that guidons measure "three feet five inches from the lance to the end of the swallow-tail; fifteen inches to the fork of the swallow tail, and two feet three inches on the lance. To be half red and half white, dividing at the fork, the red above." Unofficially, guidons were also designed that resembled the national banner. Thus the regulation was amended on January 18, 1862, to direct that "guidons and camp colors for the Army will be made like the United States flag, with stars and stripes."

guidon bearer. A trooper designated to carry a GUIDON.

gum blanket. A blanket coated with INDIA RUBBER so as to make it waterproof.

gum coat. An outer garment treated with rubber so as to make it waterproof.

gump. A fool or dolt.

gun. Although used to refer to REVOLVERS, MUSKETS, and RIFLES, this term properly designated a SMOOTHBORE or rifled CANNON (such as those in the image at the top of the next column).

gunboat. A vessel fitted with a GUN in the bow or amidships. The term was also applied to shallow-draft armed steamers or to IRONCLADS. Generally, such boats were limited to operations on inland or coastal waterways.

gunboats. Slang for clumsy and unwieldy shoes. Also called "mudscows."

gunn. Southern slang for a gunnysack made of jute or some other coarse material.

gunpowder. See powder.

gun sling. A narrow canvas or leather strip equipped with loops and hooks that attached to a RIFLE stock; it was designed to make it easier for marching men to carry their MUSKETS or rifles.

gunwale. N. Originally the *wale*, or boat's side, close to one or more gunports. By 1860 the term was used to designate the upper edge or side of a commercial vessel or warship.

H

habeas corpus. A time-honored legal instrument aimed at preventing imprisonment without a hearing. Meaning "deliver the body," it had for centuries been used to secure the release of suspects who had not been tried or convicted. First suspended during the war by Abraham Lincoln for military reasons "on a line between Washington and Baltimore," it was later suspended on numerous occasions. For a time the presidential edict applied to the entire Union. Lincoln's *Collected Works* include twenty-two sections dealing with this matter. Suspension of the writ is generally credited with having saved Maryland for the Union, but it also resulted in the arbitrary imprisonment of an estimated eighteen thousand civilians. Congress passed legislation in March 1863 that gave Lincoln's actions post facto legality. In the Confederacy, Jefferson Davis attempted a similar ploy but had limited success. His effort was approved by the Confederate Congress to enforce the 1862 draft act. This highly unpopular measure extended the enlistment period from twelve months to the duration of the conflict. Military leaders were briefly authorized to arrest subversive civilians, but public indignation was so high that the measure was never effectively enforced in the South. Habeas corpus was suspended once during the administration of Andrew Johnson to prevent moves aimed at sparing the life of convicted Lincoln coconspirator Mary Surratt.

Hale rocket. The Hale rocket was a refinement of the CONGREVE ROCKET in that it eliminated the need for a guidestick by utilizing exhaust to rotate the rocket and obtain more stable flight. Early models had a series of spin-jet holes, but this limited the rocket's range because too much gas escaped too quickly. Hale resorted to placing guide vanes at the base and found that the range increased significantly. First used in combat during the Mexican War of 1846–48, Hale rockets were used by both sides in the Civil War and manufactured in a variety of sizes. Made of rolled sheet iron, cast iron, or wrought iron, a 14-pound rocket was nearly seventeen inches long and had an effective range of two thousand yards. Nevertheless, Hale rockets were somewhat erratic in flight. They were fired from a tube on a stand, and although used in combat, they defied all efforts to make the launching process uniform. As a result they were far from reliable.

half-mast. A position approximately halfway between the deck of a ship and the top of its tallest mast. It was at this point that naval vessels displayed their flags as a token of respect for a dead officer or high-ranking political leader. The custom was adopted for use on land.

halliard, halyard, or haul-yard. N. A line used to raise or lower a flag, a sail, a spar, or a YARD.

halter. (1) A leather and metal bridle. Fastened to the nose, chin, and throat, it was used to lead and to tie mounts. (2) Slang for noose or "hangman's halter."

Hampton Legion. Early in 1861, South Carolina planter Wade Hampton raised a mixed body of INFANTRY, CAVALRY, and ARTILLERY. He spent a substantial part of his fortune on uniforms and weapons, including artillery. The infantry was dispatched to fight at the July 21, 1861, battle of First Manassas with Hampton in command. Despite suf-

Wade Hampton postbellum

fering 20 percent casualties on the field, the legion was commended. Afterward the legion's many branches were reassigned to their respective branches in the Confederate army, but the infantry, which had reached battalion strength, retained the original designation throughout the war. The Hampton Legion fought in the Seven Days' battles, Second Manassas, Antietam, Gettysburg, Chickamauga, Knoxville, the Overland campaign, and Appomattox.

Hampton Roads Conference. Missouri politician and editor Francis P. Blair Sr. believed by 1864 the war could be ended by negotiation. Abraham Lincoln allowed Blair to present his idea to Jefferson Davis in Richmond and agreed to meet with a Confederate delegation in Hampton Roads, Virginia, on February 3, 1865. The Southern embassy consisted of Vice President Alexander Stephens, former Supreme Court associate justice John A. Campbell, and Robert M. T. Hunter. Davis had instructed his representatives to settle for nothing less than independence. Lincoln, however, demanded unconditional surrender, reunion, and emancipation. Nothing was accomplished, but Davis fanned the embers of Southern pride by publicizing the hard line dictated by Lincoln, and

RADICAL REPUBLICANS refuted the generous terms implied in Lincoln's plan for RECONSTRUCTION.

hand grenade. During the early months of the war, this term was applied to fused powder-filled shells that were dropped over the ramparts of a fortress under attack. Soon, however, a number of cast-iron devices equipped with percussion caps were manufactured to be thrown at the enemy. The most satisfactory version was equipped with cardboard wings that served to stabilize the grenades in flight.

hand litter. A portable platform for transporting wounded men a short distance. Based on the horse-drawn litter, it was an immediate predecessor of the stretcher.

handcuffed volunteer. A contemptuous term used to designate recruits who had been forced into uniform. Many of these men were substitutes and others were BOUNTY JUMPERS who were sometimes brought into camp under armed guard.

handsel. (1) The first money received during a business day by a person engaged in buying and selling CONTRABAND goods. (2) The first blood spilled during an engagement.

handsome. Having a pleasing appearance and used in regard to women as well as men. Usage suggests that handsome was an intermediate term between pretty and beautiful.

handspike. A fifty- to eighty-inch wooden device used to move a GUN horizontally.

hang fire, to. A misfire of a FLINTLOCK musket. There might be a brief flash in the lock pan, where the priming powder was placed, but no subsequent explosion of the charge in the gun barrel.

Hard Backsides. A nickname for Union Gen. George Armstrong Custer, whose horsemen performed legendary exploits during the war.

Hardee hat. A tall black hat with a wide brim, the right side of which was usually turned up and attached to the crown with a brass pin. The felt hat was adopted by the U.S. Army in 1858 and named for Maj. William J. Hardee, who served on the review board that recommended it. The headgear was also known as the JEFF DAVIS HAT because Jefferson Davis was secretary of war at the time of its adoption. The stiff-brimmed hat was not popular in the ranks but remained regulation headwear until the outbreak of the Civil War. During the war, the distinctive hat was adopted by the Union's Western Brigade, also known as the IRON BRIGADE.

Hardee's *Tactics*. In 1853, at the behest of Secretary of War Jefferson Davis, Maj. William J. Hardee accepted the task of revising American tactics to reflect the shift in military science from precision formations to quick maneuvering. Hardee's work, completed in just eight months, was based on  an 1848 French manual. Hardee's *Rifle and Light Infantry Tactics* quickly became a standard textbook for officers but did not anticipate the developments in weapons technology. It directed action at the BATTALION level, leaving much to be addressed in directing REGIMENTS and COMPANIES in battle. Hardee resigned his commission in January 1861 to accept a brigadier's commission in the Confederate army. Subsequently, several Confederate editions were printed, but there were few additions to the original text. Commanders on both sides relied upon Hardee's *Tactics,* and this fact alone may account in part for the frequency with which soldiers on both sides mimicked each other's goals in combat with identical maneuvers.

hardtack. In universal use throughout the war, this quarter-inch-thick three-inch-square biscuit of unleavened flour was a staple of both armies. Officially issued as "hard bread," this inedible foodstuff was also known as "a castle for worms." Rations of hardtack were not uniform. Men received between eight to ten biscuits and prepared them in many ways. When it was mentioned in letters or diaries, it was always described disparagingly. At Point Lookout and other prisons, hardtack was used as a medium of exchange. Several biscuits were traded for a loaf of bread or a "chaw" of chewing tobacco.

hardware. Slang for a weapon—a REVOLVER, SWORD, SABER, or BAYONET.

harness. Tackle and gear used with a horse or mule. The equipment for a single draft animal consisted of at least nineteen separate pieces. Double harness, designed for a pair of animals used in pulling a wagon or a GUN, usually had at least thirty separate components. Harnesses of every variety were often listed simply as ACCOUTREMENTS, without attempting to itemize the individual components. During the fiscal year that ended on June 30, 1864, 27,480 sets of accoutrements were supplied to Federal CAVALRY units. More than 152,000 sets of "horse equipments" were issued in the North that year. Artillery units received 2,243 sets of harness designed for use with pairs of animals.

Harpers Ferry rifle. This .58-caliber U.S. Model 1855 RIFLE was manufactured at the U.S. Arsenal

Wartime ruins of the Harpers Ferry Arsenal

in western Virginia with a thirty-three-inch barrel and weighed nearly ten pounds. It was distinguished from earlier models in that only two iron bands held the stock and barrel together (other models had three). Accurate up to a thousand yards, the percussion-cap MUZZLELOADER was utilized by both sides during the war. The North, however, ceased manufacturing the model in favor of the U.S. Model 1861 rifle. Confederate armories produced the Model 1855 throughout the war.

Harper's Weekly. An illustrated weekly newspaper published in New York by Fletcher Harper, who was also affiliated with the publishing firm of Harper and Brothers. The publication was only four years old at the outbreak of hostilities and sold nationwide for six cents an issue. Editorially, the paper was unabashedly pro-Union and consistently depicted Federal soldiers as heroes and Confederates as rogues. One of the newspaper's most important contributions to the study of the Civil War was its depiction of the conflict through the woodcuts and engravings based on the frontline drawings of Alfred Waud, Henry Mosler, Theodore Davis, Winslow Homer, and Thomas Nast. The art served to bring the war into the living rooms and parlors of the North like no other media. Publication continued long after the war, but *Harper's* popularity faded with the development of technologies that allowed newspapers to print photographs.

Harwood's Tobacco Factory. This structure stood for many years at the intersection of Main and Twenty-sixth Streets in Richmond. Federal prisoners from the July 21, 1861, battle of First Manassas were held here briefly before being transferred to more permanent quarters in LIBBY PRISON. Because the short-term inmates of Harwood's were the South's first prisoners of war, the place gained notoriety. Its prewar functions probably contributed to the myth that Libby was a converted tobacco warehouse.

haul fire, to, or **haul, to.** N. To permit coal in a ship's furnace to go out or to cool so that fresh coal thrown on top would not catch fire.

haul off, to. N. To retreat quickly or withdrawal.

hausse. A graduated sight installed on the BREECH of a GUN TUBE.

havelock. A white linen covering with a short cape or apron designed to be worn over a soldier's cap so as to protect the wearer's neck from the sun. The headgear was named after Sir Henry Havelock, who popularized its usage during India's Sepoy Mutiny of 1857. Havelocks were quite fashionable at the time of the Civil War, and many recruits proudly marched off to war with two of them. Artist Winslow Homer produced a painting showing patriotic Northern women busily making havelocks for volunteers from their community. Scornfully called "head bags" by some to whom they were given, havelocks proved to be encumbrances instead of assets in the eastern theater of the war. Thousands were discarded after having

been worn a short time. Many soldiers salvaged the cloth for gun patches or coffee strainers.

haversack. A kind of backpack, haversacks were a carryall usually slung over the right shoulder so as to hang over the wearer's  left hip. There was no standard shapes or sizes or material. Foot soldiers used their haversacks to transport personal items and daily rations. On occasion, gunners used leather haversacks to carry ammunition from the LIMBERS to the GUNS; some were especially made for this purpose.

havoc. Complete destruction or devastation, a term derived from a medieval verb meaning "to plunder."

hawser. N. A thick line of hemp used in mooring a ship or in towing one vessel by another.

"Hayfoot! Strawfoot!" A camp command reputedly resorted to by frustrated sergeants whose recruits did not know left from right.

hazard, to. To enter an enterprise or an operation involving great risk.

hazards, at all. Regardless of consequences.

HBM. An abbreviation for "Her Britannic Majesty," or Queen Victoria. The name of a British commercial vessel was often prefaced with these initials.

head. N. The forward end of a ship.

headlight. A light with a reflector that was carried at the front of a locomotive to throw light on the track at night.

head logs. Logs at either end of a simple defensive work and elevated so that weapons could be fired

through a small aperture without permitting the enemy to view the heads of the riflemen.

head money. The pay of a recruitment officer or money such officials might embezzle during the execution of their duty.

headquarters. Any structure used as a command post by the commanding officer in the field. Not limited to buildings, officers were occasionally required to establish their headquarters under a tree.

headquarters flag. When a HEADQUARTERS was expected to be occupied for days or weeks, it was customary to fly a special flag. The banner supplemented but did not supplant the national flag. Distinctive flags were designed for the headquarters of ARMIES, CORPS, DIVISIONS, and BRIGADES. Some of these bore easily recognized insignia. In the Union army an elaborate color scheme was used to indicate corps and brigades.

headquarters in the saddle. A fairly common phrase meant to imply that the commanding officer would be in the field with his troops. When Union Gen. John Pope was given command of the Army of  Virginia in 1862, he repeated the phrase to assure his superiors that he would be in the field and on the march. Following Pope's embarrassment at the August 29–30, 1862, battle of Second Manassas, the general's critics commented that his headquarters were where his hindquarters should have been.

headstall. The leather segment of a halter or bridle that encircled the head of a horse or mule.

heave, to. N. Although this verb signified any act in which hard pulling was necessary, it is particularly linked with sailors pulling up a ship's anchor. In its past tense, this verb became "hove."

heavy metal. An enemy's large ammunition or GUNS against which lighter projectiles and pieces were ineffective.

heavy regiment. An ARTILLERY regiment substantially larger than normal. Some of these units were organized initially with more than the standard number of men; others were enlarged through consolidating remnants of other units after battle.

Hell Hole. A prominent feature of the battlefield at Pickett's Mill, Georgia.

Hell's Half Acre. A small tree-covered segment of the Stones River, Tennessee, battlefield. Before it became the focus of a furious struggle during the battle, nearby residents knew the site as the Round Forest.

Hell's Hollow. A slight depression in the Shiloh, Tennessee, battlefield.

Hellcat in Calico. A nickname for nurse Clara Barton, later founder of the American Red Cross.

Hellcat. A derisive reference to Abraham Lincoln.

***Henry Dodge*, CSS.** Seized in Texas shortly before the artillery duel at FORT SUMTER, this U.S. REVENUE CUTTER was armed with a single gun. It was surrendered at Houston.

Henry house. A modest farmhouse on the First Manassas battlefield. When the home drew artillery fire early in the fighting, the ailing Mrs. Judith Henry was carried by her children to the nearby Matthews house. At a time when the ebb and flow of battle seemed to have passed her home, Mrs. Henry returned. Soon afterward artillery again struck the little structure. Shrapnel struck the woman, and she died shortly after the battle ended, making her the first woman known to have been a victim of Civil War gunners.

***Henry Janes*, USS.** Purchased at New York during the summer of 1861, this wooden SCHOONER was rated at 260 tons. By February 1862 she carried a 13-inch MORTAR and two 32-pounders. Sold at public auction in July 1865, the vessel brought $10,100. That was only $2,900 below her purchase price, but wartime repairs cost the U.S. government $33,121.

Henry rifle. While working for the Winchester Firearms Company in New Haven, Connecticut, B. Tyler Henry developed and patented a .44-caliber RIFLE capable of firing fifteen rounds. When the War Department reviewed it, the examiners concluded it was too light for combat use. Nevertheless, the army purchased 1,730 rifles during the course of the war. The 66th Illinois, also known as Birge's Sharpshooters, equipped themselves with Henrys at their own expense, about fifty dollars apiece. Cartridges for the rifles, however, were supplied by the Federal government. At least two other units, the 7th Illinois and the 97th Indiana, also used Henrys. Other individuals and several state governments purchased at least ten thousand Henrys during the war, and most who used the rifle praised its copper rimfire CARTRIDGES. Very late in the conflict, Federal quartermasters realized that the copper cartridges were impervious to rain. As a result, Henrys were acquired and issued to troops, but this shift in official attitudes to repeating rifles came too late to have much of an impact on the war.

hermaphrodite brig. N. A two-masted SCHOONER, square-rigged forward and schooner-rigged aft. British sailors referred to it as a brigantine.

Hero of Pea Ridge. A nickname for Union Gen. Franz Sigel, who commanded the 1st Division of the Army of Southwest Missouri in the March 7–8, 1862, battle of Pea Ridge, Arkansas. A German refugee and one of the Union's political generals, Sigel was transferred to the east where he did not repeat his earlier successes. The low point of his career was the May 15, 1864, battle of New Market, Virginia, after which he was relieved of command.

Hero of the Crater. (1) A nickname for Confederate Gen. William "Little Billy" Mahone, whose lasting reputation was made at Petersburg. (2) A nickname for Confederate Col. Davis A. Weisiger, whose leadership at the July 30, 1864, battle of the Crater led Robert E. Lee to promote him to brigadier on the spot.

Hero, **USS.** This little SCHOONER was purchased for six hundred dollars at Baltimore during the summer of 1861 for use in the STONE FLEET.

Heroes of America. A secret Southern society whose goal was the restoration of Federal rule.

Herr Ridge. An elevated spot about 1.5 miles west of Gettysburg, Pennsylvania, only about nine hundred yards from McPherson's Ridge. The latter was crowned with a fifteen-acre tract of timber and was the scene of bitter fighting.

high bridge. A span across the Appomattox River at a point where it was necessary to build upon sixty-foot piers. A town named for the structure was the site of an April 1865 engagement that cost Federals about eight hundred casualties.

high tide of the Confederacy. A designation for the deepest penetration of the Union line by PICK-ETT'S CHARGE on July 3, 1863, at Gettysburg.

Highfly. One of the favorite mounts of Confederate Gen. Jeb Stuart.

Highlanders. A nickname of the 79th New York, which was comprised largely of Scottish volunteers. The unit entered Federal service on May 29, 1861. At the July 21, 1861, battle of First Manassas they appeared on the field in tartan trousers and marched to the cadence of bagpipes; nevertheless, the men distinguished themselves in providing the rear guard for the Federal retreat. In camp at Washington, a mutiny broke out and was quashed when U.S. Army regulars surrounded the 79th. As a result the regimental flag was confiscated until the unit had proved itself worthy in battle. In the spring of 1862 the REGIMENT was shipped to Port Royal, South Carolina, and participated in the battle of Secessionville. Recalled to Virginia, the 79th saw action at the battles of Second Manassas (Bull Run), Chantilly, Antietam, and Fredericksburg, before being sent to the western theater, where the unit was engaged in the siege of Vicksburg and fighting at Jackson. Attached to Ambrose E. Burnside's army, the Highlanders fought in East Tennessee, and in early 1864 were transferred back to the eastern theater in time for the battles of the Wilderness and Spotsylvania and the siege of Petersburg. The regiment was mustered out on July 14, 1865.

hireling. A contemptuous Southern label for Union soldiers who were believed to be in uniform solely for the sake of a regular paycheck.

hish and hash. A meal of whatever edibles were at hand.

***H. L. Hunley,* CSS.** Built with private funds at Mobile, Alabama, in 1863, this vessel was officially classified as a submarine torpedo boat. It is listed as the world's first submarine despite the fact that an earlier Federal vessel was completed but never put into service. The thirty-four-foot craft was fashioned from a cylindrical iron steam boiler that was lengthened and tapered on the ends.

NAVAL HISTORICAL CENTER

Ballast tanks were placed on both ends, and an iron weight was attached to the bottom to serve as supplemental ballast. The cramped vessel was manned by a crew of nine—eight to work the hand-crank propeller shaft and one to steer. Twenty-two of the men who volunteered to serve aboard the craft perished aboard her; the vessel sank four times and was raised three times. The vessel's lone armament was a SPAR TORPEDO that was to be embedded in the hull of an enemy vessel and triggered as the submarine withdrew. The *Hunley*'s crowning achievement was the sinking of the USS *Housatonic* near Charleston on February 17, 1864, but the small submarine was lost during the action. The vessel was recovered from the ocean bottom on August 8, 2000, but the question of what sank the *Hunley* remains unanswered.

hog and hominy. A succinct designation for all Southern food.

hog drivers. Natives of Tennessee.

Hold Fast. A nickname for Union Gen. William S. Rosecrans. This laudatory title came into use after his successful repulse of Confederates at the December 31, 1862–January 1, 1863, battle of Stones River. There is a tradition that Rosecrans coined the name himself.

"Hold the Fort." A popular song of the war that was inspired by a series of incidents on October 5, 1864, around Allatoona, Georgia. At this village not far from the Tennessee state line, Confederate forces on the move toward the north swarmed around lightly defended Allatoona and demanded

its surrender. The Union commander, Gen. John M. Corse, reputedly received a telegram from Sherman ordering him to hold the fort at all costs. When Corse and his men did that, their heroism inspired the song. Despite its martial background, the song soon became a favorite at camp meetings in both the North and the South.

holster pistol. An early name for a revolver, also called a DRAGOON PISTOL.

Holy Joe. Slang for a chaplain.

holystone. N. Any variety of soft sandstone judged suitable for scrubbing decks.

homegrown Yankee. A UNIONIST native-born in the South.

Homestead Act. For generations many Americans had worked for legislation that allowed settlers to possess public land without payment. Southern opposition to this act was so strong that when it was passed in 1860, President James Buchanan vetoed it. According to him, twenty-five cents an acre was not quite enough for good land. The fledgling Republican Party espoused passage of a "complete and satisfactory Homestead measure," and such legislation became law when Abraham Lincoln signed it on May 20, 1862. Under its terms, citizens could own 160 acres of public land by living on the tract for five years and paying a token filing fee of ten dollars. By 1864 more than 1.2 million acres had been claimed in tracts extending from Michigan to the Dakota Territory and from Missouri to Minnesota.

hooker. Slang for a prostitute. The name was not derived from Union Gen. Joseph Hooker but dates from a time before the war and possibly comes from a red-light district in New York City known as Hooker.

Hooker's Horse Marines. The 3d Indiana Cavalry, which was used as a scouting force soon after

Union Gen. Joseph Hooker was given command of the Army of the Potomac in January 1863.

hoopskirt. N. Heavy TORPEDO netting of ropes supported by numerous spars projecting from the sides of a Federal warship. Use of this homemade contrivance designed to push torpedoes aside was made necessary by the explosives set adrift by Southerners.

hop, step, and jump. Slang for a two-wheeled AMBULANCE vehicle known to career on even the best roads.

horizontal refreshment. Sexual intercourse.

horizontal shot tower. A Confederate term of admiration for the seven-shot SPENCER RIFLE. The term stems from the fact that shot towers were used to make ammunition for MUSKETS and RIFLES. Some users claimed that a Spencer rifle could be "loaded on Sunday and fired through Saturday."

Hornet's Nest. During the April 6–7, 1862, battle of Shiloh, a Union battle line was established next to a peach orchard after the southernmost Federal camps had been overrun on the morning of April 6. The line held for almost six hours before surrendering. Confederates dubbed this sector of the Shiloh battlefield the "Hornet's Nest" because the sound of the bullets from the massed fire of the Union defenders was like that of angry hornets.

hornwork. An OUTWORK of a defensive position constructed by joining two BASTIONS.

horological torpedo. A TORPEDO set to explode at a predetermined time by a clock FUSE. A Confederate agent claimed to have used such a device in the August 1864 explosion at City Point, Virginia, that caused approximately two hundred Federal casualties.

hors de combat. Literally, "out of combat." During the war the phrase was used to describe a

soldier whose wounds prevented him from continuing to fight.

horse artillery. FIELD ARTILLERY drawn by horses. Six animals were allocated to pull a light CANNON and its LIMBER. Other teams of horses were used to pull limbers to which caissons were attached. When guns were moved up steep slopes or through deep mud, it was often necessary to have them pulled by squads of soldiers. Although the 12-POUNDER NAPOLEON was the favorite GUN used by horse artillery on both sides, some PIECES as light as 6-pounders and as heavy as 24-pounders were used in the field.

horse collar. A designation for a bedroll draped around a soldier's neck and held in place by straps. This device allowed many soldiers to discard their cumbersome HAVERSACKS.

horse furniture. An inclusive term for the many pieces of gear needed with horses.

horse holder. In general, CAVALRY units fought, not on horseback, but dismounted, which meant that one out of every four horse soldiers held his own mount and those of his three comrades in the rear of the battle line. Such necessities meant that an engagement by cavalry reduced the effective fighting force by 25 percent. During the opening combat at Gettysburg between Union Gen. John Buford's horsemen and Confederate Gen. Henry Heth's corps, which outnumbered the Federals by nearly three to one, of Buford's 2,700 men, 675 were out of the fight because they were required to hold the horses.

Horseshoe. A salient, also known as the MULE SHOE, in the middle of the Confederate line during the May 10, 1864, engagement near Spotsylvania Court House.

Horseshoe Ridge. A prominent elevation on the west end of Snodgrass Hill, held by a handful of Union soldiers at the beginning of the September

19–20, 1863, battle of Chickamauga. On the second day of the struggle, the ridge was defended by redeployed BRIGADES of Union Gen. George H. Thomas's command led by Brig. Gen. James B. Steedman and reinforcements led by Maj. Gen. Gordon Granger while the remainder of William S. Rosecrans's Army of the Cumberland retreated from the field. When ammunition was exhausted, the last three companies of the Federal rear guard held off the advancing Confederates at bayonet point until the last remaining Union soldiers were forced to surrender.

George H. Thomas

hospital bullet. Oral tradition suggests that, lacking anesthesia, many patients bit a bullet during amputations and other battlefield surgeries.

hospital car. Northern railroads improvised several kinds of cars to transport wounded men. Most were modified sleeping cars in which there were few if any special amenities. Early in 1863, however, the Philadelphia Railroad Company introduced a hospital car equipped with stretcherlike berths, a stove, a toilet, and a water tank.

hospital flag. In late 1863 a flag was adopted to mark hospital facilities and vehicles carrying medical personnel—yellow bunting with a green letter H in the center.

hospital tent. Since all sides of tents used as field hospitals were vertical, these tents were considerably higher than tents generally used in camps and on fields. By war's end every Federal regiment was assigned three hospital tents, which had a combined capacity of twenty-four.

hostage. A person held as an EQUIVALENT for someone in the hands of the enemy. Although officially hostage-taking was not endorsed, there were numerous instances of hostage-taking throughout the war. At least 150 incidents are reported in the *Official Records.* Some of these involved soldiers only, but civilians were also seized and held. In the early months of the war, Abraham Lincoln indicated that captured Rebel PRIVATEERS would be treated as pirates rather than prisoners of war. When a number of these men were captured and stood to be executed, Jefferson Davis ordered that an equal number of Federal prisoners of war would be chosen by lottery to receive the same punishment. Lincoln relented. Numerous hostage incidents were one-on-one, as was the case with Robert E. Lee's son Rooney, who had been captured after having been wounded at the June 9, 1863, battle of Brandy Station. Rooney was held hostage for a Federal officer in Rebel hands until both men were exchanged. Dozens of soldiers and civilians were treated as hostages. Most of them were exchanged, but in a few instances captors shot hostages in cold blood.

hot shot. Originally designed for use against naval targets, this artillery ammunition was solid shot that had been heated in a furnace and fired against wooden targets. Ideally, hot shot would penetrate a ship's hull and ignite a fire. The evolution of ironclads and other metal-sheathed vessels limited the effectiveness of hot shot, but it proved effective in some situations. During the bombardment of FORT SUMTER in April 1861, hot shot sparked fires within the fort. Hot shot was also used against the Union fleet during the battle for FORT FISHER, North Carolina, in December 1864 and January 1865.

Hotchkiss projectile. Benjamin B. Hotchkiss designed this artillery ammunition to be cast in two segments then joined by a lead band. The round expanded in the GUN TUBE when fired, and the lead strip filled the rifling of the tube, spinning the shell into a smooth arc. Adding a psychological effect, the ragged lead bands generated a distinctive, eerie whine in flight.

Housatonic, **USS.** Launched on November 20, 1861, at the Boston Navy Yard, this 1,930-ton Ossipee-class steam screw sloop of war was destined to join the Federal BLOCKADE of Southern ports. Her battery consisted of one 100-POUNDER PARROTT, three 30-pounders, one 11-inch DAHLGREN, two 32-pounders SMOOTHBORES, two 24-pounders, one 12-pounder HOWITZER, and one 12-pounder RIFLE. The vessel participated in the blockade of Charleston, South Carolina, in many ways, including raiding parties, the shelling of the Confederate coastal defenses, and the capture of BLOCKADE-RUNNERS. Despite the enormous firepower of the 207-foot warship, she was sunk just outside the bar of Charleston Harbor on the night of February, 17, 1864, in the first successful submarine attack in history, which was launched by the Confederate torpedo boat CSS *HUNLEY.* The water was shallow enough that the masts of the Federal ship protruded above the surface, which minimized the loss of life. Of the ship's company, only five were lost. The *Hunley* was also lost in the action.

A house divided against itself. During his series of debates with Stephen Douglas for a seat in the U.S. Senate in 1858, Abraham Lincoln made this remarkable statement about the issue of SLAVERY: "A house divided against itself cannot stand. I believe this government cannot endure, permanently half slave and half free. I do not expect the Union to be dissolved—I do not expect the house to fall—but I do expect it will cease to be divided. It will become all one thing or all the other." That statement helped to push the South toward war, since Lincoln's words were interpreted to mean

that he would be committed to the abolition of SLAVERY by force. In fact, Lincoln's position was not so violent. He was a firm believer in Providence and in the Declaration of Independence and the U.S. Constitution. He expected slavery to die a natural death—after which the house would no longer be divided.

house of bondage. Northern slang for the COTTON BELT; also known as the Land of Jeff.

housewife. Slang for a soldier's kit containing the essentials needed to mend uniforms and other clothing. At first regarded as a luxury, a few months of combat caused the little sewing kit to be regarded as essential. Women were not that far from the army camps, and ZOUAVE units with VIVANDIÈRES often allowed the women to charge for patching clothing. The majority of fighting men, however, mended their own garments with needles, thread, and buttons from their housewives. There are some reports that the sewing kits blocked bullets on the battlefield and saved lives, such as an incident involving Confederate Gen. Clement A. Evans during the July 9, 1864, battle of Monocacy.

hove. N. A variant of the past tense of the verb "TO HEAVE."

Hovey's Babies. A unit of youthful unmarried men recruited by Union Gen. Alvin Peterson Hovey in 1864. There is no record that Hovey came close to his goal of bringing ten thousand single men into the regiment.

how come you so. A home-brewed alcoholic beverage.

howitzer. An artillery piece developed in the Netherlands in the early eighteenth century. The majority were made of bronze and manufactured in three standard sizes designed to throw charges of 12, 24, or 32 pounds. A few large pieces could fire 50-pound ammunition. The howitzer's short tube was chambered, which allowed a small charge to lob a shell a considerable distance. Depending on the type of ammunition used, howitzers were effective anti-personnel and siege weapons.

hubble-bubble. A vernacular phrase for the Far Eastern hookah, a tobacco pipe designed to pass smoke through water—allegedly to cool it—before the smoker inhaled.

huckleberry cavalry. The Missouri State Guard, many of whom eventually enlisted in the Confederate army. Their first major experience of combat was at the August 10, 1861, battle of Wilson's Creek, Missouri.

hulk. N. The rotting or damaged shell of a ship.

hundred circling camps. Volunteers from the East who responded to Abraham Lincoln's early calls for troops were put into camps that encircled the Federal capital at Washington. A view of the campfires of these citizen-soldiers served as one of the inspirations for Julia Ward Howe's "BATTLE HYMN OF THE REPUBLIC." The poem was published in the *Atlantic Monthly* in February 1862, for which Howe received four dollars for the rights. When the lyrics were set to music, the result was the most popular song of the war.

Julia Ward Howe

hundred-day men. Soldiers who enlisted for no fewer and no more than one hundred days of service in the Federal army. Ten days longer than nearly standard ninety-day enlistments, this period was used when Pennsylvania hurriedly called out volunteers to help repel the expected Confederate invasion of the state in 1862.

hunt gold, to. A variant of the phrase "TO SEE THE ELEPHANT," meaning to engage in combat for the first time.

Huntsville. The Texas state prison in Huntsville was used to confine captured Federal officers. All inmates were confined to cells but were sometimes permitted to mingle with the prison population.

hurdle. Fashioned of wickerlike GABIONS, hurdles were rectangular instead of round and were also used to strengthen defensive works as well as to help men ford creeks and rivers when no bridges or pontoons were available.

husband, to. Once meaning to save or to stint, this term was widely used during the war.

***Hydrangea*, USS.** The *Hydrangea* was a former commercial carrier known as the *Hippodome*. Purchased in October 1863 at Erie, New York, the 254-ton wooden screw-steamer was given a battery of three guns—one 20-POUNDER PARROTT RIFLE and two 12-pounder HOWITZERS. Sold at auction after the war, she brought $10,300, which was little more than 20 percent of the purchase price and the cost of repairs while in the service of the U.S. Navy.

I

ice calks. Special devices fastened to the feet of horses and sometimes mules to enable them to traverse ice and snow.

Idaho, **USS.** This screw-steamer was built in Brooklyn at a cost of $298,955. Rated at 2,854 tons, when loaded she required more than 16 feet of water in order to navigate. Launched in October 1864, she went out of service in just eighteen months. Her net cost to the government at the time of her postwar sale was $692,000.

identification tags. Late in the war the U.S. Christian Commission made metal identification tags available to Federal soldiers. These tags were stamped with the soldier's name and unit, and some carried the name of his wife and her place of residence. Prior to this, soldiers wrote their names and units on slips of paper that they pinned to their hats or uniforms so that their bodies could be identified if they were killed in action. More affluent soldiers purchased silver identification badges from SUTLERS or newspaper advertisements.

Île à Vache colony. During the spring of 1863, 468 former slaves embarked from FORT MONROE aboard the *Ocean Ranger* for Île à Vache, a Haitian island, which had been leased by New York financiers for COLONIZATION. Abraham Lincoln was a supporter of the colonization movement, and promoters of this particular scheme promised to provide homes and communities for former slaves who would cultivate cotton. The first proposal was offered by a promoter with a questionable background, so a second proposal was submitted with sponsors who passed congressional muster. Yet when the colonists arrived on the island, they found the land to be mostly jungle and with none of the houses that had been promised. In short order the financiers learned they had made a bad investment and withdrew their support, also abandoning the colonists. In November an agent arrived to inspect the colony and found that nothing could be salvaged from the effort. Less than one year after leaving Virginia, 368 survivors of the ill-fated experiment returned to Union soil aboard the *Marcia C. Day.* Only then did Federal lawmakers learn of the extremely high death rate among the colonists and end all funding of colonization efforts.

Illinois Baboon. A disparaging moniker for Abraham Lincoln. This imagery was exploited to satirize both the man and his administration in Northern newspapers.

immigration. A steady flow of immigrants from Europe continued to reach the Northern states throughout the war. An estimated eight hundred thousand arrived during the course of the war. More than one-fourth of this number came from Germany and almost as many were Irish refugees. Nearly one hundred thousand came from England. No one knows how many immigrants were recruited as they disembarked in the New World, but their number was substantial and they did make a significant contribution to the Union war effort.

Immortal 600. To relieve overcrowding at ANDERSONVILLE in the summer of 1864, 600 Federal prisoners of war were transferred to temporary detention in Charleston pending the availability of sufficient housing in Columbia, South Carolina. The Union captives were dispersed throughout the port city, which at the time was under siege. The Federal commander, Maj. Gen. John G. Foster, took exception to this, claiming that the placement of Union prisoners in Charleston violated the stipulation between the two warring parties not to confine captives in harm's way. Foster chose to retaliate for this and for the mistreatment of Union prisoners in the South by placing Confederate prisoners in an equally dangerous position, and he requested 600 prisoners from the prisoner-of-war camp at FORT DELAWARE. A hand-picked band of Confederate officers was dispatched on August 20 in answer to Foster's request and was confined in an open stockade directly in front of the Union batteries on Morris Island and in the line of fire from Forts Sumter and Moultrie. The Confederate gunners, however, were not deterred in their firing on the Union position. Even after the Federal prisoners were removed from Charleston, Foster left the 600 under fire for a little two more weeks. Incredibly, not a man

The stockade at Morris Island

An area of Fort Pulaski, where the 600 were kept for a while

within the stockade was killed during the time the 600 were exposed to the Confederate guns, despite the fact that eighteen shells exploded over the area and duds fell within the holding area. When the 600 had served their purpose, Foster suggested exchanging the prisoners, but his request was denied by the War Department. They were instead transferred to FORT PULASKI in Savannah, where they stayed from October 23, 1864, to March 4, 1865. Arrangements were finally made for an exchange at City Point, Virginia, and the 600 were transported to that area. Only a handful were exchanged, because the majority of the Confederate prisoners were in extremely bad health and appeared as bad or worse than the survivors recently freed from Andersonville. To save face, the Federal authorities shuttled the remnant of the 600 to Fort Delaware, where they were put on full rations and eventually exchanged in July 1865. Out of the original number, 290 emerged from the Federal prison at the end of the war. Of the other 310 men, 44 had died of disease and exposure, 7 had escaped, and 259 had been exchanged. Remarkably, at any time any one of the prisoners could have taken the OATH OF ALLEGIANCE to end the hardship, but none did. When the prisoners returned home they were accorded hero status and hailed throughout the South as "The Immortal 600"—a name coined by one of the 600 in his published account of the ordeal.

impact fuse. Ordinary FUSES were lighted before a projectile was fired. Impact fuses, however, were designed to explode when the shell struck its target.

Impending Crisis, The. Twenty-seven-year-old Hinton R. Helper, a native of North Carolina, published a scathing critique of Southern SLAVERY in 1857 in a book entitled *The Impending Crisis in the South: How to Meet It.* Basing his argument on a comprehensive study of the 1850 census, Helper compared and contrasted the economies of the North and the South and the roles of laborers in the two sections. He concluded that slaves had an unfair advantage in the competition with poor whites for nonskilled and low-skilled jobs. Bristling with statistics, the volume was addressed to Southern white laborers who owned no slaves. Helper also outlined an eleven-point plan for the abolition of slavery by 1876 that included organizing a political party for nonslaveholding whites, denying the vote to slaveholders, boycotting the services of slaveholders, banning the hiring of slaves by nonslaveholders, and a tax on every slave. The book was published in New York with the assistance of Horace Greeley, and it generated a furor in the COTTON BELT. Southern postmasters refused to deliver the book and allegedly burned any copies they saw; in many places it was illegal to own a copy of the book. Partly because of this reaction in the South, the book sold well in the North. Thirteen thousand copies were sold in the first year of publication. In 1859 Republicans circulated a one-hundred-page abridged version of Helper's material to counter accusations that the party sought the ruin of the South rather than its renovation. The political fallout from the alignment of the party and the book was seen in the House of Representatives. Ohio Congressman John Sherman, a brother of William T. Sherman, was the frontrunner for the position of Speaker of the House. Opposition from slaveholding states was keyed to Sherman's having endorsed Helper's book. After two months of debate, during which time the representatives carried pistols and knives into the chamber, Sherman

was turned out. Similarly, William Seward's bid for the presidency in 1860 foundered—and Abraham Lincoln's candidacy rose—in part because Seward was allegedly linked to the Helper volume. In 1861 Helper sought a position within the Lincoln administration and was named U.S. Consul to Buenos Aires. He did not return to the United States until after the war, in 1866. Once again he

Hinton R. Helper

addressed the ills of the South, focusing on the danger posed by FREEDMEN to the southern working class. Helper wrote three books expounding his own racism and embarrassing Republican politicians. Discredited as a writer and social scientist, he became an agent for American businesses with claims against South American countries. The rest of his life was devoted to the building of a Pan-American railroad, but his accomplishments in this pursuit were minor. On March 8, 1909, he committed suicide. His book, *The Impending Crisis,* ranks alongside Harriet Beecher Stowe's *Uncle Tom's Cabin* and John Brown's raid on Harpers Ferry as major contributors to the heightened tensions that erupted into civil war.

impressment. A synonym for seizure and commandeering private property. Federal legislation empowered the military to seize from civilians any item or article of property that might be needed under emergency conditions. What constituted such emergencies was left to the discretion of the military. After the first few months of relatively gentlemanly conflict, many Union commanders freely exercised their impressment power in their own territory. When martial law was declared in occupied areas, almost anything of use or value was susceptible to impressment. In the South, numerous state legislatures authorized impressment. By 1863 such commandeering of private property was so common that the Confederate Congress authorized the military's seizure of private property when such was deemed necessary. Opposition to this statute, based upon an appeal to STATES' RIGHTS, led to speedy repeal. State and local laws and customs remained in effect, however. As a result, Southern officers authorized the impressment of animals and supplies throughout their jurisdictions. The laws that permitted impressment, however, also addressed compensation. In practice, these laws were difficult to follow and rarely resulted in a fair settlement. In several instances, Southern impressment was enlarged to include the mandatory enlistment of UNIONISTS in the Confederate army.

income tax. No combat of consequence had yet taken place when the special session of Congress called by Abraham Lincoln convened in the summer of 1861. Yet on July 4, 1861, U.S. Secretary of the Treasury Salmon P. Chase of Ohio estimated that he would need more than $300 million to finance the war during the coming fiscal year. The House Ways and Means Committee decided to increase a number of existing taxes but knew that this revenue would not meet demands created by war. Imposition of the first U.S. tax on the income of corporations and individuals was seen as a logical means to secure additional revenue. Yearly incomes between $600 and $10,000 became subject to a 3 percent tax. The initial levy on higher incomes was 5 percent, and in 1864 the rates were raised. During 1863 and 1864 this new revenue measure, which met strenuous opposition throughout the North, yielded only about $22 million. Income tax revenue never met the demands of the Union military, but the measure was not enforced uniformly. Suspended after a decade, the tax was later ruled unconstitutional. A similar income tax plan was implemented in the South in April 1863, but the revenue generated was too little to address the needs of the Confederate government.

in detail. A movement of troops that involved sending one unit after another toward the enemy.

Indian. A nickname for Donehogawa, a full-blooded Seneca who fought in the Union army as Ely S. Parker. He had known Grant casually in Galena, Illinois, and became more acquainted with the general during the siege of Vicksburg. Parker accepted a position as a secretary on Grant's staff and was present at the surrender ceremonies at Appomattox Court House. He wrote the only official record of the proceedings.

***Indianola*, USS.** Built by contract with Joseph Brown at Cincinnati, this GUNBOAT displaced only 511 tons. Gen. Lew Wallace seized the vessel and manned her for what he described as "the protection of Cincinnati." Heavily laden, she could navigate in water a trifle more than five feet deep. A hybrid having two side-wheels plus a screw, the steamer's five boilers gave her unusual speed. She was among the vessels that successfully ran the gamut of Confederate batteries at Vicksburg in February, 1863, but was subsequently captured and sunk. Few river boats in Federal service had a longer or more colorful career. Obsolete and useless at war's end, the *Indianola* was raised and towed to Mound City, Illinois. Put on the auction block there, the once-valiant warship was sold for $3,000.

NAVAL HISTORICAL CENTER

India rubber. Natives of Brazil, Peru, and Guiana had long ago harvested a sap they called *cahuchu* (later *caoutchouc*) and used to make bottles and tubes. Europeans used the substance in making shoes. When the material was adopted in the U.S. domestic market, it was referred to as rubber because erasing pencil marks was among its first practical applications. Processed India rubber was used to make machine belting, water hoses, life preservers, furniture coverings, travel bags, and tents. Because of its water-repellent qualities and its elasticity, the substance (also called "gum elastic") was used during the Civil War to waterproof tents, pontoons, bedrolls, raincoats, shoes, and other essentials. Although the imported material was more readily available in the North than in the South, Confederates were able to exchange cotton for the rubber needs of their military.

indifferent. An adjective used to denote the inferior quality of either workmanship or finished products.

infantry. Soldiers trained, armed, and equipped to fight on foot. The word is derived from the European reference to foot soldiers who had in their youth formerly been servants and followers of knights.

infernal machine. A term used to designate any and all relatively new weapons that were considered to be less than sporting in character. TORPEDOES (though never self-propelled during the war), land MINES fashioned from artillery shells, and incendiaries that used GREEK FIRE fell into this category.

inflammation of the lungs. Pneumonia, so common by the time of the war that doctors could accurately predict a patient's death.

In God We Trust. Leaders on both sides were fervent in their expressions of faith that God would bring them victory. Possibly as a concession to this widely held belief by political and military leaders and the public, the U.S. Treasury incorporated the brief statement of faith on Federal currency for the first time in 1864 on the two-cent bronze coin.

in ordinary. N. A designation for a warship out of commission or lying at a dock.

insignia—enlisted men and noncommissioned officers. On both sides, privates fought without any insignia of rank. Two narrow *V*-shaped chevrons designated a corporal, three indicated a sergeant. First sergeants wore three chevrons above a diamond-shaped piece. A Federal quartermaster sergeant displayed three horizontal strips of cloth across the top of his chevrons. Three cloth arches designated the highest noncommissioned rank, sergeant major. The insignia of INFANTRY were made of light blue cloth, ARTILLERY wore red insignia, and CAVALRY displayed yellow emblems. This color scheme was standard among all combatants, Northern as well as Southern.

insignia—officers. An officer's emblem of rank was displayed on his SHOULDER STRAPS. A second lieutenant wore unadorned rectangular shoulder straps. Two short horizontal bars indicated a first lieutenant and four a captain. Oak leaves denoted majors (silver) and lieutenant colonels (gold). An eagle distinguished colonels, and a star identified generals. One star marked a brigadier, two a major general, and three a lieutenant general. Southern officers wore their distinguishing insignia on their collars. One bar designated a second lieutenant, two a first lieutenant, and three a captain. Above this rank the Confederates used stars: one for a major, two for a lieutenant colonel, and three for a colonel. Unlike their Union counterparts, Confederate generals did not use insignia to distinguish between the grades of generals. All of them, from brigadiers to full generals, wore three stars within a wreath. Union naval officers wore time-honored insignias on their sleeves. An ensign wore a horizontal bar topped by a star. Two bars and a star designated a master, and three bars and a star identified a lieutenant. A lieutenant commander wore four bars, a commander five, and a captain displayed two sets of three bars. Commodores wore a seventh bar between two sets of three bars. Eight bars distinguished a rear admiral. Numerous

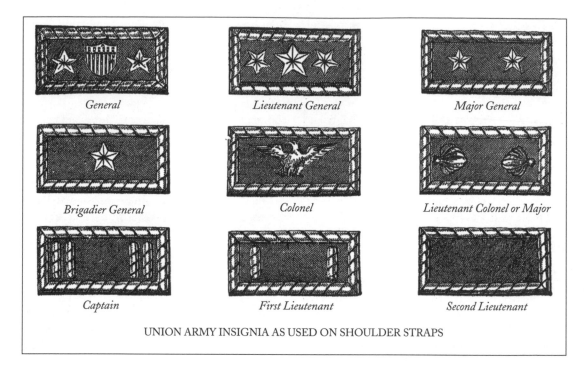

General	Lieutenant General	Major General
Brigadier General	Colonel	Lieutenant Colonel or Major
Captain	First Lieutenant	Second Lieutenant

UNION ARMY INSIGNIA AS USED ON SHOULDER STRAPS

high-ranking officers, among whom Grant was notable and conspicuous, paid little or no attention to the trappings of rank.

instant. A designation meaning "a day of the current month." For example, in his record of the defense of FORT SUMTER, Samuel W. Crawford noted that—following a meeting of the officers in early April 1861—their food would enable them to hold out until "the 15th instant" (i.e., April 15).

instrument. A telescopic sight.

insurrection. The term preferred by Abraham Lincoln to designate the conflict of 1861–65. The Northern president did not call it a war because, in his opinion, that terminology implied that he recognized the Confederacy as a nation separate from the United States.

intelligence. Information conveyed by word of mouth, written messages, telegraph messages, signal flags, newspapers, or other sources.

intelligent. Synonymous with *intelligence*. For example, an account of the New York draft riots asserted that ignorance prevailed at the HEADQUARTERS of Gen. John E. Wool "despite the intelligent staff with which he was surrounded."

interchangeable parts. Until manufacturers began producing uniform machine parts, nearly every machine component had to be fashioned individually. Eli Whitney is credited with the idea of interchangeable parts, but considerable evidence suggests that this practice was first implemented at the U.S. Arsenal in Harpers Ferry, Virginia, or at a Waltham, Massachusetts, factory that mass produced watches.

intercourse. An exchange of conversation or a process of negotiation between persons or governments. Some used the phrase to label the forbidden practice more widely known as FRATERNIZATION.

interior lines. Any situation in which a commander had the capacity to send orders and move troops rapidly. Such lines were often created when forces on one side were deployed more skillfully than the other. Other instances resulted from superior communications, such as the telegraph, or from better transportation by railroads or wagon trains.

intrenching (entrenching) tools. Gear needed to dig trenches. Civil War soldiers learned almost by accident the value of trenches in warfare. In the early battles of Shiloh, Antietam, and Fredericksburg, sunken roads were used as natural rifle pits. By 1864 both armies resorted to trenches to fortify their camps. In later combat, trenches played a valuable role in the Wilderness, Spotsylvania, northern Georgia, and Petersburg. As a result, attacking forces were fully exposed on open ground while the defenders barely showed themselves.

Intrepid. Thaddeus Sobieski Constantine Lowe's best-known observation balloon. Made chief of army aeronautics by Abraham Lincoln in the aftermath of First Manassas, "Professor" Lowe eventually controlled a fleet of seven observation balloons. Of these, the 32,000 cubic foot *Intrepid* was the largest. See also BALLOON CORPS.

inundations. Dammed waterways in front of defensive works. These pools were usually six feet deep, but if that depth could not be achieved, a TROUS DE LOUP was dug into the waterway. The only instance in which inundations were recorded during the war was at Knoxville, Tennessee, where segments of the Federal line were faced with dammed streams.

Invalid Corps. Initially, soldiers incapacitated by wounds or disease were medically discharged from the service. As the war dragged on, disabled soldiers were reassigned to noncombat duty so that others could fight. In April 1863 the Union War Department created the Invalid Corps, two BATTALIONS of disabled men. The first comprised of men with disabilities who qualified for GARRISON duty; the second was made up of those whose handicaps limited their labors to hospital duties. The two battalions were organized into companies and regiments, and eventually the surgeon general was placed in command of the second battalion. In the spring of 1864 the corps was renamed the VETERAN RESERVE CORPS, and an estimated sixty thousand men filled its ranks prior to its being disbanded at the end of the war. In the South, an Invalid Corps was established in 1864. It was not structured as BATTALIONS, REGIMENTS, and COMPANIES, but functioned in much the same manner as its counterpart.

invest, to. The essential and preliminary steps necessary prior to a siege, including the control of all roads, canals, and railroads that might be used to resupply the besieged.

investment. A full-blown siege, short or long. During the lengthy siege of Vicksburg, the Federal investment of Port Hudson, Louisiana, began on May 27, 1863, and lasted until July 9.

Irish Brigade. Thomas F. Meagher, a self-styled Irish revolutionary, hoped to lead a body of seasoned soldiers to his native land to fight for independence. He seized the opportunity presented by the conflict between the North and the South to call together Irish immigrants from the ranks of the New York Militia, and the Irish Brigade was formed of the 63d, 69th, and 88th New York regiments. Organized soon after the battle of First Manassas, the Irish unit was subjected to considerable derision until it proved itself in battle. FLAG-BEARERS of each company carried a green regimental flag in addition to the national emblem. During the Peninsula campaign, the Irish Brigade was reinforced with the addition

Thomas F. Meagher

of the non-Irish 29th Massachusetts, which was replaced by the Irish 28th Massachusetts in November 1862. A month earlier the Irish 116th Pennsylvania was also added to the brigade. Even with these additions, however, the Irish Brigade flirted with annihilation. By distinguishing itself in the battles of Antietam, Fredericksburg, Chancellorsville, and Gettysburg, high casualties almost dissolved the brigade. Despite the high rate of attrition, the Irish Brigade maintained its identity although it lost its exclusive Irish fraternity. A reorganization of the Army of the Potomac in 1864 shuffled the regiments into separate brigades, but in November of that year the Irish Brigade was reconstituted. The Irish Brigade was widely praised for its participation in some of the most gallant charges of the war, and three of its five commanders were killed in combat or died of mortal wounds. At war's end, the brigade was mustered out—the INFANTRY in June 1865 and the ARTILLERY in September 1865. The soldiers returned to the North and, as far as is known, did little for the cause of Irish independence.

Iron Brigade (Black Hat Brigade). Soon after the July 21, 1861, battle of First Manassas (Bull Run), the 2d, 6th, and 7th Wisconsin and the 19th Indiana were formed into the only all-western BRIGADE in the Federal Army of the Potomac. Command of the brigade, known initially as the Western Brigade, went to Gen. Rufus King, but failing health forced him to resign. In May 1862 Gen. John Gibbon was assigned to command. By then the distinctive uniform of the Western Brigade had been pro-

cured by Col. Lysander Cutler of the 6th Wisconsin: oversized frock coats, sky-blue trousers, and tall, black Hardee hats. Fierce fighting at Groveton, South Mountain, and Antietam contributed to the unit's nickname as the "Iron Brigade," allegedly coined by Gen. Joseph Hooker. The 24th Michigan was joined to the brigade during the autumn of 1862, but the brigade played only a minor role in the battles of Fredericksburg and Chancellorsville. At Gettysburg, however, the Iron Brigade lived up to its name. More than 1,200 of its 1,800 men became casualties during the fighting at McPherson's Ridge and Seminary Ridge, buying valuable time for the rest of the Union army to be deployed in the field. After Gettysburg, the nickname remained but the regiments were virtually gone. Most were absorbed into other brigades. The 2d Wisconsin was disbanded in July 1864. The 6th and 7th Wisconsin served until the end of the war. The 19th Indiana was merged with the 20th Indiana in October 1864. The 24th Michigan had dwindled to 120 men by the time the siege of Petersburg had begun in June 1864. It was withdrawn from the field in February 1865. The last act of the Michigan regiment was to serve as the military escort for Abraham Lincoln's funeral procession in Springfield in April 1865.

ironclad. N. A vessel either made of metal or whose wooden sides were shielded with metal

USS Galena, *one of the first ironclads*

USS Choctaw, *one of the ironclad gunboats*

plating. Although the French and British had experimented with ironclad warships prior to the American Civil War, it was not until the March 8, 1862, battle of the ironclads CSS *Virginia* and USS *Monitor* that wooden warships were proved obsolete. The South contracted the construction of sixty ironclads during the war, but only twenty-two were commissioned. Most of these were designed for river and harbor protection rather than as an oceangoing fleet designed to break the wartime BLOCKADE of Southern ports. The North constructed approximately sixty ironclads, but only one of them—the USS *New Ironsides*—qualified as a seaworthy warship.

Ironclad Oath. The oath had its roots in a loyalty oath prescribed by Federal legislation of July 2, 1862, but it was overshadowed during the war by Abraham Lincoln's benign approach to postwar plans for RECONSTRUCTION. Wartime loyalty oaths had required future allegiance; the Ironclad Oath, however, included a pledge of past loyalty as well as future fidelity. As far as loyalty oaths were concerned with postwar measures, the president favored a ONE-TENTH PLAN, that is, among the qualifications for the reestablishment of self-governing state governments in the seceded states, a loyalty oath was required by a number of voters equal to 10 percent of the number of voters who had participated in the election of 1860 in that state. Congressional opponents of the president's plan outlined a plan of reconstruction that, first,

stipulated that reconstruction would be controlled by Congress, not the president, and second, that 50 percent of the voters be required to take an ironclad oath that they had never been disloyal to the government. These measures were included in the Wade-Davis Bill in the spring of 1864, which passed both houses of Congress by close votes but was pocket vetoed by Lincoln. Several elements of the Wade-Davis Bill, however, were revived after the war in the Reconstruction Act of March 23, 1867. Subsequent legislation gave wide latitude to administrators of the oath in determining if an individual, on the basis of past activities, was eligible to declare loyalty to the Union. Few Southerners could or would swear to past allegiance, and this barred them from voting and from holding political office, which was one of the objectives of the legislation. UNIONISTS were also frustrated in that they could not always prove their wartime faithfulness to the Federal government. Also complicating the matter was the provision in the legislation that allowed the oath to be waived on an individual basis by a two-thirds vote of Congress. As a result, much of the rebuilding of the South's infrastructure was entrusted to Northerners who moved south after the war (derided as carpetbaggers) and a small number of Southern Republicans (labeled scalawags).

iron doughnut. See SHERMAN'S HAIRPINS (NECKTIES). Also known as JEFF DAVIS NECKTIES.

iron horse. A nickname for a railroad locomotive.

iron stove. A derisive alias for body ARMOR.

ironed. To be restrained by handcuffs, leg irons, or both.

irrepressible conflict. The phrase is attributed to William H. Seward from an address he delivered at Rochester, New York, on October 25, 1858, in which he described the sectional tension in the country as "an irrepressible conflict between opposing and enduring forces, and it means that the United States must and will, sooner or later, become either entirely a slaveholding nation, or entirely a free-labor nation." Seward went on to say, "It is the failure to apprehend this great truth that induces so many unsuccessful attempts at final compromises between the slave and free States, and it is the existence of this great fact that renders all such pre-tended compromises, when made, vain and ephemeral." Earlier, on June 16, 1858, in seeking his party's senatorial nomination, Abraham Lincoln drew upon the imagery of "a HOUSE DIVIDED" in stating his conviction that "this government cannot endure permanently half slave and half free. . . . It will become all one thing, or all the other." The comments of both men reflect the changing attitudes in the North in the latter half of the 1850s. The public had become disenchanted with the idea of further political compromise, and the bitter fighting in Kansas in the mid-1850s was viewed as a harbinger of things to

William H. Seward

come. The "irrepressible conflict" became a catch phrase in both sections of the nation, and the presidential election of 1860 proved to be the flash point for the approaching civil war.

issue. In military parlance, the outcome of a charge, a feint, or other confrontation with the enemy.

***Ivy,* CSS.** A side-wheel steamer, this vessel was purchased at New Orleans in 1861. She was 191 feet long, displaced 454 tons, and had an engine with a cylinder that was 44 inches in diameter. Mounting only two guns and restricted to river service, the steamer was burned in the Yazoo River to prevent her capture.

***Ivy,* USS.** Compared with the Rebel vessel of the same name, this steamer was a midget. In September 1862 she was transferred from the War Department to the U.S. Navy for use as a tug. Originally privately owned and named *Terror,* the *Ivy* was kept in such good condition that she fetched a surprising $5,650 when sold at auction in August 1865.

J

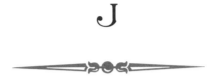

Jack. N. A naval ensign flown by a ship of war only when it was moored and anchored and always in conjunction with the national flag; it designated the ship's nationality. The ensign was so named because it flew from the jack staff at the ship's bow. Often the canton of the national flag served as the Jack. The Union Jack was blue with thirty-four white stars; the Confederate Jack was a rectangular version of the Southern battle flag, a blue St. Andrew's cross with eleven white stars on a red field.

Jack. A horse used by Ulysses S. Grant.

jackboot. A large, heavy boot that extended well above the knee, offering some protection to its wearer.

jackass gun. A mountain HOWITZER, used in difficult terrain that required it to be carried by mules rather than pulled by horses.

Jackass Regiment. The 1st Indiana Heavy Artillery, so-called because its field PIECES were drawn by mules rather than horses. Originally the unit had entered Federal service as the 21st Indiana Infantry, but was reorganized as the 1st Heavy Artillery in February 1863. The REGIMENT saw action primarily in Mississippi, Louisiana, and Alabama, participating in the battles of Port Hudson and Sabine Pass, joining the operations against Mobile, and serving GARRISON duty in

Baton Rouge and New Orleans. The men were mustered out on January 10, 1866.

jacknife. A knife with two or more blades that folded into its case when not in use. Almost all soldiers carried one, and because it was regarded as essential, captors occasionally permitted prisoners to keep theirs.

Jaeger rifle. The U.S. Model 1841 RIFLE, also known as the MISSISSIPPI and YAGER rifle.

jambiers. Black leather leggings worn over GAITERS by some early ZOUAVE units.

James rifle. This was a 3.8-inch caliber, 14-POUNDER RIFLED bronze CANNON designed by Charles T. James—an expert machinist and mechanic, superintendent of a number of cotton mills in Providence, Rhode Island, an officer of the Rhode Island Militia, and a former U.S. senator. James developed a rifling process for artillery PIECES so they would accommodate an elongated shell of his own design (see JAMES SHELL). The new pieces weighed approximately 900 pounds and had a range of 1,700 yards and required only a dozen ounces of gunpowder. The weapons were produced by the Ames Manufacturing Company of Chicopee, Massachusetts, and used a bronze GUN TUBE that was similar to the 3-inch ORD-NANCE RIFLE, which was made of wrought iron. The James rifling system was also used to adapt existing SMOOTHBORES to fire rifled ammunition, and most of these were bronze Model 1841 6-pounders, which were occasionally and mistakenly referred to as James rifles. In addition to field pieces, rebored smoothbores of the James system were also used on Union GUNBOATS. In April 1862, James rifles were used in the attack on Fort Pulaski, Georgia, and their accuracy and effectiveness were exaggerated. As a result, this experiment with rifled bronze pieces was short-lived, because the friction from the projectiles quickly wore down the soft bronze, in effect turning the guns into smoothbores. Yet as late as the July 1863 battle of Gettysburg, the 2d Connecticut Artillery was still equipped with four James rifles, making it the only battery in the Army of the Potomac not to be equipped with 12-pounder NAPOLEONS or iron rifles.

James River Bridge. One of the engineering marvels of the period, this 2,100-foot structure—at the time, the longest PONTOON BRIDGE ever built—spanned the James River, linking Fort Powhatan with Wyanoke Landing. It was erected during a single day as Ulysses S. Grant shifted his army from Cold Harbor, to the northeast of Richmond, to the southern bank of the James to lay siege to the railroad center at Petersburg, southeast of Richmond. The construction of the bridge was the result of two months' planning as 450 engineers, working from both banks on June

A pontoon bridge over the James River

14, 1864, linked more than 100 pontoons in less than eight hours. The designers had to address the strong tidal current to which the bridge would be subjected and the depth of the river at the site of the crossing—approximately ninety feet. As soon as the bridge was completed, it took almost four days for the Union army to cross the bridge. When the crossing was completed, the engineers dismantled the bridge into three barges and moved them downriver to City Point, Grant's new HEADQUARTERS.

James shell. This artillery ammunition was developed by Charles T. James for rifled field PIECES. The seven-inch-long projectile weighed almost eleven pounds and displayed a distinctive rib pattern at its base. The base was covered with a tin sleeve, secured with a lead ring. When fired, gas was forced into the base of the shell and through the ribbed slots in the lower part of the projectile, forcing the thin metal sabot to expand and engage the rifling, which made the shell rotate. A significant problem with the ammunition occurred when the shell was fired over friendly troops: After leaving the GUN TUBE, the shells lost their SABOTS, which fell into the ranks. A redesigned shell addressed this shortcoming and weighed almost fifteen pounds. In the field, however, James shells had a history of poor fragmentation.

***Jamestown*, CSS.** Earlier known as the *Thomas Jefferson*, this side-wheel river steamer was detained in June 1861 by Gen. Robert E. Lee while he was in command of Virginia's military. The vessel was seized at Richmond by Confederates a few weeks later. Armed with only two guns, in May 1862 the steamer was sunk in the James River near Drewry's Bluff in an unsuccessful attempt to close the river to Federal vessels. In September 1864 the ship was found to be still lying on the riverbed, along with at least four smaller vessels.

***Jamestown* (schooner).** Hired by the government to transport coal very early in the war, this craft may have been the vessel that was boarded by men of the USS *Dale* on August 24, 1861.

***Jamestown* (steamer).** Previously known as the *Patrick Henry* (not the CSS *Patrick Henry*) when purchased or seized by Federals, this vessel mounted six or seven guns. It was operating in the James River during the summer of 1863.

***Jamestown*, USS.** This sloop of war, built by government contract and launched in 1844, cost $303,807 on June 1, 1851. A wooden sailing sloop of 1,150 tons, in 1861 she was given a battery of six 8-inch guns and fourteen 32-pounders. The vessel was decommissioned after the war and sold at auction for $20,200.

***Java*, USS.** The hull of this 2,354-ton SLOOP was built at New York at a cost of $400,000. Since the vessel was not ready to be launched at war's end, construction was halted and was never resumed. Eventually the hulk was broken up at the New York Navy Yard.

Jayhawker. Antislavery zealots in Kansas during the 1850s. Their goal was to keep SLAVERY out of the territory that hoped soon to be a state. The abolitionist John Brown did not consider himself a Jayhawker since he directed his own antislavery program. The fighting that made the region Bloody Kansas for nearly a decade was pointless: after Kansas gained statehood, a census revealed only two slaves in the state. Neither the climate nor the dominant crops was suitable for slave labor.

Jeff Davis. (1) A small black horse seized at the Mississippi plantation owned by Joseph Davis, brother of the Confederate president, and presented to Ulysses S. Grant. (2) The original name of Robert E. Lee's horse, Traveller.

Jeff Davis Hat. See HARDEE HAT.

Jeff Davis neckties. See SHERMAN'S HAIRPINS (NECKTIES). Also known as IRON DOUGHNUTS.

Jeff Davis's Pet Wolves. The nickname of the 1st Louisiana Battalion, a ZOUAVE unit also known as Coppens Zouaves. The BATTALION was organized by George Auguste Gaston Coppens in February 1861 and trained and garrisoned at Pensacola, Florida. In early 1862 the unit was ordered to Virginia, where it participated in almost every battle of the year, from Williamsburg through Antietam, and in the process almost annihilated itself. The remnants of the command were reassigned to Brig. Gen. Harry Hays's Louisiana Brigade, and the 1st Louisiana was officially disbanded on January 18, 1865.

Jefferson boots. This was the regulation footwear used by Federal INFANTRY during the Civil War. The military terminology is somewhat vague, but in 1854 the U.S. Army quartermaster general asserted that footwear for mounted soldiers would be termed "boots" and footwear for the infantry would be called "bootees." (The term "shoe" was applied to civilian footwear.) Regulations thereafter mention only the "ankle boot" (likely a mid-calf-high boot without lacing) and the "Jefferson boot." The term "Jefferson" implied that the boot was laced (stemming from Thomas Jefferson's wearing laced shoes—rather than buckled shoes, a distinction of aristocrats—to his 1801 inauguration). Jefferson boots were available in varying ankle-high styles and were the only contract shoe issued by the Union army. The basic three-part bootee varied from four or five lace holes but had no eyelets. Although serviceable, the shoes were exceptionally heavy and subject to tearing. On an average, a pair of these low-cut "bootees" lasted between twenty and thirty days in the field. The Confederate army copied the shoe style.

Jefferson Davis. A life-size image of the Confederate president, painted on boards, that was used for target practice by the 4th Illinois Cavalry.

***Jefferson Davis*, CSS.** A full-rigged BARK that was fitted out at Charleston in June 1861, this PRIVATEER vessel displaced 187 tons. The five old iron guns she carried were manufactured in England and were ineffective except at very close range. Many U.S. Navy crews clamored for a chance to hunt her down, for the privateer's career was launched as the slaver *Echo*.

Jenifer saddle. During Jefferson Davis's tenure as U.S. secretary of war, measures were taken to improve equipment in almost all branches of the military, especially for mounted soldiers. Lt. Walter H. Jenifer, a native of Baltimore then in the 2d U.S. Cavalry, focused on the efforts to redesign the military saddle. Although he was late in submitting his design for consideration, he did secure a patent. When the Southern states seceded, he offered his services and his saddle to the Confederacy. In short order, Jenifer's design was adopted and prescribed as the official saddle for Southern cavalry. In practice, however, the saddle was hugely unpopular. The flat seat was acceptable under normal conditions, but the rigors of campaigning wore heavily on horses, and the Jenifer saddle irritated the animals' withers and backbone. By 1863 the saddle was so abhorred by the military that Robert E. Lee addressed the Ordnance Department and recommended that the saddle be changed. In the meantime, Jenifer sued the Confederate government for patent infringement when many saddlers in the South took liberties with his design, few of which did anything to improve it. Eventually, Jenifer was paid off and his design was replaced with others patterned after the McClellan and Hope saddles.

Jennie. This was a 12-POUNDER HOWITZER of the Troup Artillery attached to Cobb's Brigade. The piece was captured by the 95th Pennsylvania at Crampton's Gap, Maryland, on September 14, 1862, in the fighting for South Mountain. Cobb reported that the piece had been "lost by an accident of axle," but Union Col. Gustavus W. Town reported that the Confederate artillerists "merely disabled it temporarily by throwing off one wheel from the LIMBER, which was left with the horses

near at hand," then fled as his Pennsylvanians advanced on the position.

Jennison's monuments. Charlie "Doc" Jennison, a prominent JAYHAWKER, defined his life's mission as keeping SLAVERY out of Kansas. He shot, slashed, and burned a wide swath through the territory, and his raids on farmhouses and settlements left behind so many lone chimneys standing among blackened ruins that they came to be viewed as his personal monuments. Later serving in the Federal army as a colonel, Jennison's 7th and 17th Kansas Cavalry were notorious for horse theft and pillaging.

Jessie Scouts. Scouts under Union Gen. John C. Frémont who operated chiefly in Missouri, often wearing Confederate uniforms. Frémont named this group for his wife, the former Jessie Benton.

jewelry attached. A prisoner having an iron ball and chain attached to a leg or having been "double ironed," with both legs so confined.

***J. J. Crittenden*, USS.** Desperation must have prompted the man who agreed to buy this vessel for the U.S. Navy on May 19, 1863. Officials were obligated to pay only $1,500 for the captured hulk, but she was worthless for naval service. Although the purchase contract was honored, the ship never sailed. Unfit to serve any other useful function, it was sunk as an obstruction.

Joe Brown's Pets. The Georgia State Militia, so-called because Gov. Joseph E. Brown tried repeatedly and usually successfully to keep its members out of Confederate service.

Joe Brown's Pikes. The scarceness of weapons in the South at the beginning of the war led Georgia Gov. Joseph E. Brown to arm his state troops with what came to be known as "Joe Brown's Pikes," which Confederate Gen. John B. Gordon described as "a sort of rude BAYONET, or steel lance, fastened . . . to long poles or handles, and were given to men who had no other arms." In addressing how the pikes were to be used, Brown said, "Let every army have a large reserve, armed with a good pike, and a long heavy SIDE KNIFE, to be brought upon the field, with a shout for victory, or when the time comes for a charge with bayonets." To follow up the anticipated rout of the Union army, Brown observed, "When the retreat commences, let the pursuit be rapid, and if the enemy throw down their guns and are likely to outrun us, if need be, throw down the pike and keep close at their heels with the knife, till each man has hewed down, at least, one of his adversaries." Two patterns of pikes were manufactured in answer to Brown's call. One was a cloverleaf design, with a ten-inch main blade and two leaf-shaped blades to be used as bridle cutters. The other was a spring-loaded retractable blade that was triggered to spear an enemy. The state paid five dollars per pike. Yet while Brown was convinced that the pikes would be an effective weapon in combat, few troops were willing to test the efficiency of the pike against the massed firepower of Union soldiers. Less than ten months after Brown had issued the call for the weapons, he was summoned before the state assembly to account for the "squandering" of limited funds on pikes as opposed to more practical weapons. The governor cited examples of the successful use of pikes in warfare then explained that these were temporary measures until guns became available. Records indicated that the state had acquired 7,099 pikes and, at the request of Jefferson Davis, had sent 1,229 to the Confederate armies in the west. Although the remaining pikes were duly issued to the state militia, there is no record that these weapons were ever used in combat. During the infamous Andrews Raid in April 1862, the soldiers encamped at Big Shanty complained that they could do little to thwart the theft of the Confederate train because they had only pikes with which to fight.

Johnny Shiloh. A nickname bestowed on drummer boy John Lincoln Clem; see DRUMMER BOY OF CHICKAMAUGA.

Johnson's Island. Most Civil War prison camps had previously been training camps established at the beginning of the war. The prison at Johnson's Island, however, was planned from the beginning to be a detention camp for Southern captives. The three-hundred-acre heavily wooded island in Lake Erie's Sandusky Bay, about a mile offshore and a little more than two miles from Sandusky, Ohio, was leased by the Federal government for this purpose. When construction began in 1861, planners estimated that the forty-acre prison site should accommodate about one thousand captives, who were to be housed in three-room barracks designed to hold 180 men each. The facility also included quarters for guards, a washroom, a hospital, two mess halls (Johnson's Island was one of the few prison camps in which prisoners did not do their own cooking), a blockhouse, and a guardboat. The first few hundred prisoners arrived in February 1862. Although these included political prisoners, the majority of the captives were Confederate officers. Soon the camp housed many more than the one thousand for which it had been planned. Shelter was adequate, but food and clothing were scarce. In 1863 a prisoner escaped to Canada, and his news of the situation in the camp contributed to a far-fetched scheme to liberate the camp. The exploit was entrusted in 1864 to Confederate naval Capt. John Y. Beall, but the plot was foiled and Beall was captured. He was tried, sentenced, and hanged in New York in February 1865. By the end of the war, the prison population at Johnson's Island had swollen to three thousand.

join in battle, to. To engage in combat rather than TO FEINT or demonstrate against the enemy.

Joint Committee on the Conduct of the War. Established in December 1861 as an investigating committee of the House of Representatives, this board was founded in the aftermath of the Federal debacle at the battle of Ball's Bluff on October 21, 1861. Over the course of the war, the membership of the committee expanded and eventually included Andrew Johnson, but from the beginning it was clearly a partisan committee with a political agenda that did little good and little harm. The committee was dominated by RADICAL REPUBLICANS, particularly Benjamin Wade, Zachariah Chandler, and George W. Julian, and it assumed broad investigative powers into the military misadventures of the Federal war effort. In particular, the committee scrutinized generals who were perceived as conservative or Democrats and specifically directed their efforts on ridding the army of Gen. George B. McClellan. To accomplish this, they examined many of McClellan's subordinates, such as Gen. Charles P. Stone for the Ball's Bluff mishap and Fitz John Porter for the defeat at Second Manassas. Both men's careers were ruined as a result. On the other hand, the committee did what it could to support Republican and ABOLITIONIST generals even after their incompetence had been demonstrated in the field. Among this group were Benjamin F. Butler, John C. Frémont, and Joseph Hooker. In 1864 the committee's power was enlarged, and the members probed such atrocities as the April 12, 1864, massacre at Fort Pillow and the treatment of Union prisoners. Overall, however, the committee was not so much focused on the successes and failures of the Union army in the field as it was on managing Lincoln's military decisions. The members of this committee, however, had no more military skill or genius than the president. Lincoln cooperated with the committee when it suited his purposes and ignored it when he disagreed with its findings. Thus committee was frustrated in its efforts to dispose of George Gordon Meade, Ulysses S. Grant, and William H. Seward. Nevertheless, until the group was disbanded in June 1865, the committee vigorously advocated Radical Republican causes and harsh RECONSTRUCTION for the last year of the war.

jolly boat. N. A small boat used by a ship's crew for general work.

Josh. A Southern soldier from Arkansas.

Joslyn carbine. This breechloading weapon was widely used by Union CAVALRY in the latter years of the war. Manufactured by the Joslyn Firearms Company of Stonington, Connecticut, this sturdy seven-pound single-shot CARBINE fired a .52-caliber rimfire CARTRIDGE. During 1864 and 1865, the Federal government purchased eleven thousand Joslyn carbines. Private parties—states, units, and individuals—purchased another forty-five hundred.

Journal of the Southern Historical Society. A periodical largely devoted to Southern views and accounts of the war. Launched in Richmond in 1876, publication continued until forty-nine volumes had been issued. Now available in reprint form, some editions of which include detailed indexes, these volumes include a great deal of material not easily found elsewhere.

Jubilee, **USS.** Although purchased at Portland, Maine, by the U.S. Navy, there was never any thought of using this vessel in combat. Instead, she was loaded with an estimated two hundred tons of scrap granite and sailed southward to be scuttled as a member of the STONE FLEET.

jumper. A BOUNTY JUMPER.

Junaluska, **CSS.** Purchased at Norfolk in 1861, this steam-driven tug was given a battery of two guns that were never used in combat. After a single year of operation, the vessel was dismantled and sold. It was named for a Cherokee leader who reputedly saved the life of Andrew Jackson at Horseshoe Bend, Alabama.

June rise. The Upper Mississippi River's semiannual increase in depth brought about by spring rains. This rising began in mid- or late June and continued for several weeks.

junk. N. Beef that had been preserved by heavy salting. It was said to be about as edible as old rope.

K

Kangaroo. A horse found on the field after the April 6–7, 1862, battle of Shiloh. The animal likely belonged to a Confederate officer, and it was noted that it excelled at jumping fences and ditches. Ulysses S. Grant claimed it as his own and gave it the name Kangaroo.

katydid. A term for Virginia Military Institute cadets and other young and inexperienced soldiers. The word stems from the green color of the insect, which seemed to make its name appropriate for GREEN TROOPS.

Kearny Medal. At an engagement near Chantilly, Virginia, on September 1, 1862, Union Gen. Philip Kearney mistakenly rode into a Confederate position and was killed. Grieving subordinates commissioned a medal in his honor from the New York City firm of Ball, Black, and Company. The medal was made of gold in the form of a Maltese cross with a circle that contained the words *dulce et decorum est pro patria mori* and another with Kearny's name. The name of the recipient was engraved on the back of the cross, which was suspended by a ribbon from a clasp. More than three hundred were distributed to

Philip Kearny

officers of Kearny's division who had served honorably under Kearny's leadership. Later, Kearny's successor, Brig. Gen. David B. Birney, authorized a divisional decoration for enlisted men. Dubbed the Kearny Cross, the bronze "cross of valor" was also suspended by a ribbon. The medal was inscribed "Kearny Cross" on one side and "Birney's Division" on the obverse. No one knows how many of these divisional decorations were awarded, but at least two were given to women— one being Marie Tebe, a VIVANDIÈRE, after the May 1863 battle of Chancellorsville, and the other a nurse.

***Kearsarge*, USS.** This 1,500-ton Mohican-class steam sloop of war was built at the Portsmouth Navy Yard in Kittery, Maine, and was commissioned in January 1862. Immediately the ship was dispatched to European waters to patrol for Confederate COMMERCE RAIDERS. In June 1864 the ship detected CSS *Alabama* at Cherbourg, and on June 19 the two ships engaged in one of the most memorable sea battles of the war. Both vessels were comparable in size and weaponry, but after

NAVAL HISTORICAL CENTER

The engagement between Kearsarge *and* Alabama

an hour's fight the Southern ship was heavily damaged and sinking. *Kearsarge* also pursued CSS *Florida* and ended the war in European waters, awaiting the appearance of CSS *Stonewall*. After the war the Union ship had at least four other tours of duty until she wrecked on February 2, 1894, in the Caribbean.

kedge, to. N. To move a vessel by pulling it toward a special anchor known as a kedge.

keelson. N. A stout timber laid over the middle of the floor timbers over the keel so as to bind the floor timbers to the keel.

keening. To many who heard the famous REBEL YELL for the first time, it seemed much like a Irish wail called keening. Although these collective sounds were quite different, the battlefield scream was often given the Irish name.

***Keokuk*, USS.** Originally named the *Moodna* and built in New York City by contract, this twin-screw experimental iron steamer cost $228,244. Her twin stationary GUN towers confused many

into believing that the craft was a double-turreted MONITOR. Although she displaced only 677 tons, her draft was nearly nine feet. Powered by nine engines, the vessel was armed with two 11-inch DAHLGRENS. On March 11, 1863, *Keokuk* was commissioned and assigned to the South Atlantic Blockading Squadron. The vessel arrived at Port Royal, South Carolina, on Match 26, in time for the April 7 attack on Charleston to be spearheaded by a flotilla of ironclads. *Keokuk* helped to clear the approach for the small naval force, but the assault floundered on the obstacles in the channels and contrary currents. The vessel took more than ninety hits in the action, eighteen at or below the water line. *Keokuk*'s crew struggled to keep the ship afloat, but on April 8, the vessel sank near the south end of Morris Island—a short distance away from Charleston Harbor.

kepi. The word "kepi" is a French word meaning "cap" and denotes a French-style short, round, and leather-visored CAP with a flat crown. It refers to any variation of the 1858 U.S. Army forage cap, whose most distinctive feature was the angle or height of the crown. The 1858 model had a tall crown that flopped toward a narrow leather visor. Other styles included Zouave, chasseur, and McClellan patterns. The chasseur was perhaps the most elegant style in that it was cut lower on the sides so that the crown did not flop onto the visor, which was broader. Decorative gold or black silk braid might be added, climaxing with a trefoil on the crown. Generally speaking, the U.S. Army issued the McClellan-style forage cap to enlisted men; officers and state-supported volunteer units were free to acquire other styles. Regulations, which were not always strictly followed, allowed that the color of a kepi's crown should indicate the wearer's branch of service. In addition, gold-braid patterns on the crown of a Confederate officer's kepi denoted the RANK of its wearer.

Kerr revolver. This was a .44-caliber five-shot handgun manufactured by the London Armoury

Company, which was probably the largest single producer of handguns used by Southern forces. Allegedly equal to any REVOLVER produced in the North, the Kerr could be used as both a single- and a double-action handgun and was a favorite of Confederate horsemen.

kersey. A type of coarse, thick, ribbed woolen fabric with a diagonal weave used to make Federal uniforms, particularly trousers.

ketch. N. A sailing vessel with only two masts—main and mizzen.

Ketchum grenade. Devised by William F. Ketchum of Buffalo, this grenade was patented five weeks after the July 21, 1861, battle of First Manassas (Bull Run). Manufactured in three- and five-pound weights, the three-piece weapon—plunger, casing, and tailpiece—was front-percussion fused and fin-stabilized for throwing. Since its percussion CAP was activated by a blow from a plunger, this segment of the grenade was not inserted until the missile was ready to be thrown. The Ketchum grenade was used by Federal forces in Virginia, Kentucky, Louisiana, and Mississippi. It was not known to be a reliable ORDNANCE, because if the grenade failed to detonate on impact, it could be and usually was thrown back at the user.

Kickapoo, **USS.** Built under contract at St. Louis, this IRONCLAD steamer was commissioned on July 8, 1864. Her initial battery consisted of four 11-inch guns, to which four 12-pounders were added.

The *Kickapoo* was removed from service during the summer of 1865. Sold at public auction in New Orleans a decade after hostilities ended, the vessel brought the U.S. Treasury less than 2 percent of her initial cost.

Kid-glove Dandies. Derisive nickname for the huge escort and personal guards of Union Gen. John C. Frémont. At the beginning of the war, Frémont was one of the most celebrated national heroes in the country and one of the first generals to be appointed by Abraham Lincoln. He was further promoted to head the Western Department,

John C. Frémont

but his decision making did not translated into success on the battlefield and he failed to live up to his reputation.

kill ratio. The percentage of enemy dead compared to the original body of soldiers, a specified kind of ammunition, or some other defined variable. All published kill ratios were loose estimates since exact data was not known, but the kill ratio was nearly always low.

Kill-Cavalry. A derisive nickname for Union Gen. Hugh Judson Kilpatrick, based on the reckless way in which he drove his command. After the Atlanta campaign and the March to the Sea and through the Carolinas, Union Gen. William T. Sherman called Kilpatrick "a hell of a damned fool."

Kilpatrick's monument. Fire-blackened chimneys towering over the ashes of a Georgia home. Union Gen. Hugh Judson Kilpatrick operated on the fringes of William T. Sherman's armies during the MARCH TO THE SEA. From the perspective of his command, it seemed that Kilpatrick delighted in ordering the destruction of property belonging to an avowed or suspected Secessionist.

kilts. This traditional Scottish dress was supposedly worn prior to the war by the 79th New York; see HIGHLANDERS.

King Jeff the First. A calumny of many of the strictest states' rights advocates—such as Govs. Joseph E. Brown of Georgia and Zebulon Vance of North Carolina and outspoken newspaper editor Edward Pollard of the *Richmond Examiner*—against Jefferson Davis and any attempt to further centralize the Confederate government.

King of Spades. A derisive nickname applied to Gen. Robert E. Lee during his 1861 tour of Southern coastal defenses that was revived shortly after he was given command of the Confederate army defending Richmond in 1862. To some Lee seemed obsessed with digging trenches and building earthworks, but Lee responded, "There is nothing so military as labor, and nothing so important to an army as to save the lives of its soldiers."

Kingdom of Jones. A wartime nickname for sparsely populated, swampy, and heavily wooded Jones County in southeast Mississippi, close to a small island in the Leaf River. Somewhat UNIONIST, although probably better described as anti-secessionist, in nature, many of the residents argued against SECESSION and later claimed that their region—which was known before the war as the Free State of Jones and the Republic of Jones—was not part of the Confederacy. Although many men from this area enlisted in the Southern army, most deserted to return to their families and farms or after legislation allowed slave owners to claim exemption from military service. Several GUERRILLA bands were formed by the DESERTERS and dominated the area, but the largest of these was led by a former shoemaker named Newton Knight. Unlike the other bands, which also had a criminal element, Knight's organization survived intact until the end of the war. His men occasionally ran off tax collectors, burned bridges, and ambushed Confederate columns, but only when state and military authorities threatened to claim either their property or move against their people. Records indicated that of those Jones Countians who wished to fight for the North, several enlisted or tried to enlist in the Union army in New Orleans and Vicksburg.

***Klamath*, USS.** Built at S. T. Hambleton and Company, Cincinnati, by contract, this Casco-class light-draft MONITOR was delivered to the Union navy after the war, on May 6, 1866, at a cost of $602,986. Casco coastal monitors were designed with extra ballast tanks so that the ships could reduce their freeboard (the part of the hull above the water line) when they went into action. The designers, however, miscalculated, and so most of these ships were overweight and had very little freeboard at all. Many of the vessels—including *Klamath*—were never commissioned but placed in reserve. On June 15, 1869, *Klamath* was renamed *Harpy* and two months later reverted to her original name. The vessel was sold at auction in September 1874, yielding only 1.2 percent of the price of construction.

knapsack. Usually made of canvas and designed to be worn as a backpack, this all-purpose container was less versatile than the HAVERSACK. When packed in light marching order, it held little more than a blanket, leftover food, and whatever CARTRIDGES a soldier could not stuff into his cartridge pouch. Many members of BERDAN'S SHARPSHOOTERS (1st U.S. Sharpshooters) attached a cooking kit to their knapsacks. Complaints against knapsacks centered on their wooden frames, which wore heavily on a soldier's back. Like haversacks, these backpacks were discarded when their wearers became weary or were running for their lives. Eventually soldiers rolled their belongings in a blanket and carried that over the shoulder.

knapsack drill. A contemptuous term for a "full inspection" that involved examination of each soldier's person, dress, and weapons. Many officers required the men to open their knapsacks on such occasions so that their contents could be checked.

knife-fork-spoon. A contraption touted as serving all functions of the three primary eating utensils. In practice, the item could only be used awkwardly and slowly.

Knight of the Valley. A nickname for wealthy and dashing Confederate Gen. Turner Ashby.

Knights of the Golden Circle. This secret ANTEBELLUM organization was founded in 1854 in Cincinnati by George W. L. Bickley—a Virginia-born doctor, editor, and adventurer—with the goal of facilitating an empire in which a slave-based agricultural economy would flourish, beginning with the annexation of Mexico and including the southern United States, the West Indies, and parts of Central America. The venture was poorly financed and poorly led. Little of note occurred in pursuit of the goal, but in 1859 chapters, known as castles, sprang up in Kentucky, Indiana, Ohio, Illinois, Missouri, and Texas. After two attempts to invade Mexico were planned but never implemented, the Mexico issue subsided and the KGC focused on the issue of SECESSION. In the Border States the KGC shared a common cause with the Peace Democrats, and in the political climate of the times the KGC was blamed for a wide range of subversive activities from sabotage to providing intelligence to Southern commanders. In all likelihood, a minority of the membership was only radical enough to discourage enlistment, resist CONSCRIPTION, and hide DESERTERS. The Knights were reorganized in late 1863 as the Order of American Knights and again in early 1864 as the Order of the Sons of Liberty. At that time, Bickley was no longer affiliated with the group. He had enlisted in the Confederate army as a surgeon, and in July 1863 he was apprehended in Indiana and charged with spying. Bickley remained under arrest until October 1865 and died two years later. In his place, the controversial Ohio congressman Clement L. Vallandigham took over the group's leadership. Discussion turned to the possibility of a revolt in the old Northwest Territory, but Union successes on the battlefield undercut the credibility of any such talk. As the potential for a negotiated peace between North and South diminished, so did the Order of the Sons of Liberty, née the Knights of the Golden Circle. Estimates of their wartime numbers in Missouri range from 10,000 to 40,000 and as many as 20,000 in Illinois, but these figures were based on the common practice during the war of ascribing all mishaps and accidents to the Knights or some other group of Southern sympathizers. By the end of the war, the Knights/Sons organization had ceased to exist.

knots. Since 1859 cross-shaped gold shoulder cords, called quatrefoils, were used by the U.S. Marine Corps on all officers uniforms, except the full-dress uniform, and CAPS. Company-grade officers—second and first lieutenants and captains—displayed three gold cords; field-grade officers—majors, lieutenant colonels, and colonels—wore four gold cords. Second lieutenants and majors displayed no INSIGNIA on their knots; however, insignia were attached to the knots of the other RANKS: first lieutenants wore a single embroidered bar, captains wore two bars, lieutenant colonels wore a silver embroidered oak leaf, colonels a spread eagle, and the commandant colonel wore a silver five-pointed star.

Know-nothings. This was a popular designation of the American Party, a mid-nineteenth-century political organization that tried to operate secretly. When questioned about the party, its goals, or its activities, members swore they knew nothing about such things. This common response led editor Horace Greeley of the *New York Tribune* to coin the name.

knucks. A band of New York thieves who robbed soldiers and sailors after getting them drunk,

Kriz. A nickname for Polish-born Union Col. Wladimir Krzyzanowski. At the beginning of the war he helped to organize a regiment of Polish and German immigrants as the 58th New York

Infantry. His men were engaged in the 1862 Shenandoah Valley campaign (where they distinguished themselves at the June 8 battle of Cross Keys) and later participated in the battles of Second Manassas  (Bull Run), Chancellorsville, and Gettysburg. (When his appointment as a brigadier general expired in March 1863 and was not renewed by the Senate, Maj. Gen. Carl Schurz complained that the commission lapsed because no senator could pronounce the name.) After Gettysburg, Krzyzanowski was dispatched to the western theater along with the predominately German-American 11th Corps. There they helped to relieve the Union forces bottled up at Chattanooga, but controversies arose over how well the 11th had followed orders at the October 28–29, 1863, battle of Wauhatchee. Krzyzanowski spent the remainder of the war at Stevenson and Bridgeport, Alabama. He was mustered out in May 1865 and brevetted a brigadier general in recognition of his war service.

L

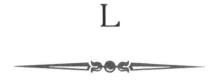

Lackawanna, **USS.** Built at the New York Navy Yard by government contract, the 1,533-ton screw-driven sloop of war was completed on August 9, 1862. Constructed of white oak, live oak, and yellow pine, she cost $459,385. Measuring 237 feet in length, the *Lackawanna* drew more than 16 feet of water when loaded. Her battery was made up of fourteen guns that saw a great deal of action during the war. The vessel was assigned to the West Gulf Blockading Squadron, principally off Mobile Bay. Although obsolete as a warship at the end of the war, *Lackawanna* remained in use—mostly in the Pacific and the Far East—for two decades and was then sold to W. T. Garratt and Company on July 30, 1887. This transaction recovered for the government almost 4 percent of her construction cost.

Ladies Aid Society. A women's organization in the North established to help Union soldiers. Through this group, soldiers received packages of soap, coffee, tobacco, and clothing. The founding of the U.S SANITARY COMMISSION led to a decline in its membership.

Ladies' Gunboat Societies. Patriotic women in several port cities of the South formed societies to raise funds for the construction of IRONCLADS. The first was established in 1861 in New Orleans, and others arose across the South. Their fundraising efforts included auctions, concerts, raffles, and fairs. Three Confederate ironclads—the *Charleston,*

Fredericksburg, and *GEORGIA*—were built with these funds and were informally known as "ladies' gunboats." These efforts reached their apogee in 1862, but the captures of New Orleans, Memphis, and Norfolk dampened the enthusiasm of the societies. Finally, all but five of the gunboats were lost or destroyed. By 1863 the societies were no more.

lading. N. The naval variant of "loading." A lading might be an entire cargo or a portion of it.

ladle. (1) A corkscrew implement used by gunners to extract a projectile from the GUN TUBE of a CANNON because it would be likely that firing the charge as loaded would damage the piece. (2) An implement used to convey molten metal, lead in particular, in manufacturing plants and foundries as well as on warships.

Lady Bell. At Confederate FORT DONELSON, site of the first great Union victory of the war, the largest of the defenders' cannon—an eight-ton DAHLGREN—was known as the Lady Bell. The piece was named for the wife of John Bell, a candidate for the presidency of the United States in 1860. Postwar recollections of Maj. E. C. Lewis include the comment, "as Mrs. Bell was a very large woman, the gun appeared well named."

Lady Breckinridge. A Confederate GUN named for the wife of former U.S. vice president John C. Breckinridge, a major general in the Confederate army. This weapon played a prominent role in the heavy fighting at the November 25, 1863, battle of Missionary Ridge.

Lady Buckner. This companion piece to the Lady Breckinridge honored the wife of Kentucky's Simon Bolivar Buckner, a Confederate brigadier general. Like the brass piece that honored Mrs. Breckinridge, the Lady Buckner was captured in the fighting at Missionary Ridge.

Lady Davis. Named for Varina Howell Davis, the first lady of the Confederacy, this 10-inch COLUMBIAD at Port Hudson, Louisiana, became known to the Union soldiers as Old Demoralizer. The weapon had also been stationed on Island No. 10 for a while, along with a 128-POUNDER known as the Lady Polk Jr.

Lady Polk. Episcopal bishop and Confederate Gen. Leonidas Polk was gratified that his men had named a 10-inch DAHLGREN in honor of his wife, Frances. The rifled PIECE required a specially trained nine-man GUN crew. It was first fired during the November 7, 1861, battle of Belmont, Missouri, in which the gunners noted the accuracy of the weapon. Its projectiles were enormous, and some referred to them as "iron gateposts." When the Federals withdrew, the fully loaded Lady Polk was left in place. A few days later, Polk arrived and asked to see the gun. He was warned that since the loaded cannon had cooled with a charge primed to fire, there was a danger the weapon would explode if it was fired again. Nevertheless the order was given, and the huge cannon burst, killing ten of the thirteen men in the gun crew as well as observers. Polk was knocked to the ground and his horse was killed.

Lady Richardson. Named for the wife of Sen. William A. Richardson of Illinois, this Federal PARROTT gun delivered 20-pound missiles. After having been in service earlier, it arrived at Corinth, Mississippi, in September 1862. On October 3 a furious Rebel charge from the west culminated in

the capture of the Federal lady by members of the 35th Alabama and 9th Arkansas.

Lady Slocomb. Named for a prominent Secessionist of the region, this COLUMBIAD was involved in the August 5, 1864, battle of Mobile Bay.

Lafayette, La Garde. The 55th New York Infantry, also known as LES GARDE FOURCHETTES. See GARDE LAFAYETTE, LA.

NAVAL HISTORICAL CENTER

Lafayette, USS. Originally built in 1848 as the side-wheel merchant steamer *Alick Scott,* the vessel was used by the Union army as a quartermaster ship under the name *Fort Henry* from 1861 to 1862. When the ship was transferred to the navy in September 1862, she was being converted into an IRONCLAD. The work was supervised by Como. William D. Porter but proved to be disappointing. Although her appearance was impressive, the ship was overweight and too slow to be a RAM. Attached to the Mississippi Squadron, she was involved in the run past Vicksburg on April 16, 1863, participated in the bombardment of Grand Gulf, Mississippi, and in the Red River campaign. Despite her long and distinguished career, when sold at New Orleans in 1866 the warship brought only $10,770.

Laird Rams. During the summer of 1862, British shipbuilder John Laird and Son secretly contracted to produce a pair of double-turreted vessels for the Confederacy. Each was to have an iron RAM that extended seven feet beyond its prow and below the water line. Confederate agent James D.

Bulloch made arrangements to name these vessels the CSS *North Carolina* and *Mississippi* while construction was in progress. The British government seized the vessels, claiming that their production violated Great Britain's neutrality in the U.S. conflict. Both rams became the property of the royal navy and were renamed HMS *Scorpion* and *Wivern*.

laminated plates. Thin sheets of iron attached to the earliest Federal MONITORS in five-inch layers. This plating was considerably more vulnerable to gunfire than was the solid 4.5-inch forged plating used on the USS *New Ironsides* and other warships.

lamppost. An artillery shell glimpsed while in flight.

***Lancaster,* USS.** This 257-ton side-wheel towboat was built in Cincinnati, Ohio, in 1855 and known as *Lancaster Number 3* and *Kosciusko.* She was converted into a ram for Charles Ellet's ram fleet and participated in the June 6, 1862, battle of Memphis, Tennessee. Later the vessel joined the Federal fleet clustered at Vicksburg, Mississippi. There on June 15 *Lancaster* was disabled by the Confederate ironclad *Arkansas* and departed for repairs. Upon her return *Lancaster* accompanied another ram, USS *Switzerland,* in a dash past the Southern batteries at Vicksburg but was sunk after numerous hits to her steam drum and hull.

lance. (1) An obsolete weapon similar to a pike. A lance consisted of a wooden staff about nine feet long tipped with a triple-edged foot-long blade. A few units, such as RUSH'S LANCERS, carried these weapons for a time and sometimes used them in battle. At Valverde, New Mexico, Union Gen. H. H. Sibley used lances but found them to be ineffective. (2) Any lengthy pole of small diameter to be used as a flagstaff.

lance corporal. A private temporarily promoted to act as a sergeant (the change in rank did not include an increase in pay).

land mines. During the May 1862 Confederate retreat from Yorktown, Gen. Gabriel James Rains improvised land mines by shallowly burying 8- and 10-inch COLUMBIAD shells in the path of the advancing Federal army. Both sides denounced the use of such munitions as INFERNAL MACHINES. Confederate Gen. James Longstreet was so appalled by what newspapers called a "fiendish innovation" that he ordered Rains to stop using these TORPEDOES. Yet the Confederate government in October 1862 created the Torpedo Service, and Rains was later the head of this department. His

Gabriel James Raines

mines were used, despite the objections of officers in the field, at Richmond, Mobile, Charleston, and in the James River.

land pirate. One who attempted to seize tracts of land not belonging to him.

land sickness. N. Among sailors, this was an acute longing to feel solid ground under one's feet.

landsman. N. The lowest rating of a ship's crewman. When the U.S. Navy began to put CONTRABANDS aboard warships, Gideon Welles forbade them to have an initial rating higher than that of landsman.

langrage. N. Improvised CANISTER shot—fashioned by dumping nails, bolts, and other metal odds and ends into an empty shell—designed to tear the sails and rigging of an opponent.

lantern. A portable hand-held lighting device.

lanyard. A length of rope with a small hook at one end and a wooden handle at the other. It was attached to a FRICTION PRIMER to trigger a large-caliber weapon.

***Lapwing,* CSS.** This BARK was captured by the CSS *FLORIDA* late in March 1863 and served as a tender to the raider afterward. Although the vessel carried two HOWITZERS, she never played a significant role in any engagement. After less than a month in Rebel service, she was burned by her commander and abandoned.

***Larkspur,* USS.** Purchased at Wilmington in the fall of 1863 for $31,000, this tug had earlier been named the *Pontiac.* The ninety-foot craft was armed with two 12-pounders, drew nine feet of water, and had a top speed of nine knots. Sold at public auction near Philadelphia, she returned to the U.S. Treasury slightly more than one-fourth of her purchase price.

Latin farmers. A nickname for the well-educated German immigrants in the Union army. Some of them had participated in the German revolutionary movements of the 1840s and were very much at ease with Greek and Latin. When forced to flee their native country, those who came to the United States were rarely able to find any work other than farming. Shortly after the war began in 1861, substantial numbers of these elite military veterans entered Federal service.

launch. N. An open boat, typically large and without cover, principally used to transport men and supplies between ship and shore.

Laurel Brigade. This *nom de guerre* was bestowed on the 7th, 11th, and 12th Virginia Cavalry Regiments and the 35th Virginia Cavalry Battalion in February 1864 following two highly successful raids. In his report, Confederate Gen. J. E. B. "Jeb" Stuart wrote that this success "adds fresh laurels to that veteran brigade so signalized for valor already." Formerly these units had been commanded by Turner Ashby and William E. "Grumble" Jones, but at this time they were led by Thomas L. Rosser. Following Stuart's report, Rosser proclaimed that the BRIGADE was to be known as the Laurel Brigade and the men were ordered to wear laurel leaves on their headgear.

lay. N. A short time during which a vessel awaited a potential opponent without moving its position.

lay-outs. Southern ruffians who hid in the swamps to escape conscription. From their lairs they plundered the nearby countryside and travelers.

lead. This soft metal was essential for the manufacture of CARTRIDGES and MINIÉ BALLS as well as "shoes," or SABOTS, that were attached to a variety of shells. In the Confederacy, lead was so scarce that a drive was organized in Charleston in which 200,000 pounds of lead window-weights was contributed to the war effort.

lead mine. A dead or badly wounded soldier with several wounds.

Lead Mine Regiment. The nickname of the 45th Illinois Infantry, a unit formed at Galena, Illinois, the majority of whose members were miners. The regiment, also known as the Washburne Lead Mine Regiment (named after E. B. Washburne, the Congressman from the Galena district), was MUSTERED IN on December 25, 1861, and attached to the Army of the Tennessee from February 1862 to July 1865. During the war, the unit participated in the battles of Fort Donelson, Shiloh, Corinth, Vicksburg, the Atlanta campaign, the March to the Sea, and the Carolinas campaign.

lead pair. Although the spelling is suggestive of metal, this term refers to horses. Under ordinary circumstances, three teams of two horses were used to pull the two-wheel ammunition chest known as a LIMBER. The first two animals constituted the lead pair. The next set of horses were known as the swing pair, and the final duo was called the wheel pair.

leap the bounty, to. To enlist for military service in exchange for a BOUNTY, collect the money, then flee.

Leather Breeches (or Britches). The nickname of Capt. Hubert Dilger of the 1st Ohio Artillery. Although he was never made a general officer, he was a prominent and well-known artillerist of the Army of the Potomac. Dilger was once an officer in the armed forces of Baden, and he wore a distinctive uniform that included doeskin trousers.

Leech and Rigdon revolver. This Southern-manufactured .36-caliber six-shot percussion pistol was considered the finest of the Confederate-made Colt Model 1851. First produced by the Memphis Novelty Works, at least fifteen hundred were manufactured during the war. Although they were made well, the weapons suffered from inferior metal castings since steel was extremely rare in the South. Gunsmiths were forced to resort to weaker metals, such as iron and brass scavenged from church bells and candlesticks.

Lee's Lost Order. Of all the misplaced pieces of paper during the Civil War, none is more famous than Robert E. Lee's Special Order No. 191 of

September 9, 1862. The orders were directed to the various commands during the Antietam campaign from Lee's HEADQUARTERS near Frederick, Maryland. All were signed in Lee's name by Robert H. Chilton, the ADJUTANT general of the Army of

Daniel H. Hill

Northern Virginia. Through a set of circumstances never explained, the copy destined for Gen. Daniel H. Hill was lost. Days later, when the Union army bivouacked on the same field in pursuit of Lee, the document was found wrapped around three cigars and was sent to Gen. George B. McClellan's HEADQUARTERS, where a staff officer confirmed Chilton's handwriting. Despite knowing Lee's plans, McClellan was slow to act and catch the scattered elements of the Confederate army before the command could

regroup. While Hill's division fought a delaying action at South Mountain on September 14, 1862, the main body of the Confederate army was able to reassemble near Sharpsburg, Maryland. The battle of Antietam, on September 17, 1862, was the bloodiest day in American history, and although tactically a stalemate, Lee's first invasion of the North was thwarted and he retreated to Virginia on September 19. The commander of the Army of Northern Virginia, however, did not learn that a copy of his orders had been discovered until several months later.

Lee's Old War Horse. A nickname for Gen. James Longstreet.

legal tender. A series of Congressional acts resulted in the production and circulation of paper GREENBACKS. Under the terms of the legislation, no public or private creditor except a revenue collector could refuse to accept payment in these certificates not redeemable in gold or silver. Although only about $450 million worth of this form of legal tender entered circulation during the war, it was enough to facilitate once-constricted trade. Challenges to the use of this form of money were not resolved until five years after the war ended. Once the U.S. Supreme Court ruled that Congress had acted within its authority, subsequent issues of paper money became increasingly larger.

leg case. Slang for desertion. Abraham Lincoln allegedly coined the phrase after he had been inundated with scores of petitions to commute the death sentences of deserters.

Leggett's Hill. A small elevated spot near Atlanta that commemorates Gen. Mortimer D. Leggett, a Federal officer who led an attack on the site during the battle of Atlanta in 1864. Leggett was a New Yorker who had grown up in Ohio and in 1861 joined the staff of Gen. George B. McClellan. He later organized and commanded the 78th Ohio then headed a

BRIGADE during the 1863 siege of Vicksburg. On the third anniversary of the battle of First Manassas (Bull Run), July 21, 1864, Leggett led the assault on Atlanta's Bald Hill, which was subsequently named for him.

Mortimer D. Leggett

legion. A military unit designation that was loosely used during the Civil War, but usually designated a comparatively large force that included elements of all three branches of the military—INFANTRY, CAVALRY, and ARTILLERY. One of the most colorful of these special bodies was South Carolina's HAMPTON LEGION.

NAVAL HISTORICAL CENTER

***Lehigh*, USS.** This 1,875-ton Passaic-class monitor was built by Reany, Son and Archbold at Chester, Pennsylvania. The Passaic class was a refinement of John Ericsson's original *Monitor* design, especially in terms of seaworthiness (*Lehigh* survived a force-ten gale off Cape Hatteras). Each had a single turret with two guns: a 15- and an 11-inch DAHLGREN, but *Lehigh's* 11-inch gun was replaced with an 8-inch PARROTT. *Lehigh* was launched on January 17, 1863, and commissioned on April 15. She was first sent to Hampton Roads to operate on the James River and was dispatched later to Charleston. There the ship ran aground under fire on November 16, 1863. After the war *Lehigh* served as a training

ship and during the Spanish-American War. She was sold for scrap in 1904.

LeMat revolver. This .40-caliber nine-shot REVOLVER was perfected in New Orleans shortly before the outbreak of hostilities. One of the earliest models included an 18-gauge shotgun load under the pistol's barrel. Because production facilities in the South were extremely limited, the inventor, Dr. Jean Alexandre François LeMat, licensed his design for manufacture in France by C. Girard and Company. The first weapons were presented to influential Confederates as promotional gifts. There were two models—one having a half-octagonal barrel and the other a full-octagon—and two variations of each—relating to the shotgun barrel. The mass-produced versions were perceived as inferior to the handcrafted presentation guns, which led buyers to reject whole lots prior to taking delivery. Richmond placed an order for 5,000 LeMats but only received 1,500.

***Leonidas*, USS.** Purchased at New Bedford, Massachusetts, in November 1861, this vessel was a worn-out whaler costing only $3,050. Her one and only mission, however, was to carry a load of scrap granite to the South as a member of the ill-fated STONE FLEET.

Leopard. A moniker for Confederate Gen. John H. Morgan, who was captured and confined in the OHIO STATE PENITENTIARY. The *Richmond Enquirer* assured readers that the captive wouldn't be there long. According to the newspaper, the "Leopard" was far too cunning and strong to remain in confinement. Morgan effected a daring escape.

Let her go, Gallagher! This enigmatic command meant to fire at will and with anything at hand.

Letter of Marque. A Confederate document authorizing a ship's captain to act as a PRIVATEER and prey upon Yankee commercial shipping. The first Letter of Marque was issued by Jefferson

Davis in answer to Abraham Lincoln's announcement of the Federal BLOCKADE of Southern ports. Wealthy Southerners, especially those in major ports such as New Orleans, Charleston, and Savannah, exploited the opportunity to invest in the privateering enterprise. Recognized under international law as a valid and legal document, Letters of Marque were nevertheless roundly denounced by Union leaders.

Level Eye. A nickname for Union Gen. Grenville M. Dodge, who gave that impression to Native American tribesmen during his work as a railroad surveyor in Iowa prior to the war.

levies or **levys.** Conscripted soldiers. When a Federal call for troops was issued, Abraham Lincoln or a cabinet member decided what levy should be assigned to each state. Governors and other officials took pride in promptly meeting these quotas. In August 1862, General in Chief Henry W. Halleck regretfully notified Gen. Benjamin F. Butler, "The new levies are only just beginning to come in and are still unorganized." Confederates used the same term but also implied that such were GREEN TROOPS. In Jackson, Mississippi, city leaders voiced their concern to Gov. Thomas O. Moore in May 1862 that, of the thirty-two hundred troops on hand, nearly all of them were new levies.

Lewis Cass, **CSS.** This U.S. REVENUE CUTTER was seized by Alabama authorities nearly ninety days before the confrontation at FORT SUMTER. The vessel had been named for a governor of the Michigan Territory, who was also a U.S. senator and a Democratic candidate for the presidency. The little SCHOONER carried only one GUN, but it was a 68-POUNDER. Transferred to the Confederate navy, the *Lewis Cass* was too small to engage a warship, so it was relegated to patrol duty.

Lexington. A Kentucky thoroughbred ridden by Union Gen. William Tecumseh Sherman during the GRAND REVIEW.

Lexington, **USS.** This 448-ton side-wheel commercial steamer was built in 1860 at Belle Vernon, Pennsylvania. In June 1861 the Union army acquired the vessel for its Western Gunboat Flotilla, and the steamer was converted into a timberclad river GUNBOAT. Although under army command, the ship's officers were supplied by the Federal navy. *Lexington* patroled the Mississippi River and its tributaries until early 1862, when it participated in the attack on FORT HENRY, Tennessee. Later the vessel supported Ulysses S. Grant's army during the April 1862 battle of Shiloh. In November 1862 *Lexington* was transferred to navy command entirely. She participated in actions in Arkansas, Tennessee, and Louisiana during the remainder of the war, including the battles of Forts Hindman and DONELSON and expeditions on the White, Black, Ouachita, and Red Rivers. The vessel was decommissioned after the war, in July 1865, and sold.

Libby Prison. Of all Confederate prisons, Libby's reputation was second only to that of ANDERSON-VILLE. Whereas most prison facilities in Richmond had been tobacco warehouses prior to the war, Libby had been instead a firm of ship chandlers and grocers before being taken over by the Confederate government. Only Federal officers and high-ranking civilians were confined in this three-story eight-room building. At first the prisoners were allowed to receive parcels of food, clothing, and blankets, but such privileges did not continue. By the winter of 1863 more than one thousand officers were confined here, and the place was so crowded that the men slept on their

sides so as to take up as little space as possible. There were escape attempts, but the most successful was engineered by Col. Thomas E. Rose on February 9, 1864; 109 escaped, but 48 were recaptured, including Rose. Long after the war, the building was dismantled and reassembled as a museum at the 1889 Chicago Exposition.

libel. N. In admiralty courts this legal term for defamation also referred to a plaintiff's written plea, including the stipulation of the relief being sought.

Liberator, The. This was perhaps the best-known ABOLITIONIST newspaper of the mid-nineteenth century. It was founded on January 1, 1831, in Boston by William Lloyd Garrison but never had more than three thousand subscribers. Through the *Liberator*'s startling and quotable editorials, Garrison made an uncompromising argument for the immediate and complete abolition of SLAVERY. Deliberately inflammatory in nature, the publication helped to arouse and focus antislavery senti-

William Lloyd Garrison

ment in the North. But the *Liberator* went beyond the issue of slavery to champion other causes and also attacked discrimination against women, smoking, drinking, political and military abuses of

power, and cruelty to animals. The last issue appeared on December 29, 1865.

Liberator of Kansas. A title given to James H. Lane by fellow JAYHAWKERS and others who desired that the Kansas Territory would be awarded statehood as a free state. Lane was a political opportunist and gained Abraham Lincoln's favor early in the war. He was elected to the U.S. Senate in 1860

and also organized several regiments in Kansas, including a unit of black soldiers.

lie on arms, to. This order instructed soldiers to sleep with their RIFLES or MUSKETS in their hands, loaded and at the ready.

lie on oars, to. N. An order to oarsmen to keep their hands on their oars and to be ready to use them.

light ball. An oval artillery projectile made of a canvas sack and filled with a flammable substance. An iron platform was attached to the bottom of the sack to prevent the shot from bursting. It differed from a FIRE BALL in that it was used to illuminate the countryside. For that reason, it did not contain an explosive.

Light Division. A special unit of the Army of Northern Virginia created in early 1862 as part of the Richmond defenses. The division was comprised of Virginia, North Carolina, South Carolina, Georgia, Alabama, and Tennessee troops and led by A. P. Hill. The designation "light" may mean that it was to be a rapid-response force or that the DIVISION traveled with as little gear as possible. It participated in the Seven Days' battles and Second Manassas (Bull Run), but the Light Division's greatest contribution to the Confederate cause was perhaps its timely arrival on the Antietam battlefield late on the afternoon of September

17, 1862, as the right side of the Confederate line was on the verge of collapse. The division served with distinction at the battle of Gettysburg and also fought at the Wilderness and during the siege of Petersburg. Hill's unit

A. P. Hill

was absorbed into James Longstreet's corps during the Appomattox campaign.

lighter. (1) N. Usually a flat-bottomed barge or boat used to move freight over short distances, such as loading or unloading a vessel. (2) A standard of measure for rice.

light metal. A single GUN or a BATTERY whose guns were 12-pounders or smaller.

Lightning Eyes. A nickname for Union Bvt. Gen. Henry L. Burnett, a chief prosecutor in the trials of the Lincoln conspirators, which was coined by Capt. William McKinley.

Lightning Brigade. A MOUNTED INFANTRY unit of the Army of the Tennessee formed by the 17th, 72d, and 75th Indiana, the 98th Illinois, and the 18th Indiana Light Artillery. The 123d Illinois replaced the 75th Indiana, and during the Chickamauga-Chattanooga campaign the 92d Illinois was added to the brigade. Prior to the MUSTERING IN of the 17th Indiana, the regiment's organizer, John T. Wilder, also tried to donate two 6-POUNDER cannon that had been cast in his Greenberg, Indiana, foundry. The PIECES were rejected but the men—many of whom were armed with seven-shot SPENCER RIFLES—were accepted. The massed firepower of these Spencer-armed mounted troops during the fighting at the June 24–26, 1863, engagement at Hoover's Gap, Tennessee, seemed to the attacking Confederates to be like lightning—thus naming the BRIGADE.

lignum vitae. A designation for wood considered to be harder than oak. Such lumber was used in constructing trucks on which heavy naval and SIEGE GUNS were moved.

Ligon's Warehouse and Tobacco Factory. This three-story brick building at the southwest corner of Richmond's Main and Twenty-fifth Streets was the first non-jail facility in the Confederate capital to be confiscated to hold Federal prisoners of war. Initial plans limited occupancy to five hundred, but the number of prisoners detained here exceeded six hundred. At first, the ground floor was used to hold officers and the second and third were relegated for enlisted men, but then confinement was limited to officers. Escape was rather easy in the beginning, and the guards were very lax. In late 1862 the prisoners were transferred to other facilities, and the warehouse was converted to hospital use.

limber. A two-wheeled horse-drawn carriage that was used to haul a CANNON and its CARRIAGE. The limber also contained an AMMUNITION CHEST, a tool chest, tar and water buckets, and a tarpaulin.

linchpin. A metal pin inserted into an axle tree to secure a wheel.

Lincoln Cavalry. A nickname of the 1st New York Cavalry, which was also known as the Carbine Rangers, the 1st U.S. Volunteers Cavalry, and the Sabre Regiment. The unit was MUSTERED INTO Federal service between July 16 and August 31, 1861. It served in the eastern theater, participating in the Peninsula campaign, the Seven Days' battles, Antietam, New Market, Cedar Creek, Five Forks, Sayler's Creek, and Appomattox. The REGIMENT was mustered out on June 27, 1865.

Lincoln coffee. A Southern designation for Northern coffee, coined in envy. Virtually all Southern coffee was ersatz, made from rye, sweet potatoes, chinquapin (a nut), potatoes and persimmons, English peas, grapes, or some other substitute.

Lincoln government. According to Abraham Lincoln's plans for RECONSTRUCTION, the state government of a seceded state could be restored when 10 percent of the population who had voted in the election of 1860 subscribed to a LOYALTY OATH to the Union. The plan was in the process of implementation in Louisiana and Tennessee when Lincoln was killed. In its place, a harsher policy was adopted that required 50 percent of the voters who had voted in 1860 to take, not just a loyalty oath, but an IRONCLAD OATH—a pledge that the individual had never been disloyal to the Union.

Lincoln Gun. This prototype 15-inch RODMAN SMOOTHBORE cannon was named in honor of Abraham Lincoln. The 49,000-pound piece had a range of almost four miles and fired either a 450-pound solid shot or a 330-pound explosive shell. The weapon was cast at Knapp, Rudd and Company's Fort Pitt Foundry in Pittsburgh and sent to FORT MONROE, Virginia, for testing in March 1861.

Lincoln hirelings. Southern slang for Union soldiers.

Lincoln pie. Northern slang for HARDTACK.

Lincoln rifle. Any shoulder arm smuggled or shipped into Kentucky from the North during the time in which the state tried to maintain neutrality. Such weapons were issued to militia whose members had sworn allegiance to the Union.

Lincoln's "Secret Weapon." Anna Ella Carroll, of Baltimore, claimed to have devised the plan by which Union forces pushed down the Tennessee

River as an invasion route into the South. Carroll had circulated in Washington's social circles before the war, so she was no stranger to the capital scene. After the war she revealed that she had suggested the Tennessee River strategy to Abraham Lincoln in a letter dated January 10, 1862, and that her identity had been masked since it could have been damaging to the army's morale to know that a woman had contrived the war plan that would assure the Federal victory. While it is possible that she did write such a letter, of which there is no record, the planning for Ulysses S. Grant's operations in Tennessee had been under way for months prior to January 1862. Carroll later corresponded with Lincoln in June 1862 to claim that she was due "a substantial and liberal reward" for her suggestion, but nothing came of her claims during the war. Congressional hearings were conducted in 1870 to address Carroll's claims and did not find in her favor. Nevertheless she pressed her demands into the 1890s—and Congress still refused to acknowledge them. After her death in 1893, Carroll's cause became an issue in the growing women's suffrage movement of the early twentieth century and continues to arise from time to time in current women's studies.

***Linden*, USS.** This 177-ton stern-wheel commercial steamer was built at Belle Vernon, Pennsylvania, in 1860. The Union navy purchased the vessel in November 1862, converted her into a river GUNBOAT, and commissioned her in January 1863. *Linden* was active in operations around Vicksburg and on the Mississippi River and its tributaries. On February 22, 1864, she struck a snag on the Arkansas River and sank while attempting to aid another vessel.

Lindsay rifle-musket. This two-barreled MUZZLE-LOADER was perfected by John P. Lindsay on the eve of FORT SUMTER. Arranged one on top of the other, both barrels could be discharged simultaneously.

link boy. A youngster who carried a torch and preceded a procession or military unit. His task was to light the way for those unfamiliar with the area.

linen cartridge. A charge for a REVOLVER, MUSKET, or RIFLE with an outer covering made of fabric. Millions of these CARTRIDGES were issued, but soldiers complained that the linen was not always completely consumed when the cartridge was fired. Burning embers remaining in a chamber were annoying at best and hazardous at worst.

line of battle. (1) The shape of an attacking force only two ranks deep. (2) N. The position of warships in preparation to launch or receive an attack.

line officer. A designation for officers who functioned between field and general officers, i.e., captains and lieutenants. Line officers carried out commands but seldom issued their own.

linstock. A wooden rod, about thirty inches long, used by gunners to hold a slow match for igniting the POWDER in a gun's VENT. The rod was tipped at one end with an iron point so it could be stuck in the ground between firings.

***Lioness*, USS.** This 198-ton stern-wheel steamer was built in Brownsville, Pennsylvania, in 1859. The vessel was purchased by the Union army and converted into a ram for Charles Ellet's fleet. *Lioness* participated in the June 6, 1862, battle of Memphis, Tennessee, and in operations on the Yazoo River during the Vicksburg campaign. When the RAM fleet was reorganized as the Mississippi Marine Brigade in 1863, *Lioness* saw action for only a short time before she was taken out of service in the summer of that year.

list, to. N. To tip to one side or careen. Under such conditions, half of a vessel's guns might be too depressed to bear on the enemy.

lithography. The art of printing by means of a stone plate using ink-receptive and nonreceptive materials.

Little Alec. A nickname for Alexander H. Stephens, vice president of the Confederacy.

Little Billy. A moniker for Confederate Gen. William Mahone.

Little Cavalryman. A nickname for Confederate Gen. Lawrence S. Ross of Iowa, who had enlisted as a private.

Little Chief. A designation for Jefferson Davis by many Native Americans of the western frontier whom he encountered during his career as a young U.S. Army officer.

Little Dan. A moniker for Union Gen. Daniel Butterfield.

Little Ellick. A variant of LITTLE ALEC.

Little Gamecock. (1) A nickname for Confederate Gen. James J. Archer of Maryland. (2) A moniker for Virginia-born Confederate Gen. James R. Callers.

Little General. (1) A reference to Confederate Gen. James Henry Lane of Virginia (not to be confused with Union Gen. James Henry Lane of Kansas). (2) A nickname for Confederate Gen. George W. Randolph, who had been a midshipman in the U.S. Navy prior to the war.

Little Jove. A nickname for Union Gen. Philip H. Sheridan.

Little Mac. A nickname for Union Gen. George B. McClellan, commander of the Army of the Potomac.

Little Powell. A nickname for Confederate Gen. Ambrose Powell Hill.

Little Sorrel

Little Sorrel. The favorite mount of Confederate Gen. Thomas J. "Stonewall" Jackson, which he acquired shortly after arriving at Harpers Ferry in April 1861. Jackson named the animal Fancy, because he had originally intended to send it to his wife, but everyone else called it Little Sorrel. The horse had a smooth pace, an even temper, and extraordinary endurance, but it was an ungainly specimen and stood only fifteen hands high. Jackson rode the animal until the night of May 3, 1863, when the general was mistakenly shot by Confederate troops. Little Sorrel was lost in the melee, and the general did not hear of the horse's recovery until the day on which he died. The animal was given to Jackson's widow and ultimately was bequeathed to the Virginia Military Institute, where Jackson had been a professor prior to the war. Little Sorrel died in 1886; his hide was preserved and displayed at the VMI museum, but his bones were buried near a statue of Jackson on the campus.

Live Oak. A nickname for Confederate Gen. William S. Walker.

Lo. A nickname for Confederate Gen. Lewis A. Addison, a ladies man with a reputation of a Lothario. Gen. John B. Magruder allegedly coined the usage with regard to Addison.

load, to. This was the complicated nine-step procedure to prepare a RIFLE to be fired. It was one of the first things a recruit learned when he was issued his weapon. The soldier (1) extracted a paper CAR-TRIDGE from his CARTRIDGE BOX. (2) He bit it and deftly tore open the cartridge. (3) The POWDER was emptied from the cartridge into the barrel. (4) A bullet was placed, with its point up, in the BORE of the gun. (5) The rifle's RAMROD was removed from the stock, (6) used to push the charge into place, and (7) returned to its niche. (8) The weapon was primed by half-cocking the hammer and removing the remainder of the previous percussion CAP. (9) Finally, a percussion cap was placed on the nipple of the weapon, which was ready to be fired as soon as it was fully cocked. Under combat conditions a skilled man could execute these steps in a matter of seconds. In the heat of battle, however, many soldiers rammed multiple charges into the barrel of their rifles and never fired.

load and fire by rank, to. Military discipline required soldiers to maintain their formations in combat. Hence units were often told to load and fire by rank. This required the soldiers in the front rank to prepare their charges and fire. When they knelt to reload, the men in the second rank fired over their comrades.

loading tong. A hinged metal tool designed to insert the POWDER charge and projectile into MOR-TARS, HOWITZERS, and other GUNS.

lobscouse. A stew made of HARDTACK, vegetables, and salted meat.

lobster backs. Slang for members of the U.S. Marine Corps.

lock or **lift-lock.** A section of a canal having a gate at each end. The water level of a lock was raised or lowered to enable boats to pass from one level to another.

lock, to. To attach a wagon or other wheeled vehicle securely to the rear of another.

log line. N. A stout cord or small rope that was fastened to the log chip of a warship or commercial vessel. Typically about nine hundred feet long, log lines served to approximate the speed of a vessel.

long arms. MUSKETS, RIFLES, and CARBINES.

Long Blade. The nickname of Prussian-born Confederate Maj. Heros von Borcke, who served for a considerable period as chief of staff to Gen. J. E. B. "Jeb" Stuart. He allegedly carried the largest sword of the war. See also MAJOR ARMSTRONG.

Long Bridge. The longest of the bridges spanning the Potomac River from Washington into Virginia.

long home. Slang for a trench into which the dead were often dumped; occasionally applied to any grave.

Long-Legged Donkey. A nickname for Abraham Lincoln.

long roll. A distinctive drumbeat that called all soldiers to arms.

Long Shanks. Yet another nickname for Abraham Lincoln.

Longstreet's slippers. Footwear supplied by Confederate Gen. James Longstreet to his men during the Gettysburg campaign. Diaries and letters make frequent reference to these "slippers" but do not describe them. The term may be derogatory—for raw or less than fully tanned leather may have been used in making them.

long taw. A distance beyond the normal range of a weapon.

Long Tom. This was a huge WHITWORTH rifled cannon that was procured in England and hauled to Cumberland Gap in the aftermath of the July 21, 1861, battle of First Manassas (Bull Run). Installed on what was considered the tallest peak with a command of the famous gap, the gun was too big and too heavy to remove when the region fell from one side to the other on several occasions. As a result, it was the only named gun to have been held twice by Confederates and twice by Federal forces. On the final occasion in which the site was to change sides again, the weapon was spiked and tumbled down the mountain. Long Tom became a visitors attraction in the decade after the war until it was purchased as scrap by a Chattanooga ironworks.

Lookout. A nickname for Union Gen. Joseph Hooker after the November 24, 1863, battle of Lookout Mountain.

loophole. Gun ports cut into the walls of a building or formed of sandbags in fieldworks.

Loose Bowels. Slang for a surgeon because many soldiers associated this prevalent condition with visits to post and field hospitals.

lop-ears. Slang for German immigrant volunteers who often spoke no English and only understood a few commands.

Lost Cause. This phrase was coined by Edward A. Pollard in the 1866 book *The Lost Cause* to describe the South's failed effort to peacefully sever ties with a Union it believed to be a voluntary coalition. The South was portrayed as an idyllic agricultural Eden that had been trampled into submission by a hateful and uncultured North that betrayed the Founding Fathers and the Constitution. To counter the harsh RECONSTRUCTION forced upon the South, the people of the South venerated every aspect of the war. In the end, Northerners relented in the face of the Lost Cause psychology that gave meaning to the sacrifices related to the war and its aftermath.

Lost Children. Several men from New York REGIMENTS that participated in the 1863 siege of Charleston.

Lost Tribes of Israel. REGIMENTS once under the command of Union Gen. Andrew Jackson Smith but given this nickname when they were shuffled so rapidly and frequently that many of the soldiers did not know their commander's name.

Loudoun Rangers. A special Federal unit composed of UNIONISTS from Virginia's Piedmont region. Created to quell the activities of Confederate PARTISAN RANGERS, the Loudoun Rangers fought chiefly in the mountainous and hilly areas that came to be known as "Mosby's Confederacy," the area of operations of Confederate Maj. John S. Mosby's 43d Battalion of Virginia Partisan Rangers. The two ranger units dogged each other for two years until a few days before Lee's surrender at APPOMATTOX, when Mosby's men captured the Loudoun Rangers en masse in a final showdown.

louse comb. Made of bone and sometimes fashioned by hand, the teeth of this comb, especially valued by prisoners, were spaced very close together to help a soldier rid himself of body lice.

louse race. Soldiers with time on their hands—either in camp or in detention—entertained themselves with all manner of diversions. Gambling and drinking were commonplace in camp, and occasionally a louse race enlivened the day. The race course was a saucer or plate, and three or more body lice were placed in the center. The first louse to tumble off the edge was the winner.

***Louisiana,* CSS.** Built at New Orleans by contract, this 264-foot IRONCLAD steamer displaced 1,400 tons. She was outfitted with a battery of two 7-inch RIFLES, three 9-inch guns, four 8-inch guns, and seven 32-POUNDER rifles. Despite this formidable armament, the *Louisiana* never saw combat. After the April 1862 fall of New Orleans, the ironclad was scuttled by her commander.

Louisiana Tigers. A motley group of New Orleans cutthroats described as "the rakings and scrapings of the city." Formed into a ZOUAVE company, they fought in the 1st Louisiana Special Battalion. Scruffy as these soldiers in colorful uniforms were, they played a significant role at the July 21, 1861, battle of First Manassas (Bull Run).

NAVAL HISTORICAL CENTER

***Louisville,* USS.** One of a class of seven GUNBOATS built for river use by James B. Eads. A rather unusual center-wheel steamer, this 468-ton vessel saw a great deal of action and was a member of the Federal flotilla that went up the Red River during the early summer of 1864. After three years of hard service, the *Louisville* was auctioned for $3,600.

Lousy 33d. One of five REGIMENTS in the famous STONEWALL BRIGADE. Each of the units in Jackson's command had a nickname that was known throughout the Army of Northern Virginia. Although it was the last to be sent to Jackson, the 33d Virginia was the first of his regiments to become heavily invested with body lice.

loyal league. A loosely organized body established in a Northern community, town, or city to support the Lincoln administration and the Union. Even in the Northeast, where ABOLITIONISTS were most numerous, few early soldiers risked their lives in the hope of freeing slaves. Tens of thousands cheerfully went to war with the hope that they were playing a role in saving the Union. This sentiment was so widespread and so important that in the election of 1864, Lincoln was nominated for the presidency by the National Union Convention. Although most or all delegates were Republicans, the decision briefly to change the name of the party indicates the strength and importance of Union sentiment in the North.

loyalist. A UNIONIST in a seceded or Border State. Such persons were scattered throughout the Confederacy, sometimes in pockets or geographical areas of concentration. Abraham Lincoln counted heavily upon the support of loyalists when he initiated actions that led to war. He was right in believing they constituted a strong minority. He was wrong, however, in thinking that all of them would rally behind the Stars and Stripes and throw off the near-dictatorial hold of plantation owners and other holders of numerous slaves. Significant concentrations of loyalists were in western North Carolina, northern Alabama, Texas, and Mississippi. To many Confederates, East Tennessee—the home of William G. Brownlow—was a hotbed of Unionists. In Mississippi, citizens of one county registered formal opposition to SECESSION. More than a dozen Texas counties did the same, but their residents never came close to having enough influence to affect the course of events. Numerous prominent Southerners were outspoken opponents of secession who at the same time advocated STATES' RIGHTS. Most or all of these leaders pushed aside their objections to secession when Lincoln called for seventy-five thousand volunteers. Other related actions in Washington persuaded many wavering Southerners to support their states, sometimes reluctantly but nonetheless significantly. A loyalist, however, never wavered during the course of the war. Despite instances of SEQUESTRATION, imprisonment, and BANISHMENT from the South, loyalists laid their property and lives on the line for the Union.

loyalty oaths. (1) At the beginning of Abraham Lincoln's administration, the president and his advisers knew that pro-Southern sentiment was strong in Washington, D.C. Hence one of the first steps was to take action to remove as many Southern sympathizers as possible from influential positions. All Federal workers were required to swear their allegiance to the Union; those who refused were discharged. Such action did not take place on a large scale, however. Many Secessionists on the government payroll resigned and returned to their native states as soon as war appeared imminent. (2) A loyalty oath, the terminology of which varied from place to place, was administered in Federal-occupied areas. All citizens who took an oath of loyalty to the Union were given special privileges that often included continued ownership of slaves. In occupied regions, a document attesting that a loyalty oath had been taken was valuable. Fraud and corruption flourished in the administrations of oaths and the distribution of these papers. Many Southerners with unswerving fidelity to the Confederacy managed to obtain the documents attesting that they had sworn loyalty to the Union. (3) Another loyalty oath was fashioned and used after the unconditional surrender of Confederate military forces. This time, former holders of Confederate political and military positions were required to subscribe to the oath to have their citizenship restored. Some who refused to take such action went into voluntary exile in Mexico, Central America, South America, Great Britain, and Europe. Robert E. Lee took the oath soon after his surrender; however, the documentary proof of his action was accidentally or deliberately lost. As a result, he was not a citizen of the United States at the time of his death. More than a century later, the paper that showed he took the oath was discovered. Lee's citizenship was posthumously restored during the administration of President Jimmy Carter.

Lucy. A derisive nickname for Confederate Gen. George E. Pickett.

Lucy Long. A horse that was ridden by Robert E. Lee for a time after the August 1862 battle of Second Manassas (Bull Run).

luff, to. N. To turn the head of a vessel into the wind. This maneuver, often held briefly, was taken for such purposes as getting beyond the range of an enemy's guns.

lugger. A small vessel carrying three masts fitted with long (or "lug") sails.

lumber. A designation for anything considered to be clumsy or useless.

lumbered. Dotted with fixed obstacles or scrap material considered useless.

lunette. (1) A temporary fortification or fieldwork distinguished by having two faces that form a SALIENT ANGLE and parallel flanks. (2) A metal ring or "eye" at the end of a GUN trail. This lunette was dropped over the upright pivot pin, or pintle, of the LIMBER so it could be towed.

M

macadam road. Scottish engineer John L. McAdam was a pioneer builder of hard-surface roads in his native land. His technique spread throughout the British Isles and then to the United States. His method required the use of pulverized limestone, which was tamped by hand until the surface was hard and smooth. This made an incomparably more desirable pathway than the more common CORDUROY ROAD. At the start of hostilities, macadam roads offered the ultimate in comfortable travel.

Macedonian, **USS.** In October 1812 this British vessel was captured by the USS *United States.* Repaired and commissioned into the U.S. Navy, by 1835 it was in such poor condition that it had to be broken up and rebuilt at Norfolk. This sailing FRIGATE of 1,341 tons reputedly could reach eleven knots in a brisk wind. When captured, she had a battery of forty-nine small guns. Rebuilt as a sloop of war, the wooden vessel operated against the Barbary pirates in 1853 and went to Japan with Commodore Oliver Hazard Perry in 1853–56. In 1861 it was a significant component of the U.S. Navy with which Abraham Lincoln proposed to BLOCKADE Southern ports.

machicouilis. Fortified balconies that allowed defenders to fire down on attacking troops.

Madawaska, **USS.** Built in New York, this FRIGATE was not ready for use until too late to have a part in the war. Rated at 3,281 tons, she was equipped with ten 8-inch guns. With the South having surrendered, the name of the 355-foot screw-steamer built at a cost of $1,673,079 was changed to the *TENNESSEE.* Sold after two decades of peacetime use, the vessel brought $34,525. The cost of repairs while she was in naval service topped $865,000.

Magic. The nickname of Col. W. W. Blackford, a staff member who served under Confederate Gen. J. E. B. "Jeb" Stuart. Right or wrong, many Federal officers were convinced that Blackford's "magic" accounted for some of Stuart's stunning accomplishments.

Magnolia Regiment. The nickname of the 2d Alabama Infantry, a one-year REGIMENT raised in Calhoun, Clarke, Franklin, Jackson, Mobile, Monroe, and Pickens Counties at Fort Morgan in April 1861. The unit was attached to the GARRISON there until March 1862 then sent to Fort Pillow, Tennessee, where the regiment disbanded and the men were assigned to other units.

Magnolia, **USS.** On February 19, 1862, this vessel was captured by the USS *Brooklyn.* Taken to the Key West PRIZE COURT, she was condemned, but naval officials purchased her for $50,310. A side-wheel steamer equipped with two masts, the 843-ton *Magnolia* received two guns. Sold in July 1865, she very nearly recovered her initial cost when N. L. and G. Griswold paid $45,000 for her.

main postern. A wall built of stone and brick close to the outer gate of the PARADE GROUND of permanent fortifications.

mainsail. N. The principal canvas of a ship. In the case of a warship or large commercial vessel, the mainsail was attached to the mainmast by means of a YARD. The mainsail of a brig, however, was held in place by a boom.

Major Armstrong. A nickname for Heros Von Borcke, a professional soldier and Prussian nobleman who served for a time as Confederate Gen. J. E. B. "Jeb" Stuart's chief of staff. This title was bestowed on him as a token of admiration for his great strength. Because he was also scrupulous in his dress, he was also called Major Bandbox.

make, to. (1) To complete or reach the apex of an endeavor or movement. (2) N. To catch sight of a craft and identify her, usually at a distance and lacking any recognizable colors.

make a number, to. N. To see the number of a U.S. Navy vessel so that it could be identified.

***Manassas,* CSS.** This Boston-built 387-ton vessel was initially called the *Enoch Train* until it was purchased in 1861 by Confederate agents. Plated with iron, the vessel operated as a RAM with only one GUN. In April 1862 it was sunk in battle not far from New Orleans.

Mamelukes. A reference to B. F. Terry's TEXAS RANGERS. The original Mamelukes were Islamic soldiers who won notoriety during the Crusades.

maneuver. A movement that was planned carefully and executed flawlessly.

manhandle, to. To transport or move a heavy object, such as a GUN, by human effort.

***Manhattan,* USS.** Built at Jersey City, New Jersey, by contract, this vessel was not completed until May 1864. Listed as a light-draft MONITOR, she could not maneuver well in less than ten feet of water. Like most monitors, the 1,034-ton screw-steamer was equipped with only two guns. She remained in service until the turn of the twentieth century.

manhole. A hole barely large enough to hold a man. Such holes were excavated in stockades where prisoners had no other shelter from the weather.

BATTLES AND LEADERS

mantelet. Named for its vague resemblance to a small garment, this device was usually made of woven rope. Mounted in front of a GUN position, it was not strong enough to stop a shell or ball from the enemy. Many gunners were fond of it, however, for it served to protect them from flying debris such as splinters.

manual of arms. Prescribed movements by which soldiers loaded a weapon or completed some other operation. See LOAD, TO.

mapmaking. U.S. Army regulations, which were largely adopted by Confederates, reserved this task for specially trained topographical engineers. Some of the best maps were produced, however, by self-taught men with limited or no military backgrounds. Confederate Gen. Thomas J. "Stonewall" Jackson's renowned mapmaker, Jede-

Jedediah Hotchkiss

diah Hotchkiss, was a schoolmaster and mining geologist before he played a vital role in the 1862 Shenandoah Valley campaign.

march. (1) Distance traversed by soldiers on foot during a given interval of time or a specific operation. Confederate Gen. Thomas J. "Stonewall" Jackson developed the ten-minute break that permitted his men to march farther and faster than unrested units. (2) Distance covered by CAVALRY or other riders during a specified time. In June 1864 Union Gen. Stephen G. Burbridge and his men rode at top speed after Confederates under the command of Confederate Gen. John Hunt Morgan. These riders made a forced march of about ninety miles during twenty-four hours—but succeeded only in capturing a few dismounted Confederates.

marching order, light. This order sent INFANTRY moving as fast as possible, with the soldiers being told to abandon their KNAPSACKS and blankets for the sake of speed.

march of death. The fatal movements of Federal troops who tried repeatedly to overrun the Confederate position on MARYE'S HEIGHTS during the December 13, 1862, battle of Fredericksburg.

March to the Sea. The movement of Gen. William T. Sherman and his armies from Atlanta to Savannah from November through December 1864. Although the Federal forces did come close to the sea at Savannah, the march was continued northward through South Carolina and into North Carolina. Before reaching Atlanta, Sherman had made plans to have his men march to a port from which they would take ship to join Ulysses S. Grant's Army of the Potomac. He was initially undecided about what route to take and considered going to Mobile or another port far from Savannah.

***Maria Theresa*, USS.** She bore a name that conjured up images of European royalty, but many considered the name of this 330-ton vessel inappropriate. The old whaler was purchased at New Bedford, Massachusetts, for $4,000, and as a member of the STONE FLEET she soon went to the bottom of a Southern channel.

marker. A soldier designated to help the other members of his company to achieve the proper alignment during drill or parade. It was not unusual for drummers to be selected for this task; the marker typically carried a GUIDON.

marline spike. N. A slightly curved iron tool that tapered to a point. It was in constant use on warships that made up the first blockading squadron, since it served to separate strands of rope in preparation for splicing.

Marquedant. Capt. W. C. Marquedant of the 9th Ohio perfected a method of making photographic negative copies without a camera—tracing an image over light-sensitive paper. It was used in the reproduction of maps.

Marque, Letter of. See LETTER OF MARQUE.

Marse Bob. A nickname of Robert E. Lee, also called Marse Robert.

Marsilly Carriage. A cast-iron GUN CARRIAGE capable of bearing most weapons up to the 9-inch DAHLGREN. Heavier PIECES were less dangerous when equipped with special wrought-iron carriages. In June 1863 an inventory of the captured CSS *ATLANTA* revealed that she had on board two Marsilly carriages for broadside guns.

Marye. A nickname of admiration for Confederate Gen. John B. Gordon that was based on his action in the fighting at Marye's Heights during the December 13, 1862, battle of Fredericksburg.

Marye's Heights. An elevated region on the outskirts of Fredericksburg that became notorious for the number of Federal charges that were repelled

U.S. ARMY MILITARY HISTORY INSTITUTE

there during the December 13, 1862, battle of Fredericksburg. Confederates were protected by a stone wall fronting a SUNKEN ROAD, and the position proved invulnerable. Yet Union Gen. Ambrose E. Burnside sacrificed thousands of Union soldiers before withdrawing the next day.

Maryland. A nickname for Confederate Gen. George H. Steuart, bestowed because he was a native of the state.

mask, to. To conceal one's position or troops from the enemy.

masked battery. A concealed BATTERY of guns, disguised so as to be unnoticeable and to surprise an attacking force.

mass, to. To concentrate a body of troops, sometimes so densely that standard formations could not be maintained.

master. N. A noncommissioned officer between a "passed" MIDSHIPMAN and a lieutenant, also known as a master's mate.

materiél. Basic or raw materials needed for making goods or performing services. During the Napoleonic wars, this term became standard English as a designation for military goods, gear, and supplies of every kind.

Maumee, USS. This wooden GUNBOAT was completed at the New York Navy Yard in July 1863. A 593-ton screw-steamer, when loaded it had a draft

of eleven feet and had an average speed of only seven knots. Initially, it carried one 100-POUNDER PARROTT RIFLE, one 30-pounder Parrott rifle, four 24-pounders, and one 12-pounder rifle. Additional guns were added to its battery later. The *Maumee* went out of commission on June 17, 1865, and was sold four years later to a resident of Hong Kong.

Maurepas, CSS. Like nearly all Confederate warships, this vessel was originally in commercial service under a different name—*Grosse Tete*. The misnamed ship was puny by comparison with most Federal vessels. In November 1861 the sidewheel steamer was mounted with six guns. They proved to be of little avail; after seven months, her officers sank her in the White River in an effort to obstruct the waterway.

Maynard rifle. Favored by wealthy sportsmen before the beginning of the conflict, this may have been the earliest RIFLE for which copper rimfire CARTRIDGES were standard. These were manufactured with tiny holes in their bases so that after having been fired, they could be refilled and reused. Wax paper sealed the holes and prevented the POWDER from being lost.

McClellan cap. Headgear fashioned after the French KEPI, of which McClellan saw a great deal during his prewar period as an OBSERVER in the Crimean War.

McClellan pie. Even though McClellan managed to capture both the minds and the hearts of most of his men, they couldn't refrain from bestowing their commander's name on HARDTACK.

McClellan saddle. Now remembered chiefly for failing to show much initiative as the commander of the Army of the Potomac, before the war George B. McClellan had been assigned to an elite military commission that studied and observed the highly regarded armies of Europe during the Crimean War. McClellan was diligent in this effort to update U.S. Army policies and procedures. In particular, he noticed that Prussian cavalrymen used a saddle much lighter and more adaptable than those with which he was familiar. He redesigned the regulation U.S. saddle so that it was light enough not to burden the horse and sturdy enough to support the rider and his gear. Characteristics included a rawhide-covered open seat, a thick leather skirt, wooden stirrups, and a girth of woolen yarn. Other accessories were a nosebag for feeding, a curry comb to groom the animal, a PICKET PIN to secure the horse while grazing, saddlebags, and a hook that held the muzzle of the rider's CARBINE. The saddle was formally adopted by the War Department in 1859, and half a million McClellan saddles were manufactured over the course of the war—not including the conversion of Confederate CAVALRY from the JENIFER SADDLE to the McClellan model in 1863.

Medal of Honor. In December 1861 the U.S. Congress authorized a Medal of Honor to be awarded by the secretary of the navy to enlisted personnel in the navy and Marine Corps, and in July 1862 similar authorization created a Medal of Honor for enlisted army personnel (in March 1863 the requirements were expanded to include officers—naval officers were not eligible for the award until the twentieth century). No other medal was officially issued by the Federal government during the Civil War to recognize heroism on the battlefield. On March 25, 1863, the first army medals were awarded to six members of Andrews's Raiders, survivors of the Great Locomotive Chase; the first navy medals were

Medal of Honor (Navy)

awarded on April 3, 1863. The criteria for the award, however, were rather lax, and Medals of Honor were awarded to soldiers who captured Confederate flags and were even used as an inducement to reenlist. In 1916 a review board investigated the awards issued to army personnel, and 911 were invalidated—including the only Medal of Honor awarded to a woman during the Civil War, surgeon Mary Edwards Walker (the medal was revoked on February 21, 1919, six days before her death, and was reinstated in 1977).

meet the elephant, to. Synonymous with TO SEE THE ELEPHANT.

men's harness. A human harness to be used in instances where the terrain was too steep or miry for animals to haul vehicles or artillery. The standard issue was an eighteen-foot version, but in many circumstances the men had to improvise. Some harnesses were made of hemp rope four inches or more in diameter, and soldiers would place their shoulders in the collars or in loops of rope that were then attached to a drag rope. Thus no hill could not be conquered; no roadway was impassable. More men could always be added until the task was complete.

merlon. The solid area between gun openings in the side of a fortress or warship.

Merrill carbine. This nine-pound .54-caliber BREECHLOADER percussion weapon was manufactured by the Baltimore firm of Merrill, Thomas, and Company and fired a paper CARTRIDGE. The carbine's breech was opened with a top-loading lever that was drawn back and up and required frequent maintenance. It was among the earliest contracted carbines of the war and was captured in large numbers and widely distributed throughout the CAVALRY of the Army of Northern Virginia. Whereas the Southern horsemen were generally pleased with them, Federals favored them only when no other breechloaders were available. By late 1863 they were no longer used by Union soldiers in the East but were common in the western theater. During the war the U.S. War Department purchased fifteen thousand of these weapons.

merrimack. An improvised lean-to good enough for one night's use.

***Merrimack*, USS** (a.k.a. *Merrimac*). This 3,200-ton screw FRIGATE was launched at the Boston Navy Yard on June 15, 1855, and commissioned on February 20, 1856. The vessel was the first to be equipped with DAHLGREN cannon and was made the FLAGSHIP of the Pacific Squadron until November 1859, when the wooden frigate was brought back to Norfolk, Virginia. Soon after Lincoln's inauguration, Secretary of the Navy Gideon Welles directed that the *Merrimack* be moved to Philadelphia. On the day that the vessel's boilers were fired, Virginia seceded. Secessionists blocked the channel between Craney Island and Sewell's Point, bottling up the ships in the Norfolk Navy Yard. On April 20, 1861, the navy yard was evacuated and the *Merrimack* was burned to the water line and sunk to preclude its capture. The Confederacy was in desperate need of ships, thus the *Merrimack* was raised and rebuilt as an IRONCLAD RAM and recommissioned on February 17, 1862 as the CSS *Virginia*. On March 8, 1862, the rebuilt vessel attacked the Union fleet at Hampton Roads, sinking two FRIGATES and damaging a third. The next day the *Virginia* was confronted by the Union IRONCLAD *MONITOR*. Although neither ship won a decisive victory, the day of ironclads dawned and wooden warships were obsolete. The two ironclads did not engage again, and the fall of Norfolk forced the evacuating Confederates to scuttle the *Virginia* on May 11, 1862.

mess. A group of four to six men who ate together and took turns cooking and cleaning. A Federal soldier's standard dinnerware consisted of a tin plate, tin cup, knife, and fork. Spoons were not issued in the Union army until 1863. Confederates carried their cooking utensils in their HAVERSACKS. They too were organized into messes that seldom included fewer than five or more than ten men. Much the same practice was carried out by naval crews.

metal. A laudatory synonym for *courage*.

metal, weight of. The weight of projectiles that could be fired by a BATTERY, a warship, or a fort. USS *New Ironsides* carried sixteen 11-inch DAHLGRENS, two 200-POUNDER PARROTTS, and four 24-pounder HOWITZERS, which gave the vessel a weight of metal of 284,800 pounds.

miasma. Unpleasant air, sometimes dark enough to see, that was believed to rise out of swamps or from other decaying matter. This phenomenon was also believed to cause a host of maladies. Considered a potential deadly exhaust, miasma was said to consist of "effluvia or fine particles of any putrefying bodies" that floated freely in the air.

midshipman. A student at the U.S. Naval Academy, comparable to a cadet at West Point. While still in training, a midshipman had none of the prerogatives of an officer, but once the course of study was completed and the midshipman was assigned to duty on a warship, he outranked all noncommissioned officers. A "passed" midshipman had finished his training and was ready for a lieutenancy whenever a vacancy should occur.

military crest. The highest elevation at a given point from which to see an approaching opponent and to deliver maximum fire upon him. Also known as the geographic crest, the highest point in an area.

Military Order of the Loyal Legion of the United States. Numerous Federal officers expressed concern that the peace achieved by the surrender of Confederate forces would not last. When news spread of the assassination of Abraham Lincoln, three Union officers in Philadelphia proposed to found an organization to frustrate any future attempts to overthrow the Federal government. On April 20, 1865, veterans in Philadelphia met to pledge their renewed allegiance to the Union and to discuss the city's Lincoln funeral ceremony. Afterward the three Union officers met again to found a permanent society, modeled after the Society of Cincinnati, which had been established after the Revolutionary War; they named it the Military Order of the Loyal Legion of the United States. The first called meeting occurred on May 31, 1865, at Independence Hall. Membership was open to any officer, as well as his descendants, who had served honorably in the army, navy, or Marine Corps. The members pledged unconditional fidelity to the Federal government and a willingness to respond against any future insurrection. Chapters, called commanderies, were established at the local, state, and national levels. When the South did not rise again, the focus of the organization turned toward the needs of veterans and their families, although it never rivaled the GRAND ARMY OF THE REPUBLIC in this respect. Since many of the MOLLUS leaders were comparatively affluent and influential, the group also launched a publishing program of first-person accounts of the campaigns of the war.

Milroy. A black stallion captured from the Federals and ridden by Confederate Gen. John B. Gordon.

mine. Strictly speaking, an explosive charge lodged in a tunnel or some other underground placement. The Union army resorted to mines during the sieges of Vicksburg and Petersburg, the latter leading to the July 30, 1864, battle of the Crater. The words *mine* and *TORPEDO* were also used to designate explosives placed in floating containers and set adrift on riverways.

Minié ball. During the 1840s French Capts. Henri-Gustave Delvigne and Claude-Étienne Minié developed an elongated soft-lead projectile with a hollow cone-shaped base as an ammunition for RIFLES, which at the time were slow and awkward to load. Prior to Delvigne and Minié's bullet, rifle ammunition had to be loaded carefully so it would engage the rifling of the barrel when fired. The French captains' bullet was easier to load, and the hollow base of the bullet expanded and forced the projectile into the rifled grooves of the barrel to gain the desired effect of improved accuracy and

range. The bullet was adopted by the U.S. Army in 1855. Those who saw these projectiles strike their comrades described the bullet as exploding on impact. Regardless of where a man might be struck, the misshapen lead did a great deal of damage, shattering limbs and splintering bones. Arm or leg wounds almost always led to amputation.

NATIONAL ARCHIVES

***Minnesota*, USS.** Built at the Washington Navy Yard at a cost of $691,408, this wooden FRIGATE was launched in 1855. Equipped with both sails and engines, her maximum speed under steam was about six knots. On May 2, 1861, her battery consisted of one 10-inch RIFLE, twenty-eight 9-inch rifles and DAHLGRENS, and fourteen 8-inch pieces. When a combined army and navy force was assembled to attack Cape Hatteras in August 1861, the *Minnesota* was selected as the FLAGSHIP of the expedition. Attacked in Hampton Roads, Virginia, by the CSS *Virginia* the following March, she tried to defend herself but grounded. When the *Virginia* returned the next day to attack, the *Minnesota* was defended by the USS *MONITOR* and the first battle between IRONCLADS ensued. The frigate *Minnesota* survived the affair and participated in the combined operation toward the end of the war to take FORT FISHER, the last significant Confederate defensive work on the Atlantic coast.

minnie. A misspelling of Minié in reference to both the projectile and the RIFLES designed to use them.

Minnie Ball. The maiden name of the wife of Confederate spymaster Thomas N. Conrad.

miscegenation. The word was coined in an anonymous 1863 pamphlet titled *Miscegenation: The Theory of the Blending of the Races.* The author thought the term more scientific than the word *AMALGAMATION,* which had been in use previously to describe interracial mixing. The pamphlet argued that intermarriage was the best solution to race relations and further suggested that this should be an issue in the upcoming 1864 presidential campaign. Abolitionists responded favorably to the pamphlet although they were somewhat reticent to endorse the political aspect, and Democrats tried to exploit the pamphlet to their advantage. On the eve of the election a London newspaper published the claim that the pamphlet had not been written by a Republican ABOLITIONIST but rather a couple of Democratic newspapermen who had wanted to make the issue an element in the election. Years later, after the war, the identities of the authors surfaced—George Wakeman and David Goodman Croly—both of whom worked for the pro-Democratic *New York World.*

Mississippi, **CSS.** This river GUNBOAT was built at a cost of $397,000 by N. and A. F. Tift in Jefferson City, Louisiana. Construction began on October 14, 1861, and the vessel was launched on April 19, 1862. A fast triple-screw-steamer, the 260-foot vessel was rated at 1,400 tons. Her double furnaces, each of which had double flues, generated a top speed of fourteen knots. Initially armed with a battery of eighteen guns in November 1861, additional armament was added to the bow and stern in January 1862, resulting in a total of twenty guns. Completion of the vessel was delayed while the propeller shaft and ship's armor were en route to New Orleans. Thus it was not able to contest Farragut's attack on New Orleans. To preclude her capture in April 1862, the Confederate gunboat was stripped of her battery and set afire. Her hulk drifted to Southwest Pass and grounded, where she was salvaged by the Union navy and taken to the Brooklyn Navy Yard for scrap.

Mississippi Butchers. A nickname of the 15th Mississippi Infantry, which was organized at Corinth on May 27, 1861, with 1,070 men. The unit saw action across the western theater, including the battles of Mill Springs, Shiloh, Vicksburg, the Atlanta campaign, Franklin, and Nashville. After the Tennessee campaign, the REGIMENT was consolidated with the 6th, 20th, and 23d Mississippi but retained the designation of the 15th. These men fought at Bentonville and surrendered with Joseph E. Johnston at Durham Station, North Carolina.

Mississippi rifle. A nickname for the .54-caliber Model 1841 RIFLE, which was the first rifle designed and manufactured with a percussion cap system that was issued to the U.S. Army. The original model was not designed to mount a BAYONET. More than one hundred thousand were produced by the Harpers Ferry and Springfield armories as well as private contractors such as Remington, Robbins, Kendall and Lawrence, Robbins and Lawrence, Tyron, and Whitney. Troops nicknamed the rifle JAGER, after the German word for hunter and light INFANTRY. The model was called Mississippi after early versions were issued to Jefferson Davis's 1st Mississippi Regiment during the Mexican War.

Mobile, **CSS.** This screw-steamer GUNBOAT was awaiting the installation of her iron armor in April 1863 when Union forces began to encircle Vicksburg. She was burned in the Yazoo River in early May 1863.

mobile telegraph. A telegraph system that was easily moved and usable in combat. No other communication device aided the Federal cause as much as this one. Lack of requisite raw materials from which to make suitable wire, plus an acute shortage of operators, greatly hampered Confederate commanders.

Modoc, **USS.** Built in New York by contract by J. S. Underhill, this 614-ton light-draft MONITOR was not completed before the end of the war. After a decade of idleness, she was broken up by contract with John Roach. Exclusive of pay for her crew and the cost of provisions, this ironclad cost the Federal government $523,197.

MOLLUS. See MILITARY ORDER OF THE LOYAL LEGION OF THE UNITED STATES.

Molly Maguires. Originally called Sleepers and Buckshots, this loose association of Irish coal miners in eastern Pennsylvania was opposed to the draft and many other actions taken by the Federal government during the Civil War, fearing that if they left the coal fields for the front lines, they would lose their jobs to cheaper labor, especially freedmen and former slaves. In 1862 and 1863 the miners halted the drafting of troops from among their number. After the New York City draft riots of 1863, reports circulated that two to three thousand miners drilled daily in Schuylkill County to resist future conscription efforts. Furthermore, the Mollies allegedly threatened to burn the homes and mines of prominent Republicans to resist the drafting of the miners.

moment. A synonym for "importance" and "urgency."

monition. Rooted in admiralty and ecclesiastical courts, this legal process and/or document was similar to a summons or notice to appear and answer charges. This order was used widely in the North in those areas with significant numbers of Southern sympathizers.

monitor. A term used to designate a class of Northern IRONCLAD that was similar in design to the USS *MONITOR,* a mostly submerged vessel with a two-gun turret.

***Monitor,* USS.** This first-of-its kind warship was contracted on October 4, 1861, and construction was accelerated by subcontracting the hull, the engines, and the turret to three New York firms.

NAVAL HISTORICAL CENTER

The single-turret screw-steamer was launched on January 30, 1862, and she was commissioned on February 25. Her unconventional appearance led to her description as a CHEESEBOX ON A RAFT. Her displacement was variously estimated as between 776 and 987 tons, and her armament was limited to two 11-inch DAHLGREN SMOOTHBORES. In the aftermath of her epic battle with the CSS *Virginia* the John Ericsson–designed craft remained on station at Hampton Roads until the Confederate IRONCLAD was destroyed during the evacuation of Norfolk, Virginia. The *Monitor* was part of a flotilla dispatched up the James River, but the Federal ships were turned back at Drewry's Bluff. For the rest of the year the *Monitor* was assigned to the blockading fleet off the Virginia coast. On Christmas Eve the vessel was dispatched to join the BLOCKADE off Wilmington, North Carolina. During a heavy gale she foundered off Cape Hatteras shortly after midnight December 31, losing sixteen of her forty-seven crewmen.

Morse carbine. Designed by George W. Morse, superintendent of the Nashville Armoury, this CARBINE was the most advanced BREECHLOADER in the Confederate arsenal. Initially manufactured in Nashville until the city was abandoned in 1862, the carbine came to be produced specifically for the South Carolina Militia by the Greenville Military Works and H. Marshall and Company in Atlanta, but fewer than one thousand of these technologically advanced weapons were manufactured during the war. A hinged lever over the breech opened the chamber, but the weapon fired specialized ammunition—a .50-caliber center-fire

Morse CARTRIDGE—which was difficult to make and thus not always available. The metallic cartridge carried both projectile and charge and could be refilled several times.

mortar. A large-caliber GUN with a very short tube designed to fire shells at a high elevation (as much as 45 degrees) using a small POWDER charge. Mortars were classified by the size of their BORE, which ranged from almost six inches to sixteen inches. They threw extremely heavy projectiles in a relatively high arc over comparatively short distances, and their destructive work stemmed from the explosion of the projectile in midair and the fragments that rained down on an opponent's position. Considered by many to be a siege gun, they performed well in the Mississippi River campaigns aboard so-called mortar schooners and in the sieges of Vicksburg and Petersburg. In the latter siege, during the July 30, 1864, battle of the Crater, the Confederate defenders resorted to highly portable Coehorn mortars to seal the breech in their lines.

Moscow. A white horse, considered somewhat nervous under fire, ridden by Union Gen. Philip Kearney.

mossyback. A nickname for a draft dodger who evaded military service by seeking refuge in a swamp or similar refuge.

mountain artillery. Light artillery that could be disassembled, carried on pack animals, and reassembled quickly. Ammunition was also carried by animal, so LIMBERS were not needed. A battery consisted of six GUNS, seven CARRIAGES, thirty-six AMMUNITION CHESTS, tools, and thirty-three pack animals. The Union army used 12-POUNDER MOUNTAIN HOWITZERS; the Confederates deployed 2.25-inch mountain RIFLES.

mountain howitzer. A 12-POUNDER HOWITZER designed to be disassembled and reassembled quickly, for use in rugged terrain.

mount. A quadruped—not always a horse—used to transport a soldier.

mounted charge. Although such a movement was a perennial subject of artists, relatively few SABER charges were made during the war. At the beginning of the conflict, this tactic was almost exclusively used by Confederate horsemen against Union INFANTRY; the Federal CAVALRY was used mainly as escorts and messengers. One early, ill-fated Union effort was executed during the Peninsula campaign at Gaines's Mill by a detail from the 5th U.S. Cavalry to save the ARTILLERY of Gen. Fitz John Porter's command. When the Confederates countercharged, most of the Federal officers on horseback were killed or wounded and about fifty Union cavalrymen were lost. By far the largest cavalry clash of the war occurred at the June 9, 1863, battle of Brandy Station, Virginia. For the first time, Federal horse soldiers acquitted themselves on the field so as to earn a grudging respect from their Southern counterparts who had heretofore easily and consistently embarrassed them in combat. In general, however, most saber charges were the work of a few horsemen rather than entire cavalry REGIMENTS or BRIGADES.

mounted infantry. Although most prewar CAVALRY tactics basically defined the horsemen as little more than mounted infantry—namely, DRAGOONS who fought both from the saddle or dismounted—those tactics changed as units were trained to fight on horseback. Yet the old ways died hard, and some units of INFANTRY were provided with horses. The increased mobility allowed the men to cover the ground faster, but they still fought on foot.

movable electric train. A mobile telegraph unit or FIELD TELEGRAPH.

moved, to be. To be in a highly emotional state.

Mozarts. The nickname of the 40th New York Infantry Regiment, dubbed after the Mozart Hall political faction of New York's Democratic Party. The 40th New York was MUSTERED IN June 21–July 1, 1861, at Yonkers, and participated in the Federal disaster at Ball's Bluff. Beginning with the Peninsula campaign in the spring of 1862, the Mozarts were involved in every major battle of the eastern theater. The REGIMENT was MUSTERED OUT on June 27, 1865, near Washington, D.C. The unit was also known as the United States Constitution Guard.

Mud Heads. Slang for natives of Mississippi.

Mud March. After the defeat of the Federal army at Fredericksburg in December 1862, the Union army commander, Ambrose E. Burnside, launched a second campaign, proposing to outflank the Confederate army behind Fredericksburg. Politics and the weather, however, turned against him. Burnside attempted to initiate the campaign in late December but was recalled to Washington when two of his generals expressed their concerns to Abraham Lincoln. After meeting with the president and gaining his approval, Burnside began again on January 20, 1863. Four days of rain, however, had turned the roads to mud and the fields into muck. Animals and wagons sank into the quagmires, and the men were exhausted. Three times Burnside attempted to march out of Washington, and three times he had to turn back. When the weather cleared, the army was expended and the campaign—called the Mud March—was canceled.

LIBRARY OF CONGRESS

mudscows. Slang for shoes, usually in reference to the square-toed BROGANS.

mud sills. Confederate slang for Union soldiers, who were derided as lacking both courage and chivalry.

Mudwall. The nickname of Confederate Gen. William L. Jackson, a second cousin of Thomas J. "Stonewall" Jackson. Prior to the war William L. Jackson had been a successful jurist in western Virginia. He enlisted as a private but was quickly promoted to lieutenant colonel and attached to the 31st Virginia Infantry. Mudwall served on Stonewall's staff during the Shenandoah campaign of 1862, the Seven Days' battles, and the battles of Antietam and Second Manassas (Bull Run). After his cousin's death, William L. Jackson continued to serve in western Virginia, the Shenandoah Valley, and southwestern areas of the state. He participated in the battles of Monocacy, Third Winchester, Fisher's Hill, and Cedar Creek. In April 1865 Jackson did not surrender but rather disbanded his command and emigrated to Mexico. After a brief stay there, he returned to West Virginia but found that RECONSTRUCTION laws forbade him from reviving his law practice. So he moved to Kentucky and remained there until his death in 1890.

mule. (1) A hybrid animal between a horse and a donkey, known for both its strength and its temper. Rarely used in combat, mules were central to Union Col. Abel D. Streight's failed April 11–May 3, 1863, raid through northern Alabama and western Georgia. These animals also played prominent roles at Valverde, New Mexico, and in the Wauhatchie night attack of the Chattanooga campaign. They were used more widely than horses for pulling wagons and were preferred to horses when BATTERIES were ordered over steep terrain. (2) A MUSKET, so-called because of its harsh recoil. (3) Tough salted meat that was almost inedible.

Mule Shoe. A Confederate salient near Spotsylvania Court House, whose shape was somewhat reminiscent of the iron shoe of a mule. The Union army attacked the salient twice during the twelve-day battle of Spotsylvania Court House, May 7–19, 1864, penetrating the Southern lines the first time, on May 10, but unable to hold on, and crushing the works the second time, on May 12.

Mullane shell. A 3-inch shell used by Confederate gunners. A copper SABOT was attached to the base of the shell to engage the rifling of the GUN TUBE, and the shell itself was made of wrought iron. Gunners could use either a WOODEN FUSE PLUG or a timed paper FUSE. In an article written after the war, Confederate artillerist Edward Porter Alexander stated that the Mullane shell failed three out of four times by either losing its sabot in the gun or by exploding in the gun tube. Of those that were successfully fired, Porter estimated that only 25 percent detonated. Mullane shells were also called "Tennessee Sabots."

Multiform. Slang for the attire of the Army of Northern Virginia prior to the 1862 invasion of Maryland. Few Confederate soldiers had uniforms of any type, and those who did had worn them to tatters. Many wore whatever clothes had been scavenged from Federal casualties on the battlefield or captured supplies. After the battle of Antietam, Union burial crews noted that no two Confederates seemed to be dressed alike.

musicians. Music was everywhere in the war. At the beginning of the conflict, recruiting officers targeted a town's band leader to launch their enlistment efforts. Thus almost every unit had its own musicians, and their music set the rhythm for the march and made camp life tolerable. At the beginning of an engagement, bands played the men into battle. When the fighting had begun, bands put away their instruments and picked up the litters to carry the wounded from the field.

musket. These were SMOOTHBORE shoulder arms with an effective range of one hundred yards. The early years of the Civil War were among the last to see muskets used in combat. Advances in firearms technology in the 1850s, however, had refined rifled barrels, which extended the effective range to six hundred yards, but the U.S. military was not in the forefront of these developments. The twenty-four U.S. arsenals were filled with old-style .69-caliber muskets, although most FLINTLOCKS had been converted to percussion firing systems. When the seceded states seized the arsenals within their borders, they gained almost a quarter of a million shoulder arms—mostly muskets. The Union army's ORDNANCE department authorized increased production of RIFLE-MUSKETS, but production would take time. Both North and South sent agents abroad to procure weapons from Europe, and the British, French, Austrian, and Belgian armorers emptied their stock of outdated muskets, including their shoddiest weapons. It took a year for Northern manufacturers to meet the demand for weapons in terms of both quantity and quality; in the South the need was constant because the eighteen firms founded during the war could not match the output of the Northern manufacturers. Overseas procurements also improved, thus providing the armies with more accurate RIFLES and displacing muskets entirely.

musketoon. A short musket with a large BORE, sometimes called "pumpkin rollers" and "stovepipes."

musket sling. A strap of leather used to carry a MUSKET.

mustang. Several commanders compared the wild and unbroken horse to their subordinates.

muster, to. To assemble an orderly body as governed by long-standing precedent. See GENERAL MUSTER.

mustered in, to be. To be accepted formally and enrolled for military service and thus ready to participate in the next muster of the COMPANY or REGIMENT involved. At least in theory, the mustering in of officers was determined by the rate at which the general muster process proceeded. Once

half of a company was mustered in, a first lieutenant could be named. A captain was not supposed to be mustered in until a company had been mustered in full. Four companies were required to be on muster rolls before a lieutenant colonel could be added, and six companies were needed for a major. A colonel and his staff were to be added only when a regiment had been filled. In practice, many men who served as recruiting agents were rewarded by being elected as captains or colonels.

mustered out, to be. (1) To be discharged formally from military service as a result of a unit's dissolution or the expiration of a soldier's term of enlistment. Discharge could also result from severe illness, a physical handicap, or an order by a superior officer. Because Union Gen. Robert Patterson failed to attack Confederates in the Shenandoah Valley before the July 1861 battle of First Manassas (Bull Run), he was mustered out six days after the battle. Union Gen. Edward R. S. Canby, whose RANK was in volunteer forces, was not mustered out until September 1, 1866. (2) Slang for being killed or severely wounded.

mutatis mutandis. A legal phrase frequently attached to orders, reports, and other documents of which copies were made and sent to persons other than the addressee. Use of the Latin phrase was shorthand for indicating that "all necessary changes have been made."

mutilation. Deliberate abuse of one's body or amputation of body parts to avoid conscription. Some lost front teeth, a finger or two, or a big toe. Others applied medicinal, chemical, or other agents so as to appear to have a skin disease or respiratory condition.

mutiny. Any act or defiance against authority. Scores of mutinies, clearly labeled as such, took place during 1861–65. Some of these involved violence but others were instances of passive resistance. There was no standard by which a commander could easily determine if he was confronted by a mutiny. Some soldiers and units were severely punished for actions that went unnoticed in other commands. The most common causes were bad food or no food, no pay, orders to move to a new geographical region or a new unit, harsh discipline, and extending terms of enlistment. During the war the term was also applied to civilians, Indians, and slaves. Confederate Fort Jackson, which was one of two installations protecting New Orleans, may have been the only scene of two separate mutinies.

muzzleloader. A weapon that had to be loaded from its muzzle rather than its BREECH. Although BREECHLOADERS were predominant among REVOLVERS and RIFLES long before the war ended, the majority of CANNON were muzzleloaders.

muzzle velocity. A measure of the speed at which a bullet, ball, or shell left the muzzle of the weapon from which it was fired.

N

nail ball. A cannonball with a protuberance like a nail, the purpose of which was to keep the projectile from rotating in the BORE of the GUN.

Nansemond, CSS. This 166-ton twin-screw GUN-BOAT was built at Norfolk, Virginia, and commissioned shortly before that city was abandoned in May 1862. For the remainder of the war, she served on the James River, taking part in the engagements at Trent's Reach, Dutch Gap, and Fort Harrison from June to October 1864. On April 3, 1865, the gunboat was burned during the evacuation of Richmond.

Nansemond, USS. Desperate for vessels of any kind, the U.S. Navy purchased this wooden side-wheel steamer in August 1863. It took more than a year to mount one 30-POUNDER PARROTT RIFLE and a pair of 24-pounders on the clumsy 340-ton vessel. Two years after her purchase, she was sold to the Treasury Department, and the Navy Department recovered nearly one-third of the initial investment.

Nantucket, USS. Built by contract at the Atlantic Iron Works, East Boston, this Passaic-class one-turret MONITOR, which mounted two GUNS—11-inch and 15-inch DAHLGREN SMOOTHBORES—cost $408,091. She drew 10.5 feet of water and had a speed of only seven knots. The craft was launched on December 6, 1862, and commissioned on February 26, 1863. Having a displacement of 844 tons, the vessel was assigned to the South Atlantic Blockading Squadron and participated in the attack on the Charleston forts on April 7, 1863. During that unsuccessful action, Nantucket was struck fifty-one times and sent for repairs to Port Royal. When she returned to active duty, she joined in the support of operations on Morris Island in July 1863. While on blockade duty, Nantucket captured the British steamer Jupiter and again challenged the Charleston forts in May 1864. The vessel survived the war, was recommissioned twice, including coastal duty during the Spanish-American War, and was sold for scrap on November 14, 1900.

Napa, USS. Built at Wilmington, Delaware, by contract, this steamer was classified as a light-draft MONITOR, costing $503,897 in December 1864. Evidently unsatisfactory for this use, she was converted into a Casco-class TORPEDO and GUNBOAT that saw wartime service of about ninety days. When John Roach broke up the Napa at New York in 1875, he charged $2,502 for his services.

LIBRARY OF CONGRESS

Napoleon. A field GUN named for Napoleon III (Louis Napoleon) who had assisted in the design. This 12-POUNDER bronze SMOOTHBORE fired a variety of ammunition: SOLID SHOT, SPHERICAL CASE SHOT, and CANISTER. The guns had a range of 1,500 yards with solid shot; canister range was about 200 yards. Napoleons were roughly 500 pounds lighter than other 12-pounders, and they were highly effective in the field because of the increased mobility facilitated by the lighter weight. The 1857 model, which was predominant in the war, was technically classified as a HOWITZER, but it did not arc its shells and did not have a chambered gun TUBE. Both sides addressed their ARTILLERY needs with these smoothbores, as well as other rifled CANNON. The Northern version had a slightly flared muzzle, and some Southern versions added a band to reinforce the BREECH.

Nashville, **CSS.** (1) Built at Greenpoint, New York, in 1853 as a BRIG-rigged side-wheel passenger steamer, this vessel was seized at Charleston, South Carolina, in 1861 and converted to a lightly armed cruiser. As such she made one combat cruise, capturing and burning the merchantman *Harvey Birch* in the English Channel on November 19, 1861. Upon her return to American waters, she captured and burned the SCHOONER *Robert Gilfillan* on February 26, 1862, en route to Beaufort, North Carolina, and then Georgetown, South Carolina. She was sold for use as a BLOCKADE-RUNNER and renamed *Thomas L. Wragg,* but her deep draft was a problem in her newfound pursuits. So she was again sold, and in November 1862, near Savannah, Georgia, became a PRIVATEER and was renamed *Rattlesnake.* In February 1863 she was destroyed by the MONITOR-class USS *Montauk.* (2) The second CSS *Nashville* was an IRONCLAD RAM converted from a side-wheel steam SLOOP in Montgomery in 1864. Construction, however, was completed in Mobile. The vessel measured 271 feet in length, and the added weight of her armor—which was found to be greater than the ship could bear—increased her draft to eleven feet. The battery was installed on November 5, 1864, consisting of six guns, including three 7-inch BROOKE RIFLES and one 24-POUNDER. The Confederate ironclad was surrendered at Nanna Hubba Bluff on the Tombigbee River in Alabama on May 10, 1865. Later the vessel was sold for scrap on November 22, 1867.

National Covenant. An organization of Northern women who founded the first significant boycott of anything not made in the United States.

Nationals. Slang for Union soldiers.

National Union Convention of 1864. The midterm House elections of 1862 went badly for the Republican Party and Abraham Lincoln, forcing the Republicans into an informal coalition with the sixteen members of the pro-war, pro-emancipation Unconditional Union Party from the Border States of Missouri, Kentucky, Maryland, and West Virginia. By mid-1863 many Republicans began to identify themselves as the Union Party and focused on a bipartisan alignment of moderate Republicans and so-

NAVAL HISTORICAL CENTER

called War Democrats. Through the Union Party, they also supported the Union League of American and other patriotic organizations so as to define themselves to the public as the party that represented the restoration of the Union at all costs. In so doing, they won several key political contests throughout the North and the Midwest. To further unite Republicans, Abraham Lincoln used the Union Party label to ensure his renomination, despite the recent history in which no president since 1832 had won a second term and the last incumbent to be nominated had been in 1840—and he had lost. His likely rivals were Salmon P. Chase and John C. Frémont, but both men withdrew from consideration. To underline the bipartisan position of this revived Union Party, Lincoln left the selection of his running mate to the convention meeting in Baltimore on June 7–8, 1864. The delegates chose a Democrat, Andrew Johnson. In the meantime, Ulysses S. Grant's army had bogged down before Petersburg and William T. Sherman's army had stalled in Georgia. To compound matters, Robert E. Lee dispatched Jubal Early's army to threaten Washington. Democrats argued that Lincoln's war policies were a failure, and by the end of August, Lincoln believed the election might be lost as well. In mid-July Early's army was repulsed, and on September 2 Sherman captured Atlanta. Lincoln's opponent and former general, George B. McClellan, was further limited by the peace plank in his campaign. Thus, in the midst of Union victories in the field, the landslide reelection of Lincoln also gave the president a mandate to win the war.

***Nausett*, USS.** This Casco-class light-draft MONITOR was built by contract at a cost of $565,160, but she was not delivered at the Boston Navy Yard until the war was over. As a result she went out of commission only four days after having hit the waves. Listed as a fourth-rate screw-steamer, she survived the war by a decade. In August 1875 John Roach was paid $3,666 for breaking up the warship.

naval flags. (1) The principal ensign of Confederate naval vessels was the same as the national flag. From 1861 to 1863 this was the Stars and Bars, which was flown from the stern of a ship. Naval ensigns varied, as did the national banner, both in the arrangement and number of white stars—varying from seven to thirteen—on a blue field. The Confederate naval JACK followed the custom of the British Royal Navy in that the jack was the same as the union of the ensign (the design in the upper inner corner). Thus from 1861 to 1863, following the pattern of the Stars and Bars, the jack was a blue banner with white stars. In 1863 the design of the naval ensign was changed to the so-called Stainless Banner—a white flag with a union that resembled the Confederate Battle Flag—a blue St. Andrew's cross trimmed in white with thirteen white stars against a red field. The navy jack was also changed to a rectangular version of the battle flag. (2) The Union navy ensign was the Stars and Stripes, displaying from thirty-three to thirty-six stars. Likewise, following the Royal Navy tradition, the jack was patterned after the blue canton and displayed the same number of white stars as the ship's national ensign.

navy. Tobacco cut specifically for sailors.

Navy Yard Bridge. A Washington bridge near the navy yard that spanned an eastern branch of the Potomac River and crossed into Maryland. During much of the war, the Washington bridges were usually closed after 9 P.M. On the night of Abraham Lincoln's assassination, a guard was posted here, but no passes had been required to cross the bridge since April 1, 1865. Thus John Wilkes Booth and co-conspirator David Herold, who arrived separately, were not prevented from crossing.

navvy. A construction laborer, usually associated with public works. During the nineteenth century, canal work and other waterway construction was performed by workers who were called navigators (since the waterways were called navigations). The word *navvy* first appeared in Great Britain in the 1830s and spread from there.

near-firing charge. A small charge of gunpowder estimated to throw projectiles into targets at close range.

Neighbor. A nickname for Confederate Gen. David R. Jones, who his men claimed was just like the neighbor at the farm next door.

Nellie Bly. A horse used by Ulysses S. Grant just after his graduation from the U.S. Military Academy at West Point.

Nellie Gray. A fast mare used by Confederate Gen. Fitzhugh Lee.

Neptune. A nickname for U.S. Secretary of the Navy Gideon Welles, coined by Abraham Lincoln. While Welles lacked a naval background, he was an excellent administrator and was ably served by a number of subordinates, notably Gustavus V. Fox. At the beginning of the war, Welles resourcefully implemented the blockade of Southern ports, pursued the development of ironclads, and encouraged the development of armored ships, heavier naval ordnance, and steam-driven vessels.

Neptune, **CSS.** A wooden steamer fitted out at Galveston, Texas, in 1862. During the January 1, 1863, battle of Galveston, the Neptune—refitted as a COTTONCLAD—sank after ramming the USS *Harriet Lane,* but the Federal ship was boarded and taken in subsequent action.

Nero. A large and fierce guard dog belonging to Confederate Capt. George W. Alexander, commandant of Richmond's CASTLE THUNDER prison. During the winter of 1864 Alexander was transferred to LIBBY PRISON, and Nero patrolled the grounds at night to prevent escapes. At one time Alexander was offered $700 in gold for the dog, but declined. Nevertheless he abandoned the dog during the evacuation of Richmond, and Nero was confiscated by Union authorities and taken to New York.

New Era, **USS.** See USS ESSEX.

New Hampshire, **USS.** Nine ships were authorized to be built by Congress on April 29, 1816, "to rate not less than 74 guns each," and work began on the one named *Alabama* in June 1819. Built of white oak at the Portsmouth Navy Yard, the warship was rated at 2,633 tons and had a draft of eighteen feet. The ship was set to be launched in 1825, but she was left on the stocks until the Civil War. Renamed *New Hampshire* on October 28, 1863. she was launched on April 23, 1864, and fitted out as a stores and depot ship of the South Atlantic Blockading Squadron. Although initially planned as a ship of the line with a vast battery, the *New Hampshire* sailed with only four 100-POUNDER PARROTT RIFLES and six 9-inch DAHLGRENS. Commissioned on May 13, 1864, she was sent to Port Royal, South Carolina, and on July 29, 1864, relieved her sister ship, *VERMONT.* After the war she served as a receiving ship and a training ship. On November 30, 1904, she was renamed *Granite State* to release the state name for a newly authorized battleship. *Granite State* caught fire in May 1921, and the hull was sold for salvage. In 1922 the remains were refloated and taken in tow, but the hulk caught fire and was lost in a storm off the Massachusetts coast.

newspaper leaks. Military information regularly appeared in the newspapers of both North and South and often proved to be of value to the other side. Partly because all communication was slow, editors frequently printed news of value to the enemy. One such incident involved the *New York Evening Post* in September 1863. Washington's military planners had decided to send reinforcements to Gen. William S. Rosecrans, whose forces were bottled up at Chattanooga. Although news correspondents were briefed on the plan, they were asked not to print anything. Shortly afterward the *Post* ran a story revealing that the 11th and 12th Corps were en route to Tennessee. When called to account for this breach of faith, the paper's editors claimed that the account had been based on rumors and that their Washington correspondent had nothing to do with the story. During Gen. William T. Sherman's March to the Sea, there were no lines of communication between Washington and Sherman. Thus news of the Federal advance from Atlanta to Savannah had to be gleaned from Southern papers. Such information appeared throughout the war and was never effectively controlled.

New Uncle Sam, USS. See USS *BLACK HAWK*.

New York Times. The *Times* was founded in 1851, and by the time of the war had become the second-largest newspaper in New York. Its editors were among the pioneers in impartial reporting, as opposed to the partisan editorializing to which most other papers were prone. During the war, the *Times* supported the Lincoln administration and sent its correspondents into the field with the Northern armies. At a time when news was usually days old before it appeared in the paper, the *Times* printed accounts of some battles within twenty-four hours of the engagement.

New York Tribune. The *Tribune* was founded in 1841 and came to be perhaps the most influential newspaper in the nation during the editorship of Horace Greeley, who made no pretension of objectivity. When the paper echoed the "ON TO RICHMOND!" cry, it was heard in Washington and may have been a factor in the premature launching of the army into Virginia and onto the Manassas countryside. When the paper intoned the "PRAYER OF TWENTY MILLIONS," advocating emancipation of Southern slaves, most in the North responded well to Abraham Lincoln's proclamation of January 1863. Yet Greeley's volatile editorials at times advo-

cated positions contrary to those that he had taken previously: one day championing RADICAL REPUBLICANS, the next favoring Liberal Democrats, and later promoting various peace initiatives. The paper's fortunes were tied to Greeley, and so, over time, it lost ground in New York to the *Herald* and the *Times*.

Nicodemus house. A square white-framed dwelling that stood in a depression on the west end of the battlefield of Antietam. Caught between the two armies, several civilians who had taken refuge in the home ran from the structure during the early morning fighting. Most of them would almost certainly have been killed had not both sides suddenly ceased fire.

nice. Accurate to the point of exactness. During Confederate Gen. John H. Morgan's raid into Indiana and Ohio, he initially dispatched numerous units in many directions. Gen. Basil W. Duke later wrote that "very nice calculation was necessary" to prevent these men from becoming separated from the main body of raiders.

niddering. A synonym for *cowardly* or *base*, prevalent in the COTTON BELT.

night action. Any movement that took place after the sun had set and "black dark" descended. Except when the moon was bright, most commanders considered the risk of night action to outweigh the advantages of surprising the enemy. Describing a move near Resaca, Georgia, in 1864, newspaper correspondent A. J. Daugherty wrote: "Of all the fearful things in the world, a night attack, I truly believe, is the most dreaded by the soldier." At Chancellorsville, Thomas J. "Stonewall" Jackson undertook a reconnoiter of the Union positions himself to assess the practicality of further night action. As he rode through the darkness, at about 9:30 P.M., a North Carolina unit fired on the party and wounded Jackson, who died a week later. A scouting excursion to assess the merits of a night attack cost the Confederate army one of its most dynamic generals.

nine-month man. A soldier who enlisted for no less and no more than nine months. Some early units went to war on this basis, but it was apparent that such enlistments were both awkward and inadequate. Most of the men who marched off for a little bit of fighting were forced to fight for the duration of the war.

nines, by the. The step-by-step process by which soldiers loaded their MUSKETS and RIFLES.

ninety-day gunboat. A term of praise for the GUN-BOATS built by James B. Eads in ninety days or any similar craft that was hurriedly constructed for Federal use.

nipple. With regard to shoulder arms, this was part of the percussion firing system, a small round device with a hole in the center upon which soldiers placed a percussion CAP. When the hammer struck the cap, the flash was channeled into the gun barrel, igniting the POWDER and firing the bullet. With regard to artillery, similar nipples were attached to the contact end of a percussion FUSE and held the percussion cap in place. When the percussion cap was detonated, the spark traveled through the nipple and ignited the charge.

Nipsic, **USS.** This wooden GUNBOAT was built at Portsmouth Navy Yard at the comparatively low cost of $231,127. A brigantine of only 593 tons, the vessel had a draft of nearly twelve feet. Her initial battery included one 150-POUNDER RIFLE, one 30-pounder, two 9-inch DAHLGRENS, two 24-pounder HOWITZERS, and two 12-pounder RIFLES. Commissioned in September 1863, the *Nipsic* did not play a significant role in any Civil War battles. Her career ended in 1889, when she was beached at Samoa. Later refloated, the vessel was sold to George J. Willy of Seattle for $7,375.

"No Bottom!" N. The cry of a LEADSMAN whose line was not long enough to measure the depth of water at a given point.

nockum stiff. A home-brewed alcoholic beverage.

no quarter. A condition under which prisoners were not to be taken. At times, both sides accepted this stipulation despite the fact that few ever acknowledged such a BLACK FLAG POLICY.

nostalgia. This diagnosis appears in several surgeons' reports and may best be seen as a kind of extreme depression. This synonym for homesickness was sometimes listed as a cause of death.

Northwest Conspiracy. In early 1864 two officers who had been with John Hunt Morgan in Tennessee and Kentucky—Thomas Hines and George St. Leger Grenfel—were given the task of fomenting revolt in the western states of the Union, an area formerly known as the Northwest Territory. From Richmond it appeared that Southern sympathizers, known in the North as COPPERHEADS, in Illinois, Indiana, and Ohio were on the verge of insurrection. Hines and Grenfel were dispatched to coordinate the effort and pull these states out of the Union, which supposedly would force the North to negotiate an end to the war. Confederate agents in Canada were to launch a series of raids in Northern cities, including efforts to release Confederate prisoners and arm them from the arsenals near the camps in which they were being held. The most ambitious of these prison breaks was to be timed to coincide with the Democratic National Convention meeting in Chicago in August 1864. While the leaders of the plot were devoted to the cause, and these included many from the Sons of Liberty (see KNIGHTS OF THE GOLDEN CIRCLE) and other Copperhead organizations, the Confederate agents found there were fewer followers than they had been led to believe and few who were willing to risk their lives. At the same time, the Copperhead groups were rife with informers who passed information on to the Union military authorities. Shortly before the uprising was to begin in Chicago, three thousand additional Federal troops arrived in the city and many of the leaders of the groups were arrested and imprisoned. Faced with the realities of the situation, the Confederate agents scaled down the operation and focused on the state of Illinois, rescheduling the uprising for November 8, 1864, the day of the presidential election. Again information was leaked to the Federal military and a series of arrests were made, nabbing virtually all of the agents. In December 1864 eight men, including Hines and Grenfel, were taken to McLean Barracks in Cincinnati for trial. By the time guilty verdicts were returned for all of them, one had escaped and another had committed suicide. All received prison terms except Grenfel, who was sentenced to hang. President Andrew Johnson later commuted his sentence to life imprisonment. No one knows just how influential the Copperhead groups in the Midwest were during the war. Indiana Gov. Oliver P. Morton and other politicians of the Midwest were panicked by what they heard and by the dissent they saw demonstrated in their streets. As the Northwest Conspiracy played out, it appeared that these fears were exaggerated almost as much as the claims and promises made to the Confederate government by the Copperhead leaders of these small pockets of dissent.

Nottoway Grays. The nickname of Company G of the 18th Virginia Infantry, which had begun the war as the Nottoway (County) Rifle Guards. The COMPANY began the war with 100 men, and muster rolls indicate that 473 served in the unit during the war. Beginning with the battle of First Manassas (Bull Run), the company participated in most of the major battles of the eastern theater. At APPOMATTOX the ranks of the Nottoway Grays held only 28 men, of which only 3 were original members.

noxious effluvia. A term similar to MIASMA used by medical personnel to designate extremely strong unpleasant odors.

number. An identification assigned to each vessel of the U.S. Navy in addition to a name. Signalmen using semaphore flags on vessels out of voice range exchanged numbers rather than names, because numbers were shorter and more rapidly transmitted. Also several vessels were renamed during the war, but they retained their number, which made numbers a better means of identification than names.

Number Ones. The members of GUN crews were numbered according to their role in the loading and firing of their gun. Number ones were responsible for loading, and because of their vital role, not to mention their being toward the front of the weapon, these men were easier targets for the oncoming enemy. During the September 17, 1862, battle of Antietam, four number ones in a Federal BATTERY were picked off during a span of five minutes.

numbers on caps. Federal soldiers wore various INSIGNIA on the crown of their caps to identify their REGIMENT.

nurse. At the beginning of the war all army nurses were men. Through the efforts of Dorothy Dix and Mary Anne Bickerdyke, women were allowed to serve as nurses in U.S. military hospitals. By the end of the war, far more women than men served as army nurses.

Nyanza, **USS.** In 1863 Rear Adm. David D. Porter purchased this 203-ton wooden side-wheel steamer at Cincinnati for $33,500. Armed with six 24-POUNDER HOWITZERS, the vessel could easily be used against Confederate batteries on bluffs overlooking the inland waterways. The *Nyanza* suffered no serious damage during the two years she spent in naval service; thus this was one of a handful of ships the U.S. government did not sell at a loss after the war. When sold at auction in New Orleans, she brought $34,000.

O

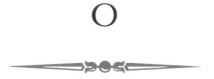

oath of allegiance. See LOYALTY OATH.

oblique order. A sequence of troops in which one FLANK of an attacking force is held back, or REFUSED, while another flank moves forward to press the assault. This strategy was designed to have the refused flank in position so that it could rapidly support the attacking flank.

observer. A military representative from a foreign country. Observers were often attached to a commander's staff as aides-de-camp and moved with the troops but did not take part in combat. Their role was to note what weapons and strategies were most effective and report their findings to their governments. A substantial number of foreign observers traveled with the Federal and Confederate armies, but no one knows how many. Some of these men were soldiers of fortune; others were aristocrats and minor nobles. Many were here at the behest of their governments, but others came without credentials. In April 1863 Lt. Col. Arthur James Lyon Fremantle of the Coldstream Guards, a British officer, began a three-month trek across the country, from Brownsville, Texas, to New York. Along the way he met Joseph E. Johnston, Braxton Bragg, P. G. T. Beauregard, Jefferson Davis, Robert E. Lee, and James Longstreet and witnessed the July 1–3, 1863, battle of Gettysburg. Another Englishman, G. F. R. Henderson, spent time with both Lee and Thomas J. "Stonewall" Jackson and wrote a biography of the latter. France was represented by the Prince de Joinville and two of his nephews, the Comte de Paris and the Duc de Chartres. All three were attached to the Army of the Potomac for about a year. Joinville wrote a

LIBRARY OF CONGRESS

book about this army and its commander, George B. McClellan, and the Comte de Paris wrote a history of the war that appeared in both French and English. Francois Adolphe Victor de Chanel was dispatched to Ulysses S. Grant's army by the French government in 1864 and remained until the Confederate surrender. His official report was published nearly a decade later. Switzerland sent Col. Augusto Fogliardi in 1863, and he met several members of Lincoln's cabinet then went into the field just before the May 2–3, 1863, battle of Chancellorsville. Prussia sent Justus Schiebert, an army engineer, and he entered the country at Charleston and later joined the Army of Northern Virginia. He too wrote a book of his experiences. Another Prussian, Count Ferdinand von Zeppelin, came to observe the war, but not as a representative of his government. He met with Lincoln and received a pass to move freely among the Union forces. Zeppelin served briefly on the staff of Alfred Pleasanton and then moved into the Midwest. On August 13, 1863, the self-appointed military observer ascended in a balloon at St. Paul, Minnesota. He noted the military aspect of balloon observation, but it was not until thirty-seven years later (1891) that he began to experiment with rigid navigable balloons, later called dirigibles. Zeppelin's refinement of dirigible building introduced a class of aircraft that carried his name for the following thirty-seven years.

occupy, to. To maintain an engagement with an enemy.

oh-be-joyful. A home-brewed alcoholic beverage.

Ohio State Penitentiary. This three-story facility in downtown Columbus began preparing to receive its first Confederate prisoners of war on July 30, 1863, following the capture of Gen. John Hunt Morgan and thirty men near New Lisbon, Ohio. The limestone structure had been built in the early 1830s with five tiers of thirty-five cells, and was overcrowded when the first sixty-eight Confederate prisoners arrived. The prisoners were kept separate from the rest of the prison population, but discipline was enforced without regard to the privileges normally afforded prisoners of war. On this point, the warden, Nathaniel Merion, proved to be intractable, even consigning POWs to solitary confinement when rules were broken. The Federal government assumed responsibility for the prisoners on November 4 and relaxed several of the prison policies for the Confederates, notably daily cell inspections. On November 28 Morgan and six other prisoners escaped, having tunneled out; it was later deduced that the tunneling had begun as soon as the Federal authorities had taken over the supervision of the Southerners. Two of the escapees were apprehended in Louisville, Kentucky, and Morgan appeared on December 23 in Franklin, Tennessee, well beyond the reach of Union authorities. Meanwhile the Confederate prisoners remaining in the Ohio Penitentiary were moved to another cell block and watched more closely. An escape attempt similar to Morgan's was thwarted in February 1864, and by mid-March the remaining sixty-five POWs were transferred to FORT DELAWARE.

oil. Civil War references to oil generally refer to whale oil.

oil of gladness. A home-brewed alcoholic beverage.

Old Abe. (1) Abraham Lincoln. (2) The eagle mascot of Company C of the 8th Wisconsin, also known as the Eagle Regiment. By far the most famous mascot of the war, the bird witnessed more than forty battles and skirmishes. In battle he flew over the fighting and screeched at the Southerners, and afterward he would return to his perch. To the Confederates, he was known as the "Yankee buzzard."

LIBRARY OF CONGRESS

Old Abe was retired from front-line duty in September 1864 and presented to the state of Wisconsin, which kept him in a cage in the state capitol. The bird made countless appearances at war benefits and afterward to raise funds for orphans. He died of smoke inhalation during a fire at the capitol in 1881. (3) A nickname for Confederate Gen. Abraham Buford who served in Braxton Bragg's 1862 Kentucky campaign and with Nathan Bedford Forrest during John Bell Hood's 1864 Tennessee campaign.

Old Allegheny. A nickname for Confederate Gen. Edward Johnson, also known as "Allegheny Ed." He participated in Thomas J. "Stonewall" Jackson's 1862 Shenandoah campaign and the Gettysburg, Wilderness, and Spotsylvania campaigns, where he was captured at the "Bloody Angle." Paroled, Johnson was assigned to John Bell Hood's ill-fated 1864 Tennessee campaign and was captured again during the battle of Nashville.

Old Artillery. A nickname for Confederate Gen. P. G. T. Beauregard, whose artillery skill was legendary. After graduating from the U.S. Military Academy at West Point in 1838, he was appointed as an assistant to the artillery instructor, Robert Anderson, whom Beauregard faced later in the 1861 crisis at FORT SUMTER in Charleston, South Carolina.

Old Bald Head. A nickname for one-legged Confederate Gen. Richard S. Ewell.

Old Beeswax. A nickname for Confederate Adm. Raphael Semmes, who became a MIDSHIPMAN at age seventeen and during the war commanded the famous COMMERCE RAIDER CSS *ALABAMA*. Beeswax was a reference to his meticulously groomed and lengthy mustache.

Old Blinkey. A nickname for Union Gen. William H. French. Stationed in Texas when the war began, he was one of the few officers in the

state who refused to leave the U.S. Army. He served well as a brigade commander in the Peninsula and Seven Days' campaigns and a division commander at Antietam, Fredericksburg, and Chancellorsville, but he proved a poor corps commander following Gettysburg and the Mine Run campaigns. Thus he was removed from field command and ended the war with garrison and administrative duties.

Old Blizzards. A nickname for Confederate Gen. William W. Loring based on his successful repulse of Ulysses S. Grant's effort to approach Vicksburg through the tangle of waterways to the north of the city. During a spirited engagement at Fort Pemberton at Yahoo Pass, Loring ordered his gunners to fire with the excited command: "Give 'em blizzards, boys! Give 'em blizzards!"

Old Blue Light. An alleged nickname of Thomas J. "Stonewall" Jackson.

old bull. Derisive slang for salted horse meat.

Old Bob. A nickname for Robert E. Lee.

Old Boy. A nickname for Confederate Gen. P. G. T. Beauregard.

Old Brains. A nickname for Union Gen. Henry W. Halleck, who was known to have an intellect but feared to use it on the battlefield. In July 1862 Abraham Lincoln appointed him the nominal head of the Federal army so as to take advantage of his administrative skills and leave the fighting to the

men who were proving themselves in the field. When Ulysses S. Grant was elevated to the rank of lieutenant general and named supreme commander of all Union armies, Lincoln named Halleck his chief of staff.

Old Buck. (1) A nickname for Confederate Gen. William Terry, who was a member of the militia company that went to Harpers Ferry in 1859 to subdue and capture John Brown. He fought under Thomas J. "Stonewall" Jackson and commanded a REGIMENT from First Manassas through Spotsylvania, after which he commanded the Stonewall Brigade through the siege of Petersburg. (2) A nickname for Union Col. Robert C. Buchanan, who commanded the 4th U.S. Infantry, the regiment from which Ulysses S. Grant resigned in 1854. Although named a brigadier for the Seven Days' campaign, Second Manassas (Bull Run), and Fredericksburg, this promotion was not confirmed by the Senate—likely due to his friendship with Fitz John Porter, who was court-martialed for the defeat at Second Manassas. (3) A nickname for James Buchanan, the fifteenth president of the United States.

Old Bush. A nickname for Confederate Gen. Bushrod R. Johnson.

Old Capitol Prison. This three-story brick structure in Washington, D.C., at the corner of First and A Streets, was built in 1800 as a tavern and boarding house, but both ventures failed and the building stood empty when the city was put to the torch by the British in 1814. The government purchased the structure and renovated the interior for use by Congress until 1819, when the new Capitol was completed. The First Street building came to be known as the Old Capitol, and for the next forty years served various purposes, including use as a boarding house and a school. In 1861 the provost marshal commandeered the structure, and on August 8 the first Confederate prisoners of war arrived. Occupancy, however, was not limited to POWs, and the Old Capitol came to be the primary holding facility for political prisoners, Southern sympathizers, and spies. By October 1861 the structure was full and a row of adjoining houses was added to the complex. The annex became known as the Carroll Prison and brought capacity to about 1,500. Among the spies housed

in the Old Capitol Prison were Rose O'Neal Greenhow and Belle Boyd. The prison operated throughout the war, and records show that 5,761 prisoners at one time or another were kept here. Of that number 457 died while in custody, but these numbers are considered low since the first reports were not filed by the officials of the prison until May 1863. In 1865 the Old Capitol was used to detain anyone accused of complicity in the Lincoln assassination; it also was the scene of the hanging of Henry Wirz, the commandant of ANDERSONVILLE and the only individual convicted of war crimes during the war. On November 29, 1865, two weeks after Wirz's hanging, the Old Capitol Prison was ordered dismantled and the Carroll Prison Annex was also torn down.

Old Cerro Gordo. A nickname for Confederate Gen. John S. Williams that stemmed from his role in the battle of Cerro Gordo during the Mexican War.

Old Clubby. A nickname for Confederate Gen. Edward Johnson; see OLD ALLEGHENY.

Old Cock Eye. A nickname for Union Gen. Benjamin F. Butler.

Old Demoralizer. A nickname given by Union soldiers for a Confederate 10-inch COLUMBIAD at Port Hudson. The Confederates named the gun LADY DAVIS.

oldest. Slang for the veterans within a unit.

Old Figgers. A nickname for Union Gen. Charles H. Grosvenor, who had a penchant for odds making.

Old Flintlock. A nickname for Confederate Gen. Roger W. Hanson, who was criticized for being prone to old-fashioned notions and ways. He fought at FORT DONELSON and in Braxton Bragg's Kentucky campaign and was mortally wounded at the battle of Stones River.

Roger W. Hanson   *Louis M. Goldsborough*

Old Four Eyes. A nickname for Union Gen. George G. Meade; see also OLD SNAPPING TURTLE.

Old Glory. The Union banner known as the Stars and Stripes.

Old Granny. A nickname for Confederate Gen. William S. Pendleton. Prior to the war he had been the rector of Grace Episcopal Church in Lexington, Virginia, but at the beginning of the conflict he was elected the captain of the Rockbridge Artillery. He served as chief of artillery to Joseph E. Johnston and was chosen by Robert E. Lee to be chief of artillery for the Army of Northern Virginia. Pendleton's son, Alexander "Sandie" Pendleton, was on the staff of Thomas J. "Stonewall" Jackson.

Old Gridiron. Southern slang for the Union Stars and Stripes.

Old Gun Barrel. A nickname for Union Gen. William H. French. See OLD BLINKEY.

Old Guts. A nickname for Union Rear Adm. Louis M. Goldsborough, who commanded the North Atlantic Blockading Squadron from April 1861 to July 1862. He received the THANKS OF CONGRESS for the capture of Roanoke Island although it had been necessary for his command to fire on Union soldiers who were engaged in hand-to-hand fighting with the Confederate defenders.

Old Heart of Oak. A nickname for Union Adm. David G. Farragut, who was regarded with

U.S. ARMY MILITARY HISTORY INSTITUTE

David W. Farragut   *Thomas J. Jackson*   *James Longstreet*   *William T. Sherman*

suspicion at the beginning of hostilities because of his strong southern ties. Such fears were repudiated with Farragut's April 1862 capture of New Orleans, Mississippi River operations, and the August 1864 battle of Mobile Bay.

Old Hike. A guard at FORT DELAWARE who had a reputation for cruelty. Prisoners reported that he was from Vermont and that his name was Adams, but no one knew his full name. The captives also claimed that Adams was the first prisoner sent to Fort Delaware because he was the first Union soldier to reach Washington after the great skedaddle from the First Manassas battlefield. The nickname came from his constantly yelling "Hike out!" to groups of prisoners as he marched them from their barracks to search the men and their bunks for contraband.

Old Jack. A nickname for Confederate Gen. Thomas J. "Stonewall" Jackson. Also called Old Jack the Sleepless.

Old Jack's Commissary General. A nickname for Union Gen. Nathaniel P. Banks who amassed several depots of supplies in the Shenandoah Valley and saw many of them captured by Stonewall Jackson's men.

Old Jubilee. A nickname for Confederate Gen. Jubal Early.

Old Lundy. A nickname for Union Gen. Winfield Scott, whom many commented as being one year older than the Constitution.

Old One Wing. A nickname for Confederate Gen. John G. Martin, who lost his right arm at Churubusco during the Mexican War.

Old Pap. (1) A nickname for Confederate Gen. Sterling Price; also known as OLD SKEDADDLE. (2) A nickname for Union Gen. Alpheus Williams, whose command discovered Robert E. Lee's LOST ORDER prior to the September 17, 1862, battle of Antietam.

Old Pete. A nickname for Confederate Gen. James Longstreet, who was also known as Lee's Old War Horse.

Old Pills. A nickname for Union Gen. William T. Sherman.

Old Prayer Book. A nickname for Union Gen. Oliver O. Howard, who was known for his piety.

Old Probabilities. A nickname for Union Col. Albert J. Meyer, chief signal officer of Federal forces.

Old Quinine. Slang for Federal surgeons who often had no medication to offer except quinine.

old regular. Any soldier who had enlisted in the regular army prior to the war was considered an old regular. Men who enlisted in the U.S. Army after the battle of FORT SUMTER were assigned to long-established units rather than into newly formed volunteer and state units. Throughout the war, regular army units maintained their identity apart from the volunteers.

Old Reliable. (1) A nickname for Confederate Gen. John Bratton, who succeeded Micah Jenkins when Jenkins was killed during the battle of the Wilderness. (2) A nickname for Confederate Gen. William J. Hardee, whose book on tactics was the standard of martial conduct used by both sides in the war; see also OLD SLOW TROT.

Old Rock. A nickname for Confederate Gen. Henry L. Benning, who, after the mortal wounding of Robert A. Toombs, commanded the Confederate defenders at Burnside's Bridge during the September 17, 1862, battle of Antietam.

Old Sacramento. A nickname for a cannon that was seized during the Mexican War by Americans at Sacramento, California. It was used against the Union army at Carthage, Wilson's Creek, and Lexington but was captured at Pea Ridge.

Old Skedaddle. A nickname for Confederate Gen. Sterling Price, see also OLD PAP.

Old Slow Trot. A nickname for Confederate Gen. William J. Hardee, see also OLD RELIABLE.

Old Snapping Turtle. A nickname for Union Gen. George G. Meade, see also OLD FOUR EYES.

old soldier's disease. See SOLDIER'S DISEASE.

Old Soldiers' Home. See SOLDIERS' HOME.

Old Spectacles. A nickname for Union Gen. Henry W. Halleck; see also OLD BRAINS.

Old Stars. A nickname for Union Gen. Ormsby M. Mitchel who received his brigadier's star in August 1861 and wore his insignia of rank day and night.

Old Tecumseh. A nickname for Gen. William T. Sherman, after his middle name.

Old Thad. A nickname for Vermont-born Congressman Thaddeus Stevens. A proud RADICAL REPUBLICAN, Stevens clashed with Abraham Lincoln over the civil rights of freed and former slaves. After the war, Stevens initiated the process that led to the impeachment of Andrew Johnson.

Old Tom Fool. A nickname for Thomas J. "Stonewall" Jackson dating from his tenure as an artillery and physics professor at the Virginia Military Institute.

Old Tycoon. (1) A nickname for Abraham Lincoln. (2) A nickname for Confederate Gen. Sterling G. Price of Missouri.

Old Whitey. The name of the horse used by Mary Anne "Mother" Bickerdyke.

Old Wooden Head. A nickname for Union Gen. Henry W. Halleck.

old wristbreaker. A heavy SABER with a curved single-edged blade and a large brass guard; it was first used by the U.S. CAVALRY in the decades before the war.

one-hundred-day men. In response to Robert E. Lee's second invasion of the North, many Pennsylvanians volunteered for one hundred days' service within the state to repel the Southerners.

***Oneida,* USS.** This vessel, a three-masted wooden SCHOONER also equipped with steam power, was commissioned early in 1862. She had a displacement of 1,032 tons, a draft on nine feet, and a top speed of 12 knots. The ship's battery consisted of three 30-POUNDER DAHLGREN RIFLES, two 9-inch Dahlgren SMOOTHBORES, four 32-pounders, and one 12-pounder boat howitzer. The warship was not seriously damaged during the war, but five years afterward the vessel was run down in Yokohama Bay by the steamer *Bombay.* Forced to sell the hulk in Japan, the U.S. Navy recovered $1,505 of the ship's $294,697 original construction cost.

One-legged Dick. A nickname for Confederate Gen. Richard Ewell.

One-tenth Plan. Abraham Lincoln's proposal for the restoration of the seceded states to the Union was based on one-tenth of a state's 1860 electorate taking a LOYALTY OATH. Although the plan was implemented briefly in Louisiana, it was scrapped by Congress soon after the president's assassination.

onion day. In many parts of the North, a day was designated for children to bring onions and non-perishable foods to school to be sent to soldiers by the U.S. SANITARY COMMISSION or some other soldiers aid organization.

On to Richmond! A slogan popularized by the *NEW YORK TRIBUNE* in a wartime editorial by Charles A. Dana. This challenge appeared on the front page of the *Tribune* for many days during the summer of 1861 and played a role in the timing of the Union army's July advance on Manassas.

open, to. To fire at the enemy, usually in regard to ARTILLERY.

open the ball. To initiate a battle.

operate on, to. To direct fire at a specific position, unit, BATTERY, or warship.

OR. See *WAR OF THE REBELLION, THE: OFFICIAL RECORDS OF THE UNION AND CONFEDERATE ARMIES.*

Orange Blossoms. The 124th New York Infantry, which was recruited and organized in Orange County.

Orange Plank Road. This east-west PLANK ROAD linked Orange Court House with Fredericksburg, Virginia. In the midst of this heavily wooded region, eleven miles west of Fredericksburg, the road passed the Chancellor farmhouse and inn, which was the focal point of the May 1–4, 1863, battle of Chancellorsville.

order arms. According to the MANUAL OF ARMS, this position required the RIFLE to be placed with its butt on the ground and held vertically next to a soldier's right leg.

orderly. An aide, typically a private, assigned to perform various tasks for an officer.

order of battle. A specific and detailed battle plan, listing each unit of the army for which it was prepared. Such orders could also contain specific directives concerning the sequence in which these units would engage the enemy.

ordnance. Although widely used to designate a BATTERY or a group of GUNS, this term also included vehicles used in combat, ammunition, and equipment. Every BATTALION and CORPS had its own ordnance unit whose members were responsible for maintaining this gear and storing and transporting it as needed.

ordnance gun. This 3-inch wrought-iron rifled CANNON was one of the mainstays of the FIELD ARTILLERY of both Union and Confederate armies. While 12-POUNDER SMOOTHBORE NAPOLEONS were excellent for short-range fighting, ordnance guns were valued for their long-range accuracy. Production was inexpensive compared to other cannon since sheets of iron were wrapped around a core, and these were less prone to explode when fired, as was the case with many cast-iron cannon. Ordnance guns were also called 6-pounders or Rodmans, but neither term is accurate.

Original Gorilla. A harsh nickname for Abraham Lincoln, referring to his ungainly limbs.

Oriole, **USS.** This 137-ton TINCLAD was purchased in Cincinnati on December 7, 1864, to be used on the western rivers. Originally named *Florence Miller,* she cost only $40,000 but required repairs cost $24,500. The vessel was commissioned in March 1865 at Mound City, Illinois, but never saw combat. Eight months after its purchase, it was sold for one-fourth the cost it took to get it ready for use.

Orphan Brigade. The Confederate 1st Kentucky came to be known as the Orphan Brigade when the state remained in the Union and these four thousand men departed in February 1862, never to return until the end of the war. They fought at Shiloh, Corinth, Vicksburg, Baton Rouge, Stones River, Jackson, Chickamauga, Missionary Ridge, and throughout Georgia during the Atlanta campaign and MARCH TO THE SEA. Because of their peculiar situation, the BRIGADE could not recruit additional Kentuckians to fill its battle-depleted ranks, so the unit dwindled to five hundred men by the end of the war. Former U.S. vice president and Confederate Gen. John C. Breckinridge is believed to have given the brigade its nickname after the battle of Stones River, where the unit suffered 35 percent casualties. One of the brigade's generals, Ben Hardin Helm, was Abraham Lincoln's brother-in-law. When Helm was killed at Chickamauga, he was mourned at the Lincoln White House. In the last months of the war, the surviving members of the brigade were made MOUNTED INFANTRY. They were among the last Confederates to surrender, postponing the inevitable until May 1865 at Washington, Georgia.

***Osage*, USS.** The 523-ton Neosho-class USS *Osage* (smallest of her class) and her sister ship, USS *Neosho*, were designed by James B. Eads and built at his shipyard at Carondelet, Missouri. These shallow-draft, wooden-hulled, single-turret MONITORS were commissioned in July 1863 and armed with two 11-inch SMOOTHBORES. They were the only stern-wheel monitors built during the war. *Osage* was assigned to Mississippi River operations and participated in an expedition up the Black and Ouachita Rivers and in the Red River campaign. In February 1865 she was transferred to the West Gulf Blockading Squadron for use in Mobile Bay operations. A month later, on March 29, 1865, during the attack on Spanish Fort, *Osage* was sunk by a TORPEDO (mine) in the Blakely River. The hull was raised and sold at public auction in 1867, recovering $20,467 of its original cost of $119,678.

osnaburg. A heavy, coarse cotton fabric used for the linings of HAVERSACKS. Less coarse versions were used for undergarments.

Our Stanley. A nickname for Union Gen. David S. Stanley, a career officer who served as the chief of cavalry of the Army of the Cumberland and became a divisional commander during the Atlanta campaign. He received the highest praise for his conduct at Columbia, Spring Hill, and Franklin, Tennessee.

outbreak. A euphemism in the South for slave trouble. In 1863, near Thibodeaux, Louisiana, Union Gen. Godfrey Weitzel was alerted to an outbreak, which seized the surrounding community with an "hourly expectation and terror of a general rising," he wrote.

outworks. Defensive positions—such as RIFLE PITS, RAVELINS, and LUNETTES—designed to hinder an enemy's advance on a fortification.

overhaul, to. N. To inspect the contents of a ship carefully.

overslaughed, to be. To be bypassed for promotion by an officer junior in RANK or prestige. After

having won the largest battle ever fought in North America, George Gordon Meade was over-slaughed by Abraham Lincoln, who made Ulysses S. Grant the first full lieutenant general since George Washington.

Owl-eyed Billy. A nickname for Confederate Gen. William E. "Grumble" Jones.

oysters. A Southern dish made of coarse corn-meal, eggs, and butter.

P

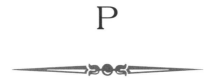

pack saddle. A saddle for a donkey, mule, or horse that was designed to carry a burden rather than a rider.

Paddy. (1) A nickname for Union Gen. Joshua T. Owen, a native of Wales, which in the United States was not always distinguished from Ireland. After raising a ninety-day REGIMENT he became the colonel of the 24th Pennsylvania. At Antietam he led a BRIGADE and earned a star by his performance. Although present at Gettysburg, he took no part in the battle because he was under arrest. At his own request, he relinquished his commission and was MUSTERED OUT in July 1864. (2) A nickname for James Graydon, a native of Ireland and a soldier in the U.S. Army. Apparently without a commission, he organized and led what he called a "spy company" in New Mexico and Arizona. Most of his recruits were Hispanics and lacked any military training. Nevertheless they were successful in harassing Confederate movements prior to the battle of Glorietta Pass.

Joshua T. Owen

pads. These organized gangs in New York, Boston, and Philadelphia preyed on Union soldiers on leave.

painter. N. A stout line fastened at the bow of a ship or boat and used to moor the vessel. A mooring line attached to the stern was known as a stern fast.

palisade. A line of wooden stakes driven into the ground to form a defensive bulwark in front of earthworks.

***Palmetto State*, CSS.** This Richmond-class IRON-CLAD RAM was built by the Charleston firm of Cameron and Company in January 1862 and ready for service in September of that year. Initially her battery consisted of two 7-inch RIFLES and two 9-inch SMOOTHBORES. On the morning of January 31, 1863, in concert with her sister ship, CSS *Chicora*, she attacked the Union blockading fleet off Charleston, capturing the USS *Mercedita* and disabling the USS *Keystone State*. *Palmetto State* also participated in the defense of Charleston Harbor during the attack of April 1–7, 1863, and also assisted in removing troops from Morris Island on the night of September 6–7, 1863. By February 1865 *Palmetto State*'s battery was upgraded to ten 7-inch rifles, but the vessel was burned when Charleston was evacuated on February 18.

panada. Also known as BULLY SOUP, this gruel of cornmeal, army crackers mashed in boiling water, ginger, and wine or medicinal whiskey was usually administered in hospitals. Some say that it first appeared during the Mexican War, and others claim that it was concocted by Eliza Harris of the U.S.

SANITARY COMMISSION. Mary Anne "Mother" Bickerdyke was known to dispense it to her patients.

panniers. These baskets were used to carry non-perishable foods and medical supplies on the backs of horses and mules.

***Pansy,* USS.** Formerly known as *Samson,* this steam tug was renamed when it was transferred to the War Department on September 30, 1862. Never armed, she performed useful service on the western rivers. After the war, the 50-ton vessel was sold at Mound City, Illinois, for $450.

Pap. (1) A nickname for Confederate Gen. Sterling Price. (2) A nickname for Confederate Gen. Felix Zollicoffer. (3) A nickname for Union Gen. George H. Thomas, also known as Slow Trot, the ROCK OF CHICKAMAUGA, and the Hammer of Nashville.

Felix Zollicoffer

paper-collar soldiers. Soldiers on GARRISON duty where the probability of fighting was considered remote.

parade. (1) An open space within a fortress that was large enough for units to practice marching drills. During the battle of FORT SUMTER, four 8-inch COLUMBIADS and one 10-inch PIECE were mounted on the parade as MORTARS. (2) An unusually large and orderly display of men and equipment such as the postwar GRAND REVIEW in Washington.

parallel. A trench dug to link all of a fortification's SAPS so that men could be moved from one to another relatively secure from enemy fire. When a prolonged attack was expected, some commanders ordered a SECOND PARALLEL dug closer to the walls or earthworks of the fortification.

parapet. A defensive work, usually of stout masonry, erected above the RAMPART of a fortress to protect gunners and their PIECES. In the field, logs were used to form a parapet. Special parapet BAYONETS could be attached to the logs as deterrents to attempts to scale the parapet.

parbuckle. A heavy rope, usually twelve feet long, with a loop at one end and a hook at the other. Parbuckles were hitched to a GUN to move it to a new site. Like the MEN'S HARNESS that was often used in steep or rugged terrain, parbuckles were supposed to be made of rope four inches or more thick.

park, to. To place GUNS, wagons, AMBULANCES, or other wheeled vehicles at a set location and unhitch the animals used to pull them.

Parlor Pets. A nickname for Union Gen. John C. Frémont's ESCORT, who were envied by their comrades for the special treatment accorded to them as well as to the general.

parole of honor. Derived from the French *parole de'honneur,* this status for prisoners taken in battle allowed the captives to be released with the understanding that they would not bear arms again until they were formally EXCHANGED for an EQUIVALENT captive from the other side. Because the negotiations for exchanges sometimes took many months, many parolees were unsure as to when they had been exchanged properly and could rejoin their units. The benefit of the parole system was that prisoners did not need to be guarded, sheltered, and fed, but the confusion of the exchange system offset the benefits and led to the 1864 abandonment of the system of paroles and exchanges. Perhaps the largest body of soldiers paroled during the war occurred in July 1863 at Vicksburg, Mississippi, in which twenty-two thousand men were involved.

Parrott gun. These CANNONS were distinguished by a distinctive reinforcing band around the BREECH. Developed in 1860 at the West Point

John S. Mosby

J. H. McNeill

Foundry in Cold Spring, New York, by Robert P. Parrott, an 1824 graduate of the U.S. Military Academy, the first models were 10-, 20-, and 30-pounders. By the end of the war 300-pounders were in production. Never a competitor with the NAPOLEON for field use, Parrotts were used in all theaters of the war and by both army and navy and produced in Confederate versions. Manufacturing costs were low and the guns were easily operated, but the larger PIECES were prone to bursting. During the lengthy siege of Charleston in July 1863, Union Gen. Quincy A. Gillmore noted that twenty-three Parrotts exploded. In most cases, however, a broken muzzle could be smoothed and the gun put back into service.

partial rations. Slang for less than the daily allowance of food for soldiers.

partisan rangers. In April 1862 the Confederate Congress authorized the formation of partisan rangers to infiltrate and raid behind the Union lines. The rangers were to be part of the Confederate military, wear uniforms, and be paid much as PRIVATEERS were for arms and munitions captured and turned over to the government. By September 1862 six REGIMENTS, nine BATTALIONS, and several COMPANIES of rangers had been organized in eight states. Confederate regulars, however, were resentful of the freedom afforded the irregular partisans, particularly for the compensation they received in capturing Federal supplies. To address the shortcomings of the original authorization, transfers were prohibited from the regular army to

the partisans and the rangers were placed under the discipline and regulations of the regular army. Furthermore, no additional partisan units were authorized after early 1863. Notable bands were formed by John S. Mosby, J. H. McNeill, and Harry Gilmor. In early 1864 the partisan ranger legislation was repealed but Secretary of War James Seddon was given the authority to allow specific bands of rangers to continue operations. Seddon retained only Mosby's and McNeill's commands. During the last year of the war, the partisan rangers operated to a large extent in the Shenandoah Valley and occupied the Union army of Philip H. Sheridan to the extent that only a scorched-earth policy effectively curtailed their efforts.

pas de charge. The drumbeat by which a charge was signaled.

pass. A written authorization for a person or group to travel through military lines. The recipients of passes were expected to be loyal to the government that had authorized its issuance, and acceptance of a pass included the understanding that if the recipient should be discovered to have borne arms against the government issuing the pass, the penalty was death. In Washington, Drake De Kay, a youthful forger, achieved a sort of notoriety by affixing unusually bold signatures to passes.

***Passaconaway*, USS.** This ship was one of four Kalamazoo-class seagoing MONITORS authorized for construction in 1863. Double-turreted with four 15-inch SMOOTHBORES, these were to be the largest warships ordered by the U.S. Navy during the war. They were 345 feet long with a draft of almost eighteen feet and promised a speed of up to ten knots. The Kalamazoo monitors, however, were never finished; construction was suspended on November 27, 1865.

passing box. A name for the white-pine boxes used in passing out CARTRIDGES or carrying balls and shells from magazines to GUNS.

Pathfinder. A prewar nickname for Union Gen. John C. Frémont, based on his explorations of the Rocky Mountains.

Pathfinder of the Sea. A nickname for Matthew F. Maury of Virginia, whose reputation as a oceanographer and cartographer preceded the outbreak of the war. During the conflict he served under Stephen R. Mallory in the Confederate Navy Department, and in 1862 he went to England as a naval procurement agent.

Patrick Henry, CSS. This 1,300-ton brigantine-rigged side-wheel steamer was formerly known as *Yorktown* before it was seized on April 17, 1861, and turned over to the Confederate navy. She was refitted and added to the James River Squadron, which was used to support the Confederate FLANK during the Peninsula campaign of 1862. On March 8, 1862, she supported the CSS *Virginia* during its engagement with the USS *Cumberland* and *Congress,* but she had to be towed from the scene after a shell penetrated her boiler. After the evacuation of Norfolk on May 10, 1862, *Patrick Henry* became the school ship for the Confederate Naval Academy and was stationed near Drewry's Bluff. Several times she was used to block Union naval incursions up the James River,

which gave the students combat experience in addition to their regular course of study. During the April 2 evacuation of Richmond, the vessel was sunk with others to obstruct the river at Drewry's Bluff.

paulins. Canvas used to cover light wooden frames and produce pontoons. Although useful in many instances, these were unsuitable for fast-flowing rivers.

***Paw Paw,* USS.** In April 1863 J. Van Vortwick sold this 175-ton boat, originally named *Fanny,* to the U.S. Navy for $8,000, and it was converted into a GUNBOAT with a battery of two RIFLES and six HOWITZERS. The little ship performed well for the remainder of the war and was sold at auction for $5,850, making the former *Fanny* one of the least expensive Federal gunboats of the war.

pay. Monthly compensation in cash, rations, and a clothing allowance. Volunteers who flocked to defend the Union in 1861 as enlisted men received $11 per month, which was later raised to $13. BLACK TROOPS who enlisted after January 1, 1863, were paid $10 per month at first and then an amount equal to the regular enlisted men's rate. Confederate rates varied. On both sides, paymasters were often several months behind. Slow pay and no pay triggered many protests in the ranks and led to several MUTINIES. In a few instances, commandants of prisons authorized pay for labor performed by inmates. At Rock Island, Illinois, prisoners were put to work building a reservoir and were told they would receive a credit of 40 cents per day at the prison SUTLER. This rate was quickly reduced to 10 cents per day for mechanics and five cents for common laborers.

pay tribute to Neptune, to. N. Shipboard slang for nausea and vomiting.

Peach Orchard. (1) A sector of the Shiloh battlefield near which Confederate Gen. Albert Sydney Johnston was wounded and died. (2) An area of the Gettysburg battlefield to which Union Gen. Daniel E. Sickles moved his corps without orders on July 2 and blunted a Confederate assault.

peas on a trencher. The Federal bugle call for breakfast.

peculiar institution. A euphemism for SLAVERY—the paramount social, political, and economic cause of the war. Some trace the origin of the phrase to the florid oratory of John C. Calhoun of South Carolina.

pedegral. Also known as the *mal pais,* this cartographical term referred to a rough area that separated segments of a valley or mesa.

Pelican Rifles. (1) Company D of the 2d Louisiana (Confederate), which served in the eastern theater in most major engagements beginning with the Peninsula campaign and climaxing at APPOMATTOX. (2) Three companies of the 3d Louisiana Infantry (Confederate) bore this designation, and eventually the nickname was applied to the REGIMENT. The unit was organized at New Orleans on May 11, 1861, and participated in the engagements at Wilson's Creek, Pea Ridge, Corinth, Iuka, and Vicksburg. After being paroled at Vicksburg, some elements were reorganized within the 22d Louisiana Consolidated Infantry on January 26, 1864, and the remainder were reorganized as the 3d Louisiana in July 1864 and assigned to GARRISON duty in Shreveport. Portions of the units disbanded in May 1865, and the rest surrendered on May 26, 1865, with E. Kirby Smith.

pendulum-hausse sight. A gunner's tool, also known as a HAUSSE sight, this free-swinging sighting piece complemented a GUN'S BREECH SIGHT on rough ground and uneven terrain. Weighted at the bottom, an upright piece of brass swung on a pivot, or GIMBAL, and designated a true vertical plane. A slider moved over the graduated markings on the upright to indicate elevation. Different versions of the sight were manufactured for specific gun types.

pennant. N. A tapered flag ending in either a point or a swallowtail. Military vessels displayed a commission pennant, indicating that the craft was under commission to its government. The commission pennants of both Federal and Confederate vessels were similar in that the elements of the Stars and Stripes and the Stars and Bars were comparable.

***Pennsylvania,* USS.** This ship-of-the-line was one of the nine vessels authorized by Congress in 1816 "to rate not less than 74 guns each." She was designed and built in the Philadelphia Navy Yard, with construction beginning in September 1821, but tight budgets delayed her launch until July 18, 1837. *Pennsylvania* was the largest sailing ship ever built for the U.S. Navy and boasted four gun decks for 136 guns. She never received the full battery and was instead redesignated in 1842 a receiving ship for the Norfolk Navy Yard. *Pennsylvania* remained in Norfolk until April 20, 1861, when she was burned to the water line to prevent her capture by Confederates.

penny packet. A disparaging term for anything used in very small quantities.

People's Ellsworth Regiment. The 44th New York Infantry was named as a tribute to Col. Elmer Ellsworth, believed to be the first Federal officer killed in the war. When the unit was MUSTERED, its organizers planned for it to be an elite REGIMENT, composed entirely of unmarried men between the ages of eighteen and thirty. Each recruit was to be at least five feet eight inches tall and had to donate twenty dollars to the regimental fund. Many of the officers had formerly served in Ellsworth's original regiment, the Fire ZOUAVES, and requested the transfer to the 44th. The unit was attached to the Army of the Potomac in October 1861 and participated in the Peninsula campaign, the Seven Days' battles, Second Manassas (Bull Run), Fredericksburg, and Chancellorsville. During the July 2, 1863, defense of Little Round Top at Gettysburg, the 44th New York held the line to the right of the 20th Maine and Joshua Lawrence Chamberlain. The regiment was engaged in the battles of the Wilderness, Laurel Hill, and Cold Harbor. Of the 1,061 men of the unit in 1861, 184 were mustered out on October 11, 1864.

pepperbox. One of the best-selling weapons of the prewar years, especially from 1840 to 1860, pepperboxes featured a number of barrels that rotated around a single firing mechanism. Most of these were double-action, which made their rate of fire faster than other pistols. The primary American manufacturer was Allen and Thurber in Worcester, Massachusetts, and overseas makers included J. R. Cooper, Cogswell, and Mariette. REVOLVERS with fixed barrels and revolving cylinders were slightly more reliable than pepperboxes and less muzzle-heavy and quickly displaced them.

percussion bullet. A bullet with a charge that is detonated by striking; an EXPLOSIVE BULLET.

percussion fuse. A FUSE that is detonated by impact.

percussion lock. A refinement of the firing mechanism of a MUZZLELOADER in which a percussion CAP replaced the flint and frizzen of FLINTLOCKS. By using fulminate of mercury in percussion caps, these RIFLES became the first all-weather shoulder arms.

Peripatetic Coffin, the. A nickname for the CSS *H. L. HUNLEY*, the world's first submarine to sink an enemy vessel in battle. It sank several times during its trial runs in Charleston Harbor and claimed the lives of thirteen men, including the craft's designer and namesake. On its only mission, on the night of February 17, 1864, the *Hunley* attacked and sank the USS *HOUSATONIC*, but the Confederate crew and the submarine were lost as well.

Perry's Saints. The 48th New York, whose organizer and first commander, James H. Perry, was a Methodist minister and therefore able to enlist a large number of seminary students and others with strong religious backgrounds. The unit was MUSTERED IN the summer of 1861, after the battle of First Manassas (Bull Run), and assigned to the Department of the South where it participated in the siege of Fort Pulaski, the assault on Fort Wagner, the battle of Olustee, and the assault on FORT FISHER. The 48th was also known as the Continental Guards Regiment.

Persimmon Regiment. In all instances, the derivation of this nickname was based on soldiers breaking ranks while on the march to pluck persimmons. It was applied to (1) the 73d Illinois, also known as the PREACHER REGIMENT, (2) the 35th Ohio Infantry, a three-year REGIMENT (for whom the nickname was an embarrassing reminder of a December 1861 skirmish in which fifteen men were captured when they strayed from the regiment to search for persimmons), and (3) the 100th Indiana.

personation, false. To impersonate.

pest house. Any holding area used to isolate soldiers or civilians believed to have contagious diseases.

Pet. A family nickname for John Wilkes Booth.

Peter. A nickname for Pierre Gustave Toutant Beauregard.

Petersburg Express. A nickname for the 13-inch seacoast MORTAR known as the DICTATOR, which was mounted on a railroad car and shelled Confederate positions near Petersburg.

Petersburg Progress. A newspaper briefly printed by Union soldiers after occupying Petersburg in April 1865. Issue no. 4, which circulated on April 10, carried the news of Robert E. Lee's surrender at Appomattox Court House.

Philippi Races. A satirical nickname for the brief battle of Philippi, Virginia, on June 3, 1861. At dawn five Federal regiments approached a camp of one thousand raw Virginia recruits. The Confederate commander, Col. George A. Porterfield, reasoned that retreat was better than suicide and ordered his men to flee the field.

Phil Kearney's Thieves. A nickname for the First Division of the Federal 3d Corps, which was led by Gen. Philip Kearney.

phonography. A system of phonetic writing believed to have been developed before 1840 by Isaac Pitman. The Federal intelligence service briefly experimented with this as a way to transmit messages in code.

phosphorus. This yellowish semitransparent element was so widely used in FRICTION PRIMERS for GUNS that they were often simply called "phosphorus." When a LANYARD was pulled, a wire was drawn through a tube containing phosphorus. Friction caused ignition, which sent a flash through the vent to detonate the charge.

picket. A soldier on guard, alone or with others. His most urgent duty was to give warning of an approaching enemy to prevent a surprise attack.

Picket Boat No. 1. This steam launch was built in 1864 and attached to the Federal blockading fleet. To attack the Confederate IRONCLAD *ALBEMARLE,* the boat was outfitted with a SPAR TORPEDO. On the night of October 27–28, 1864, an all-volunteer crew of fourteen under Lt. William B. Cushing

launched the assault at Plymouth, North Carolina, where the Southern ship was moored. The attack was successful—the ironclad was sunk—but *Picket Boat No. 1* and its crew, except Cushing and another man, were also lost.

picket pin. These foot-long iron pins were standard CAVALRY issue. They were designed to be driven into the ground and used to tether a horse so that the animal could graze unattended.

Pickett's Charge. This is the most widely known of all charges made during the Civil War, but the name should more accurately be Pickett-Pettigrew-Trimble after the primary divisional commanders on the field—George Pickett, James Johnson Pettigrew, and Isaac Trimble. The mile-long line of thirteen thousand Confederates had to cross a mile of open field before they could attack, but the Union gunners opened on them long before the Federal line was threatened. Although the Southerners breached the line in a few places, they were hurled back—and somehow half of them returned to their own line. It was over in less than an hour. The survivors of the Army of Northern Virginia began to retreat from Gettysburg the next day.

pickled sardine. Slang for a prisoner of war who had endured imprisonment for many months.

piece. A general term for a field GUN and occasionally reserved as a designation for light artillery.

piecemeal. A strategy that commits portions of an army to attack as they became available; also known as a meeting engagement. The gamble inherent in the MANEUVER is that the attacking side can build up its forces faster than the other.

pigeon roost. Slang for a sentry box on top of a prison wall or overlooking a high fence around a stockade.

pilaster. N. A cylindrical metal cover applied to the bolt heads of IRONCLAD ships.

pill. Slang for a cannonball or other artillery projectiles.

pilot. A civilian who served as pilot or guide to refugees from the Confederate states.

pioneers. These were skilled soldiers who were given detached duty to clear roads, construct bridges, dig trenches, and erect fortifications. In the Union army, initially, there was no formal organization for pioneer COMPANIES. As the war dragged on, pioneers were drawn from the Veteran Reserve Corps and the U.S. Colored Troops. Some army commanders formed pioneer companies by reassigning two or three men from each company. There were few formal pioneer units in the Confederate army, which at the beginning of the war had commandeered slaves for such work. In time pioneer duties fell to Southern engineers, since the duties were similar.

pinnance. N. A small two-masted boat propelled by both oars and sails.

pipe. N. The smokestack of a steamer.

pirogue. Originally referring to dugout canoes, this term came to designate any canoelike craft. Troops used pirogues when they could not wade across streams.

pivot gun. N. A GUN mounted on a warship so it could be swung across a considerable arc, giving it a greater field of fire than a fixed gun.

place of arms. A designated point outside an enemy position at which the attacking troops were to assemble. Most commanders preferred the place of arms to be under cover.

plank road. These were wagon highways, usually twelve to fifteen feet wide, surfaced with thick pine planks.

plant the flag, to. To place one's banner inside an enemy line or position. Since flags marked the position of a COMPANY or REGIMENT, such an achievement indicated the successful occupation of the enemy's works.

Planter, **USS.** The 300-ton side-wheel steamer was a commercial ship before the war, and from 1861 to 1862 it served as a transport and dispatch vessel for the Confederate army in Charleston Harbor. At this time the ship's pilot and crew were slaves. On May 13, 1862, pilot Robert Smalls took the vessel out without the ship's captain but with members of Smalls's family and the families of the crew. He steamed past the Southern forts without being challenged and then turned toward the Federal blockading fleet and surrendered the vessel. Smalls and the crew were awarded half the value of the ship and its cargo. The steamer then operated with the South Atlantic Blockading Squadron until she was reassigned to the U.S. Army with Smalls still the ship's pilot. During RECONSTRUCTION, Smalls was elected to the U.S.

Congress. The *Planter* returned to commercial service and was lost in 1876.

play, to. A gunners' term signifying any firing on the enemy.

play bayonets, to. This deadly mock combat involved two or more men with BAYONETS and loaded RIFLES or MUSKETS and usually had fatal consequences or serious injury.

play off, to. To feign illness or injury so as to be given a few hours or a few days in the camp or field hospital or sick bay.

plebe. A West Point cadet in his first year at the U.S. Military Academy.

plug, to. A gunners' expression for maintaining a sustained fire on a single target.

plume. A feather or feathers worn as an ornament and in some cases as a sign of RANK. Federal commanders were allowed to wear yellow swan feathers; their subordinates could wear plumes fashioned from rooster or vulture feathers and dyed red.

plunging fire. Gunfire from a position overlooking the enemy.

plys. Folded sections of cloth, canvas, or carpet.

pocket. A synonym for an opening or pass over a mountain or through a range of mountains.

pocketknife. A knife with one or more blades that folded into a case and could be carried safely in one's pocket.

point blank. A distance so short that a projectile travels in a straight line to the target with no degradation in the flight of the bullet, shot, or shell.

point d'appui. The French phrase means "point of support" and designates sites in a fortress, town, or

battlefield at which an army secures its position with a definite advantage over an opponent.

Point Lookout. This Union prison was named CAMP HOFFMAN but was better known by the name of its location in Maryland—Point Lookout, which had been a resort before the war. The prison was established after the July 1–3, 1863, battle of Gettysburg, when the need for Federal prisons mushroomed. The forty-acre site was set up with no buildings on the grounds but a cook and mess halls; the captives were to live in tents. Initial plans anticipated a population of ten thousand, a quarter of which were to be officers. The first prisoners arrived on July 25 before the compound was finished and were used to complete the work. By the end of the war the facility came to be the largest prisoner-of-war camp in the North; more than twenty-two thousand captives had been crammed onto the grounds. Winters were particularly harsh on the Southerners, especially because the compound was prone to flooding and blankets were scarce. At least 3,584 Confederates died here; there were only fifty escapes.

poleaxe. A short-handled ax or hatchet used by soldiers or by sailors to board a vessel.

Polecat. A nickname for Confederate Gen. Camille Armand Jules Marie de Polignac, a native of France who served on P. G. T. Beauregard's staff at the beginning of the war and who went on to command a BRIGADE and later a division under E. Kirby Smith in the western theater. In 1865 he was sent to Europe to seek aid from France and was still there when news arrived of Robert E. Lee's surrender in April.

police, to. Any effort to remove litter and trash and improve the appearance of a camp, barracks, or prison.

political generals. These were Federal GENERAL OFFICERS who received their commissions because of their political influence. While many were

Republicans, several were Democrats, and their absence from the home front also served to weaken the opposition to the Lincoln administration. If any of them faltered on the field, they weakened their status within the party, and if they succeeded, the Union was that much stronger for their contributions. Among this group were Nathaniel Banks, Francis P. Blair, Benjamin F. Butler, Samuel Curtis, John A. Logan, John McClernand, John A. Rawlins, Carl Schurz, Daniel E. Sickles, and Franz Sigel.

Polly. A nickname for Confederate Gen. Jerome B. Robertson, who had fought in the  Texas revolution of 1835 and joined the 5th Texas Infantry at the beginning of the war. Robertson served in the Texas Brigade in the eastern theater from the Seven Days', Second Manassas, Antietam, Fredericksburg, Gettysburg, and Knoxville campaigns. He was transferred to Texas and commanded reserve forces there until the end of the war. His son, Felix, had participated in the shelling of FORT SUMTER and served in the western theater, earning a general's rank during the Atlanta campaign.

poncho. A capelike outer garment of waterproof material with an opening in the center for the wearer's head. Often made of muslin coated with INDIA RUBBER, the underside readily lent itself to marking with anything from charcoal to pencil. Thus thousands of ponchos came to be used also as checkerboards.

pontoon bridges. Pontoons were flat-bottomed boats of wood or canvas that were anchored and connected to form a temporary causeway for men and equipment to cross over water barriers. These bridges were adapted from a French model in which the wooden pontoons were overlaid with large timbers upon which boards about a dozen feet long were placed crosswise. Whenever possible, the wooden surface was cushioned with a layer of earth or straw. A Russian model used buoyant canvas over wooden frames to achieve a similar purpose. In June 1864 Federal engineers used 101 French-style pontoons to erect a span across the James River in just eight hours and allow Ulysses S. Grant's army to cross the waterway and seal off the escape route of the Army of Northern Virginia. Other notable pontoon bridges include an 880-foot span over the Osage River and the bridges erected at Fredericksburg in December 1863 leading to the Federal defeat there. One of the most notorious instances of pontoon bridge building occurred on December 9, 1864, during William T. Sherman's MARCH TO THE SEA, when Union Gen. Jefferson C. Davis had to pull up a pontoon bridge as soon as his army had crossed Ebenezer Creek in Georgia to stave off the pursuit of Confederate CAVALRY. In doing so Davis stranded hundreds of slaves who had been following his men. Untold numbers threw themselves into the river and drowned rather than face the Southern horsemen and a return to servitude.

Ponchartrain, **CSS.** Formerly known as *Lizzie Simmons,* this side-wheel river steamer was purchased at New Orleans on October 12, 1861, and converted into a warship in early 1862. She carried a battery of six guns at first, but only five after her conversion. When she was commissioned she was dispatched to the fleet then commanded by Flag Off. G. N. Hollins for the defense of the Mississippi River and the Louisiana coast. During March and April 1862 she participated in the actions at Island No. 10 and New Madrid, Missouri. During the battle of St. Charles, Arkansas, on June 17, 1862, two of her rifled 32-pounders were transferred to the fort, and several crewmen were among the prisoners taken there. While on the Arkansas River in 1863, the vessel was burned by her crew to avoid capture. As the hulk settled downward, her battery tore loose and went to the bottom.

Pook Turtle. A nickname for the seven city-class sternwheel GUNBOATS—*CAIRO, CARONDELET, Cincinnati, Louisville, Mound City, Pittsburg,* and *ST. LOUIS* (*BARON DE KALB*)—designed by Samuel M. Pook, an employee of James B. Eads of St. Louis. Three were built by Hambleton and Collier of Mound City, Illinois—*Cairo, Mound City,* and *Cincinnati.* The other four were constructed at Eads's shipyard in Carondelet, Missouri. All were delivered to Cairo, Illinois, in the fall of 1861. Pook's 512-ton "turtles" were round-nosed and flat-bottomed; they were assigned to the Western Gunboat Fleet and played an important role in securing Federal successes on the inland waterways.

Pop. A nickname for Union Gen. George S. Greene.

pop, to. To discharge a single GUN or a BATTERY a single time.

pop-skull. A nickname for bootleg whiskey.

portcullis. At permanent installations, this holdover from medieval castles hung over the gateway. It was either a metal grate or a heavy wooden gate that could be lowered to impede a frontal attack upon the fortress.

Porte Crayon. The pen name of artist David H. Strother, who was probably the best-known graphic artist in American prior to the Civil War. Strother was a regular contributor to *HARPER'S WEEKLY* and served as a topographer and staff officer to several Federal generals during the war.

portfire. Used to fire CANNON before the introduction of FRICTION PRIMERS, portfires were manufactured by saturating paper FUSES with a solution of nitre, sulfur, and mealed powder. Even after the development of friction primers, portfires were still used in emergencies and to fire ROCKETS. A lengthy portfire would burn for ten minutes. These early fuses were essentially waterproof and could not be extinguished.

possum beer. A variety of homebrew made from persimmons.

posted, to be. To be given an assignment at a specific location.

postern. A passageway, usually covered, that linked the body of a fortification with an outerwork. In permanent installations, posterns were designed to withstand artillery but also included escapeways to the surface.

Potomac, **USS.** Construction of this 1,726-ton wooden FRIGATE began at the Washington Navy Yard in August 1819, and the fifty-two-gun vessel was launched in March 1822. She served in the Pacific and Atlantic prior to the war, including service during the Mexican War at the battles of Palo Alto and Vera Cruz. In the mid-1850s *Potomac* was also the FLAGSHIP of the Home Squadron, but at the outbreak of the Civil War she was dispatched to the West Gulf Blockading Squadron and later became the stores ship for the squadron and remained in Pensacola as a receiving ship until after the war. Sold at Philadelphia in 1877, the old vessel brought only $12,400.

potshot. Random shots at irregular intervals, distinguished from a volley in which a line of soldiers fires simultaneously.

pounder. Prior to the war artillery was classified in two ways: the weight of the solid shot fired from the GUN TUBE and the diameter of the gun's BORE in inches (which was also known as CALIBER). The use of the ammunition's weight in conjunction with the word "pounder" (e.g., a 32-pounder) implied that the PIECE was a SMOOTHBORE. This designation was not uniformly applied after the introduction of rifled weapons, because the weight of projectiles varied since ammunition could be elongated or shortened. It should also be noted that despite having a rifled bore, PARROTT GUNS were designated initially by the traditional pounder method of reference. An 8-inch PARROTT RIFLE, however, was designated a 200-pounder by the army but a 150-pounder by the navy, because the original projectile was shortened, which reduced its weight. The army retained the original designation, but the navy adopted the latter. Similarly, the 10-inch Parrott was categorized as a 300-pounder although its shell weighed only 250 pounds. Because these disparities became so numerous between the different Parrott models, these guns, especially the larger weapons, came to be classified by their bore diameters—their caliber.

pour, to. To order several units to move against an adversary so that their ranks are mingled and they are able to overrun a numerically smaller force.

powder. During the war, the composition of gunpowder was 75 percent saltpeter, 15 percent charcoal, and 10 percent sulfur. Charcoal served as the combustible component, and sulfur provided the oxygen necessary for sudden combustion and transformed the gunpowder into a propellant that forced a projectile through the GUN TUBE. Coarse-grained gunpowder was used in ARTILLERY and fine grains for small arms. The largest supplier of gunpowder to the Union army was Elutherian Mills owned by the duPont family in Delaware; the largest manufacturer in the South was the Augusta (Ga.) Powder Works, an enterprise wholly owned and operated by the Confederate government and designed and maintained by Col. George W. Rains.

powder barrel. A wooden or metal container used to ship gunpowder. Typical barrels were about one foot tall and ten to twelve inches in diameter.

powder flask. A portable metal container, with a capacity ranging from two to ten ounces, used to hold gunpowder used with a REVOLVER.

powder measure. A round copper device with a flanged bottom. It was used to measure the gunpowder used in both projectiles and weapons.

powder monkey. N. Young boys who conveyed gunpowder from a ship's cramped magazine to the GUN crews. Their size was their main asset since this task required them to pass through small spaces not easily traversed by men.

LIBRARY OF CONGRESS

powder tank. N. A wooden container with a capacity of two hundred pounds, used to hold gunpowder.

practible breach. A hole created in a defensive structure by ARTILLERY fire. Once breached, an attacking force had access to the interior lines of an adversary. Hence a practible breach signaled the climax of an engagement.

Prairie Dog Village. A nickname for the besieged Confederate stronghold at Vicksburg. The name stems from the fact that the artillery siege had driven many of the townspeople from their homes and into caves dug into the hillsides.

prayer. A legal petition or formal request. This term was frequently used by parties negotiating the disposition of a PRIZE.

"Prayer of Twenty Millions, The." In an open-letter editorial to Abraham Lincoln on August 20, 1862, editor Horace Greeley of the NEW YORK  TRIBUNE encouraged the president to exploit the recently enacted Second Confiscation Act to emancipate the slaves and punish slave owners in the occupied territory of the South. The editor signed the letter in the name of the twenty million people of the North. Although Lincoln had been drafting the EMANCIPATION PROCLAMATION at the time, the president believed it would be premature to announce it. He did, however, respond to Greeley's editorial in an open letter that was published in the *Tribune* on August 25 in which he stated that the task before him was focused not on SLAVERY but on the restoration of the Union. When the preliminary Emancipation Proclamation was announced following the September 17, 1862, battle of Antietam, many believed that it was due to Greeley's original editorial.

Preacher Regiment. A nickname for the 73d Illinois Infantry, also known as one of the PERSIMMON REGIMENTS, but distinguished by the number of clergymen and theological students in its ranks. This unit was organized in August 1862 and was initially led by the Reverend James Jaquess, a Methodist minister. It participated in thwarting Braxton Bragg's Kentucky campaign in October 1862, the battles of Stones River, Chickamauga, Missionary Ridge, the Atlanta campaign, and against John Bell Hood's Tennessee campaign that climaxed at Nashville in December 1864.

press. A hand-powered device by which its contents could be compacted. It was essential in the bookbinding trade but became paramount when it was adapted to compress loose cotton into bales.

press, to. (1) Slang for impressment, which involved the seizure of horses, vehicles, supplies, and other MATERIÉL needed by armies in the field. Previous owners were often given receipts but few of these were ever honored. (2) N. To put one's shoes on the deck of a warship.

Priest Cap. An elevated position in the center of the Confederate line on the Port Hudson, Louisiana, battlefield and the focus of an unsuccessful Union attack on June 14, 1863.

Prime Minister. A nickname for William H. Seward, the U.S. secretary of state. Seward had been confident that he would win the Republican nomination for the presidency in 1860 and came close to doing so on the first ballot. He later accepted a cabinet post in the new administration and tried to exercise power as the primary policy maker.

priming wire. An iron wire pointed at one end and looped at the other. Gunners inserted the wire into the VENT of the GUN TUBE to puncture the CARTRIDGE bag seated in the gun's BORE. This allowed the spark of the FUSE or FRICTION PRIMER to ignite the propellant and discharge the gun.

prison fund. The Federal prisoner-of-war camps were administered by Col. William H. Hoffman who authorized a plan to withhold a portion of the prisoners' rations and place the savings in a fund to be used to purchase vegetables and fruits for the captives. In practice, however, many commandants and wardens put as much as they could into the fund

William H. Hoffman

and spent as little as possible. In several camps these funds grew to staggering sums—but authorization was rarely given to use them. At the end of the war Hoffman returned $1.8 million to the Treasury from the prison funds, but several camps lost money through graft and corruption. One praiseworthy allocation was at ROCK ISLAND, Illinois, where a hospital facility was built with $30,000 from the prison fund.

privateer. A privately owned vessel whose mission was to prey upon the warships and merchant vessels of an adversary. This enterprise was granted by LETTERS OF MARQUE and reprisal, and the right to issue such authorizations was granted by the U.S. Constitution to Congress but specifically denied the states. The 1856 Declaration of Paris abolished privateering, and while the United States observed the treaty, the country had not adopted it. Thus when the Confederacy issued letters of marque in 1861, the North could not protest the action too strenuously. The Union navy, however, did regard privateers as pirates, and a conviction of piracy carried a sentence of death. In all, the Confederacy granted fifty-two letters of marque to

vessels operating mostly out of New Orleans and Charleston. Records indicate that only twenty-eight actually pressed claims as privateers, but their impact on the commerce of Northern shipping was negligible.

prize. A captured commercial vessel or warship of one's enemy. In some instances this term was applied to captives who confessed their involvement in BLOCKADE-RUNNING. Custom dictated that crews involved in the seizure of an enemy vessel were entitled to a cash prize equivalent to the value of the ship and its cargo. An elaborate scale stipulated how the prize money was distributed among the seizing ship's crew.

Prize Cases. The most important case of the Civil War to reach the U.S. Supreme Court centered on the question of when a state of war existed between the United States and those states that had seceded in 1860–61. The Union navy had seized four ships and their cargoes before July 13, 1861, when Congress authorized the president to announce that a state of insurrection existed. One of the vessels in question, the *Amy Warwick,* had a cargo of coffee and was bound for Richmond. The *Hathaway,* caught in Richmond when the conflict began, was a British vessel that had been given fifteen-days' notice to depart after the Northern BLOCKADE had begun. A Mexican vessel, the *Brilliance,* took a cargo to New Orleans about a month after the blockade had been announced. The *Creashak,* operated by Richmond businessmen, was captured en route to England with a cargo of tobacco. The owners of these four vessels argued that Abraham Lincoln was not empowered to order a blockade without congressional sanction. Attorneys for the administration, however, asserted that as soon as FORT SUMTER had been fired upon, the president had the authority to impose the blockade. The Prize Cases were argued in February 1863, and the five-to-four ruling announced on March 10 that a state of war had existed when the four ships were seized. The verdict affirmed that a state of war had existed in July 1861 despite the fact that war was never declared by Congress.

prize court. A judicial body whose sole function was to determine the value of captured vessels and crews and to arrange their disposal. Numerous prize courts were established at Union ports, and a few were instituted at Confederate ports.

prize crew. A skeleton crew placed aboard a captured vessel and charged with the responsibility to take her to the nearest friendly port.

prize money. Funds apportioned among the officers and crew of a vessel or vessels that had captured an enemy ship.

produce loan. A congressionally authorized procedure by which plantation owners could purchase Confederate bonds with the produce of their fields.

prolonge. This sturdy twelve-foot length of rope with a hook at one end and a toggle at the other was used to connect a GUN to its LIMBER and move both pieces quickly on the battlefield. Although designed specifically for use with guns, prolonges were also used to upright wagons or other vehicles that had tumbled over.

propeller. A shortened reference to a steam-powered vessel that was driven by a screw propeller.

prosecute, to. To move forward vigorously.

provost. The military police.

provost guard. A police detail usually charged with guarding prisoners or retrieving STRAGGLERS.

Provost Marshal. A nickname for a large shark that patrolled the seventy-foot-wide, thirty-foot-deep moat of Fort Jefferson on Garden Key in the Dry Tortugas. The guards often fed the shark by throwing stray cats into the moat and on several

occasions watched the creature "capture" an escaping prisoner, sometimes shooting the prisoner to get the scent of blood in the water and attract the beast.

provost marshal. A military officer charged with suppressing insurrection and preserving order. Both North and South appointed provost marshals for each military district to enforce martial law and ensure that violators were prosecuted or court-martialed and that all sentences were carried out.

provost marshal general. This Federal office was created in conjunction with the Federal Enrollment Act of March 1863. Union Col. James B. Fry, a distinguished veteran of the Mexican War, was named to this office on March 17, and he was charged with enforcing the DRAFT, fostering voluntary enlistment, and apprehending DESERTERS.

puke. Slang in Kansas and other western regions for a Southern sympathizer.

pumpkin rind. Union army slang for a lieutenant, based on the bare SHOULDER STRAPS that indicated his rank.

pumpkin shell. A floating MINE often tethered to a slender post.

pumpkin slinger. (1) A nickname for the Model 1842 .69-caliber percussion SMOOTHBORE, which fired the largest ammunition of the shoulder arms. (2) A nickname for heavy and inaccurate RIFLES imported by Union authorities from

Belgium early in the war. The name stems from the large ball that the weapon fired. These rifles were inexpensively priced because their makers had been unable to sell them in Europe. Many of these weapons recoiled so hard that they were also called "MULES."

punch through, to. To create a hole through the armor of MONITORS and other IRONCLADS. Originally, gunners used relatively small shot to penetrate armor so they would hit at maximum velocity. Naval authorities later determined that heavier projectiles were needed to pierce metal plating, which led to the decision to produce both 20-inch RODMANS and DAHLGRENS rather than the long-standard maximum of 15-inch GUNS.

pungy. N. A small, nondescript vessel or a small wind-driven SLOOP or shallop.

punt. A small flat-bottomed boat propelled by oars and used in the repair work on the hulls of wooden ships.

Puritans. A nickname for the 1st Maine Cavalry, which was organized at Augusta and MUSTERED IN as a three-year unit on October 31, 1861. Throughout the course of the war, the horsemen of the 1st Maine participated in more engagements than any other unit in the Army of the Potomac and lost the greatest number of men killed in action of any other CAVALRY REGIMENT in the Union army. The unit was MUSTERED OUT on August 1, 1865.

Q

quadrant. A gunner's tool made of wood or metal with a ninety-degree arc and a rule almost two feet long. A plumb line was attached to the center of the curve to provide a factor in determining the necessary elevation of the GUN TUBE.

Quaker gun. An imitation gun made of wood, painted black, and positioned to look like artillery and deceive the enemy. Confederates installed such "pieces" at Centreville prior to the July 21, 1861, battle of First Manassas (Bull Run) and at several positions to buy time for a withdrawal. When Federal forces entered Corinth, Mississippi, they found the BASTION empty except for a few Quaker guns. An innovative variation was devised in 1862 by Confederate partisan Adam R. Johnson at Newburgh, Indiana. With fewer than thirty men, he mounted a set of stovepipes on wagon gear, pointed these Quaker guns toward the town, gained the surrender of the town, and confiscated a sizable cache of munitions. The nickname "Stovepipe" stuck to Johnson for the rest of his life.

Quaker oath. A vow taken during the summer of 1864 by some BLACK TROOPS under the guidance of their officers in which the former slaves swore that they were free when Abraham Lincoln proclaimed the BLOCKADE of Southern ports. By doing so, these men were paid on the same scale as white soldiers. The higher rate was retroactive to April 19, 1861.

quarantine. N. A landing spot for vessels at which a quarantine officer checked the crew and passengers for contagious diseases.

quarter. Clemency granted to a defeated enemy by sparing the lives of those who had surrendered. Inherited from the age of chivalry, many considered this term obsolete by the middle of the nineteenth century, but according to Federal reports about the October 1861 battle of Santa Rosa Island, Florida, the expression was still in use. The report claimed that the Confederates who burned the camp of Col. William Wilson's zouaves repeatedly cried, "No quarter to Wilson's men!" Failure to give quarter was equivalent to a BLACK FLAG POLICY.

quarter, to. N. To assign men to battle stations in preparation for an engagement.

quartering. N. The arrangement of PIVOT GUNS on a warship so they could be used as bow and stern chasers. The design for the CSS *VIRGINIA* required that her fore and aft guns be positioned in this fashion

quartermaster. An officer whose primary duty was to provide quarters, food, clothing, transportation for troops and FORAGE for their animals.

quartermaster shot or **quartermaster hunter.** A sardonic gunnery term that labeled a shot sent far over the heads of the enemy. Such a shot was only a threat to QUARTERMASTERS in the rear.

Queen of the Confederacy. A nickname for Lucy Holcombe Pickens, who was so honored for the actions of her husband, Francis W. Pickens. When they married in 1858, Pickens was a South Carolina congressman, but he was governor of the state when it seceded in December 1860. Lucy's appearance was less than regal, but the sobriquet probably had an impact upon officials in Richmond since hers was the only portrait of a woman to adorn Confederate currency.

Queen of the West. One of nine steamers procured by Charles Ellet for his fleet of RAMS designed to cripple and sink Confederate vessels by crashing into them. Ellet's modifications were carried out in Cincinnati, and the ships were assigned to Charles H. Davis's flotilla. The *Queen* was rated at 406 tons and carried a battery of one 30-POUNDER and three 12-pounder HOWITZERS. Her first engagement was the June 6, 1862, battle of Memphis in which Ellet was killed and the *Queen,* Ellet's flagship, was run aground. Twice the *Queen* encountered the CSS *ARKANSAS* near Vicksburg. On July 15, 1862, she fled from the Confederate

NAVAL HISTORICAL CENTER

IRONCLAD, but on July 22 they engaged, leaving the *Queen* so badly damaged that she was sent north for repairs. When she reappeared near Vicksburg in early 1863 she made a name for herself by destroying four Southern steamers, including the CSS *City of Vicksburg.* Several days later, however, she ran aground at Fort de Russy, Louisiana, and was captured. While in Confederate service the *Queen* participated in the pursuit and capture of the USS *INDIANOLA.* During action on the Atchafalaya River on April 14, 1863, she caught fire and exploded.

quick-match. A segment of cotton yarn, much like the wick of a candle, which was saturated with a flammable substance. Although kerosene or pitch was sometimes used, the most common substance employed to make cotton burn quickly was a mixture of gunpowder and starch. Used to launch SIGNAL ROCKETS, one foot of quick-match burned in the open air for about four seconds. When used to prime a gun, it was usually lighted with a SLOW MATCH held in a LINSTOCK.

quickstep. (1) A fast rate of march, usually dictated by the beat of martial music. This pace was about 110 steps per minute, during which soldiers covered about 85 to 90 yards. (2) Slang for diarrhea.

quill, to. To write up a West Point cadet for an infraction of rules. Class standing at the time of graduation was all-important in terms of a graduate's first assignment. Good grades could be offset by misconduct, so cadets tried to avoid being quilled.

quintal. A Mexican unit of weight equivalent to approximately one hundred pounds.

quoin. A wedge of oak used like an elevating screw for MORTARS and large HOWITZERS. During an engagement between the USS *Lexington* and a Confederate GUNBOAT near Mound City, Illinois, the Union gunners removed their quoins to get more elevation. Using fifteen-second FUSES, they had the satisfaction of seeing the enemy vessel's smokestack careen from their first shot at her.

R

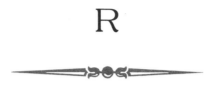

race. An engagement ending in the rapid withdrawal of one side. When Confederate troops failed to put up a fight on June 3, 1861, at Philippi, Virginia, the Federals derided the action as the PHILIPPI RACES. A five-mile CAVALRY chase at Buckland, Virginia, on October 19, 1863, resulted in 150 Union captives and concluded the Bristoe campaign. It came to be known as the "Buckland Races."

rack, to. A form of camp punishment in which a soldier's hands and feet were spread and attached to the FELLOES of the right rear wheel and his other hand and foot to the left. This position threw a culprit's entire weight against his chest, which was positioned against the edge of the rack—usually made of boards about an inch thick, whose edges were sharp. Few punishments were so severe as this one, which took its name from medieval instruments of torture. Even a very strong battle-hardened veteran seldom remained conscious for more than a few minutes after having been bound to the rack.

rake. N. To rake an enemy's vessel with heavy shot, preferably from a short distance. SMOOTHBORE GUNS were usually employed in raking, since their heavy balls hit with enormous impact—up to 4,000 foot-tons or more. When subjected to repeated blows of this magnitude, the skeleton of the enemy vessel was likely to shed its armor plating and become a helpless sitting duck. Union Rear Adm. Samuel F. Du Pont made a FRONTAL ATTACK upon besieged Charleston in April, 1863. During this engagement, the USS *Weehawken* took a great many heavy blows then retired from the action. Members of her crew quickly discovered that raking had so shattered her armor that pieces of it could be lifted off in a man's fingers.

radical. An individual who favored harsh, punitive measures against the defeated Confederacy.

Radical Party. Southern slang for the Republican Party.

Radical Republicans. The smallest of three factions within the Republican Party, these politicians exerted an influence that belied their numbers. They were aggressive advocates of the immediate abolition of SLAVERY and viewed the war as a crusade for emancipation. Although they formed a minority within the party, their members were skillful, talented, and held key positions in the Federal government. Many but not all were New Englanders. They included Speaker of the House Galusha A. Grow, Ways and Means Committee chairman Thaddeus Stevens, Sen. Charles Sumner, Sen. Henry Wilson, Sen. Benjamin Wade, Secretary of the Treasury Salmon P. Chase, and Secretary of war Edwin M. Stanton. During the war they championed the various confiscation acts, emancipation, the enlistment of BLACK TROOPS, and punitive RECONSTRUCTION of the

Benjamin Wade   *Edwin M. Stanton*

South. Although Abraham Lincoln was in agreement with them on several measures, the Radical Republicans did not favor his renomination in 1864. They dominated the COMMITTEE ON THE CONDUCT OF THE WAR, through which they tried to dictate military policy and also examined the political views of many generals. After the ASSASSINATION OF THE PRESIDENT, they shaped the course of Reconstruction in the South, which they viewed as a legislative function rather than an executive task. They were also in the forefront of the impeachment of Andrew Johnson.

rag out, to. Slang for formal dress.

raid. In contrast to a SIEGE or FRONTAL ATTACK, which was designed to gain possession of an enemy's position and hold it, a raid focused on a fast-moving strike behind the lines to burn, wreck, or confiscate a strategic target and then retire. Raids were conducted by CAVALRY, so many reputations were won on horseback. Among Union ranks, these included Philip H. Sheridan, Benjamin Grierson, Abel Streight, and James H. Wilson. Their Confederate counterparts encompassed Jeb Stuart, Nathan Bedford Forrest, John Hunt Morgan, and Thomas L. Rosser. Not all raids, however, were successful and some were notorious, such as the raid on Richmond led by H. Judson Kilpatrick and Ulric Dahlgren.

railroad artillery. Federal forces made good use of existing RAILROADS in moving ARTILLERY from place to place. Some short lines were constructed specifically for this purpose. Two kinds of heavy artillery were mobilized by rail. One was a 32-POUNDER cannon, which was bolted to the bed of a flatcar, allowing the gun to be fired from the railroad car on which it sat. The other PIECE was the 13-inch siege MORTAR, which could be transported by standard flatcar. Both weapons appeared near Richmond. In 1862 a railcar-mounted Confederate 32-pounder participated in the opening of the Seven Days' battles. Two years later a railcar-mounted Federal 13-inch mortar shelled the Confederate line at Petersburg.

railroad monitor. An armored railroad car designed to protect construction and repair crews from Confederate raiders. Although heavily armed, these movable forts were only effective against small arms fire. They did not prove to be effective and saw only limited use. One of the best-known groups of these wheeled vehicles was commanded in 1863 by Lt. John Rodgers Meigs, son of Union Q.M. Gen. Montgomery C. Meigs and chief engineer to Philip H. Sheridan in the Shenandoah Valley during the summer of 1864.

railroads. At the beginning of the conflict, railroad mileage in the North greatly exceeded that of the South and this disparity never changed. Thousands of miles of railroad track were torn up during the war, but most were speedily rebuilt. Although construction of a transcontinental railroad was authorized by the Federal Congress in mid-1862, the war

prevented any major construction until after the South's surrender. In terms of the strategic value of railroads, the Confederates were the first to use their railroad to transport troops to the scene of a battle in progress. The timely arrival of Brig. Gen. Edmund Kirby Smith's troops on July 21, 1861, at Manassas Junction turned the tide of battle in favor of the Southern army. Perhaps the most significant movement of Confederate troops by train occurred in the fall of 1863 when James Longstreet's eighteen thousand men were transported from Virginia to north Georgia in time to join in the battle of Chickamauga. Yet by far the most massive troop movements by rail were conducted by Union forces, such as the relocation in October 1863 of two corps from the Virginia front to bolster the defense of Chattanooga.

Railsplitter, the. A nickname for Abraham Lincoln that originated during the Republican Convention of 1860 in Chicago. John Hanks, a cousin of Lincoln's, appeared with a pair of weather-beaten fence rails and a sign indicating that Lincoln, as a youth, had split the wood for the fences. It was a bit of political theater, because at the time Lincoln was known as a highly effective railroad attorney. The Railsplitter image effectively portrayed the candidate as a common man of the people, which went over well during the campaign and helped Lincoln win the White House.

raincoat. Raincoats made with INDIA RUBBER saw limited use among Union soldiers. Most such outer-

wear was provided by civilian benefactors, but the comfort was often sacrificed by the inconvenience of having to carry it on the march. Properly known as caoutchouc, this crude form of rubber was used on a very large scale before war broke out.

Rains torpedoes. See TORPEDO.

raking. N. A distinctive slanted smokestack on a steamer, characteristic of BLOCKADE-RUNNERS.

Raleigh, CSS. (1) This 65-ton steamer GUNBOAT had formerly been an iron-hulled propeller-driven towing steamer that had been seized by the state of North Carolina at the beginning of the war and transferred to the Confederate navy. She participated in the defense of Forts Hatteras and Clark and Roanoke Island before moving to Norfolk, from which she supported the CSS VIRGINIA during the March 8–9, 1862, battle of the IRON-CLADS. When Norfolk was evacuated in May 1862, *Raleigh* was moved up the James River to patrol service around Richmond. Renamed *Roanoke* toward the end of the war, the gunboat was scuttled on April 4, 1865, during the evacuation of the Confederate capital. (2) Built at the Wilmington shipyard of J. L. Cassidy and Sons in 1863–64, this Richmond-class ironclad RAM carried a battery of four 6-inch RIFLES. Commissioned into Confederate service on April 30, 1864, she was part of a three-vessel attack force that engaged six Federal blockading ships on May 6 off New Inlet, North Carolina. The next day, when *Raleigh* withdrew toward Cape Fear River, she ran aground on the Wilmington bar and fractured her keel. The ironclad was classified as a wreck and salvaged for her iron plating.

ram. N. A warship equipped with a massive iron arm projecting from its prow, designed to cripple and sink an enemy vessel by crashing into it. The CSS VIRGINIA was among the earliest Civil War rams. In early 1862 the Confederacy purchased seven riverboats to be converted into COTTON-CLAD rams. On May 10, 1862, these rams engaged

NAVAL HISTORICAL CENTER

a Federal flotilla near Fort Pillow, Tennessee, and aided in the evacuation of the fort. At about the same time, Charles Ellet converted nine river steamers into rams for the Union navy. The Federal rams engaged the Confederate rams on June 6, 1862, near Memphis and captured or sank all but one of the Southern ships. Other Confederate rams were built and engaged Union ships, with varied results, at Galveston, on the Mississippi River, in Mobile Bay, and off the North and South Carolina coasts. The South also considered oceangoing rams to break the Northern BLOCKADE and contracted two such vessels to be built by John Laird and Sons in England. The British government seized the ships before completion on the grounds that their construction violated the country's neutrality. Confederate agents, however, were able to contract with a French builder for the oceangoing STONEWALL, but the vessel did not arrive in American waters until the war was over. In general, the Confederate rams were underpowered, and the rams themselves frequently broke off after penetrating the hull of an enemy vessel. Occasionally, a sinking ship threatened to take the attacking ram down with her, and usually the only way the Confederate warship remained afloat was if the ram detached.

ram fever. After the March 8, 1862, engagement at Hampton Roads, Virginia, between the CSS *VIRGINIA* and the USS *Congress, Cumberland,* and *MINNESOTA,* a state of near hysteria swept through the Federal capital. Even though the Confederate craft had lost its ram in the fighting, many politicians feared that this unstoppable "monster" would smash through the blockading fleet, sail to the major Northern ports, and shell them with impunity. Gideon Welles, the Union secretary of the navy, recounted a hastily called cabinet meeting in which Edwin M. Stanton, the secretary of war, warned of the catastrophes the Confederate IRONCLAD could wreak on Washington. Despite Welles's assurances that the Federal ironclad *MONITOR* was en route to protect the fleet at Hampton Roads, Stanton solicited the assistance of shipping magnate Cornelius Vanderbilt, who volunteered to send his own 3,360-ton sidewheel-steamer to ram the *Virginia.* The secretary of war also procured every ship in the area so they could obstruct the approaches to Washington from the Potomac River. When the *Virginia* and the *Monitor* battled to a stalemate, Stanton ordered several vessels to Hampton Roads to await the next approach by the Confederate ironclad. The ships never encountered the *Virginia;* she was destroyed during the May 1862 evacuation of Norfolk.

rammer. A cylinder of wood at the end of a wooden staff, the opposite end of which held a SPONGE that was used to drive the charge and projectile to the base of the BORE of a GUN in preparation for firing. The center of the rammer was concave so as not to make contact with the FUSE of the projectile.

rampart. A protective wall on which the PARAPET of a fort was raised, hence a general term for a defensive work. It also described an earthen embankment that surrounded a fortification.

rampart gun. Any large-caliber GUN considered inappropriate or unwieldy for field service.

ramrod. A slender metal or hardwood shaft used to ram a charge into the base of the BORE of a MUZZLELOADING MUSKET or RIFLE.

ramrod bread. A form of cornbread made by plastering a RAMROD with a coating of cornmeal batter and baking it over an open fire.

rank. (1) a body of soldiers standing side by side. (2) A soldier's official position or grade, usually certified by commissions in the case of officers.

rank, brevet. A long-standing custom of the Union army provided that an officer who had exhibited unusual courage or leadership in the field could be promoted to an honorary rank known as a brevet. Prewar regulations specified that brevetted ranks had no significance within an officer's own unit and branch of service (that is, INFANTRY, ARTILLERY, CAVALRY, engineers) but were recognized if he were part of a mixed command or serving on a court-martial board. Likewise, brevet ranks did not carry an increase in pay or authority. Most wartime brevets were of limited duration, after which officers reverted to their previous ranks. In March 1863 Congress authorized brevet promotions of the officers of the U.S. Volunteers. By the end of the war, approximately seventeen hundred Union officers held brevet ranks as major generals and brigadier generals of the regular army and the volunteers. Most of these were dated March 13, 1865, when Congress conferred the honor wholesale, but this abuse led to the termination of brevet promotions. The highest brevet rank conferred was lieutenant general, which was given to Winfield Scott. The Confederate army also had a system of brevet promotions, but they were rarely awarded.

rank and file. A collective term referring to all enlisted men and noncommissioned officers as opposed to commissioned officers.

ransom. (1) A sum demanded and/or paid in exchange for the release of a captive. (2) N. A sum promised by the master of a captured ship, acting in the name of or on behalf of the vessel's owners. Ransom of this sort usually led the capturing vessel to release its PRIZE rather than burn it at sea. Once a ransomed vessel had reached port, the owners usually repudiated the agreement.

***Rappahannock*, CSS.** (1) This 1,200-ton side-wheel steamer formerly had been the passenger steamer *St. Nicholas*. She was captured on June 28, 1861, at Point Lookout, Maryland, and sailed to Chesapeake Bay, where she took three PRIZES on June 29. Relinquished as a prize herself, *Rappahannock* operated on the Potomac and Rappahannock until April 1862, when she was burned at Fredericksburg. (2) This 1,042-ton wooden screw cruiser was built in 1857 for the British navy as the *Victor* and served as a dispatch carrier. She was sold to the Confederacy as a China trader, but the British government was suspicious of the transaction and ordered the vessel to remain in port. On November 24 the vessel escaped with workmen still aboard and a skeleton crew. Defective machinery required that she put into Calais for repairs, but the French government refused to grant permission for her return to sea and the vessel remained in France until the end of the war.

rations. Food provided to soldiers and sailors was treated as part of their pay. This practice prevailed regardless of whether or not the men in a given unit were fed according to regulations. Early in the war food was comparatively abundant in both South and North, so most soldiers fared about as well as if they had been at home. As the conflict widened and intensified, it was not uncommon for a COMPANY or a REGIMENT to be without food for several days. Federal regulations called for issuing two different rations—one for camp and the other when the men were on the march. In camp every soldier was supposed to get twenty-two ounces of bread or flour or a pound of HARDTACK daily. The basic component of the marching ration was hardtack. When other foodstuffs were available, they were added to the starch doled out, but such additions varied widely from time to time and from unit to unit. The Confederate army formally adopted the Federal ration plan but could not adhere to it after the spring of 1862. When possible, men who knew they were going into battle were issued two or three days' rations at a time. Some of them devoured everything at a single meal, but others ate sparingly on the first day and saved something for the next two. Tasteless dried, DESICCATED VEGETABLES were issued when available. In the prisons of the North and South, commandants and wardens rarely made a pretense of adhering to military standards. Some of the most gruesome photographs of starved prisoners were made on BELLE ISLE in Richmond and at ANDERSONVILLE, Georgia.

ratline. N. A small line that linked the shrouds of a ship, forming the steps of a ladder by which the mastheads could be reached.

rattle. N. A noisemaker of sturdy wood, usually about twelve inches long, was standard equipment aboard warships. Sailors used them to transmit basic signals to the rest of the crew.

ravelin. A defensive work not attached to a fortification. Its two embankments formed a SALIENT ANGLE.

razorback. A prisoner of war who served as an informer.

readmission. The process by which a seceded state was readmitted to the Union. As envisioned by Abraham Lincoln, this would have been a simple process, requiring only 10 percent of the number of persons in a state who had voted in 1860 to take an OATH OF ALLEGIANCE to the Federal government. The president's assassination, followed by the increased political power of the RADICAL REPUBLICANS, caused the ONE-TENTH PLAN to be abandoned. Readmission then became a long and difficult process.

rear admiral. N. The grade just above that of commodore. David G. Farragut's chief reward for his April 1862 capture of New Orleans was his promotion to the rank of rear admiral. This new rank was symbolized by SHOULDER STRAPS that showed an anchor flanked by stars.

ready finder. Scavengers who scoured battlefields for salvageable material such as MUSKETS, RIFLES, and SHOES.

rear-guard action. Any defensive action taken as a body of troops withdrew from the scene of a SKIRMISH, engagement, or battle.

Reb. Derisive slang for a Confederate soldier or Southern citizen.

Rebel Conch. Slang for a soldier or resident of coastal Florida.

Rebel Gray. See CONFEDERATE GRAY.

Rebel Rag. Derisive slang for a Confederate flag.

Rebel yell. A high-pitched holler, reminiscent of hunting, shouted by attacking Confederates to unnerve Federal soldiers.

reconciliation. The long and difficult process of bringing about healing between warring sections. Because the Confederacy was forced into unconditional military surrender, animosity between the North and South remained high for generations due to the harsh RECONSTRUCTION measures imposed by Congress.

reconnaissance. A systematic attempt to gather information about an opponent's position, size, and movements. A strictly military operation, reconnaissance did not include espionage but was part of the routine of every army. CAVALRY normally scouted in advance of an army in regions where terrain made this feasible. Reconnaissance was relegated to INFANTRY units in mountainous and heavily wooded areas. On both sides, some cavalry units were noted for their skill in reconnoitering.

Reconstruction. A general term used to label the process of restoring the seceded Southern states to the Union. Three plans characterized the process, one proposed by Abraham Lincoln, one by Andrew Johnson, and one by the RADICAL REPUBLICANS who controlled Congress in the postwar years. In the end, Congress adopted a repressive and punitive set of programs that mandated constitutional conventions in the defeated states that recognized the right of Freedmen to vote and banned former Confederate leaders from holding public office. In the defeated South, the planter class and the landed gentry retained little of their prewar affluence, and former slaves had their freedom but little else. With no significant help from the North, the decimated South slowly and painfully rebuilt its cities and transportation infrastructure. Freedmen were forced into a new kind of servitude—sharecropping. Most of the former Confederate states adopted constitutions as required, but they also enacted laws that restricted the freedoms of the former slaves. Home rule was returned to the Southern states in 1877.

recruiting card. A printed appeal for men to enlist in the Union army. Like the more common BROADSIDES issued to foster recruitment, these cards typically listed BOUNTIES and other benefits.

BATTLES AND LEADERS

recruitment. Once the surge of war fever subsided in the North, recruitment became increasingly difficult and complex. Because the South viewed the war as an invasion, Southerners saw themselves as defending their homes and families. As a result, Confederate recruitment was less difficult than in the North. In both regions, patriotism and financial inducements eventually lost their appeal and CONSCRIPTION became the primary means of recruitment.

recusant. A rejection or refusal to conform to social conventions or to the orders of a superior.

redan. A small FIELDWORK with two walls set at a SALIENT ANGLE against the enemy; the rear was usually open. Such fortifications were usually constructed to protect a camp, a line on a battlefield, advanced posts, and along roadways near towns, bridges, or other strategic sites.

red-eye. Inferior whiskey.

red leg. A band of FREE-SOILER partisans in Kansas. Early in the struggle for dominance known as Bloody Kansas, these men adopted the practice of wearing red leggings.

Red Legs. The 55th New York, in reference to the red trousers of their ZOUAVE uniforms. See GARDES DES FOURCHETTES, LES.

redoubt. (1) An addition to a permanent fortress. (2) A small field fortification, often hastily constructed, that was enclosed on all sides.

Red Rover, **USS.** This 786-ton side-wheel steamer was built in 1859 at Cape Girardeau, Missouri, and purchased by the Confederacy on November 7, 1861, to serve as a barracks ship for a floating battery. The vessel was damaged on March 15, 1862, during the fighting at Island No. 10 and abandoned on March 25. The Federal GUNBOAT *Mound City* seized the ship on April 7. She was repaired and taken to St. Louis, where the vessel was converted into a hospital boat for the Union army's Western Flotilla. *Red Rover* began that mission on June 10, 1862, and received her first patient on June 11. She was attached to the Federal flotilla around Vicksburg. On September 30

NAVAL HISTORICAL CENTER

the hospital ship was purchased by the navy and with the rest of the Western Flotilla became a part of the Mississippi Squadron. *Red Rover* participated in the assault on Fort Hindeman and the siege of Vicksburg. Through the fall of 1864 she took on sick and wounded and delivered medical supplies to units along the waterways. *Red Rover* returned to Mound City on December 11 and remained there until she was decommissioned on November 17, 1865. She had served twenty-four hundred patients during the war. The ship was sold at public auction to A. M. Carpenter for $4,500.

reduce, to. To compel an enemy to surrender.

Reed projectile. One of the first shells manufactured for rifled PARROTT artillery, it continued to be a staple in Confederate arsenals because it was easily produced and could be adapted to several rifled PIECES. A wrought-iron ring at the base expanded on firing to fit the rifling of the GUN TUBE.

reentering angle. The junction of two faces of a FIELDWORK or fortification whose apex points toward the interior of the work. The opposite of a SALIENT ANGLE.

refuse, to. To hold back a segment of a line—the center, a WING, or a FLANK—so as to force an enemy to keep troops there. This tactic sometimes created an opportunity to attack a vulnerable point in the opponent's line because he was unable to move troops from the point of refusal.

regiment. The basic organizational unit of both Confederate and Union forces. As soon as they were organized, regiments had an identity of their own since their recruits tended to come from one region or area and were generally known to each other before the war. Individual states were responsible for recruiting, organizing, and to some extent, equipping each unit and designating it with a number. In the Federal army, an INFANTRY regiment was made up of ten COMPANIES of 100 men (3 officers and 97 enlisted

men and noncommissioned officers). Heavy ARTILLERY and CAVALRY regiments were comprised of twelve companies. There were no infantry or cavalry BATTALIONS, but heavy artillery regiments incorporated three battalions of four companies each. The Confederate army followed the same regimental structure although some Southern regiments had battalions and at least one infantry regiment included two companies of cavalry. Federal regulations dictated that regiments should have no more than 1,025 men and no fewer than 845. Since new recruits were assigned to new companies rather than distributed among existing units as replacements, regimental manpower steadily declined over time. By the end of the war the North had fielded 2,144 infantry regiments, 61 heavy artillery, 272 cavalry, 13 engineers, 9 light infantry, and 432 artillery BATTERIES. The South had raised 642 infantry regiments, 137 cavalry, 16 artillery, and 227 batteries.

regulators. A vigilante group established among the Union prisoners at ANDERSONVILLE to end the extortion and brutality by gangs of fellow prisoners who preyed on those weakened by imprisonment as well as new arrivals.

reimbursement. For more than a decade after the war, the U.S. Congress wrestled with tens of thousands of claims for compensation for damages incurred during the war. Many were never acted upon; others were paid a fraction of their claims.

Usually any reimbursement depended upon the interest and influence of the claimant's congressman. In January 1873 an act was passed guaranteeing reimbursement to "loyal citizens of Loudoun County, Virginia, for their property taken by Military Authorities of the United States." The list of payments included several hundred names. One of the smallest settlements was $25, and one of the largest was $1,437.

relic. A souvenir. A scrap of an enemy flag was among the rarest and most prized relics, but almost anything—a belt buckle, button, SHOULDER STRAP, CANTEEN, or shell fragment—fell into this category. Some of the most bizarre relics were skeletal remains.

***Relief,* USS.** This 468-ton wooden storeship was commissioned by the Union navy late in January 1861 and given a battery of two 32-pounders. She went out of commission in less than a year despite building costs and repairs in the amount of $207,826.

relieved, to be. (1) To be released from a post of duty, such as a sentry. (2) To be withdrawn from a position or point of battle when replaced by another unit. (3) To lose one's command when replaced by an officer of higher rank or by order of a higher authority, such as a commanding general, the secretary of war, or the president.

remand, to. To order or otherwise specify that an individual or unit should return to a previous position or stance.

Remington. (1) A .50-caliber single-shot CARBINE built to use the rimfire SPENCER CARTRIDGE. Remington received a patent for this weapon in December 1863, and the Union War Department purchased 15,000. (2) This .44- (army) and a .35-caliber (navy) six-shot percussion REVOLVER was one of the most popular handguns of the war. Weighing less than three pounds, two models were produced and designated 1861 and 1863.

One of the most sought-after weapons of its kind, the U.S. government purchased 125,314 Model 1863 revolvers during the war.

removed, to be. The removal of an officer from a command position was much more severe than just relieving him. When removed from command, such officers were seldom reassigned. Partly a result of rivalry and jealousy, Col. A. J. Myer was removed from the Union Signal Service in July 1864, and his commission vacated. Confederate Gen. Daniel H. Hill was removed from command by President Jefferson Davis as a result of charges brought against Hill by Gen. Braxton Bragg. Since his commission was not vacated, Hill was given another command. Union Gen. Robert Patterson was removed much earlier as a result of his failure to prevent the reallocation of Confederate forces from the Shenandoah Valley to the Manassas battlefield. In this instance, the aggrieved Patterson demanded a court of inquiry but never got it.

reportial corps. A nickname for newspaper correspondents.

representative recruit. Slang for a conscript.

reprise, to. To retake a position for the second or third time. Frequently some kind of retaliation was implied.

republics, seceded. The SECESSION movement gained great momentum before the Confederacy was organized. As a result, a number of COTTON BELT states were briefly treated as independent republics. In the case of the Republic of South Carolina, formal organization as an independent political entity began in December 1860. Plans to send representatives to this republic were abandoned when other states seceded and voiced interest in banding together into a political confederation.

restitution. Similar to REIMBURSEMENT, issues of restitution typically dealt with significant sums. F. B. Carter kept meticulous records of the damages to his property caused during the November 30, 1864, battle of Franklin and also produced a memorandum signed by a Union officer concerning the destruction. As a result, the Carter estate eventually received a settlement in the amount of $20,061.10.

retaliation. An act to avenge an enemy act. In the fall of 1862 Confederate Gen. John H. Morgan burned the village of Olive Hill, Kentucky, and forty-five other houses in retaliation for BUSH-WHACKERS who fired on his men. Near Bayou Sara, Louisiana, the Federal gunboat *SUMTER* was fired on, and David D. Porter retaliated by shelling several homes in the region. When another vessel was fired upon, Porter leveled the town. Confederate Gen. Jubal Early was enraged by actions of Union Gen. David Hunter's command in the Shenandoah Valley. In retaliation Early demanded an impossible RANSOM from the city of Chambersburg, Pennsylvania, then torched the town. Comparable acts of REPRISAL and retaliation took place in every theater of the war.

retire, to. To withdraw, retreat, or fall back.

retired flank. A curved flank whose convex point turned toward the fortress or position it was ordered to REDUCE.

retrenchment. A secondary or covering trench to which defenders could withdraw should they be driven from the forward or outer PARAPET; it provided a second line of defense.

retrograde. Movement toward the rear or away from the enemy. Retrograde movements were not synonymous with retreats; they were efforts to maneuver into better position.

revenue cutter. A sizable vessel owned and operated by the U.S. Revenue Service. Ships were widely employed because most DUTIES or TARIFFS were collected at port cities. At the outbreak of hostilities, only one revenue cutter, the *HARRIET LANE,* was steam powered. Several of these vessels were seized by Secessionists early in 1861, and some were incorporated into the fledgling Confederate navy.

reverse fire. Fire delivered from positions to the rear of the enemy's front line.

revetment. A retaining wall that was usually but not always part of a permanent fortification. The same term was used to name a layer of stone or other permanent material used to line the FACE of an earthen embankment and strengthen it.

review. A display of martial skill in executing MANEUVERS before an audience.

revolver. A pistol with a revolving chamber that fired several shots in rapid succession.

***Rhode Island,* USS.** This 1,517-ton wooden side-wheel steamer was built in New York in 1860 by Lupton and McDermut as *John P. King,* but burned and was rebuilt and renamed *Eagle* when purchased by the navy on June 27, 1861 from Spofford, Tileston and Company in New York. Renamed *Rhode Island,* the vessel was commissioned on July 29, 1861, at the New York Navy Yard. She was used as a supply ship during the war but was also involved in capturing BLOCKADE-RUNNERS. When she returned to northern waters, *Rhode Island* was used to tow several MONITORS from Hampton Roads,

NATIONAL ARCHIVES

Virginia, to Beaufort, North Carolina. On December 29, 1862, she had the MONITOR in tow when they encountered a heavy storm, and the IRONCLAD sank. In 1863 she returned to southern waters and blockade duty until she was forced to sail for Boston to have her engines overhauled and other extensive modifications that transformed the ship into an auxiliary cruiser. Aside from returning to blockade duty, the vessel participated in both the December 1864 and January 1865 attacks on FORT FISHER, North Carolina. After the war, *Rhode Island* was dispatched to escort the French-built Confederate armored RAM *STONEWALL* to the United States. The ship was decommissioned in 1867 and sold to G. W. Quintard at New York in 1867. Subsequently the ship was renamed *Charleston* and entered the merchant service until 1885.

rodomontade. Empty bluster or vain talk. Also spelled *rhodomontade*.

Richmond, **USS.** Although not launched until after Maj. Robert Anderson and his men occupied previously unused FORT SUMTER, this wooden screw-steamer retained the name of the Confederate capital throughout the conflict. She was 225 feet long, had a maximum speed of almost ten knots, and required at least seventeen feet of water to operate. Built by government contract, the vessel cost $566,259, exclusive of her battery, which never included fewer than sixteen GUNS. At the Boston Navy Yard she went out of commission on July 14, 1865.

ricochet fire. Fire delivered at a low angle, just clearing the PARAPET and then bouncing into the interior of a FIELDWORK.

Rider's tent-knapsack. This patented device made of heavy gutta-percha was touted as both a tent and a KNAPSACK. A huge folded burlap sheet inside the case could be pitched to form a tent that would accommodate five men. With the sheet removed, the case formed a durable waterproof large-capacity knapsack. Although the tent-knapsack was ingenious and weighed only three pounds with the sheet included, it was too bulky and cumbersome to be used much in the field.

LIBRARY OF CONGRESS

Rienzi. A very large horse acquired by Union Gen. Philip H. Sheridan in Rienzi, Mississippi, in 1862. Following the famous ride that reversed Federal fortunes in the October 19, 1864, battle of Cedar Creek, Sheridan renamed the horse WINCHESTER.

rifle. (1) Both artillery and shoulder arms were classified as rifles due to a grooved treatment of the interior of their barrels, which extended the range of the weapons and increased their accuracy. The INFANTRY rifle was more accurate than any MUSKET, and it was shorter. (2) A synonym for infantryman.

rifle-musket. This term was adopted in 1855 as SMOOTHBORES began to give way to rifled barrels.

Rifles differed from rifle-muskets in that they had shorter barrels.

rifle pit. A short, shallow trench large enough to afford protection to one or more men.

Riker's Island. This tiny island in the East River, close to New York City, held a few small storage buildings in 1861 but in 1864 was converted into a prison. Barracks built on the 87-acre island were designed to hold one thousand prisoners of war and quickly filled to capacity. After the war, the island continued to serve as a prison for the city of New York.

robbers' row. Slang for the area in camp reserved for SUTLERS to peddle their wares.

rocket. See HALE ROCKET.

Rock Island. The Rock Island military prison opened in December 1863 on an island three miles long and a half mile wide in the Mississippi River between Davenport, Iowa, and Rock Island, Illinois. Shortly after it opened, the camp became known as the worst prisoner-of-war camp in the North. When an offer of AMNESTY was made to the captive population, a record number of inmates took the OATH OF ALLEGIANCE to the Union. Most of the Confederates who switched allegiance probably did so to get better food and medical care. More than a thousand of these GALVANIZED YANKEES were formed into ten COMPANIES, each of which had about 125 men. At no other prison in the North or in the South did an equal number of inmates choose to renounce their loyalty.

Rock of Chickamauga. A nickname for Union Gen. George H. Thomas, whose actions at Snodgrass Hill averted a Federal disaster at the 20 September, 1863 battle of Chickamauga.

Rodman gun. A SMOOTHBORE CANNON developed by Capt. Thomas J. Rodman, who devised a method of casting the iron piece around a core that was cooled from the inside out, which allowed reliable larger GUNS to be made. Rodman patented the process and contracted with the Fort Pitt Foundry in Pittsburgh to produce and test his guns. The trials went on for almost a decade, but they proved that guns cast by Rodman's method were more durable than those cast by conventional methods. In 1860 the War Department authorized the casting of a 15-inch smoothbore COLUMBIAD, and the piece was sent to FORT MONROE for testing in March 1861. Eventually the War Department authorized larger guns, as large as a 20-inch smoothbore. Up to that time most artillery had a BORE length of fifteen to twenty times its caliber; Rodman was able to produce reliable and accurate guns with BORE lengths

that were only eleven times their caliber. Rodman guns were distinguished by a bottle-shaped appearance and the absence of reinforcing bands around the gun BREECH. They were adopted as a standard heavy gun for coastal artillery, fortress-siege, and shipboard use. During the war the War Department purchased 286 15-inch, 1 13-inch, 15 10-inch, and 240 8-inch Rodman guns. Most COLUMBIADS that saw service during the war were cast by the Rodman method.

roll of honor. At the beginning of the war the Confederacy authorized medals and badges for officers "conspicuous for courage and good conduct on the field of battle" and one enlisted man per REGIMENT after each victory (chosen by a regimental vote), but wartime shortages prevented the medals from being made. Thus in October 1862 the Confederate Congress authorized a roll of honor that would include all RANKS and was to be inscribed with the names of the honorees. Furthermore, the roll was to be preserved in the office of the adjutant and inspector general, the names were to be read to each regiment at the first dress parade following receipt of the roll, and the honorees' names were to be published in at least one newspaper of every state. By the end of the war, there were more than two thousand names recorded.

rotgut. Inferior whisky.

route step. Regulation indicated that this pace equal 110 steps per minute. In practice, it was almost impossible to maintain this rate. As a result, route step came to mean rapid and uncoordinated withdrawal.

rowlock. N. A wooden or metal brace designed to support an oar while it was in use.

run. A small body of water that followed a natural drainage pattern, equivalent to a branch and usually reserved for a stream smaller than a creek.

Rush's Lancers. Organized as the 6th Pennsylvania Cavalry in the summer of 1861 by Richard H. Rush, a graduate of West Point, the ranks were filled with the sons of the most prominent families of Philadelphia—the social, military, and athletic elite of the city. Their primary weapon was a nine-foot lance with an eleven-inch three-edged blade topped by a scarlet swallowtail pennant. Incredibly, the unit retained the lances until June 1863, when they were replaced with CARBINES. The first action in which the 6th Pennsylvania Cavalry participated was the Peninsula campaign, during which it was involved in the battles of Hanover Court House and Gaines's Mill. The next major action in which it participated was the June 9, 1863, battle of Brandy Station, executing two charges against the Confederate CAVALRY. During the Overland campaign of 1864, these men fought with distinction at Cold Harbor and Trevilian Station.

Russian Aid for Yankees. A sizable Russian fleet spent much of the winter of 1863–64 in New York Harbor, and rumors circulated that Alexander II was about to put his military might behind the Union war effort. The czar's interest, however, was in the development of IRONCLAD warships, and he had ordered a dozen for his navy. Other than that, he had little interest in the American conflict. Anticipating a possible conflict with Britain and France, the Russian leader elected to send his best ships to New York because it seemed

LIBRARY OF CONGRESS

improbable that the vessels would be attacked in American waters.

Russian Thunderbolt, the. A nickname for Union Gen. John Basil Turchin (born Ivan Vasilovitch Turchinoff), a native of Russia and a graduate of the imperial artillery school at St. Petersburg. After fighting in the Crimean War, Turchin and his wife came to the United States and settled in Chicago. As a colonel in the Army of the Ohio, he led his men into Missouri, Kentucky, and Alabama. During the capture of Huntsville, Alabama, Turchin was dubbed "the Russian Thunderbolt" and "the Mad Cossack." In May 1862 residents of the town of Athens, Alabama, fired on Turchin's troops, so the Russian had the town burned. Gen. Don Carlos Buell court-martialed Turchin and ordered his dismissal from the service, but the Russian's wife pled her husband's case before Abraham Lincoln, and the president not only pardoned Turchin but also promoted him to brigadier. Thereafter Turchin performed admirably in the battles of Chickamauga and Chattanooga and during the Atlanta campaign. Bad health, however, forced him to resign his commission, and he returned to Chicago.

S

saber. An edged weapon with a curved blade and a hand guard. Although designed for cavalrymen, some sabers were also issued to soldiers in other branches. Yet despite the blade's long history, cavalrymen found the weapon to be impractical and more ornamental than useful. In battle sabers became a weapon of last resort. By the end of the war they had been supplanted by the CARBINE. Nevertheless, there were occasional saber duels between massed CAVALRY, most notably at Brandy Station on June 9, 1863, and at Gettysburg on July 3, 1863.

Saber Brigade. The CAVALRY BRIGADE comprised of the 4th Michigan, 7th Pennsylvania, 5th Iowa, 3rd Indiana, and 4th U.S. regulars and led by Irish-born professional soldier Robert H. Minty.

saber-tache. An ornamental leather case worn on the left side of a CAVALRY officer's SWORD belt.

sabot. Sabots provided stability for artillery projectiles within the GUN TUBE. Made of wood, brass, copper, lead, papier-mâché, leather, rope, or wrought iron, they were used in both SMOOTHBORES and rifled guns. With smoothbore guns, wooden SABOTS were used to keep the FUSE forward and in the center of the bore. Sabots for SOLID SHOT were attached with two crossing tin straps. If it was tied to a cartridge bag, the round was referred to as fixed ammunition. Sabots for rifled ammunition were designed to expand and fill the rifling of the gun tube, causing the projectile to rotate. This spin extended the range of the gun and enhanced the accuracy of the weapon. In many instances, especially during the earliest battles of the war, sabots caused casualties among friendly troops when fragments fell into the ranks of soldiers in front of the guns.

sack, to. To plunder or pillage.

sacred dust. Slang for a corpse.

saddle tree. A saddle's wooden frame, usually made of beech.

safety-switch. A mechanical device designed to reduce the number of head-on collisions of railroad trains. A short section of track was attached to the rails in such fashion that an approaching train would cause the switch to swing into position and allow uninterrupted passage. If a train approached from the opposite direction, however, the safety switch moved it from the line to avoid a collision.

sailmaker mate. N. A petty officer who made and repaired sails on small vessels and supervised this task on larger vessels.

sail under false colors, to. N. The practice among PRIVATEERS, BLOCKADE-RUNNERS, and warships of flying the ENSIGN of an enemy or a neutral power so as to avoid a confrontation or lull the enemy into a state of trust that could be exploited.

St. John the Baptist Regiment. A Confederate unit whose members were from the Louisiana parish of St. John the Baptist. This REGIMENT was commanded for a time by Gen. Jean Jacques Alfred Alexander Mouton, a member of the West Point Class of 1850.

***St. Louis,* USS.** See BARON DE KALB, USS.

St. Louis Riot. An omnibus title referring to a series of violent clashes in St. Louis between Federal soldiers and Southern sympathizers. Beginning on May 9, 1861, and continuing for more than two days, these encounters claimed an estimated fifty lives. Both Ulysses S. Grant and William T. Sherman were in the city at the time, and Grant wrote of his visit there but did not mention the deadly riot.

***St. Philip,* CSS.** This 1,172-ton side-wheel steamer was built at Greenpoint, New York, in 1852 and originally named *San Juan.* It was renamed *STAR OF THE WEST* and chartered by the Federal government, first to carry reinforcements to FORT SUMTER in January 1861 and then in April 1861 to transport troops from Texas to New York. During the latter mission, the ship was captured and sent to New Orleans. There the vessel's name was changed to *St. Philip* and she was employed as a receiving ship. When New Orleans fell to the Federals in April 1862, the ship was sent up the Mississippi. In March 1863, when a Northern naval force attempted to outflank Vicksburg through the Yazoo Pass, *St. Philip* was sunk to obstruct a channel of the Tallahatchie River, above Fort Pemberton.

salient angle. The junction of two FACES of a fortification, permanent or temporary, whose apex projects outward. The opposite of a REENTERING ANGLE.

Salisbury Prison. The Confederate prison at Salisbury, North Carolina, had formerly been a cotton factory. It was converted for use as a prison in November 1861 and was originally designed to hold 2,000 prisoners: spies, soldiers charged with military offenses, and DESERTERS as well as Federal prisoners of war. The eleven-acre site included a four-story brick building and six small cottages, all of which were enclosed by an eight-foot-high fence. In many ways the camp was situated ideally near a railroad crossroads in an area rich in produce. During the first two years of operation, the camp had abundant food and spacious quarters for its captives. In fact there was but one death among the prisoners. The townspeople brought home-cooked meals to the captives, and the Northerners reciprocated with drill parades and introduced many of their captors to the game of baseball. All in all, Salisbury was one of the South's principal prisons, and thanks to the EXCHANGE CARTEL it was empty of Union prisoners by the end of 1863. That situation, however, changed radically in the latter half of 1864. Five thousand Federal prisoners arrived at the camp on October 5, 1864, and a total of 10,321 were imprisoned there by the end of that month. Overcrowding created an intensely hostile environment, and gang fights erupted between the

Images of Salisbury Prison include this depiction of a baseball game.

Confederate prisoners and the Union captives. The worst offenders were eventually transferred to ANDERSONVILLE, and many of these became the infamous "raiders" of that prison camp. To address the lack of shelter, prisoners were issued tents and many Northerners dug trenches and shelter holes. Further complicating the situation, the winter of 1864–65 was particularly severe, and the prisoners were faced with drastic food and water shortages. At least 3,419 inmates died of hunger and disease. On February 22, 1865, 2,800 prisoners were marched to Greensboro to be exchanged at Wilmington; only 1,800 survived the march. By March 2, 5,149 had been removed from Salisbury for the exchange. When Federal troops arrived at the prison in April 1865, they burned the camp.

sally, to. To rush out (from a fortification) and attack (a besieging enemy).

sally port. A postern gate, or underground passage, from innerworks to the outerworks of a fortification. It was designed to allow troops to exit a facility without being exposed to fire.

salt, to eat. Union army slang for a meal of government RATIONS.

salt horse. Slang for beef preserved by salt or pickling.

salt fish. A term of honor reserved for hardened veterans or experienced prisoners of war.

Samson's Post. N. (1) A strong post that rested on the keelson of a ship and supported a beam of the deck. (2) A temporary or portable support for a leading block or pulley.

sandlapper. A native of South Carolina.

Sangamon, USS. This 1,875-ton Passaic-class single-turret MONITOR was built under the name *Conestoga* at Chester, Pennsylvania, by John Ericsson in the summer of 1862. Renamed *Sangamon*, she was commissioned on February 9, 1863 and assigned to the North Atlantic Blockading Squadron to support the Federal army in the waterways of northern Virginia. In early 1864 she

NAVAL HISTORICAL CENTER

was reassigned to the South Atlantic Blockading Squadron for duty off Charleston, South Carolina, but *Sangamon* returned to Hampton Roads to support the Overland campaign. After the war she was decommissioned until May 13, 1898, when she served in the Spanish-American War. The vessel was sold in 1905.

Sanitary Commission, U.S. Several prominent civilians in the North recognized the need for a nonmilitary organization to care for sick and wounded soldiers and founded the commission in June 1861. These aims were soon expanded to include providing food, clothing, and other essentials to Federal troops and their dependents beyond what the military was empowered to do. A central office was set up in Washington, D.C., and main branches were opened in the ten largest cities in the North, which eventually sponsored seven thousand aid societies. The facilities and supplies made available to Union soldiers were financed by private donations and special fund-raising fairs. By war's end the commission had raised more than $7 million and distributed supplies worth more than $15 million.

sap. A trench dug in a zigzag pattern, connecting a succession of PARALLELS necessary to advance on an enemy fortification. Often created under fire from the defenders, the workmen were protected by movable shields. There were several types of sap trenches—the simple sap, the flying sap, the full sap, the half-full sap, the double sap, and the half-double sap—depending on their method of construction. All were designed to protect the troops from the point of attack of a besieged fortification.

sap parallel. A trench parallel to a defensive work that linked all SAPS emanating from the position.

sapper. A workman whose task was to dig SAPS.

sap roller. A cylinder of wood or wicker that was rolled ahead of sappers (those who dug the trenches) to shield them from enemy fire.

sap up, to. To excavate a SAP or saps very close to the enemy's line.

sauerkraut. A nickname for a German immigrant in the Union army. Many of these men spoke little English and responded only to German-language commands.

Saviour of the Valley. A nickname for Confederate Gen. Thomas L. Rosser, who was lauded for his service in the summer of 1864 against the Union armies in the Shenandoah Valley.

Sawbones. A nickname for a surgeon.

Sawyer gun. This MUZZLELOADING rifled CANNON was developed in the mid-1850s by Sylvanus Sawyer of Fitchburg, Massachusetts, in 6-, 24-, and 30-POUNDER sizes. Sawyer also designed six-ribbed lead-coated shells for his weapon; the lead ribs were engineered to engage the rifling of the BORE. These GUNS were deployed early in the war, but they were awkward to load and had a tendency to burst. The larger guns were Sawyer's most successful models, and these were eventually utilized as seacoast artillery.

scarp. The side of a defensive ditch that lay next to the PARAPET of an installation. It was often cut vertically so it would be difficult to scale.

scarp wall. Constructed only at permanent installations, these structures were designed to prevent the weight of the fortification from causing a cave-in and to prevent an adversary from surmounting the scarp. The scarp walls of Fort Jackson, Louisiana, towered twenty-two feet.

Schenkl shell. This artillery projectile was designed and manufactured by John H. Schenkl in Boston. The shell was made of a cast-iron body, of which the lower half was a tapered cone with raised ribs against which a papier-mâché SABOT was attached. This design addressed the fact that sabots had caused injuries among friendly troops; the papier-mâché sabot was blown to pieces as soon as it cleared the muzzle. The tapered tail, however, restricted the size of the shell's charge, and damp weather tended to cause the papier-mâché sabots to swell, which prevented loading. Confederate versions of the Schenkl shell substituted wood for papier-mâché.

schooner. N. A sailing vessel rigged only with a foremast and mainmast. As steam propulsion technology progressed, many schooners added steam-powered plants but carried collapsible masts for emergency use.

***Sciota*, USS.** Built by contract at Philadelphia, this 507-ton two-masted screw-steamer GUNBOAT was equipped with two tubular boilers, each of which had two furnaces. The costs of Sciota's construction amounted to $96,000, she was sunk in Mobile Bay by a TORPEDO.

scorbutic diathesis. A medical term for SCURVY.

scout. (1) A RECONNAISSANCE, usually in force and carried out by CAVALRY. (2) An individual— either military personnel or civilian—sent out to gather information; a euphemism for SPY.

scraper. An twenty-seven-inch-long iron implement with a spoon at one end and a spade-shaped scraper at the other. It was used to remove

A group of scouts for the Union Army of the Potomac

POWDER residue from the BORES of MORTARS and large HOWITZERS.

Scrappy Bill. A nickname for Confederate Gen. William Mahone, whose admirers claimed that he had never dodged a fight, regardless of the odds.

scratch. Slang for a test of character, such as a soldier's first experience under fire.

scrip. Tickets issued by SUTLERS as change for purchases, but honored only by the same seller.

scurvy. A nutritional malady caused by a lack of vitamin C due to a lack of fresh vegetables and fruit. Traditionally the bane of seamen who were often at sea for months, it became a major illness among the soldiers of the Civil War during the last year of the conflict. Scurvy causes spongy gums, loose teeth, and bleeding in the skin and mucous membranes.

scuttlebutt. N. Gossip or idle talk. To sailors this referred to the butt or cask of fresh water around which men lingered and talked.

seacoast guns. These heavy weapons were permanently mounted in forts or other defensive areas along rivers and coastal waterways. Such guns were mounted on BARBETTE, CASEMATE, flank casemate, and on CARRIAGES. MORTARS were mounted on beds. The primary seacoast guns were 10-inch COLUMBIADS and 15-inch RODMAN SMOOTHBORES.

Sealer. A unique MUSKET projectile that saw only limited action. Sealers were designed to split into three segments after they were fired, but in practice this fragmentation rarely happened. The War Department did not buy the peculiar ammunition in quantity, but individuals were allowed to purchase it for their own use.

sea pie. N. A mixture of meat and vegetables cooked with several layers of crust.

secess or **secesh boys.** Northern slang for Confederate civilians as well as soldiers.

Secessia. Northern slang for the Confederacy.

secession. Formal withdrawal from a governmental entity or organized body. In North America, the first act of secession took place in Massachusetts. Citizens of Suffield, Somers, Enfield, and Woodstock found the level of taxation to be burdensome and asked to withdraw from the colony so they could be annexed by Connecticut. When the request was ignored, they seceded from Massachusetts and became a part of the neighboring colony. The earliest talk of a state's seceding from the Union also occurred in New England, but no action followed. New York City flirted with the notion of seceding from the state in January 1861. During the war to repair the Union, the Federal government encouraged and supported the secession of West Virginia from Virginia. As far as the law of the land was concerned, the constitutionality of secession was never examined by the U.S. Supreme Court.

secession bread. Bread made from rice flour rather than wheat flour.

Secessionville. Despite its name, this South Carolina village was not a product of the state's withdrawal from the Union. It originated as a village of summer homes built by Charlestonians who wanted to get away from the city. Residents who joked that they spent their vacation time seceding from the society life of the city were responsible for the name of the town.

second parallel. In laying SIEGE to an opponent's fortification, a series of interconnected trenches—eight to twelve feet wide—allowed the besieging army to advance and hold the ground gained in the approach. Succeeding PARALLELS served as forward supply depots for the next. The second parallel was excavated within CANISTER range (about 300 yards) of the first parallel, which was opened between 1,500 to 600 yards from the point of attack.

see the elephant, to. Slang for combat experience. The phrase is believed to have originated during the Mexican War. See also ELEPHANT and MEET THE ELEPHANT.

see the tiger, to. A variation of TO SEE THE ELEPHANT.

seed tick coffee. A substitute coffee made by Confederates. In this instance, the substitute looked like the larvae of ticks.

NAVAL HISTORICAL CENTER

***Selma*, CSS.** This 320-ton side-wheel GUNBOAT was built in Mobile, Alabama, in 1856 as the coastal steamer *Florida*. The Confederate government seized the ship in 1861 and converted her into a warship, which eventually cruised the area between New Orleans and Mobile. In July 1862 the vessel was renamed *Selma*. During the August 5, 1864, battle of Mobile Bay, *Selma* joined the IRONCLAD *TENNESSEE* in action around Fort Morgan, and *Selma* was captured and adopted by the Federal navy.

Seminary Ridge. An elevated area west of Gettysburg around which most of the Confederate army deployed. Since the Federal army occupied Cemetery Ridge, east of the town, the area between the two positions was the major focus of the July 1–3, 1863, battle.

Seminole. A nickname for Confederate Gen. Edmund Kirby Smith.

semi-Yankee. Disparaging Confederate slang for a UNIONIST Southerner. In the South, the number of civilians arrested and jailed without a hearing was small in comparison to the "prisoners of state" in the North. Richmond's CASTLE THUNDER was the primary facility for holding Southern political prisoners, but almost all prison facilities held some of those whose loyalties were suspect.

senior. (1) Holding RANK at least one grade above other officers. During combat, numerous officers were killed and a surviving lieutenant might be briefly the senior regimental officer. (2) Holding a commission issued before other officers of the same rank. (3) N. Being in permanent or temporary command of a station aboard ship. Unlike battlefield seniority, which came as a result of attrition, naval seniority was conferred by a superior officer.

sequestration. A euphemism for seizing money, property, or goods for the use of the state. Despite the issuance of receipts, sequestrations made by Confederates were not recognized by Union officials, and those made by the latter had no legal standing in the Confederacy. The matter was debated in both the U.S. and Confederate Congresses, and attempts were made to regulate the process. Although pronounced legal by courts on both sides, laws concerning sequestration were generally ignored after 1863. In theory, a person whose gold or cotton or horses had been confiscated could expect to be indemnified, but in practice, this rarely happened.

serfs. Derisive Confederate slang for Union soldiers, whom the Southerners claimed had less freedom than the lowest class of Russians.

serpent's egg. Northern slang for SECESSION.

sergeant. A noncommissioned officer next in RANK above a corporal. Several levels of the rank were created, establishing a hierarchy of power within the grade.

sergeant of the floor. A prisoner of war with the RANK of private who was designated in charge of a floor holding several other men of equal rank.

serve, to. To fire into the ranks of the enemy. Thus an artillerist during the battle of Brandy Station said that his battery served GRAPE and CANISTER to enemy INFANTRY at a range of twenty yards.

set, to. (1) To establish permanently or to firmly affix. Cloth makers used this term to designate the process for making colors fast, or tenacious. Unfortunately, haste plus inferior coloring substances often entered into the setting process. Thus many soldiers—especially Southerners—went into battle with a nearly colorless uniform. Such garb contributed to numerous instances in which comrades fired upon comrades, believing them to be enemies. (2) N. To hoist the flag on the mainmast of a vessel. Many Union blockade ships were hesitant to attack suspected BLOCKADE-RUNNERS who had set the colors of a neutral country.

set-piece battle. A precisely planned engagement or campaign between two maneuvering forces. Most of the battles of the Civil War were set pieces played out between two opposing commanders.

seven knots. Tradition required a hangman to tie seven knots in a noose to be used to execute a woman. Hangman Christian Rath, however, tied only five knots in the noose he prepared for convicted Lincoln assassination co-conspirator Mary Surratt. Like many others, Rath anticipated that her sentence would be commuted, and so her noose would not be used. Yet no clemency was forthcoming, and although her noose was two knots short of standard, it accomplished the purpose for which it was fashioned.

shade. Slang for an African American.

shako. Patterned after French models that had been popular since the Napoleonic wars, this formal military headgear was distinguished by a stiff high crown and decoration. Although U.S. Q.M. Gen. Montgomery Meigs acquired ten thousand shakos as part of a chasseur uniform ordered from France, the style was not adopted by the army. It had, however, enjoyed a popular status among state militia units and thus was worn into many early battles of the war. Made of bearskin or other leather from which fur had not been removed, this distinctive piece of gear was highly visible but low in functional value.

Shanks. A nickname for Confederate Gen. Nathan G. Evans, who was known for his unusually long and lean legs. A West Pointer who was posted to the DRAGOONS upon his graduation, Evans resigned his commission in February 1861. For his leadership at Ball's Bluff eight months later, he received the THANKS OF THE CONFEDERATE CONGRESS.

Shark. A nickname for Union Como. William D. Porter, also known as "Dirty Bill." A brother of Adm. David D. Porter and a half brother of Adm. David G. Farragut, Porter divorced his Southern wife to demonstrate his loyalty to the Union, but two sons fought for the South. He participated in the battles of FORTS HENRY and DONELSON and the initial campaigns along the Mississippi River before ill health forced him to leave active service.

Sharps carbine. Developed by Christian Sharps prior to the war, this .52-caliber BREECHLOADING single-shot percussion CARBINE did not gain widespread acceptance until it had proved itself in combat. The weapon fired a paper or linen CARTRIDGE, but after the war it was adapted to use rimfire metallic cartridges. At least eighty thousand carbines were purchased by the War Department and made the standard issue of Federal CAVALRY. Confederates purchased more than fifteen hundred before the war began, and S. C. Robinson in Richmond fabricated a version of the Sharps carbine for Southern cavalry.

Sharps rifle. The Sharps Rifle Manufacturing Company in Hartford, Connecticut, was based on a .52-caliber BREECHLOADING single-shot percussion RIFLE. Accurate up to six hundred yards, the rifle could be fired from eight to ten times a minute. A high price tag and belief that infantrymen would expend ammunition carelessly limited distribution to special SHARPSHOOTER REGIMENTS, such as BERDAN'S. The War Department purchased less than ten thousand units, but individuals and states were not precluded from acquiring the highly accurate, fast-firing weapons.

sharpshooter. At the beginning of the war Hiram G. BERDAN, a renowned marksman, organized two regiments of skilled riflemen as the 1st and 2d U.S. Sharpshooters, which were attached to the army rather than the Union VOLUNTEERS service. The 1st Sharpshooters was organized on November 29, 1861, and consisted of ten COMPANIES of proven marksmen from New York, New Hampshire, Vermont, Michigan, and Wisconsin—each company was comprised of men from the same state. The 2d Sharpshooters was orga-

nized at the same time, of recruits from New Hampshire, Maine, Pennsylvania, Michigan, Minnesota, and Vermont, but contained only eight companies, each of which was mustered in as it formed. Originally the men provided their own weapons, but the vast array of SHARPS, WHITWORTHS, and specialized hunting and target RIFLES created an ammunition logistics problem. Berdan therefore requested that the men be issued Sharps rifles. The two regiments performed in every campaign of the eastern theater, and a similar Confederate organization was authorized by the Southern Congress in 1862. Over time, organizers saw the value in dispersing the sharpshooters in company strength throughout the regular INFANTRY regiments. In this capacity, they were used primarily as SKIRMISHERS and proved invaluable in picking off and demoralizing the soldiers of the other side as well as silencing artillery BATTERIES from a distance.

shavetail. (1) A mule whose hindquarters had been shaved in preparation for military service but who had received little or no training. (2) By extension, a recently commissioned second lieutenant.

Sheal. A nickname for FORT DELAWARE, coined by the Confederates imprisoned here. A corruption of the biblical *Sheol*, the Old Testament's shadowy realm of the spirits of the dead.

shebang. A temporary hut or shelter.

sheep dip. Slang for inferior whiskey.

sheer. N. To cause a ship to swerve or abruptly deviate from its course.

sheet iron crackers. One of several nicknames for HARDTACK.

shell. A hollow projectile packed with an explosive charge designed to be detonated by a FUSE. Shells fired at troops were set to either explode in the air above the target or to fall into the ranks before exploding. When fired at FIELDWORKS or structures, shells were set to detonate after penetration.

shellback. N. (1) A veteran sailor. (2) One who has crossed the equator and been subjected to a traditional celebration of the achievement.

shell gun. A gun designed to fire shells as well as SOLID SHOT.

shell hooks. A pair of metal tongs used to move MORTAR and other heavy artillery ammunition. The tongs were linked by means of a pivot, and one end of each hook was bent so that it could catch the "ears" of a shell.

shell plug screw. This large tapered screw was used to remove wooden or cork plugs from a FUSE hole prior to inserting a fuse holder.

Sherman's Hairpins (Neckties). During the Atlanta campaign and the MARCH TO THE SEA, William T. Sherman's armies refined the procedure for destroying sections of railroad track. The track was ripped up  then placed over a bonfire made up of the ties from the railroad bed. When the rails were warped by the heat, work crews would bend the rails around tree trunks and twist the track so it could not be easily reshaped. Depending on the tools at hand, lengths of track were sometimes bent into doughnut shapes. This debris was also known as a Jeff Davis necktie and an iron doughnut.

Sherman's Sentinels. Chimneys left standing over the ashes of homes burned by William T. Sherman's armies during the march through Georgia and the Carolinas.

shinplaster. A reference to paper money. Originally issued by banks during the Panic of 1837, the name stems from the fact that the public derided the currency as useful only for making shinplasters—pieces of paper coated with tar, soaked in vinegar or some other home medicinal, and wrapped around sore spots on one's lower legs.

ship, full rigged. A three-masted oceangoing sailing vessel.

ship, to. N. To transfer from a Federal military unit to a naval vessel. At Cairo, Illinois, U. S. Grant authorized experienced sailors and rivermen to transfer from any REGIMENT in his command. This measure was necessitated because the U.S. Navy, whose river vessels were frequently commanded by army officers, was desperately short of manpower.

shirt, bloody. Used in metaphorical fashion, this expression designated a cause that invited conflict. During the two decades before the outbreak of the war, Northern and Southern politicians waved the bloody shirt at one another.

shoat bars. The chevrons of a noncommissioned officer. This usage stemmed from the fact that shoat, the term by which a piglet was identified,

had come to mean any worthless fellow. Privates saw far more of noncommissioned than commissioned officers and took delight in designating most of them as unworthy.

shoddy. Early Union uniforms were made of an inferior wool that fell apart within a few weeks of issue. The word *shoddy* came to refer to any government issue of inferior supplies. Unscrupulous manufacturers and equally unprincipled purchasing agents pocketed enormous sums by passing off shoddy to Federal warehouses. In St. Louis, a network of thieves, headed by quartermaster Justus McKinstry, pocketed hundreds of thousands of dollars. As late as May 1864, Union General in Chief Henry W. Halleck charged that shoddy contractors infested every department of the government.

shod horses. Animals designated for CAVALRY or draft use that were equipped with metal shoes. Many horses that lacked these protective pieces were sold to QUARTERMASTERS when they bought in such numbers that individual animals could not be examined. A cautious cavalry officer was likely to stipulate that only shod horses should be taken on raids or into battle.

short-timer. A soldier whose enlistment was about to expire.

shot. Any spherical projectile designed for use in a cannon or gun.

shot across the bow, a. N. A warning shot directed from ship or shore and designed to pass close to the bow of a vessel without hitting it. It required the vessel to identify itself or change its course.

shotgun. Shotguns were never standard-issue weapons among Federal forces, but they were widely employed by Confederates. Commanders on both sides occasionally had shotguns issued to small units who were expected to lead a charge. Many Confederate CAVALRY leaders considered the shotgun to be the most versatile and useful weapon for general use after its barrel had been cut down to about twenty inches. Nathan Bedford Forrest and his riders habitually carried 12-gauge shotguns in scabbards that were attached to their saddles. When available, buckshot was the preferred charge for one of these single-barrel weapons, which was lethal at a short distance.

shot plug. N. A piece of hardwood designed to be inserted into a hole made by an enemy's shot.

Shotpouch. A nickname for Confederate Gen. W. H. T. Walker, a Georgia-born West Point graduate who earned the moniker through multiple wounds sustained during the Seminole and Mexican Wars.

shotted. CANNON loaded and ready to fire. During the lengthy siege of Charleston, Confederates gave notice of an impending attack by means of firing a shotted GUN and simultaneously dipping a flag.

shoulder strap. A device worn on each shoulder to display an officer's RANK. Dark blue shoulder straps were worn by general officers, white designated INFANTRY, yellow represented CAVALRY, and red denoted ARTILLERY. Since shoulder straps were trimmed with gold or silver embroidery, they were easily spotted by SHARPSHOOTERS. By 1863 experience had demonstrated that conspicuous shoulder straps were a hazard in battle, so officers were allowed to remove them before going into combat.

shoupade. A three-sided fort designed by Confederate Gen. Francis A. Shoup, a veteran of the Seminole Wars. Shoup was Joseph E. Johnston's chief of artillery, and he did not lose a single gun during the long retreat from Dalton to Atlanta. Typical shoupades were a double-walled crib packed with red clay. These 10- to 12-feet-high structures were impervious to artillery fire. Some shoupades supported log PARAPETS holding numerous riflemen. The structures were built at intervals of about eighty yards and situated so that each covered the rear and flanks of others. Shoup

believed that just one corps stationed in the novel works would be capable of stopping William T. Sherman's force. Atlanta's defenses proved to be too strong for a FRONTAL ASSAULT, and the Federal assailant was forced to cut the city's supply lines in order to starve occupants into submission.

Shovelry. Pro-Confederate residents of San Francisco. In California, far from fields of conflict, everyone was a newcomer. At least a generation before the war was initiated, Northerners came to be called "The CHIVALRY." Thus the jocular designation for transplanted Southerners, whose former homes were known for manual slave labor, was "The Shovelry." The Chivalry and the Shovelry never fought a pitched battle, but feelings ran high and everyone was partisan.

show of heads. A challenge to an enemy made by having the men in the trenches, or some other protected position, show their heads just enough to invite fire.

shrapnel. See SPHERICAL CASE SHOT.

Sibley stove. A cone-shaped stove designed to burn wood or coal inside a SIBLEY TENT. Theoretically airtight, this apparatus weighed only thirty pounds. The exhaust was vented through a pipe that ran through an open space in the middle of the tent. More than fifteen thousand of these stoves were used by Federal forces.

Sibley tent. A cone-shaped canvas tent designed in the decade before the war by Maj. Henry H. Sibley following his service on the frontier. Much larger than the standard-issue field tent, this structure had a center pole support and accommodated as many as twenty men. It saw limited use in the 1850s

Henry H. Sibley

but was put into the field early in the war. Because it was tall and heavy, it proved too cumbersome for many fast-moving units. An estimated forty thousand Sibleys were used by Federal and Confederate forces, primarily on training grounds and in permanent or semipermanent camps. Sibley himself resigned his commission in May 1861 and was made a Confederate brigadier.

sideburns. A style of whiskers known before the war as "muttonchops" but popularized by Union Gen. Ambrose E. Burnside, who wore a mustache and cheek whiskers but kept a clean shaven chin. The style was a radical departure from the general practice of the day, which was to shave everything but one's chin. For a while muttonchops were renamed "burnsides," but over time the general was forgotten and the word reshaped to sideburns.

side-knife. A large knife carried in a sheath on one's side. Side-knives were not issued officially by either army, but many Southerners carried BOWIE KNIVES with blades ranging in length from six to eighteen inches. Although lethal weapons, to be sure, most were used for utilitarian purposes around camp, such as skinning game and scaling fish.

siege. A partial or complete isolation of a city, port, or fortress designed to compel its surrender without resorting to a FRONTAL ASSAULT. Several sieges of Confederate-held positions were carried during the war, the best known of which were the thirty-seven-day siege of Vicksburg and the ten-month siege of Petersburg. Other notable sieges occurred at Atlanta, Knoxville, Lexington (Mo.), Port Hudson, and Charleston. By Confederate count, the siege of Charleston lasted for 567 days, but the city was never cut off from supplies and reinforcements.

siege guns. Heavy and cumbersome CANNON, MORTARS, and RIFLES that were effective but difficult to maneuver from one position to another. These commonly included 12-, 18-, and 24-pounders, 8-inch HOWITZERS, and 8- and 10-inch and COEHORN MORTARS. Until Fort Pulaski, near Savannah, was besieged in 1862, rifles had not been used in operations of this sort. Although Union Gen. Quincy A. Gillmore employed only ten rifles, these heavy GUNS punched holes in the fort's seven-foot-thick brick walls and precipitated a Confederate surrender in less than twenty-four hours. During the summer of 1863 Gillmore was dispatched to Charleston, where his siege guns facilitated the capture of Morris Island, the leveling of FORT SUMTER, and a bombarding of the city. Probably the most famous siege guns of the war were the 200-POUNDER known as the SWAMP ANGEL, which was deployed at Charleston, and the flatcar-mounted 13-inch mortar known as THE DICTATOR, which was utilized during the siege of Petersburg.

siege train. A cluster of varying numbers of artillery weapons coordinated according to size and type. In general, siege weapons were organized in groups of one hundred PIECES and their required CARRIAGES, horses, ammunition, and gunpowder. Field trains were much smaller, typically consisting of three field guns per regiment.

Signal Corps. Under the leadership of Maj. Albert J. Myer, the U.S. Army established a signal corps nearly a year before the war. From the beginning, the corps used a wigwag system of flags and torches but soon included ROCKETS and signal flares. On a clear day, wigwag signals could be distinguished at a distance of twenty miles. Working with Myer was Lt. Edward Porter Alexander, who resigned his commission when the war broke out and helped organize a Confederate signal corps that went into operation well before its counterpart in the Union army. Lacking impediments imposed by the Federal bureaucracy, some of Alexander's signalmen saw action at the July 21, 1861, battle of First Manassas (Bull Run), and at least one timely message aided in shifting troops to a critical sector of the battlefield. In both the South and the North, signal corps units were devoted full time to communications and did not participate in combat. Myer also formed FLYING TELEGRAPH TRAINS, using BEARDSLEE TELEGRAPH machines, which sparked an intense rivalry with the U.S. MILITARY TELEGRAPH—a War Department project that employed civilians as telegraphers. Finally Secretary of War Edwin M. Stanton intervened and sent Myer to Memphis to end the competition by assigning all FIELD TELEGRAPHY to the Military Telegraph. After the war, Myer headed the expanded and renovated Signal Corps.

signal rocket. A paper or pasteboard tube filled with a charge and guided by a light stick. Used by the Signal Corps, these devices conveyed messages or directions through prearranged signals. Under good conditions, a rocket could be seen from eight miles away.

U.S. ARMY MILITARY HISTORY INSTITUTE

signal tower. An elevated spot, quickly erected or occupied because of its height and position, from which Signal Corpsmen communicated to one another and their commanders.

sign over, to. To sign a document to reenlist after the termination of one's initial period of enlistment. The zeal with which Union soldiers signed over varied widely, but among the Southern ranks this practice was discarded when the Confederate Congress required all soldiers to serve for the duration of the war. Several Federal commanders did not offer their men a sign-over option but ignored the enlistment data and kept their men in uniform after their enlistments had expired.

sin away the day of grace, to. In those regions of the South that were occupied by Union troops—e.g., parts of Tennessee and Louisiana—this phrase was used by Federal commanders to describe Southerners who continued to espouse loyalty to the Confederacy after a Federal offer of AMNESTY had ended.

sinks. Trenches that served as latrines. In some commands, sinks were routinely dug whenever a command camped overnight when not under enemy fire. They were standard features of permanent installations, camps, prisons, and stockades. At some prisons their use was strictly regulated and sometimes closed at night. One captive reported that it was not unusual to see several hundred men waiting in line for the sinks; those who couldn't wait relieved themselves wherever they could. In some camps, the placement of the sinks relative to any fresh water sources led to rampant illness and disease.

sixty-day volunteers. At the beginning of the war, stipulated terms of enlistment varied. Among the first to respond to Abraham Lincoln's call for seventy-five thousand men after the loss of FORT SUMTER were units organized for sixty days' service. Only a few Federal REGIMENTS went into combat as sixty-day units.

skedaddler. Derogatory slang for a soldier who fled the battlefield, discarding his weapons and equipment in the process. Such panic was not unusual during periods of heavy or extended combat, despite the fact that skedaddlers were likely to be punished severely when caught. According to an account in the *New York Evening Post,* skedaddlers were omnipresent in the ranks during the first year of the war; the term meant "to cut stick, vamoose the ranch, clear out, slope, or cut your lucky." By the summer of 1862, when Federal conscription was violently resisted, those who tried to dodge the DRAFT were also called skedaddlers.

skiff. A small boat.

skillygalee. A dish made from HARDTACK soaked in water and fried.

skiout, to. This variant of "scoot" was used by some commanders to describe the swift occupation of abandoned enemy works.

skirmish. (1) Light combat that involved relatively few men. In DYER'S *COMPENDIUM* an attempt was made to categorize every military event according to sixteen varieties. In this work, a skirmish was larger than an operation but smaller than an assault. (2) In the jargon of prisoners of war, skirmishing was to deal with body lice or other vermin.

skirmish line. The point at which special groups of skirmishers, who moved in advance of relatively large bodies of troops, came into contact with the enemy.

skulker. Soldiers who habitually avoided combat.

skyscraper. A huge hat worn by some Confederate women. Headgear of this sort was made from whatever light and thin material was at hand, often becoming larger by adding to what may have been a simple, small hat. According to one commentator upon Civil War dress, "The bonnet reared itself higher and higher as the hopes of the Confederacy sank lower and lower."

slant fire. Fire directed at an angle, usually thirty degrees, toward the enemy's front.

Slasher. A well-trained CHARGER ridden by Union Gen. John A. "Blackjack" Logan.

Slaughter Pen, the. A wooded area between Big Round Top and the Devil's Den at Gettysburg. Since it lay close to the base of Little Round Top, it was sometimes described as just south of Hock's Ridge. A high percentage of casualties was suffered by numerous units that fought there, notably the 40th Alabama and the 4th Maine.

Slaughter's field. A sector of the Port Hudson, Louisiana, battlefield that was named for the farmer who owned it rather than the casualties suffered there.

slavery. This was the only issue dividing the North and the South for which zealots on both sides saw no possible compromise or solution. Yet most Confederates denied that slavery was the cause of the Civil War. That position had limited validity, since other issues like STATES' RIGHTS and discriminatory TARIFFS were deeply involved, but it fails to take into account the ardor with which numerous high-placed Southerners defended slavery as a divinely ordained institution. Much

that Abraham Lincoln wrote and spoke suggests that he shared the view attributed to the Founding Fathers, who expected that slavery would end of its own accord. Had there been no Civil War, it is possible that such might have happened. Also to be considered is that, without the war, the South's vaunted monopoly on cotton production might not have terminated when new producers were found in India and the Near East during the war years. Slaves in the eleven seceded states and the four cotton-producing Border States that remained in the Union numbered about 4.2 million. Virginia held substantially more slaves than any other state, but before the beginning of hostilities more than 400,000 were held in each of four other states—Alabama, Georgia, Mississippi, and South Carolina. The density of the slave population was greatest in regions adjoining the coast of South Carolina. Here it was not unusual for a county to include six blacks for every white inhabitant. In some states of the COTTON BELT, growing prewar tensions led to North-South divisions in formerly national religious bodies and to enactment of legislation making it impossible for freed slaves to reside within a given state. Increasingly strict Fugitive

Slave Laws were enacted in years preceding the war. These had the sanction of Lincoln for a time after he became president, but they also created problems for military commanders after the war broke out. Union Gen. Benjamin F. Butler's shrewd use of the label CONTRABAND effectively nullified the Fugitive Slave Laws in the North. Slavery itself was abolished by the EMANCIPATION PROCLAMATION and the adoption of the Thirteenth Amendment.

sleep on arms, to. This order required soldiers to keep their weapons at hand while they slept.

slew, to. N. (1) To maneuver a warship so that an enemy vessel was pulled from its course or from the position it expected to occupy. (2) To extricate a stranded vessel from a shoal or other spot at which it was grounded.

sloop. A one-masted sailing vessel.

slow bear. Yankee slang for pigs.

slow match. A length of three-strand rope used to ignite an explosive. The rate of burning varied from flax to hemp to cotton and the treatments with which the material was soaked. A slow match could be made to burn at the rate of four to five inches per hour. Prior to the introduction of FRICTION PRIMERS, slow matches were used to ignite the PORTFIRE, which lit a CANNON'S FUSE.

small arms. Originating in Great Britain, this term was applied to any weapon carried on a soldier's person and wielded by hand. Clubs, bows, and LANCES came under this category until they became obsolete. In Civil War usage, the term usually designated a firearm such as a REVOLVER, MUSKET, RIFLE, or CARBINE. SWORDS were also categorized as small arms. Most battlefield reports include a notation concerning the number of small arms taken from the enemy.

smart. Synonymous with "significant," e.g., smart losses.

smell powder, to. To be involved in action; roughly equivalent to the expression TO SEE THE ELEPHANT.

smoke ball. A hollow paper sphere filled with a mixture that discharged a dense and nauseous smoke. They were designed to burn for twenty-five to thirty minutes and were used to repel enemy miners seeking to undermine one's position or to mask troop movements.

smoke box. A wrought-iron compartment used with heavy GUNS on warships and in permanent fortifications. Built inside the gunport, it was situated so the gun's muzzle entered it when the PIECE was run forward to be fired. By means of the smoke box, most of the smoke and noise from the gun's blast was channeled away from the gunport.

smoothbore. A MUSKET, CANNON, or other firearm whose BORE was smooth, lacking rifling. Smoothbores were standard weapons until manufacturers developed techniques to RIFLE the bores so that projectiles would spin in flight, extending their range and increasing accuracy.

snag, to. To capture or seize.

snakes in the grass. Confederate soldiers who attempted to camouflage themselves.

snipe, to. To divert the attention of a person while eating so that some of his food could be snatched.

sniper. Expert marksmen who were accurate riflemen over great distances. Possibly because snipers were considered to be less than gentlemanly or even dishonorable, records were not kept of the accomplishments of these soldiers.

"so-called seceded states." Abraham Lincoln's preferred reference to the Confederate States, refusing to concede that any state had actually seceded from the Union.

social intercourse. Pleasant conversation.

soda-pop gun or **soda-water gun.** A nickname for a DAHLGREN GUN, widely used on warships of the Union navy. The allusion stems from the gun's resemblance to bottles then used for flavored carbonated beverages.

sold, to be. To be deceived. A civilian or an officer who was described as having been sold cheaply was considered to be a dolt who would fall for any ruse.

soldiery. A military force of undetermined size.

soldier vote. The ballots cast by Union soldiers in a political contest. With the reelection of

Abraham Lincoln being doubtful in 1864, several Federal officers took great pains to see that their men voted. Numerous REGIMENTS were furloughed home so that their members could cast their ballots; others voted at special polling places established in camps. Lincoln received overwhelming support from the soldier vote but might have been reelected without it. The same process determined the outcome of a number of other contests for places in the Confederate and the U.S. Congress.

soldier's disease. Slang for most any chronic ailment suffered by Civil War veterans but especially with reference to addictions to morphine and opium. Surgeons in the field resorted to whatever painkillers were at hand to treat badly wounded soldiers, particularly amputees. Yet there were no guidelines for pain management, so drugs were administered until patients were comfortable. After a few weeks of convalescence, the men were addicted and usually remained so for the rest of their lives.

Soldiers' Home. In 1851, after a twenty-five-year effort championed by Winfield Scott, Jefferson Davis, and Robert Anderson, an "asylum for old and disabled veterans" was established three miles north of the White House and the Capitol. It became known as the Soldiers' Home. During the Civil War, one of the facility's original buildings, a hilltop fourteen-room Gothic Revival cottage that had been built in 1842 as a residence, served as the summer White House for Abraham Lincoln as it had for his predecessor James Buchanan. The cottage, named for Anderson, who went on to command the GARRISON at FORT SUMTER, had previously been used as quarters for the first residents, as a hospital, and as a guesthouse. The bucolic atmosphere of the cottage provided Lincoln a welcome retreat from the hectic atmosphere of the Union capital, and here he composed the final draft of the EMANCIPATION PROCLAMATION. Lincoln could not escape the war here, however. Fort Stevens was only two miles away, and during Jubal Early's raid on the Washington area in the summer of 1864, the president had to flee from the cottage to avoid the risk of capture. In August 1864 the president was shot at while returning to the cottage; he was unharmed, but troops found his hat the next day with a bullet hole in the crown. Lincoln was also targeted to be kidnapped in September 1864 by a Confederate quartet lying in wait for him as he was en route to the cottage, but the attempt was thwarted when the conspirators saw the president accompanied by Union CAVALRY. It has also been claimed that Lincoln spent the last night of his life at the Anderson Cottage; the next day he attended a play at Ford's Theatre, where John Wilkes Booth shot him.

soldier's letter. A letter mailed without postage by a Union soldier. A two-word code was used in lieu of postage. Many men used printed envelopes that were given to them by representatives of the U.S. CHRISTIAN COMMISSION. Others scrawled the code by hand and found this practice to be just as effective as using the envelopes with the printed code.

solid shot. Spherical chunks of cast iron used as projectiles in SMOOTHBORE GUNS. Weapons that used solid shot were rated in terms of the weight of the projectiles they threw, so they were called 6-pounders, 12-pounders, etc.

somebody's darlin'. A reference to an unidentified corpse.

songsters. An inexpensive song book or a single page carrying the words of a popular song. Publishers produced great numbers of songsters at very low cost then sold them to SUTLERS or to such agencies as the U.S. SANITARY COMMISSION or the CHRISTIAN COMMISSION.

sortie. Borrowed from long-established European usage, the term was applied to a sudden attack against besieging forces.

soubrette. Prewar usage designated an actress who played the role of a saucy maidservant, but during the war the term was applied to any woman encountered at a SUTLER'S establishment.

sound, to. (1) Equivalent to "sound out" or "gently probe."

Southern Historical Society. See *JOURNAL OF THE SOUTHERN HISTORICAL SOCIETY.*

southern sidestep. A reference to the dance formally known as the Georgia Reel, but it was also applied to the series of withdrawals executed by Confederate Gen. Joseph E. Johnston's army during the Atlanta campaign.

Southron. A Northern designation for a Southerner.

souvenir. Virtually anything picked up at the site of combat or a significant meeting of leaders.

Southwestern Conspiracy. A reference to the purpose of the KNIGHTS OF THE GOLDEN CIRCLE, which proposed to establish an empire where the cotton-and-slave economy would flourish.

Spangler's meadow. A segment of the Gettysburg battlefield, at the eastern base of Culp's Hill, where an attack by the 2d Massachusetts and the 27th Indiana at 10 A.M. on July 3 was repulsed by four Virginia REGIMENTS. The Federals suffered almost 50 percent casualties in the action.

spanker. N. (1) An adaptable sail carried on a square-rigged vessel's aft mast. (2) The aft mast and its sail on a ship having more than four masts.

spare wheel or **fifth wheel.** CAISSONS carried a fifth wheel as a replacement. As punishment, DESERTERS and other major offenders were strapped to the wheel for hours.

spark arrester. This device fit over the top of a locomotive's smokestack to prevent the escape of sparks that might start a fire.

spar torpedo. An explosive charge attached to a spar projecting forward from the bow of a vessel and detonated on contact or by a rope trigger against the hull of an enemy vessel. A TORPEDO such as this was used by the CSS *H. L. HUNLEY* in the successful February 17, 1864, attack on the USS *HOUSATONIC* in Charleston Harbor. Small Confederate torpedo boats like the CSS *David* also utilized spar torpedoes in their attacks against Federal blockaders. An ingenious Federal variant enabled the charge to be released and guided against the side of a Confederate vessel and then triggered. On October 28, 1864, a Union raiding party successfully triggered such a torpedo under the massive CSS *ALBEMARLE* near Plymouth, North Carolina.

speak, to. N. To exchange signals between vessels. The Union navy had a system of flag signals—based on the British navy system—long before the Federal army developed its wigwag system. Because the two systems were very different, it was not possible for warships to communicate with land forces during battle. That changed following the August 27–29, 1861, engagement at Hatteras Inlet.

Spencer. A short double-breasted man's overcoat.

Spencer carbine. This was the first successful BREECHLOADING repeating RIFLE. Patented by Christopher M. Spencer on March 6, 1860, it held seven .52-caliber copper rimfire CARTRIDGES end to end in a copper tube in the buttstock. A spring advanced the ammunition into the BREECH, and a trigger-guard lever expelled spent cartridges. Each CARBINE came with a hexagonal case that held ten to thirteen bullet tubes. Despite these superior features, the War Department balked at purchasing this weapon. Factors held against it were its weight—approximately ten pounds fully loaded—and the criticism that most repeating guns wasted ammunition. In the meantime, individual units purchased the carbine as well as its special ammunition—the first self-contained cartridges. Finally, Abraham Lincoln intervened and ordered the weapon tested; initial orders were placed in mid-1863 and by the end of the war the Federal government had purchased almost eighty thousand. Federal CAVALRY performed exceptionally well when equipped with the rifle, and many soldiers claimed that the weapons were the single most influential factor in ending the war. It was also advantageous that Confederates could not operate captured weapons because they lacked the specialized ammunition required by the carbine. After the war, overproduction and declining sales led the Spencer Repeating Rifle Company of Boston into bankruptcy in 1869, and the company was purchased by the Winchester Repeating Arms Company.

Spencer rifle. A variant of the popular CARBINE manufactured by the same firm, this seven-shot .52-caliber BREECHLOADING repeater was just under four feet in length and weighed ten pounds. It also delivered fourteen rounds a minute. Despite the Spencer's superiority to many other weapons, it was initially rejected as were most repeating RIFLES. By late 1863 an eight-shot model was adopted for Federal use. Policy dictated that repeaters go to the CAVALRY, but the first Spencer rifles were shipped to MOUNTED INFANTRY— John T. Wilder's BRIGADE in Tennessee, where, during an obscure action at Hoover's Gap, the rapid-firing Spencers held off repeated Confederate advances and earned Wilder's men the nickname LIGHTNING BRIGADE.

spent ball. Originally used to designate a MUSKET ball that hit with so little force that it did little or no damage, the name came to be applied to nonspherical projectiles from RIFLES.

sperm candle. A candle made from whale spermaceti.

spherical case shot. (Also called CASE SHOT.) This most common SMOOTHBORE ammunition had been developed in 1784 by Henry Shrapnel, a British artillerist, as a way to extend the range of GRAPE SHOT and CANISTER. The shell was a thin-walled ball (Northern gunners used lead, Southerners used iron) filled with smaller lead or iron balls, arranged around a bursting charge at the center of the shell. The shot was set off by a BORMANN TIME FUSE, which had a five-second maximum delay, thus giving the shell a range of 1,200 yards. When the shell burst, the contents were propelled in a conical pattern, much like that of exploding grape and canister. Most spherical case shot was designed to be used by 12-POUNDER NAPOLEONS. Due to wartime shortages, Confederate gunners had to resort to less reliable wooden fuses.

spike, to. To disable an artillery piece so as to preclude its use by the enemy. Several methods sufficed: a nail or spike could be driven through the VENT hole, a shot could be wedged in the BORE, ammunition could be caused to explode in the bore, two weapons could be fired at one another— muzzle to muzzle, or the TRUNNIONS could be broken or shattered by firing an overloaded charge at an excessive elevation.

Spiller and Burr revolver. This reliable Confederate .36-caliber REVOLVER was patterned after the Whitney .36-caliber single-action percussion revolver. The Southern handgun differed primarily in its use of brass for the lock frame and iron for the cylinder. The lock frame was also electroplated in silver, and the muzzle was rounded off. Production was financed by Edward N. Spiller and David J. Burr and planned by James H.

Burton, a small arms expert. The trio contracted to produce fifteen thousand revolvers for Confederate CAVALRY within two and half years. Initially the revolvers were manufactured in Richmond, but the factory moved to Atlanta shortly after production began. Labor and material shortages hindered progress, and the company was sold to the Confederate government and moved to the armory at Macon, Georgia, shortly before Atlanta fell to William T. Sherman. By the end of the war, only fifteen hundred revolvers had been produced, fulfilling one-tenth of the original contract.

spiriting. N. Heavy timbers placed along the hull of wooden vessels to reinforce the planking.

Spit and Polish. A nickname for U.S. Secretary of the Navy Gideon Welles, so-called because he insisted that all things be done properly and in a timely fashion.

spitfire. Slang for a MUSKET or RIFLE used largely by Union soldiers from large cities who had little experience with firearms.

splice, to. To unite two or more pieces of rope by interweaving their strands according to any of several standard patterns.

splinter-proof. A structure designed to withstand the impact of shell fragments and SPHERICAL CASE SHOT. Like bombproofs, these were built of posts and joists covered with planking and two to three feet of tamped soil. In some instances, the side facing the enemy was reinforced with sandbags. The side facing away from the enemy's line was left open.

spoiling attack. An attack designed to disrupt or thwart an anticipated attack before or while the enemy is in the process of forming or assembling.

spondulics. A playful term that designated a quantity of money.

sponge. Made of coarse, twisted woolen yarn and shaped like a bag, sponges were used to extinguish any burning embers and to clean the BORE of a GUN of any gunpowder residue. The sponge was one end of the RAMMER staff. It was inserted in the gun TUBE then turned three times clockwise and three times counterclockwise.

sponge and rammer. A wooden staff with a SPONGE on one end and the RAMMER on the other.

sponge bucket. A sheet iron container of water used to saturate a SPONGE when washing out a GUN TUBE. The bucket measured nine inches high and almost eight inches in diameter. A wooden cover was attached to the handle, which could be secured to the axle of the carriage.

sponge cover. A canvas bag used to protect the SPONGE, which was secured with a drawstring. These covers were also marked with the size or CALIBER of the GUN for which it was made.

spoon, to. Two or more persons lying on their sides, front to back, knees slightly bent, as they "nest" like stored spoons. In cramped quarters—especially prison conditions—this was the only way in which soldiers could sleep in relative comfort.

Spoons. A derogatory nickname for Union Gen. Benjamin F. Butler, military governor of Louisiana during the occupation of New Orleans. Since the property of prominent citizens was confiscated if they did not swear LOYALTY OATHS to the Union, many avowed Southerners accused Butler of stealing silverware from their homes.

sport for Yankees, to. The wanton shooting of captives by guards in Southern prison camps.

spotted papers. Slang for playing cards.

spotter. A soldier assigned to note enemy movements and positions and determine the placement of artillery BATTERIES.

spread-eagle speech. Bombastic or unusually sentimental language.

spread-eagled, to be. To be lashed to a spare wheel with arms and legs spread apart.

Springfield rifle. This Model 1861 .58-caliber percussion shoulder arm was the most widely used RIFLE model in the Union army and the last MUZZLELOADER of the U.S. arsenal. The weapon was adopted in 1861 as the principal longarm of the U.S. INFANTRY and had an effective range of 500 yards and an extreme range of 1,000 yards. The rifle was 56 inches long with a 40-inch barrel and weighed a little less than ten pounds. The barrel was attached to the black walnut stock by three iron barrel bands and supported an 18-inch triangular BAYONET. Springfields were manufactured at the Springfield, Massachusetts, armory, but despite an average annual output of 100,000, supply could not keep up with demand, and the government contracted production with at least twenty private manufacturers. The unit cost was between fifteen and twenty dollars, and each contractor's rifle was inspected by a government ORDNANCE inspector who fired a test charge. If the weapon passed inspection, the barrel was struck with an eagle's head acceptance mark and "VP" (viewed and passed) and the inspector's initials were marked on the stock. The rifle's lockplate was stamped with the model (1861 or 1863) and the name of the manufacturer. By the end of the war, the War Department had purchased 1.5 million Springfields. They were used on all fronts and in every major battle of the war. Early seizures of U.S. arsenals and armories in the South netted approximately 150,00 Springfields for Confederate use.

squad. One-fourth of a COMPANY, anywhere from ten to twenty-five men.

squadron. Two COMPANIES of CAVALRY.

Square Box. A Virginia Military Institute nickname for Thomas J. "Stonewall" Jackson.

squirrel hunters. A disparaging nickname for Federal VOLUNTEERS from rural Ohio.

stadia. A marksman's instrument for gauging distances.

staff officer. Any officer attached to the HEADQUARTERS of a field commander.

Stainless Banner. The similarity of the STARS AND BARS (the first national flag of the Confederacy) to the Stars and Stripes led to a two-year debate in the Confederate Congress over a redesign of the national banner. The result was a plain white flag (which led to the nickname "Stainless Banner") with a square red canton that resembled the Confederate battle flag. The new banner was adopted on May 1, 1863, and one of the first flags to be made at the Richmond Depot was used to cover the casket of Thomas J. "Stonewall" Jackson while his body lay in state in the Confederate Capitol on May 12. The new design, however, could be mistaken for a flag of truce, and almost two years later a red bar was added to the fly edge.

stake torpedo. A floating MINE anchored in the path of approaching enemy vessels. The device was held in place by a weighted chain that also positioned the explosive at a specific angle to assure detonation.

stand, to. (1) To become a candidate for elective office. (2) To remain in place and be vigilant, ready to move out quickly.

standard. (1) A flag, banner, ENSIGN, colors. (2) The regimental color of a CAVALRY REGIMENT. See GUIDON.

stand in, to. N. To move a vessel into an inlet, harbor, or waterway.

stand of arms. The complete equipment of a single soldier: a MUSKET or RIFLE, RAMROD, BAYONET,

CARTRIDGE BELT, CARTRIDGE BOX, wiper, screw driver, spring vice, wire punch, and ball screw. In practice, especially after 1863, the term designated only the rifle and belt. Battlefield reports usually included a notation concerning how many stands of arms had been taken.

stand of colors. A single flag.

stand toward, to. N. To direct a vessel toward a specific objective.

star fort. An enclosed polygonal FIELDWORK with a series of alternating SALIENT and REENTERING ANGLES. These fortifications were described as either regular or irregular and by the number of salients (anywhere from four to eight). The design enabled overlapping FIELDS OF FIRE and precluded any possibility of the defenders' being outflanked. Most star forts were erected to protect isolated GARRISONS.

Stargazer. A nickname for Union Gen. Ormsby M. Mitchel.

Star of the West. A side-wheel steamer chartered by the Buchanan administration to resupply FORT SUMTER in January 1861. Her manifest indicated that her destination was New Orleans, but the details of her mission to South Carolina appeared in several newspapers. Thus when the vessel attempted to enter Charleston Harbor on the morning of January 9, a BATTERY manned by cadets from the Citadel fired a warning shot across her bow and other batteries opened from Fort Moultrie on Sullivan's Island. The Federal GARRISON in the harbor fort did not return fire—instructions to assist the ship had been sent by regular mail and were not received until after the crisis had passed—and the *Star* withdrew and returned to New York. For more information on the vessel during the war, see CSS ST. PHILIP.

Starr revolver. The Starr Arms Company of New York took advantage of the expirations of some of Samuel Colt's patents to produce one of the most popular handguns of the war. Three models were sold to the government. The Model 1858 Navy .36-caliber double-action percussion REVOLVER held six CARTRIDGES and cast a deceiving profile. What looked like a trigger was actually a cocking lever that rotated the cylinder and cocked the hammer; the trigger was mounted on the inside rear of the trigger guard. An army model—.44-caliber—was also available. A Model 1863 Army single-action revolver was introduced to compete with less-expensive revolvers being purchased by the government from Remington and Whitney. Most of these 1863 models were used in the western theater. By the end of the war, the War Department had purchased 48,000 Starr revolvers.

Stars and Bars. Adopted on March 4, 1861, the first national flag of the Confederacy consisted of two horizontal red bars separated by a white bar. The canton was a blue field on which seven five-pointed white stars—one for each state then in the Confederacy—were displayed in a circle, sometimes around a center star. In battle for the first time during the July 21, 1861, battle of First Manassas (Bull Run), the similarity of the Confederate banner and the Stars and Stripes proved a deadly confusion. As a result, a distinctive battle flag was designed by Confederate Gen. P. G. T. Beauregard and the Confederate Congress ruminated on a new design for a little more than two years before adopting a second national banner, known as the STAINLESS BANNER.

state colors and standards. According to U.S. Army regulations, each REGIMENT carried two flags—a national banner and a regimental standard. INFANTRY regimental flags were dark blue and displayed the coat of arms of the United States in the center and a red scroll with a unit's designation beneath. ARTILLERY regimental flags were yellow with two crossed CANNON in the center and a red scroll beneath with the unit's title. CAVALRY regiments carried only one flag, a regimental emblem, but each company had its own GUIDON. Although there were specifications for these unit flags, individual states did not always strictly observe them in contracting regimental flags and often combined elements of the two. In such instances, it was not unusual to see a state seal in the middle of the blue canton of stars on the national colors or in lieu of the national coat of arms on regimental flags. Many communities generated presentation flags for their recently organized units and staged formal ceremonies to bestow the colors on the company or regiment when it departed for formal muster. In 1862 the government assumed the responsibility for providing all colors and standards and contracted the work to three firms—each of which had its own style and designs. As the war continued, presentation flags were rarely taken into combat and sometimes were given to units that had reenlisted. Of all the Northern states, Pennsylvania and Massachusetts were the most consistent in providing banners for their regiments. In the South, many COMPANIES were intent on carrying their own flags into battle, and so some regiments received as many as ten flags from local sewing circles and other women of their communities. Confederate army units eventually carried a single banner, a battle flag. In the eastern theater these followed the Beauregard design (red field with a blue St. Andrew's cross filled with thirteen stars), but in the western theater there was a vast assortment of designs.

state prisoner. A political prisoner, or "prisoner of state."

states' rights. Based on the political theories of Thomas Jefferson and John C. Calhoun, this concept was based on the sovereignty of the individual states and a strict interpretation of the Constitution's delegation of all powers to the states not specifically granted to the Federal government. During the decades preceding the war, most Southern political leaders opposed the increasing centralization of power in Washington, and thus this issue was often cited as a major cause of the war. After the Confederate States of America had been founded in 1861, some Secessionists were such ardent proponents of states' rights that they were as opposed to a centralized Confederate government in Richmond as they were to the Federal government in Washington. This recalcitrance contributed to the failure of the Confederacy it had helped to found.

steam alphabet. As an alternative to a wigwag system of communication between vessels at sea, the Union navy experimented with ways of harnessing the exhaust from a ship's boilers to signal messages. Tests at the Washington Navy

Andrew A. Harwood

Yard satisfied Como. Andrew A. Harwood of the Potomac Flotilla, so in November 1862 he ordered his command to utilize the steam alphabet. The steam system failed, however, when put into practice. The wigwag system was used for the duration of the war.

steam gun. Ross Winans of Maryland, a pioneer in steam technology and a designer of railroad machinery, was involved in a proposal to design a CANNON that would use steam as a propellant rather than gunpowder. Allegedly a hopper-fed prototype was made and mounted on a railroad car, but Federal forces seized the weapon while it was en route to Harpers Ferry and supposedly headed south from there. Winans was also arrested and held at FORT McHENRY, charged with selling arms to the enemy. Tests were conducted with the steam gun, but the final report claimed the thing was inoperable.

stock. A formal neckware for Union officers.

stem. N. The prow of a vessel.

stone fleets. In July 1861 the U.S. Navy Blockade Strategy Board proposed to close Southern channels and ports by obstructing them with scuttled derelict ships filled with stone. The project

commenced in August 1861 and was headed by Comdr. H. S. Stellwagen; Flag Off. Silas H. Stringham led the effort to acquire the necessary vessels. In November three ships were sunk in North Carolina's Ocracoke Inlet. In December sixteen were sunk in the main channel at Charleston, and in January 1862 another twenty were sunk in a second Charleston channel. Within three months, however, marine worms had weakened the timbers of the sunken vessels, releasing the stone cargoes. Fast-moving currents then swept around the granite and cut new and deeper channels. This early blockading attempt failed, and the Southern ports remained open.

stone wall, the. (1) A waist-high wall next to a SUNKEN ROAD at Marye's Heights above Fredericksburg, Virginia. It was the strongest segment of the Confederate line during the December 13, 1862, battle of Fredericksburg, against which the Union attack failed. It was also prominent during the May 3, 1863, battle of Chancellorsville, in which a stronger Federal force overran the posi-

The stone wall at Fredericksburg

U.S. ARMY MILITARY HISTORY INSTITUTE

tion but stalled at Salem Church. (2) The main defensive position at the center of the Federal line during the Confederate attack known as PICKETT'S CHARGE on July 3, 1863, at Gettysburg.

Stonewall. The best-known nickname for Confederate Gen. Thomas J. Jackson, bestowed during the July 21, 1861, battle of First Manassas (Bull Run).

***Stonewall*, CSS.** This 900-ton oceangoing IRONCLAD RAM was built by L. Arman at Bordeaux, France, in 1863–64 under contract with the Confederacy. Upon completion, she was to attack the blockading fleet off Wilmington, North Carolina, intercept Northern commerce, assault New England coastal cities, and wreck the fishing fleet in the Newfoundland Banks. French authorities blocked delivery, however, when the Lincoln administration protested. Eventually the ship was sold to Denmark, which planned to use the vessel in the Schleswig-Holstein War. The ironclad did not reach Copenhagen before the unexpected conclusion of the war, so the Danish government refused to accept it. The title reverted to the builder who brokered a surreptitious deal with the Confederates. In January 1865 the ship departed Copenhagen for France then Spain. En route a severe storm caused the captain to put in to Ferrol, Spain, for repairs, and two Union ships arrived in the area. On March 24 CSS *Stonewall* steamed out to confront the Federal vessels, which avoided an engagement, suspecting that the Confederate ironclad outgunned them. *Stonewall* sailed for Lisbon for supplies and then crossed the Atlantic. On May 6 the vessel arrived in Nassau and sailed for Havana, where news of the Confederate surrenders in Virginia and North Carolina reached the captain. The vessel was turned over to Cuban authorities for money to pay the crew. In July 1866 Cuba delivered the ship to the U.S. government, which sold it to Japan.

Stonewall Brigade. The nickname and later official designation of the 1st Brigade/Virginia Volun-

CSS Stonewall *at an anchorage in Spain*

teers, whose members were raised from eighteen counties in the Shenandoah Valley. The elements of the BRIGADE were later designated the 2d, 4th, 5th, 27th, and 33d Virginia Infantry and, until October 20, 1862, included the Rockbridge Artillery. When Thomas J. Jackson assumed command of the brigade in April 1861, the ranks numbered 2,611. Their performance during the July 21, 1861, battle of First Manassas (Bull Run) earned them the same nickname bestowed on their commander by Barnard E. Bee. Despite severe losses throughout the war, the brigade played significant roles in the battles of First and Second Manassas, the 1862 Shenandoah Valley campaign, Gaines's Mill, Cedar Mountain, Antietam, Fredericksburg, Chancellorsville, the Wilderness, and Spotsylvania. Although a participant in the battle of Gettysburg, it was limited to the Culp's Hill engagement. The Stonewall nickname was made the brigade's official designation on May 30, 1863, by the War Department, but the brigade was officially ended following the battle of Spotsylvania, when all but two hundred men were casualties. The remaining members were consolidated into a single REGIMENT and participated in Jubal Early's raid on Washington during

the summer of 1864, the defense of Petersburg, and the retreat to APPOMATTOX. The brigade had seven commanders—Jackson, Richard S. Garnett, Charles S. Winder, W. H. S. Baylor, Andrew J. Grigsby, Elisha F. Paxton, and James A. Walker—but only three survived the war.

Stonewall of the West. (1) A nickname for Union Rear Adm. Andrew H. Foote, who received this nickname after the first major Federal victory of the war at FORT DONELSON, Tennessee. (2) A nickname for Confederate Gen. Patrick R. Cleburne, a fearless Irish-born commander whose command participated in the battles of Shiloh, Richmond (Kentucky), Stones River, Chickamauga, Chattanooga, the Atlanta campaign, and the Tennessee campaign. He was killed

Patrick R. Cleburne

during the November 30, 1864, battle of Franklin. During the Atlanta campaign Cleburne signed a

241

statement proposing that slaves be given their freedom in exchange for military service.

stoten-bottle. Slang for a soldier who refused to reenlist.

Stovepipe. A nickname for Confederate Brig. Gen. and PARTISAN RANGER Adam R. Johnson of Kentucky. The nickname stemmed from his use of stovepipes as QUAKER GUNS at Newburgh, Indiana, and his subsequent seizure of munitions. His success

attracted recruits, whom he called the Breckinridge Guards, and for a time he served with John Hunt Morgan. In June 1864 he received his general's commission, but on August 21 Johnson was accidentally shot and blinded by his own men.

stove rat. Prisoners of war who hogged the warmest spots near a stove during cold weather. Sometimes stove rats were so tenacious in maintaining their place that other prisoners had to form together and charge them to dislodge them from the heat source.

straggler. A soldier who deliberately wandered away from his REGIMENT, usually to avoid combat.

strake. N. A band of planking or plates on the hull of a ship.

stretcher. A frame or litter on which a wounded man could be carried from the field.

strike, to. (1) To take the necessary actions to depart from a camp. (2) To stop work on a task with little or no advance notice.

striker. A workman whose task was to wield a hammer under the direction of a blacksmith or a metalworker.

strip, to. The separation of SABOTS from shells in flight.

stripe. A strip of cloth used to designate the RANK of a noncommissioned officer.

strong grease. Slang for rancid butter.

studs. Projections from the sides of shells that were designed to fit into the rifling of a GUN'S BORE.

substitute. An individual paid to enlist on behalf of another. The usual fee for such services was three hundred dollars. In all, about eighty-six thousand Northerners paid others to fight in their place.

suck. A dangerous point on a waterway.

sucker. Slang for a native of Illinois. The nickname may be related to a variety of fish, related to the carp, which abounded in the Mississippi River on the state's border.

***Sumter,* CSS.** This 437-ton BARK-rigged SCHOONER was built in Philadelphia as the merchant steamship *Habana* but then was purchased by the Confederate government in April 1861 and converted into a COMMERCE RAIDER. Under the command of Raphael Semmes, the ship took eighteen PRIZES in its only year of service. In April 1862 the vessel put in to Gibraltar for repairs and a succession of Union naval vessels maintained a watch on the vessel. The Confederate crew was

NAVAL HISTORICAL CENTER

removed, and many of them were reassigned to the new cruiser *ALABAMA*. *Sumter* was sold, renamed *Gibraltar,* and used as a BLOCKADE-RUNNER. The vessel was lost in a storm in the English Channel in 1867.

Sumpter. A misspelling of Sumter.

sunken roads. A heavily used road eroded over time so as to be below ground level. During the war geographical features such as these presented troops with natural RIFLE PITS. At least two sunken roads played important roles in the battles of Antietam and Fredericksburg. The fighting at the sunken road at Antietam led the survivors to refer to the roadway as BLOODY LANE. At Fredericksburg, a sunken road ran next to the battlefield feature known as the STONE WALL.

Supply, **USS.** This 547-ton wooden supply ship cost the U.S. Navy $95,732.07. She was eventually mounted with four 20-POUNDER PARROTT RIFLES and two 24-pound HOWITZERS. Too slow and fragile to be effective in combat, the ship remained in service throughout the war. Sold in 1884, the old vessel brought $1,301 at Great Neck, New York.

surcingle. A girdle or band that ran around the belly of a horse and held a saddle in place. Also called a girth.

Susquehanna, **USS.** Built at a cost of $697,212 in 1850 by the government at the Philadelphia Navy Yard, this 2,450-ton side-wheel steamer participated in Como. Matthew Perry's mission to Japan prior to the war. Her 1863 battery consisted of two 150-POUNDER PARROTT RIFLES, one 9-inch DAHLGREN, and one 12-pounder rifle. She supported the Union army during the Peninsula campaign and participated in the assaults on FORT FISHER in December 1864 and January 1865.

sutler. A civilian licensed or permitted to operate a shop at a military camp or post. Sutlers often offered foodstuffs that were not included in offi-

LIBRARY OF CONGRESS

cial RATIONS and other small items, such as buttons and thread, that were in constant demand. Generally, they operated on a cash basis, but some extended credit at high rates of interest. Many issued their own fractional currency, called SCRIP or CHITS, which they used in making change.

swallow the yellow dog, to. Derisive slang for taking an OATH OF ALLEGIANCE to the Union by a Confederate—usually a prisoner of war.

U.S. ARMY MILITARY HISTORY INSTITUTE

Swamp Angel. A 200-POUNDER PARROTT gun situated on Morris Island and used on August 22–23, 1863, to shell the city of Charleston, four miles away. The discharge of the thirty-sixth round, however, disabled the gun. After the war it was shipped to New Jersey as scrap metal, but before it could be melted down it was identified. As a result, it was set on top of a granite monolith and treated as a monument.

Swamp Fox of the Confederacy. A nickname for self-appointed Confederate Gen. M. Jeff Thompson of Missouri, who fought both as part of the

Southern army and as a partisan in Missouri and Arkansas. Because he camped and RAIDED along the Mississippi, his men came to be known as "Swamp Rats."

swash. N. A shallow, narrow, twisting channel that conveyed vessels to the open sea from inland sounds or landlocked harbors.

sweeper. A device for clearing a river or channel of TORPEDOES (floating MINES).

sweet cloth. A game of chance in which players placed their money on numbers in an effort to guess the total of three thrown dice.

***Switzerland*, USS.** This 413-ton side-wheel towboat was built in Cincinnati, Ohio, in 1854 and converted into a RAM in early 1862 as one of the ELLET RAMS. She was present during the action at Memphis in which Ellet was killed and was involved later in operations on the Yazoo River against Vicksburg. On March 25, 1863, *Switzerland* and another ram ran past Vicksburg's guns; only *Switzerland* survived the run, and she went on to run the guns at Grand Gulf, Mississippi, on March 31. In May and June *Switzerland* operated on the Red and Atchafalaya Rivers. Later she was

attached to the Mississippi Marine Brigade. After the war the vessel was sold and operated as a merchant steamer until 1870.

swivel gun. A small-caliber artillery PIECE mounted on a pivot.

sword. These were the weapons of classical warfare but by the 1860s, aside from cavalrymen, they served mostly as decorative symbols of RANK. Horse soldiers, however, considered SABERS and swords their principal weapons, but battlefield conditions rendered edged weapons impractical, and mounted troops came to rely primarily on pistols and CARBINES (see SABER). Artillerists were issued short swords patterned after those carried by French gunners, but they too turned to pistols during the conflict. INFANTRY sergeants were issued swords, but they were weapons of last resort. Staff officers and generals carried swords as symbols of rank. The armories of the navies included traditional CUTLASSES for crewmen. In the Union army, swords issued to enlisted men were manufactured by private companies in the North, but most officers' swords came from European manufacturers and were based on patterns established in 1850. Confederate swords were copies of prewar U.S. Army models but also included imported blades, heirlooms, and standard prewar issues of the regular army. Rounding out these symbols of the glory of war were custom-made ceremonial swords awarded to officers and generals by community groups and special parties as units mustered for service or in recognition of battlefield accomplishments, but these were worn only on formal occasions if at all. Although swords were rarely used in battle, as contrasted with the use of firearms, commanders customarily yielded their swords when surrendering.

sword, to offer one's. A metaphor indicating one's willingness to fight for a cause.

T

tac. Slang at West Point for an instructor in tactics.

tack. A designation for any gear associated with horses.

tactics. The science (or art) of directing soldiers in combat. Because nearly all armies were too cumbersome to be directed from the commanding general's HEADQUARTERS, tactics were delegated to DIVISION and BRIGADE leaders. Until this war, battlefield tactics were based entirely on the schemes employed by Napoleon Bonaparte. Since many of the French emperor's battles were fought in open country, he succeeded by massing his men to overwhelm his opponents. Advancements in weapons technology, particularly those in shoulder arms and ammunition, made such tactics obsolete. Nevertheless, since officers in both the Union and Confederate armies had been schooled in Napoleon's tactics, many INFANTRY commanders persisted in implementing outdated strategy.

taking a twist at the tiger. Indulging in a game of chance.

Tall Pine of Mississippi. A nickname for Confederate Col. Thomas R. Stockdale.

talma. Outerwear in the form of a cape or cloak. Federal QUARTERMASTERS applied the term to the distinctive overcoat issued to CAVALRY.

tambour. A stockade of two faces with LOOP-HOLES, erected at a SALIENT ANGLE at the gorge of small FIELDWORKS or at the doorways of fortified buildings.

tangle foot. Slang for potent alcoholic beverages.

tap. The stump of an amputated leg.

"Taps." The U.S. Army's bugle call for lights out. Adopted by the other services, including many Confederate units, its composition was attributed to Union Gen. Daniel Butterfield. He did play a role in bringing the call to prominence, but he did not originate it.

Daniel Butterfield

tar. (1) N. Slang for a sailor. (2) The lubricant for CARRIAGE axles. Lard or tallow was usually mixed with tar to prevent melting during long marches and hot weather.

tar bucket. A sheet iron container for tar used by artillerymen. Also known as a grease bucket, it was just over seven inches in diameter and eight inches tall. A metal cover was attached to the bucket by a rivet, and a length of chain served as the handle.

Tardy George. A nickname for Union Maj. Gen. George Sykes, a veteran of the Seminole and Mexican Wars. His commands participated in the battles of First and Second Manassas (Bull Run), the Peninsula and

Seven Days' campaign, Antietam, Fredericksburg, Chancellorsville, and Gettysburg. He was reassigned to the Department of Kansas following the November–December 1863 Mine Run campaign.

tar heel. A native of North Carolina. The tar of the Civil War was thickened turpentine, or pine tar, which was a principal product of coastal North Carolina.

tariff. Fees (customs or duty) assessed on imported goods. For decades the tariff was the chief source of income for the federal government. Most tariffs came from the South from high importations of manufactured goods. Because of the inequity between the industrial North and the agrarian South, the tariff was a major source of contention between the sections and was considered a cause of the war. In his first inaugural address, Abraham Lincoln stated that he would continue to collect tariffs in the South. Many Southerners interpreted this as a warning that troops would be used to collect the revenue.

tattoo. A bugle call for soldiers to return to their quarters at the end of the day. It was replaced by "TAPS."

tax in kind. In much of the South, food and other supplies were in short supply as early as the summer of 1862. Before the year ended, Confederate officers began to seize what they needed from Southern farmers. In April 1863 the Confederate Congress enacted a tax-in-kind measure that required farmers to surrender 10 percent of their produce to the government.

Teachers Regiment. (1) The 33d Illinois Infantry, which was recruited by Charles E. Hovey, the president of Illinois State Normal University, who served as the REGIMENT'S colonel. Most of the recruits were students or faculty from the university and other schools in Illinois, thus the unit was also known as the Normal Regiment and the Brains Regiment. The 33d Illinois operated in Missouri, Arkansas, and Louisiana and participated in the battles of Port Gibson, Champion Hills, and Spanish Fort and the sieges of Vicksburg and Jackson. (2) The 151st Pennsylvania Infantry, whose ranks were filled with instructors and students from McAllisterville Academy and across the state. The regiment commanded by Col. George F. McFarland operated in northern Virginia and participated in the battle of Gettysburg, where it suffered 69 percent casualties.

tea kettles. N. A contemptuous reference to IRONCLAD vessels.

Telegraph Road (1) A sector of the Fredericksburg battlefield, so-called because of the telegraph lines that ran alongside it. A small hill on Telegraph Road was the highest point in the area held by James Longstreet's corps and was the point from which Robert E. Lee planned and directed his defense. (2) A sector of the Pea Ridge campaign so named because it was used to signal messages.

tell off, to. Detached duty in which a small number of soldiers were placed on special duty, requiring them to leave their REGIMENTS temporarily.

Temperance Regiment. (1) The 13th Maine Infantry, which was organized by Col. Neal Dow, a temperance crusader, and MUSTERED into service on December 13, 1861. One of its first assignments was, interestingly, provost duty in New Orleans. It operated in Texas, Louisiana, and northern Virginia, participated in the Red River campaign and the battle of Mansfield, Louisiana, and performed GARRISON work at Washington, D.C., and the Shenandoah Valley. (2) The 24th

Iowa Infantry, which was raised by Eber C. Byam of men who had not touched, tasted, or handled any alcoholic beverages and was mustered into service on September 18, 1862. It participated in the sieges of Vicksburg and Jackson, the battles of Champion Hills, Mansfield, Fisher's Hill and Cedar Creek, and the Red River and Shenandoah Valley (1864) campaigns. The regiment was MUSTERED OUT August 1865.

tennaille. A defensive work formed by a series of REDANS joined at the FLANK, creating a front of unbroken SALIENT and REENTERING ANGLES.

NAVAL HISTORICAL CENTER

Tennessee, **CSS.** This 1,273-ton IRONCLAD RAM was built in Selma, Alabama, in 1863 and commissioned in February 1864. Almost immediately she became the FLAGSHIP of the Confederate flotilla in Mobile Bay. During the August 5, 1864, battle of the bay, the ironclad fought at close quarters with the Federal fleet but was surrounded and beaten into surrendering. The Union navy was quick to adopt the ironclad and employ it in the assault on the harbor forts. USS *Tennessee* served with the Mississippi Squadron through the end of the war.

Tennessee high step. The distinctive gait of a diarrhetic soldier.

Tennessee sabot. A MULLANE SHELL.

tent peg. Slang for BAYONETS, which were seldom used in combat but often employed in pinning down a tent or holding a candle.

terebine oil. A substitute for kerosene in the South, it was produced by redistilling turpentine. Although this oil emitted considerable heat, it also generated a great deal of smoke.

terreplein. Any level surface suitable for the placement of artillery.

tete de pont. A FIELDWORK erected to protect a bridge and situated on the bank considered hostile.

Texas. A locomotive that played a major role in facilitating the capture of Andrews's Raiders.

Texas Rangers. The 8th Texas Cavalry, which was raised by Benjamin F. Terry and Thomas S. Lubbock and was MUSTERED into service in Houston on September 9, 1861. The recruits supplied their own arms and equipment, and the majority enlisted for the duration of the war. Most of the officers were former Texas Rangers. They participated in the battles of Shiloh, Perryville, Stones River, Chickamauga, Knoxville, and Bentonville and the Atlanta and Carolina campaigns. Undisciplined soldiers, they fought recklessly and courageously as one of the most effective CAVALRY units in the western theater. At different times they were under Nathan Bedford Forrest and Joseph Wheeler.

Thanks of Congress, Confederate. A formally adopted measure expressing gratitude for services rendered to the Confederacy. The first such act, in February 1861, thanked the state of Alabama for hosting the new government in Montgomery and a $500,000 donation. The first military thanks was directed to P. G. T. Beauregard for successfully dislodging the Federal GARRISON at FORT SUMTER, and such thanks was offered throughout the war for battlefield successes, funding from the states, and reenlistments. The final Thanks of Congress was issued on March 17, 1865, to Gen. Wade Hampton for the defense of Richmond.

Thanks of Congress, U.S. Federal lawmakers were parsimonious in their thanks and issued only fifteen during the war. Individual thanks, however, could honor more than one person, and thanks issued on February 22, 1862, was directed all service personnel for their contributions during a string of Federal victories. The officers honored with the Thanks of Congress include Nathaniel Lyon, William S. Rosecrans, Ulysses S. Grant, Nathaniel P. Banks, Ambrose E. Burnside, Joseph Hooker, George Gordon Meade, Oliver O. Howard, William T. Sherman (twice), Joseph Bailey, Alfred H. Terry, Philip H. Sheridan, George H. Thomas, Winfield Scott Hancock, Newton M. Curtis, David G. Farragut (two), and David Dixon Porter (four).

Thermopylae of the Civil War. A reference to the September 8, 1863, battle of Sabine Pass, Texas, in which forty-four Confederate artillerists turned back Nathaniel P. Banks's invasion of southern Texas. The Southerners took four hundred prisoners.

Thief of the Mississippi. A nickname for Union Adm. David D. Porter.

thirty-day volunteers. Federal enlistments for thirty days of service.

thirty-nine lashes. Generally understood in the North to be the typical punishment meted out to Southern slaves.

"Those People." Robert E. Lee's usual reference to Union soldiers and Northern citizens.

three days' rations. The quantity of food usually issued to Federal soldiers in anticipation of battle. Letters and diaries are filled with descriptions of the way in which hungry men dispatched three-days' food in a single meal.

through bolt. N. A heavy bolt spanning the combined thickness of armor and wood, sometimes as much as eleven inches. Such bolts could be very dangerous in combat. If one received a direct hit from enemy fire, the securing nut was usually jolted loose to ricochet within a ship's hull.

throw, to. To direct soldiers or fire against an enemy target.

thumb hanging. A barbaric punishment used in many prisons. A prisoner was suspended by his thumbs so that his toes barely touched the floor.

thumb stall. A buckskin pouch with a thumb pad stuffed with horsehair used by gunners to block the VENT while the GUN was being loaded.

Thunderbolt of War. A nickname for Confederate Gen. Nathan Bedford Forrest coined by Gen. Dabney H. Maury.

ticket to Dixie. In the North, notice that one had been selected for service by the draft lottery.

tied on the fifth wheel. A cruel punishment in which an offender was lashed to the spare wheel of a CAISSON.

tier shot. Slang for GRAPESHOT, based on the arrangement of the grapeshot in tiers.

Tige. A nickname for Confederate Gen. George T. Anderson.

tiger. Slang for the game of FARO.

Tiger. A nickname for Confederate Gen. William L. Cabell.

tigers. Natives of Louisiana.

Tiger Regiment. The 125th Ohio Infantry, which was MUSTERED into service on October 6, 1862, and commanded by Col. Emerson Opdycke. The REGIMENT was attached to the Army of the Cumberland and participated in the battles of Franklin (1863 and 1864), Chickamauga (where it was dubbed Opdycke's Tigers), Missionary Ridge,

Knoxville, Spring Hill, and Nashville and the Atlanta campaign. The unit was MUSTERED OUT on September 25, 1865.

timberclad. A riverboat armored with layers of wood rather than iron.

time fuse. A FUSE attached to a shell and designed to burn a specific number of seconds. Although fuses of this sort were marked at their place of manufacture, they were cut to length by hand just prior to being used.

tinclad. These were shallow-draft riverboats protected by light iron, less than an inch thick. The armor was sufficient protection from light arms fire and light to medium artillery.

tisanes. Household remedies made from flowers, bark, red pepper, and roots.

toad sticker. Slang for a knife, BAYONET, or SWORD.

tobacco. This basic crop of tidewater Virginia, Kentucky, the Carolinas, and other parts of the deep South was largely cut off from Union soldiers. As a result, it was a major item in both illegal commerce and in FRATERNIZATION between members of opposing forces. One of the most common trades between soldiers was tobacco for coffee, which was scarce and expensive in the Confederacy.

Tombs, The. New York City's combination criminal courts building and city jail covered two city blocks between Lafayette and Center Streets. When the four-story granite building was completed in 1838, it was named the Halls of Justice, but to New Yorkers it was known as "the Tombs" because of its similarity to Egyptian mausoleums. The structure housed 150 cells on four tiers. In 1860 the damp, unsanitary, overcrowded facility was rated one of the four worst prisons in the country. It housed Confederate prisoners for only nine months during the war, from June 15, 1861, to February 3, 1862, when twenty-one men from the pri-

vateer *Savannah* were detained here prior to being moved to the prison being set up Fort Lafayette.

Tom Fool. A Virginia Military Institute nickname for Thomas J. "Stonewall" Jackson.

tompion (or tampion). An iron or brass stopper that fit the muzzle of a GUN to protect the BORE from weather and debris. Tompions for large guns were made of wood, and many were rimmed with cork for a secure fit.

tongs. A set of iron arms with a pivoted center, used to grasp and carry ammunition.

toothpick. (1) Slang for knives with blades between four and eighteen inches long. (2) A derogatory nickname for natives of Arkansas.

top of flood. N. The crest of a rising tide.

Topographical Engineers. Mapmakers and surveyors of the Union army.

torpedo. The earliest land MINES were called torpedoes. The first of these were devised by Confederate Gen. Gabriel J. Rains during the withdrawal from Yorktown in May 1862. These torpedoes were improvised from 8- and 10-inch COLUMBIAD shells and were condemned by leaders on both sides, who called them "INFERNAL MACHINES." Nevertheless they were adopted by both sides. Later uses focused on floating torpedoes to obstruct waterways. Some of these were anchored just beneath the surface of the water, set to detonate on impact, and others were monitored to be detonated by lookouts on shore. One version of the former was known as the RAINS TORPEDO, which was fashioned from a small beer keg suspended between two wooden stabilizing cones. It was detonated by a trip wire attached to its anchor.

Tory. A UNIONIST in the South who remained in Confederate territory. Such persons were often accused of treason, making them subject to property seizures and imprisonment. Some of the most violent confrontations between Unionists and Confederates took place in Eastern Tennessee and Missouri.

tosspot. Slang for an alcohol abuser.

tot. N. A small drinking cup holding about half a pint. It was used to measure out a sailor's weekly GROG allowance.

touch, to. N. A brief layover en route to a destination.

tow hook. An iron tool with a hook at one end and a hammer at the other. It was used to open ammunition containers and for adjusting or repairing SABOT straps on fixed-ammunition shot.

trace. Well-beaten pathways inside or around a fortification.

trace chains. Short, sturdy chains used to link a horse's HARNESS with a CARRIAGE or vehicle.

trade with the enemy. Commerce between Northern and Southern interests—civilian or military. Although strictly forbidden by lawmakers on both sides, such exchanges flourished throughout the war. Cotton was the commodity most desired by the North, and manufactured goods were desperately needed by Southerners.

trail. The stock of a GUN CARRIAGE that rested on the ground when a PIECE was unlimbered.

trail handspike. A stout pole used to correct the placement of a field GUN during the aiming process.

trailed arms. MUSKETS or RIFLES carried with their stocks close to ground level, often when men were moving through rugged terrain.

train. When not a reference to RAILROADS, trains referred to four or more wagons on the road.

train tackle. N. A tackle designed to run out GUNS and aid in training them on their targets.

trajectory. The curve of a projectile in flight from the muzzle to the point of impact. It was affected by the elevation of the GUN, the weight of the shell, and the quantity of gunpowder used. Many gunners classified the paths of various shot and shell as either flat, medium, or high.

Tramp Brigade. A Confederate BRIGADE made up of the 17th, 18th, 22d, 23d, and 26th South Carolina Volunteers and led by Confederate Gen. Nathan G. "Shanks" Evans, Stephen Elliot, and William Henry Wallace. The ranging unit saw action in South Carolina, Virginia, Maryland, North Carolina, and Mississippi and marched through Georgia and Alabama.

trample upon our flag, to. A phrase coined by William T. Sherman to describe SECESSION.

Traveller. Perhaps the most famous steed of the war, Traveller was the primary animal ridden by Robert E. Lee during the conflict. An iron-gray horse with black points, the horse was born in 1857 in Greenbrier County in western Virginia. His first owner, Andrew Johnston, named him Jeff

Davis, and his second owner, Capt. Joseph M. Broun, named him Greenbrier. Lee purchased the horse in the spring of 1862 in South Carolina and named him Traveller. Although the animal was Lee's favorite, the general had other horses. Richmond, a bay stallion, was acquired in early 1861 and died after the battle of Malvern Hill. Brown Roan was purchased by Lee in western Virginia during the summer of 1861, but the animal went blind in 1862 and was retired. Lucy Long, a sorrel mare, was Lee's primary backup to Traveller and remained in the Lee family long after the general's death in 1870. Ajax, another sorrel, was a very tall animal and was used infrequently. Traveller was known to be a calm animal, but on August 31, 1862, he was startled and caused Lee to severely sprain both hands. A year later, during the fighting at Spotsylvania in May 1864, the horse reared at a critical moment and most likely saved Lee's life. The animal outlived the general for a short time and walked behind the hearse during Lee's funeral in 1870. Later Traveller stepped on a rusty nail and developed lockjaw, for which there was no cure. He was buried outside the Lee Chapel, on the grounds of Washington College (later Washington and Lee University).

traverse. (1) Portions of PARAPETS that crossed the breadth of the covered way, at the SALIENT and REENTERING ANGLES of arms. (2) A steeply sloped mound of soil, usually reinforced with GABIONS, erected to protect gunners from DEFILADE fire or REVERSE FIRE, that is, shells bursting to the rear. When used with BATTERIES, traverses were placed between each GUN or every two guns to limit the extent of damage that could be caused by either mishap or enemy fire.

trestle. A latticelike structure of piles and crossbeams that support a road or railroad spanning rivers, streams, and other geographical depressions.

trestletrees. N. One or two heavy horizontal timbers attached on opposite sides of a masthead to support the crosstrees and the frame at the top.

trews. Tight-fitting trousers made of tartan and customarily worn by Scottish Highlanders.

trim, to. N. To adjust a sailing vessel's position by shifting cargo, crew, or sails to make her sit well or take better advantage of the wind.

troop. Early in the war, this referred to a company of CAVALRY, but over time it came to be a general designation for horse soldiers.

Trostle farm. A small sector of the Gettysburg battlefield. The Abraham Trostle farm was one of the most prosperous farms in the area and stood south of town, north of the Wheat Field, east of the Peach Orchard, and between the Emmitsburg and Taneytown Roads. On July 2, 1863, the farm marked the center of the line established by Union Gen. Daniel E. Sickles, and the general set up his HEADQUARTERS in the yard of the house.

trous de loup. A field obstacle of shallow holes, roughly two feet deep, arranged in a quincunx pattern with stakes in the center of each hole.

truck. N. A small wooden cap at the top of a flagstaff or masthead. Holes were drilled into the base truck to accommodate halyards.

trunnion. Two short cylinders that projected from opposite sides of a GUN barrel, near its center of gravity, which were used to attach the barrel to a CARRIAGE.

try guns, to. To fire a few shots at a target to ascertain the ELEVATION and angle best suited to compensate for wind.

tube. (1) A CANNON barrel. (2) Rubber tubing used to launch TORPEDOES. (3) A length of powder-filled small-diameter metal pipe used to detonate MINES from a distance. Confederate Gen. Francis A. Shoup tried these during the siege of Vicksburg, and after several failures reported that the powder burst the tube before reaching the end of the tube. Word of Shoup's failures may have influenced Federals to use a FUSE to ignite the gunpowder that created the Crater at Petersburg. (4) N. A pipe used to convey water to a boiler.

tumble, to. A shell traveling end over end in flight.

tunic. A coat; the outer garment of a Union officer that extended to a point midway between the hips and knees and was always double-breasted.

turkey driver. A Federal PROVOST MARSHAL.

turncoat. A person who switched sides. Perhaps the most famous turncoat of the war was John Rowlands of Wales, who came to America, changed his name, and fought as a Confederate at Shiloh, became a Yankee artilleryman, and later a sailor in the Union navy. After the war he took the name Henry M. Stanley and worked as a newspaperman and found fame by finding David Livingstone near Lake Tanganyika in central Africa.

Turner. A member of a German fraternal society, strong and influential in St. Louis and other areas with large populations of German immigrants.

turnspit. A useless fellow.

turtle. A small GUNBOAT named for its resemblance to a tortoise. See POOK TURTLE.

Twenty-Negro Law. A provision of the April 16, 1862, Conscription Act in the South that exempted owners or overseers of twenty or more slaves from military service. One of the most hated statutes of the war, it contributed to the notion that the struggle was "a rich man's war and a poor man's fight." In May 1863 the exemption included payment of a fee of five hundred dollars.

two-wheel hearse. An artillery LIMBER.

Tycoon. (1) A derogatory nickname for Abraham Lincoln in the North, especially in the Northeast. (2) A nickname for Robert E. Lee.

tye. N. A chain or rope used to hoist or lower a sail.

NAVAL HISTORICAL CENTER

Tyler, **USS.** This 575-ton TIMBERCLAD GUNBOAT was built in 1857 at Cincinnati, Ohio, as the sidewheel steamer *A. O. Tyler.* The Union army's Western Gunboat Flotilla acquired the ship in June 1861, but she was commissioned in September with officers of the Federal navy. Because *Tyler* was one of the first warships on the river, she saw extensive action throughout the war. Her first engagement occurred in September 1861 with CSS *Jackson* near Hickman, Kentucky. The gunboat was involved on the Ohio, Mississippi, and Tennessee Rivers for the remainder of 1861 and early 1862, which included providing support during the April 6–7 battle of Shiloh. Subsequent operations on the Yazoo River involved a running battle with the Confederate IRONCLAD *ARKANSAS* on July 15. In October 1862 the vessel was transferred to the Union navy and thereafter functioned primarily on the Arkansas waterways. After the war the ship was sold.

U-V

Ulster Guard. The 20th New York State Militia, which was founded in Ulster County in 1848 and maintained this designation after entering Federal service despite being renamed the 80th New York Infantry on December 7, 1861. MUSTERED into service between September 20 and October 20, 1861, and MUSTERED OUT on January 29, 1866, the REGIMENT fought in every major battle of the eastern theater except Chancellorsville.

ultimo. A reference meaning "the previous month," also abbreviated as "ult."

Uhlans. An informal designation for foragers or pillagers.

Unadilla, **USS.** This was one of the first so-called NINETY-DAY GUNBOATS built in New York for the war. The ship was commissioned in September 1861 and participated in the capture of Port Royal,

South Carolina. Thereafter the vessel was relegated to blockading operations off South Carolina and Georgia, during which she captured three BLOCKADE-RUNNERS. In 1864 the ship was dispatched to the fleet engaged in the assault on FORT FISHER and afterward was used in operations around Wilmington, North Carolina, and on the James River in Virginia. After the war the ship remained in Federal service until it was sold in November 1869.

Uncle. A nickname usually conveying an element of admiration and respect. To many of his soldiers, William T. Sherman was Uncle Billy. In a similar fashion, Union Gen. Richard J. Oglesby was known as Uncle Dick, and Gen. George Crook was called Uncle George.

uncover, to. (1) To search an area recently occupied by an enemy for information about his strength and disposition. (2) To learn the current position of an enemy force or elements of an opponent's presence, such as PICKETS, STRAGGLERS, or other individuals.

underwrite, to. A guarantee offered by a paroled officer that his troops would observe the PAROLE that he had accepted, usually not to fight again until an EXCHANGE had been negotiated.

undress. Fatigues or any clothing other than dress uniforms. Union regulations stipulated that the

NAVAL HISTORICAL CENTER

undress coat of an officer of any grade should be dark blue. Like the dress TUNIC, it was double-breasted but a few inches longer than the tunic.

unhorsed, to be. To be temporarily on foot instead of astride an animal because of having been thrown from the saddle or because a horse had taken a serious wound.

uniform. Federal uniforms were not standardized until 1862, and until then units on both sides wore a vast array of colorful uniforms more appropriate to the parade ground than the battlefield. Union forces addressed the need by basing the clothing requirements on the regulations of the regular army, which stipulated dark blue as well as types of jackets, trousers, headwear, and footwear appropriate for officers and enlisted men in the army, navy, and marines. Enlisted men's INSIGNIA was worn on their sleeves, and officer's RANKS were displayed on their shoulders. The Confederacy adopted similar standards for uniforms for its military services, although the color was gray and officers displayed their rank on their collars. Despite these regulations, wartime shortages generally dictated that Southern soldiers appeared increasingly ragged and nondescript as the conflict progressed. Many Confederate soldiers wore combinations of uniforms and personal clothing, and shoes were rare. By 1863 most Confederate forces in the field wore some kind of homespun that had been dyed a yellowish brown, known as BUTTERNUT.

Union. (1) The canton of the U.S. national flag, the upper inner portion of the banner. (2) A designation of the North during the war.

Unionist. A resident of a seceded or Border State who either disagreed with SECESSION or espoused loyalty to the Union. Many Unionists in the South had to modify their views and their language when war broke out. Those who opposed separation from the United States were suppressed and socially ostracized.

U.S. Army. The prewar army of professional soldiers. According to E. B. Long, the U.S. Army was made up of 16,367 officers and men on January 1, 1861. Thus Abraham Lincoln's call for 75,000 VOLUNTEERS following the fall of FORT SUMTER increased the effective strength of the military fivefold. When war broke out, however, several regular army officers resigned their commissions to accept command RANK in the Confederacy. Few enlisted men did likewise. The regular army remained a separate service within the ranks of Union soldiers, and units were dispatched as needed to the many armies formed of volunteers in the eastern and western theaters. Certain units remained on the West Coast and in the Southwest, but the majority were shuffled into the war effort. Some administrative reorganization occurred during the war, and DRAGOONS came to be known as CAVALRY. ARTILLERY regiments, however, were dispersed throughout the armies as the nucleus of FIELD BATTERIES. Throughout the conflict, officers and men of the U.S. Army retained their rank and privileges even as they requested leave to transfer to and accept higher rank in the U.S. Volunteers. After the war, these men returned to the regular army and their previous rank.

U.S. Military Telegraph. This special branch of the Federal service was established after the Union defeat at the July 21, 1861, battle of First Manassas (Bull Run). It grew gradually in size and efficiency, eventually competing successfully

with the SIGNAL CORPS. Confederate telegraphers never came even close to matching their Federal rivals. Both sides developed a code system, one of which (the Southern) was broken by the other.

unmask, to. To discover the location of enemy forces or installations.

unmetaled. A reference to roads, trails, and paths that had not been hardened by heavy traffic.

up in the air. (1) Signifying a vulnerability to attack, this term was applied to permanent field fortifications, BATTERIES of GUNS, and bodies of soldiers. (2) Applied to a gun or battery, the connotation was that the weapons were too elevated to be of use.

Urbanna Plan. This campaign was devised by Union Gen. George B. McClellan to outflank the Confederate line in northern Virginia in late 1861 by moving the Union army over water from Washington, D.C., down the Potomac, into Chesapeake Bay, and up the Rappahannock River to the TOBACCO port at Urbanna, which was fifty miles from Richmond. This grand scheme came to nothing, however, when the Federal effort bogged down in planning and Joseph E. Johnston withdrew the Confederate army from Manassas to set up a new defensive line south of the Rappahannock River, which was closer to Urbanna and thus negated the tactical advantage McClellan hoped to gain by occupying the area.

used up, to be. A COMPANY, REGIMENT, or BRIGADE whose ranks were severely depleted by casualties, sickness, or desertion.

Valiant Val. A nickname for the COPPERHEAD leader Clement Vallandigham (see BANISHMENT and KNIGHTS OF THE GOLDEN CIRCLE).

Valley of Death. The portion of the Gettysburg battlefield marked by Plum Run.

van. The front of a body of soldiers or a fleet of vessels advancing toward the enemy; also known as the vanguard.

vangs. N. A pair of lines attached to the top of a GAFF and steadied it when no sail was set.

Van Van. A nickname for Ernest Jager, a German scout in Federal service known for his limited English skills. Clerks and telegraph operators dubbed him Van Van.

veal. A soldier with no combat experience.

vedette. Also spelled vidette. A mounted sentinel on PICKET or guard duty.

vent. A small hole, also known as the touch hole, at the BREECH of a GUN through which a FRICTION PRIMER transferred a spark to ignite the POWDER charge of the gun. The holes were kept small so as to limit the amount of gas leakage, which could cause a misfire or adversely affect the velocity of the discharge.

vent cover. To protect the VENT, this leather strap was fastened across the BREECH of the GUN. The strap was secured with a brass or copper pin, which fit into the vent and prevented the cover from slipping.

vent drill. N. A drill used to clear a VENT when a punch failed to do so.

vent punch. A steel tool used to clear or open a VENT if it became clogged.

***Vermont,* USS.** This 2,633-ton ship of the line was built at the Boston Navy Yard in 1818 and launched in 1848, but she was not commissioned until January 1862. For most of the war the ship was stationed at Port Royal, South Carolina, as a support vessel of the South Atlantic Blockading Squadron. In late 1864 she was reassigned as a receiving ship at the New

NAVAL HISTORICAL CENTER

York Navy Yard and remained there until she was sold in April 1902.

vertical fire. Fire delivered at a high angle, such as by MORTARS.

veteranized, to be. A reference to a soldier whose enlistment had expired and who planned to return to civilian life.

Veteran Reserve Corps. The reorganized name of the INVALID CORPS in the Union army. After the corps had been established originally by the War Department, most disabled veterans avoided assignment. The IC had been issued distinctive sky-blue uniforms, and the initials were the same as a standard military abbreviation for "Inspected-Condemned." In March 1864 the corps was renamed the Veteran Reserve Corps and the uniform was changed to the standard issue of the regular army. Those who were determined unfit for front-line duty were reassigned to the corps for garrison and other duties so as to free able-bodied soldiers for combat. The VRC was not withheld from all fighting and participated in several small engagements, but its greatest combat contribution came during Confederate Gen. Jubal Early's raid on Washington during the summer of 1864.

Veteran Volunteer Corps. To address the manpower needs of the Union army in late 1864, Secretary of War Edwin M. Stanton attempted to establish a corps of veterans to be raised from the more than one hundred thousand soldiers who

had been discharged over the course of the war. These men had enlisted earlier and were exempt from the draft, and so Stanton authorized a special bounty to entice their reenlistment. He also secured command of the corps for Maj. Gen. Winfield Scott Hancock, one of the most popular commanders in the Army of the Potomac. Despite Hancock's devotion to the corps and the generous bounties offered throughout early 1865, fewer than five thousand veterans enlisted. The corps was disbanded with little fanfare in April 1865.

veteran volunteers. (1) Elderly veterans who were either too old for combat or severely handicapped but volunteered to be used as guards and watchmen. (2) Soldiers who had been in numerous battles and campaigns who were rewarded with special FURLOUGHS.

vibrate the lines, to. To swing like a pendulum before enemy lines to note how the enemy was concentrated and where a drive could effect a breakthrough.

Vincennes rifle. Derogatory slang for an outdated .69-caliber MUSKET.

Virginia. A large and exceptionally sturdy mare ridden by Confederate Gen. J. E. B. "Jeb" Stuart.

Virginia Creeper, the. A nickname for Union Gen. George B. McClellan.

Virginia, **CSS.** The first American IRONCLAD was a Confederate innovation. The Southern secretary of the navy, Stephen R. Mallory, was a strong proponent of ironclad technology and viewed such ships as indispensable in combating the Union blockade. To expedite construction of the first ironclad, naval architects utilized the salvaged hull and engines of the scuttled USS *MERRIMACK* to create a floating gun battery of ten heavy ordnance pieces and an iron ram. The primary designers of the vessel were Lt. John M. Brooke, an expert in gun design, and John L. Porter, a naval designer. More than fifteen hundred men worked around the clock for nine months on the conversion at the Norfolk navy yard. The vessel was commissioned on February 17, 1862, and named *Virginia*. On its maiden voyage on March 8, the ship's captain, Franklin Buchanan, chose to engage the Federal fleet at Hampton Roads. By the end of the day, the ironclad had sunk a sloop of war, captured another, and left a third ship grounded. Buchanan, however, had been wounded, and so command fell to his executive officer, Catesby ap Roger Jones. When *Virginia* returned the next day, she encountered the Union ironclad MONITOR, which had arrived during the night. After two hours' combat, neither ship was able to gain an advantage or penetrate the other's hull. Both withdrew. Although *Virginia* returned to challenge *Monitor* in the following weeks, the two never again engaged. *Virginia* was essentially bottled up, and when her home port of Norfolk was abandoned on May 10, the ironclad was destroyed on May 11 to prevent her falling into Union hands. See also MERRIMACK, USS.

vivandière. Patterned after European practice, these women, usually soldier's wives or officers' daughters, were unofficially attached to a REGIMENT in the field to perform various camp and nursing duties. They were also known as daughters of a regiment and were found in both Confederate and Federal units. Typically they served with regiments of immigrant soldiers and wore a stylized uniform patterned after that of the regiment, particularly ZOUAVE units. Some were armed with SWORDS, RIFLES, and REVOLVERS, but very few followed their regiments into combat. Most of their names, however, are known. Federal vivandières included Susie Baker (33d USCT), Sarah Beasley (1st Rhode Island), Kady Brownell (1st Rhode Island), Molly Divver (7th New York), Bridget Divers (1st Michigan Cavalry), Anna Etheridge (2d, 3d, and 5th Michigan), Hannah Ewbank (7th Wisconsin), Elizabeth Cain Finnan (81st Ohio), Augusta Foster (2d Maine), Martha Francis (1st Rhode Island), Ella Gibson (49th Ohio), Virginia Hall (72d Pennsylvania), Lizzie Clawson Jones (6th Massachusetts), Sarah Taylor (1st Tennessee U.S.), Mary Tepe (27th and 114th Pennsylvania), and Eliza Wilson (5th Wisconsin). The Southern ranks included Eliza "Lide" Carico (10th Kentucky Partisan Rangers), Lucy Ann Cox (13th Virginia), Lucina Horne (14th South Carolina), Jane Claudia Johnson (1st Maryland C.S.), Leona Neville (5th Louisiana), Mary Ann Perkins (Gardes Lafayette, Mobile, Alabama), Rose Rooney (15th Louisiana), Betsy Sullivan (1st Tennessee C.S.), and Lavinia Williams (1st Louisiana). Vivandières, although somewhat rare to begin with, were a not uncommon sight before 1863, when the armies spent a great deal of time in camp and the fighting was infrequent. As the war progressed and armies campaigned, there is less evidence of vivandières. In September 1864 Ulysses S. Grant ordered all women out of the military camps in the east, so the remaining vivandières either turned to nursing in the front-line hospitals or returned home.

voltigeurs. These were light INFANTRY companies patterned after elite French units comprised of men of short stature who were extremely quick on their feet. Europeans used voltigeur units to spearhead an attack, but this model was never mimicked in combat in the New World, although the U.S. Army had established a similar regiment during the Mexican War. When volunteer REGIMENTS were being formed in the North and South, several opted to style themselves after specialized units in the various European armies, such as ZOUAVES, chasseurs, hussars, and voltigeurs. During the Civil War, voltigeur units served as regular infantry.

volunteer. The war began as a war of volunteers, for the North did not have much of an army to begin with and the South had none. For this reason the individual states were given quotas and required also to equip the soldiers for combat. Both sides also mirrored each other's actions in calling first for brief enlistments of so many days and then lengthening them to either three years or the duration before eventually turning to CONSCRIPTION.

The volunteers were idealistic and purposeful as compared to the BOUNTY soldiers and draftees who were less motivated to pursue the duties of soldiers. Even with that distinction in mind, it is interesting to note that, according to wartime figures, the rate of desertion for volunteers was only 6 percent compared to 24 percent for the regular army. Whereas the South had to eventually extend all enlistments to the duration of the war, the North could offer some reenlistment inducements to the volunteers who had fulfilled their three-year obligations, including a thirty-day FURLOUGH, transportation home, and a generous bounty.

W

Wabash, USS. This 4,808-ton steam screw FRIGATE was built at the Philadelphia Navy Yard and commissioned in 1856. During the war she served as the flagship of the South Atlantic Blockading Squadron and oversaw the captures of Hatteras Inlet, North Carolina, and Port Royal, South Carolina, the BLOCKADE of Charleston, and the assault and capture of FORT FISHER. The ship was decommissioned in February 1865 but then served in the Mediterranean Squadron in the 1870s and was converted into a receiving ship at the Boston Navy Yard in 1876, where she remained until sold in November 1912.

Wachusett, USS. This 1,032-ton Iroquois-class screw sloop of war was built at the Boston Navy Yard and commissioned in March 1862. She first saw action in Hampton Roads and on the James River in Virginia and participated in an assault on

Drewry's Bluff on May 15, 1862. From September 1862 through 1863 the vessel was the FLAGSHIP of a special squadron in the Caribbean on the lookout for Confederate COMMERCE RAIDERS. After a brief time for refitting, she ventured to South America, and on October 7, 1864, seized the cruiser *FLORIDA* from her moorings in Bahia, Brazil. After the war, the ship remained in Federal service until it was decommissioned in September 1885.

wagon dog. A soldier who feigned illness so as to be allowed to drop out of the ranks and wait for the supply trains, thus avoiding combat.

walk-over. A victory won with little effort.

walking beams. N. A pair of rocker arms that linked a ship's engines with the cranks of its paddle wheels.

walkway. An elevated path erected around the perimeters of most stockades and prisons. -

War Child. A nickname for Confederate Gen. Joseph Wheeler.

war criminal. The only soldier convicted of war crimes was Swiss-born Confederate Maj. Henry Wirz, the commandant of Andersonville, who was executed on November 10, 1865.

war, declaration of. The South interpreted Abraham Lincoln's April 1861 call for troops as a declaration of war. The Confederate Congress noted the existence of a state of war, but no such admission was made in Washington. There the struggle was termed an INSURRECTION, and a declaration of war was never issued. The invasion of the so-called seceded states was based on three factors: the restoration of the Union, the recovery of government property, and the honor of the flag. Nevertheless, Washington's refusal to issue a declaration of war was ridiculed and derided by many overseas observers. Because the conflict was officially treated as an insurrection in Washington, individuals who lost property found themselves with little legal footing on which to base any claim for RESTITUTION. The PRIZE CASES decision of the U.S. Supreme Court in March 1863 upheld the Lincoln administration's view that the insurrection, even without a declaration of war, could be suppressed according to the rules of war. The ruling also relieved the United States of any liability for any acts of war and their consequences.

War Eagle. A nickname for Union Gen. Robert H. Milroy.

war horse. A veteran.

War of the Rebellion. A designation for the war used in the North.

War of the Rebellion, The: Official Records of the Union and Confederate Armies. After encounter-ing several difficulties in locating the necessary documents with which to prepare his annual report of military operations in 1863, General in Chief Henry W. Halleck suggested to the Congressional Committee on Military Affairs that the records of the war be collated and published. On May 19, 1864, Sen. Henry Wilson of Massachusetts, the committee chairman, subsequently introduced a joint resolution to publish the correspondence and reports of Union commanders as well as other public documents relating to the war. For the next ten years, however, the project languished since the directives that authorized the work also stipulated that it should not interfere with the regular work of the clerks to whom the task was delegated. In 1874 the GRAND ARMY OF THE REPUBLIC, a veterans organization, urged that the project be completed. Funds were allocated, but the task remained with those who had as yet accomplished nothing. By the mid-1870s a trio of clerks assembled a forty-seven-volume collection of Union and Confederate reports entitled *Reports of Military Operations During the Rebellion.* The material, however, was poorly arranged and poorly received; only thirty sets were printed. On December 14, 1877, the army took over the project and appointed Capt. Robert N. Scott to head it, and Scott established the criteria for translating the vast warehouses of documents into print. The contents had to be official, that is, prepared by an individual in the course of his duties. All documents had to have been created during the war, thus minimizing any effort at revisionism. Scott established the four series into which the documents were to be categorized: military operations (including Federal and Confederate accounts), prisoners of war and political prisoners, reports and correspondence of Union officials, and reports and correspondence of Southern officials. To balance the vast preponderance of Federal documents, Scott made successful overtures to the SOUTHERN HISTORICAL SOCIETY, a valuable archive of Confederate material, and consulted with several former Southern commanders, finally hiring former Confederate Gen. Marcus J.

Wright to acquire material in the South. Editorially, Scott authorized the correction of clerical errors, grammar, and spelling. In 1880 Congress allocated funds to publish ten thousand copies of the records, and the first volume was released on July 22, 1881. Scott died in 1887, but the project continued under five different editors: Capt. Wyllys Lyman, Lt. Col. Henry M. Lazelle, Maj. George B. Davis (chairing a three-man publication board), George W. Davis, and Maj. Fred C. Ainsworth. The work took twenty years to complete, and the 128th and final volume appeared in 1901. Seven years prior to completion, the enterprise was transferred from the War Department to the Pension Branch. In the end, the undertaking generated 138,579 pages and 1,006 maps, and the cost of production totaled $2.8 million. The work was received well by both Northern and Southern veterans and stands alone as the primary source material for the study of the war. Most public libraries in the nation were offered the set at no cost, and many of these are still available. In 1884 a similar project was begun on the official naval records of the war. Thirty-one volumes later it was completed in 1927. These two projects were the largest ventures ever finished by the Government Printing Office.

war paint. Both Federal and Confederate soldiers occasionally smeared gunpowder on their faces as a kind of war paint.

warp. N. A heavy cable attached to a post or anchor. Sailors used the warp to pull vessels a short distance by muscle power rather than steam or sail.

warrant officer. A noncommissioned officer, such as a SERGEANT, corporal, bandmaster in the army or a QUARTERMASTER, gunner, or BOATSWAIN in the navy.

Washington Grays. (1) The 47th New York, which was recruited primarily from New York City and Brooklyn, was MUSTERED INTO service on September 14, 1861. The REGIMENT was sent to South Carolina in 1862 and 1863, where it was involved in operations against Charleston. The unit also participated in the battles of Secessionville, Olustee, Drewry's Bluff, Cold Harbor, the siege of Petersburg, and the attack on FORT FISHER. The New Yorkers were MUSTERED OUT on August 30, 1865. (2) A BATTERY of Confederate heavy artillery that was assigned to the 7th North Carolina on May 29, 1861, and reassigned to the 10th North Carolina State Troops (also known as the 1st North Carolina Artillery). On August 29, 1861, the battery was captured at Fort Hatteras. The men were confined at FORT WARREN (Boston), PAROLED, EXCHANGED, and reformed at Wilmington. Throughout the rest of the war they served in the Wilmington area, and most were captured at Fort Fisher on January 15, 1865. The remainder were absorbed by other commands and participated as INFANTRY under Joseph E. Johnston until the surrender at Durham Station.

water purifier. A cylindrical charcoal filter that was set in the middle of some Federal CANTEENS. Water was poured into the right side of the canteen, filtered through this core, and was poured out from the left side. Its success was very limited.

ways. N. The structure upon which a ship was built.

wear, to. N. To turn the head of a vessel away from the wind.

web-foot. A soldier without shoes.

web-footed cavalry. Slang for INFANTRY.

Wee Nee Volunteers. South Carolina Militia from Williamsburg who were attached to the 1st South Carolina, known as Gregg's Regiment. The men were raised near the Black River, which was known to Native Americans as the Wee Nee.

weigh, to. N. To pull up anchor in preparation for sailing.

weight of metal. The estimated weight of all projectiles fired in an engagement.

Wesson carbine. Manufactured in Worcester, Massachusetts, this weapon was developed by Frank Wesson, youngest brother of Daniel B. Wesson, the cofounder of Smith and Wesson. The CARBINE was a .44-caliber rimfire BREECHLOADER with a barrel only twenty-four inches long. It had a unique firing system that involved two triggers and two trigger guards. Although enthusiastically endorsed by some Union commanders, the carbine was not approved by the War Department until after Gettysburg. Prior to that, most purchases were made by individual units and soldiers.

U.S. ARMY MILITARY HISTORY INSTITUTE

West Woods. A segment of the Antietam battlefield, the scene of the initial fighting, which included the Dunker Church, the Cornfield, and the East Woods.

Westchester Chasseurs. The 17th New York Infantry, which was composed of VOLUNTEERS

NATIONAL ARCHIVES

from Westchester, Rockland, Wayne, Wyoming, Chenango, and New York Counties who signed on for two years' service. The unit fought in twelve engagements, including the Peninsula campaign, the Seven Days' battles, Second Manassas (Bull Run), Antietam, Fredericksburg, and Chancellorsville. The REGIMENT was MUSTERED OUT on June 2, 1863. It had been the largest unit in its BRIGADE, which included the 20th Maine, 12th and 44th New York, 83d Pennsylvania, and 16th Michigan—who one month later preserved the left side of the Union line on Little Round Top at Gettysburg.

wet goods. Slang for whiskey.

wharf lice. A contemptuous reference to stevedores and roustabouts who were also fit for military service.

LIBRARY OF CONGRESS

What-Is-It? The nickname for the strange-looking wagons devised by photographer Mathew B. Brady for use as portable darkrooms when his photographers were in the field.

Wheatfield. A sector of the Gettysburg battlefield, south of the town and between the Emmitsburg and Taneytown Roads, just below the Trostle farm. These nineteen acres of wheat were owned by George Rose, and they were the site of more than four thousand casualties on July 2, 1863. This tract of land changed hands at least six times during the fighting, which began in earnest at 4:30 P.M. when George Anderson's Georgians encountered Union REGIMENTS under Regis de Trobriand. The fighting was compared to a whirlpool as reinforcements arrived and each side attacked

and counterattacked. Men of the Union IRISH BRIGADE received absolution just prior to charging into the field; the Federal units were forced to withdraw to Plum Run as night fell and the fighting ended.

wheel, to. To pivot troops or a fleet of ships on an axis while maintaining the integrity of the line.

wheel horse(s). A horse or pair of horses closest to the wheels of a wagon, CAISSON, or other vehicle.

wheelhouse. (1) A storage structure for wagon wheels. (2) N. A small structure on the deck of a ship that contained the helm, or steering wheel.

Whipple hat. A felt hat with a havelock-style brim and a leather visor. This design was patented by John F. Whipple and first produced by the Seamless Clothing Company of New York in 1861. The headgear was used by troops from New England and New York and also Hiram Berdan's U.S. Sharpshooters. Confederates dubbed it the "Excelsior hat."

whippletree. A swinging or pivoted bar to which the traces of a HARNESS are fastened and by which a CARRIAGE, plow, or other vehicle or implement is drawn. Also known as a whiffletree, a swingletree, and a singletree.

Whiskey Rebellion legislation. In 1794 an uprising in western Pennsylvania by farmers opposed to a federal excise tax on whiskey led to legislation that authorized the president to call for troops from the adjoining states to quell the insurrection. The legislation, however, also limited the time of service of these troops to ninety days and released them from this obligation thirty days after the beginning of the next session of Congress. Apparently the James Buchanan administration reviewed the legislation with regard to the SECESSION crisis in South Carolina but opted not to pursue it since secession was not the same as INSURRECTION. Abraham Lincoln, however, relied on the legislation in calling for troops from the states after the fall of FORT SUMTER. At the same time, the restrictions inherent in the Whiskey Rebellion legislation may have been a factor in forcing the July 21, 1861, battle of First Manassas (Bull Run) before the army was ready. Many VOLUNTEERS had enlisted in April, and the next session of Congress began on July 4. Thus the military obligations of the volunteers would expire in early August.

Whistling Dick. An 18-POUNDER banded SMOOTHBORE manufactured at the Tredegar Iron Works in Richmond. Like several smoothbores, this piece was later rifled, but a defect in the rifling gave its shots an odd and distinctive sound. Deployed in the water battery at Vicksburg, the weapon is known to have been involved in the sinking of the Federal gunboat *Cincinnati* on May 27, 1863. The gun was disabled by Union fire from across the river, and after the fall of the Confederate stronghold, a PIECE identified as Whistling Dick was sent to West Point as a trophy. In the late 1950s that identification was proven false, and the fate of the gun remains a mystery.

white glove boys. A disdainful reference to the Union army in the eastern theater coined by Federal soldiers in the western theater.

white weapon, the. An allusion to SABERS.

Whitworth gun. Manufactured in England, this GUN was unique because it fired a hexagonal rather

than a round projectile. A BREECHLOADER, this PIECE used both solid shot and shells. Numerous 6- and 12-POUNDER Whitworths were imported by the South, and successful methods were devised by 1863 for manufacturing ammunition equal in quality to that made in Britain. The drawbacks to the weapon were rooted in the precise crafting demanded to produce both the gun and its ammunition. Interestingly, the weapon was never adopted by the Royal Army, and in the field it was noted that the BORE had to be kept exceptionally clean or the weapon would jam. At the same time, the weapons were highly accurate and had considerable range. Most large-caliber Whitworths were MUZZLELOADERS, and after 1863 most of the pieces imported were muzzleloaders. The South did not have a monopoly on Whitworths, however. During the Peninsula campaign a Federal Whitworth BATTERY was deployed but never went into action. Afterward it was assigned to the Washington defenses.

Widow Blakely. A British 7.44-inch BLAKELY RIFLE that served in the water battery at Vicksburg. Of the thirty-one PIECES in the riverfront batteries, this was the only Blakely, thus it was dubbed "widow." Originally the barrel measured 124 inches, but on May 22, 1863, during action against Union GUNBOATS, a shell burst inside the TUBE. The muzzle was trimmed, reducing the overall length to 100 inches, and the weapon was used

throughout the remainder of the siege. The gun was displayed at West Point afterward, but it was misidentified as another named gun, WHISTLING DICK. The error was discovered in the late 1950s, and the Blakely was returned to the Vicksburg National Battlefield Park, where it was installed about a mile south of its position during the siege.

Wild Riders. The 1st Kentucky Cavalry (U.S.), also known as [Col. Frank M.] Wolford's Cavalry, which was MUSTERED INTO Federal service on October 28, 1861. Twice it encountered Kentucky's most famous Confederate CAVALRY REGIMENT, led by John Hunt Morgan, and twice the Wild Riders defeated them. The unit was engaged in the 1862 battle of Mill Springs, later chased and captured Morgan, joined in the defense of Knoxville, and participated in the Atlanta campaign. The regiment was MUSTERED OUT on December 31, 1864.

Willard's Hotel. This Washington hotel at the corner of Fourteenth Street and Pennsylvania Avenue, one block from the White House, was by far the most distinguished hotel of the city. The hotel had been opened originally by Benjamin Tayloe in the 1830s as the City Hotel and was purchased from Tayloe by Henry and Edwin Willard in 1850. The Williard brothers had their own ideas about enhancing the reputation of the already distinguished and successful hotel. The six four-story rowhouses that comprised the hotel were given a single facade, and one hundred guest rooms were created. The hotel became popular with politicians and office seekers, and the presidents became regular guests. Prior to the war, Willard's hosted the February 4–27, 1861, Washington Peace Conference. President-elect Abraham Lincoln arrived at Willard's on February 23, 1861, and was a guest until his inauguration. On March 9, 1861, a fire threatened to engulf the hotel, but Elmer Ellsworth's 5th New York, a ZOUAVE REGIMENT comprised of New York firemen, extinguished the blaze. The men were hosted to breakfast by the grateful hotel management. In

1862 Julia Ward Howe was a guest in the hotel when she wrote "The Battle Hymn of the Republic." Willard's also welcomed Ulysses S. Grant in early 1864, when the general came to Washington to meet with Lincoln and accept command of the Union armies. During the 1860s Nathaniel Hawthorne wrote an article for *The Atlantic Monthly* in which he described Willard's as "the center of Washington and the nation." Patronized by hundreds of distinguished guests, Nathaniel Hawthorne wrote that the hotel could more properly be called the center of Washington than could "The Capitol, the White House, or the State Department." The hotel was razed at the turn of the century to make way for a larger Willard's, which opened in 1901.

Williams bullet. This specialized small-arms ammunition carried a zinc washer at the base. The washer expanded when the CARTRIDGE was detonated and scrapped away any potentially fouling residue that might remain from POWDER. It was remarkably successful in practice and won War Department approval in late 1861. Many soldiers were suspicious of the bullet's odd appearance and refused to use it, fearing that it would damage their RIFLES.

Winchester. One of the famous horses of the war, this animal was presented to Union Gen. Philip H. Sheridan in 1862 by the 2d Michigan Cavalry near Rienzi, Mississippi. The general named the horse Rienzi and rode him in nearly every engagement in which he participated for the rest of the war—eighty-five battles and skirmishes—including his October 19, 1864, ride from Winchester to Cedar Creek, Virginia, in which he rallied his troops to victory. After the battle, Sheridan renamed the horse Winchester.

windage. The difference between the diameter of a GUN'S BORE and that of the projectile it fired. Gunners had to consider windage so that allowances could be made for a bore's becoming fouled by use, the expansion of shot by heat, occurrences of rust, and the tin straps of fixed ammunition. By reducing windage, gunners were able to increase their accuracy and extend the range of their guns.

windlass. A heavy timber roller or cylinder that was mounted on its axis and used to wind up a rope or chain by means of a crank or lever.

windrow. In agriculture, this was a line of hay raked together to be rolled into heaps, or sheaves of grain. The sheaves were then set up in rows and resting against each other so as to allow the wind to encircle them. During the war, however, the term was applied to piles of bodies. These piles were sometimes three or four bodies deep and were formed at sites where the fighting was especially fierce.

wing. (1) A term used to designate a Confederate or Union command. (2) The left or right flanks of a line of battle.

wire road. Unlike PLANK and CORDUROY ROADS, these thoroughfares were not named for the material that covered them but rather because a telegraph line, or wire, was strung beside them.

Wizard of the Saddle. (1) A nickname for Confederate Gen. Nathan Bedford Forrest. (2) A term of respect for gifted CAVALRY commanders.

wolfhounds. A reference to ragged Confederate soldiers.

Wolverines. Natives of Michigan.

Women's Order, the. See GENERAL ORDERS NO. 28, GEN. BENJAMIN F. BUTLER.

wood road. A muddy roadway across which wooden planks were placed to allow vehicles to pass. This term embraced both the CORDUROY ROAD and the PLANK ROAD but was a very temporary situation.

woodcut. An engraving on wood. During the war, illustrated newspapers such as *HARPER'S WEEKLY* and *FRANK LESLIE'S ILLUSTRATED NEWSPAPER* dispatched sketch artists to follow the army and generate images of the fighting. These images were then engraved in wood by artisans who sometimes embellished or edited the image so as to be appropriate for publication. The published results usually appeared in the newspapers within two weeks of the action depicted.

wooden ordnance. A QUAKER GUN.

wooden overcoat. A barrel with a hole cut in its bottom so it could be slipped over an individual's head in the same fashion as a BARREL JACKET. Usually a sign on the barrel indicated the offense for which the man was being punished.

Woodruff gun. This small 2-POUNDER SMOOTH-BORE was manufactured by James Woodruff in Illinois. When his petitions that the GUN be adopted were rejected by the Union army's ORD-NANCE department, which assessed the weapon as outdated and obsolete, Woodruff utilized his political connections to gain a government contact. Thus his weapons were issued to the 10th Illinois Cavalry, the 2d and 4th Iowa Cavalry, and the 1st Illinois Light Artillery by the command of Abraham Lincoln. Col. Benjamin Grierson's command carried Woodruffs on his celebrated raid into Louisiana, but in general, the small gun did not distinguish itself in combat. One regimental historian noted: "They were of no value and were generally voted a nuisance. They were never known to hit anything, and never served any useful purpose." In every instance in which the GUN was judged to have had a positive role in combat, it was also pointed out that the enemy had no artillery. Thus the only distinction enjoyed by the Woodruff gun was that it was issued to exceptional units by order of the president.

Woodstock Races. A CAVALRY clash on October 9, 1864, at Tom's Brook, Virginia, precipitated by Philip H. Sheridan's scorched-earth program in the Shenandoah Valley. Confederate forces under Thomas L. Rosser and Lunsford Lomax harassed Sheridan's army as it was withdrawing from the valley, and finally Sheridan ordered his cavalry to engage the Southerners. Union horsemen under Wesley Merritt and George A. Custer routed the Southerners. The victory was not only an embarrassment to the Confederates, hence the use of the term "RACES," but it also resulted in the Federal cavalry attaining overall control of the valley.

work. FIELDWORKS.

worm, to. To extract an unfired projectile from a MUZZLELOADING handgun using a screwlike device on the end of a ram.

X-Y-Z

Yager. The U.S. Model 1841 RIFLE, also known as the MISSISSIPPI and JAEGER rifle.

yaller dog. (1) A coward. (2) A staff officer or courier in the Confederate army. In his account of the war, Confederate Pvt. Sam Watkins notes, "They were looked upon as simply 'hangers on,' or in other words, as yellow sheep-killing dogs, that if you say 'booh' at, would yelp and get under their master's heels."

Yankee. (1) A New Englander. (2) A Northerner.

Yankeedom. Southern slang for the North.

Yankees' devils. Federal ARTILLERY.

Yankee, to. Southern slang for lying or embellishing a story.

Yankee well. An escape tunnel dug by Union prisoners.

yard. N. A lengthy spar that supported a lug, lateen, or square sail.

yaupon tea. A Southern substitute for tea made by boiling leaves and twigs of the yaupon tree then adding molasses and milk.

yaw. A projectile's wobbling motion upon clearing a GUN's muzzle. If the ammunition and the gun's rifling were well made, the yaw was self-correcting. If the yaw was uncorrected, the shell's range and accuracy were decreased.

NAVAL HISTORICAL CENTER

Yazoo, **CSS.** This 371-ton side-wheel river steamer was built in 1860 at Jeffersonville, Indiana, and used by the Confederates as a transport on the western rivers. During the battle for Island No. 10 on April 7, 1862, the ship was captured and sunk.

Yearling. A second-year cadet at West Point.

yellowback. Inexpensive paperback books marketed to soldiers by SUTLERS.

yellow belly. A coward.

yellow hammer. A native of Alabama.

yellow sash. A Federal general, referring to his emblem of rank when in full dress.

yoke. N. A crosspiece at the head of a ship's rudder. Lines were attached to its ends so that the vessel could be directed from amidships.

Young Napoleon. A nickname for Union Gen. George B. McClellan.

yuunk. An unpopular individual. The term is prevalent in the correspondence of prisoners of war, particularly from Camp Chase and Johnson's Island. Specifically the word referred to a relative or sweetheart who either wrote only short letters or not at all.

Zouave. The original Zouaves were natives of North Africa who were recruited into the French army as light INFANTRY. They brought with them a distinctive and colorful garb, which was adopted by the French for certain units. During the Crimean War, several Zouave units distinguished themselves in combat, and the attendant publicity popularized the uniform, which of itself came to represent boldness and courage under fire. In the United States, the style became fashionable for drill units and militia companies. The Zouave image was further magnified by touring drill squads, such as Elmer Ellsworth's U.S. Zouaves. At the outbreak of war, the colorful uniforms combined with a sense of pomp and ceremony to project an image of Zouaves as premier fighting men. That perception attracted both the elite as well as the rowdiest elements to the recruiting stations. Zouave companies were formed for both the Union and Confederate armies. Their garish uniforms featured GAITERS, baggy trousers, short open jackets with elaborate piping, and turbans or fezzes. As the war wore on and shortages hit the South, many of the Confederate Zouave units relinquished the colorful uniforms for homespun or more traditional uniforms. The North continued to muster Zouave units until the end of the war, but the Zouave fashion faded quickly. The experience of war displaced the Zouave image of glorious battle.

BIBLIOGRAPHY

Adams, James T., ed. *Dictionary of American History*. 6 vols. New York: Scribner, 1940–60.

Alsager, C. Martin. *Dictionary of Business Terms*. Chicago: Callaghan, 1932.

The American Heritage Dictionary of the English Language. 3d ed. Boston: Houghton Mifflin, 1992.

Barrère, Albert M. V. *Argot and Slang*. New and revised edition. London: Whittaker, 1889.

Bartlett, John, comp. *Familiar Quotations*. 12th ed. Boston: Little, Brown, 1948.

Blunt, John H. *Dictionary of Sects, Heresies, Ecclesiastical Parties, and Schools of Religious Thought*. London: Rivingtons; Philadelphia: J. B. Lippincott, 1874.

Boatner, Mark M., III. *The Civil War Dictionary*. 1988; reprint, New York: Vintage Civil War Library, 1991.

Bombaugh, Charles C. *Facts and Fancies for the Curious from the Harvest-Fields of Literature*. 1905; reprint, Detroit: Gale Research Co., 1968.

Brand, John. *Popular Antiquities of Great Britain*. 3 vols. London: J. R. Smith, 1870.

Brewer, Ebenezer C. *A Dictionary of Miracles*. Philadelphia: J. B. Lippincott, 1934.

———. *Dictionary of Phrase and Fable*. Revised and enlarged edition. New York: Harper, 1953.

———. *The Historic Note-Book*. Philadelphia: J. B. Lippincott, 1891.

———. *The Reader's Handbook of Famous Names in Fiction, Allusions, References, Proverbs, Plots, Stories, and Poems*. Revised edition. Philadelphia: J. B. Lippincott, 1904.

Catholic Encyclopedia, The. 15 vols. New York: Robert Appleton Co., 1970–12.

Chambers, Robert. *The Book of Days*. 2 vols. London: W. & R. Chambers, 1869.

De Vore, Nicholas, ed. *Encyclopedia of Astrology*. New York: Philosophical Library, 1947.

Dictionary of National Biography. 66 vols. London: Smith, Elder, & Co., 1885–1901.

Dixon, James M., ed. *Dictionary of Idiomatic English Phrases*. London: Nelson, 1891.

The editors of Time-Life Books. *Arms and Equipment of the Confederacy*. Alexandria, Va.: Time-Life Books, 1991.

———. *Arms and Equipment of the Union.* Alexandria, Va.: Time-Life Books, 1991.

Encarta World English Dictionary. New York: St. Martin's, 1999.

Espy, Willard R. *O Thou Improper, Thou Uncommon Noun.* New York: C. N. Potter, 1978.

Farmer, John S., and William E. Henley. *Slang and Its Analogues.* 1890; reprint, New York: Arno, 1970.

Faust, Patricia, ed. *Historical Times Illustrated Encyclopedia of the Civil War.* New York: Harper & Row, 1986.

Flexner, Stuart B. *I Hear America Talking: An Illustrated Treasury of American Words and Phrases.* New York: Van Nostrand Reinhold, 1976.

———. *Listening to America: An Illustrated History of Words and Phrases from Our Lively and Splendid Past.* New York: Simon and Schuster, 1982.

Goldin, Hyman E., ed. *Dictionary of American Underworld Lingo.* New York: Twayne, 1950.

Gwatkin, H. M., and Whitney, J. P., eds. *The Cambridge Medieval History.* 8 vols. Cambridge: Cambridge University Press, 1911–36.

Hastings, James, ed. *Encyclopedia of Religion and Ethics.* 13 vols. New York: Scribner, 1924–27.

Hendrickson, Robert. *The Dictionary of Eponymns: Names That Became Words.* New York: Stein and Day, 1972.

Holt, Alfred M. *Phrase Origins: A Study of Familiar Expressions.* New York: Thomas Y. Crowell Co., 1936.

Little, Charles E. *Cyclopedia of Classified Dates.* New York: Funk & Wagnalls Co., 1900.

MacEwen, William A., and A. H. Lewis. *Encyclopedia of Nautical Knowledge.* Cambridge, Md.: Cornell Maritime Press, 1953.

Mathews, Mitford M., ed. *A Dictionary of Americanisms on Historical Principles.* 2 vols. Chicago: University of Chicago Press, 1951.

Mencken, H. L. *The American Language: An Inquiry into the Development of English in the United States.* New York: Knopf, 1936.

Menke, Frank G. *The New Encyclopedia of Sports.* New York: Barnes, 1947.

Bibliography

Morris, Richard B., ed. *Encyclopedia of American History.* New York: Harper, 1953.

Morris, William, and Mary Morris. *Dictionary of Word and Phrase Origins.* New York: Harper & Row, 1962.

Munn, Glenn G. *Encyclopedia of Banking and Finance.* New York: Bankers Publishing Co., 1924.

Onions, C. T., ed. *The Oxford Dictionary of English Etymology.* Oxford: Clarendon Press, 1966.

Patridge, Eric. *A Dictionary of Clichés.* New York: Macmillan, 1940.

———. *A Dictionary of Slang and Unconventional English.* 5th ed. London: Routledge & Paul, 1961.

———. *Origins: A Short Etymological Dictionary of Modern English.* 4th edition. London: Routledge & K. Paul, 1966.

Radford, Edwin, and Mona A. Radford. *Encyclopaedia of Superstitions.* New York: Philosophical Library, 1949.

Rose, J. Holland, A. P. Newton, and E. A. Benians, gen. eds. *The Cambridge History of the British Empire.* 7 vols. Cambridge: Cambridge University Press, 1929-40.

Runes, Dagobert D., and Harry G. Schrickel. *Encyclopedia of the Arts.* New York: Philosophical Library, 1946.

Seligman, Edwin R. A., and Alvin S. Johnson, eds. *Encyclopedia of the Social Sciences.* 15 vols. New York: Macmillan, 1935.

Serial. *Annual Register, The.* London: Longmans, annual publication.

Serial. *Notes and Queries.* London: Oxford University Press, 1849– .

Seyffert, Oskar, ed. *A Dictionary of Classical Antiquities.* London: S. Sonnenschein, 1891.

Skeat, Walter W., ed. *A Concise Etymological Dictionary of the English Language.* Oxford: Clarendon, 1901.

Smith, Benjamin E., ed. *The Century Cyclopedia of Names.* New York: Century, 1914.

Speer, Lonnie R. *Portals to Hell: Military Prisons of the Civil War.* Mechanicsburg, Pa.: Stackpole Books, 1997.

Stevenson, Burton. *The Home Book of Proverbs, Maxims, and Familiar Phrases.* New York: Macmillan, 1948.

———. *The Home Book of Quotations, Classical and Modern.* 5th edition. New York: Dodd, Mead & Co., 1947.

Thomas, Joseph. *Universal Pronouncing Dictionary of Biography and Mythology.* 5th edition. Philadelphia: J. B. Lippincott, 1930.

U.S. Navy Department. *Dictionary of American Naval Fighting Ships.* 8 vols. Washington, D.C.: Government Printing Office, 1959–81.

U.S. War Department. *The War of the Rebellion: A Compilation of the Official Records of the Union and Confederate Armies.* 128 vols. Washington, D.C.: Government Printing Office, 1880–1901.

Ward, Adolphus W., and Alfred R. Waller, eds. *The Cambridge History of English Literature.* 15 vols. Cambridge: Cambridge University Press, 1907–32.

———, G. W. Prothero, and Stanley Leathes, eds. *The Cambridge Modern History.* 13 vols. Cambridge: Cambridge University Press, 1902-12.

Webster's New International Dictionary of the English Language. 2d edition. Springfield, Mass.: G. & C. Merriam Co., 1947.

Weekley, Ernest. *A Concise Etymological Dictionary of Modern English.* London: J. Murray, 1924.

———. *The Romance of Names.* London: J. Murray, 1914.

———. *The Romance of Words.* London: J. Murray, 1917.

———. *Surnames.* 3d edition. London: J. Murray, 1936.

Weseen, Maurice H. *A Dictionary of American Slang.* New York: Thomas Y. Crowell Co., 1934.

Wright, Joseph, ed. *The English Dialect Dictionary.* 6 vols. London: H. Fowde, 1898–1905.

April 23, 2002
Albuquerque, New Mexico

#17.06
Hastings
6001 R Lomas Blvd N.